Managing Canada's Renewable Resources

Recently published

Canada's Natural Environment:
Essays in Applied Geography

G.R. McBoyle & E. Sommerville

Managing Canada's Renewable Resources

edited by

Ralph R. Krueger
University of Waterloo

and

Bruce Mitchell
University of Waterloo

Methuen

Toronto • London • Sydney • Wellington

Canadian Cataloguing in Publication Data

Main entry under title:

Managing Canada's renewable resources

ISBN 0-458-92350-8

1. Renewable natural resources - Canada.
2. Environmental policy - Canada. 3. Conservation of natural resources - Canada. I. Krueger, Ralph R., 1927- II. Mitchell, Bruce, 1944-

HC113.5.M35 333.7'0971 C77 --1128-4

Printed and bound in Canada

2 3 4 5 81 80 79

Contents

Preface

The idea for this book of readings grew out of the difficulty experienced by the editors in finding adequate reading material on Canadian environmental and resource management topics that could be made available for large university classes. The most useful reading material is spread among a variety of academic journals, government reports, conference proceedings and other fugitive sources. This book brings together a selection of readings which will partially solve the abovementioned problem. It is our hope that this collection of papers will also be found useful to secondary school teachers, resource management professionals, decision makers in the public and private sectors, and to those of the general public who are concerned with Canadian environmental issues.

The first two sections of the book provide a framework of perspectives, concepts, approaches and techniques which may be applied to resource management problems in general. Some of these are already considered as classics. Others by authors well known in the resource management field will likely also stand the test of time. The balance of the book provides case studies concerning management of specific Canadian land ad water resources. These studies provide a range of issues and problems which may be viewed in the context of the perspectives and decision-making approaches outlined earlier in the book.

Choosing papers for a book such as this is no easy task. Because of the limitations of space, we decided to include papers on renewable resources only. Within renewable resources, we were still obliged to be selective. We realize that we have excluded important Canadian management issues relating to resources such as forests, wildlife and fisheries and have neglected entirely some parts of Canada. However, we wish to emphasize that the case studies are just that; they illustrate one or more of the perspectives and approaches discussed earlier and they represent various scales ranging from local to international. In the final analysis, much of the selection was dependent upon the bias of the editors and the availability of suitable papers. In several cases, we commissioned papers to be written specially for this volume to plug important gaps that we perceived.

One criterion not specifically mentioned above was that of readability. We looked for papers which were interesting and sufficiently free from jargon so that they could be understood by readers who do not share the disciplinary background of the authors.

There is considerable range among the papers in complexity of ideas and in the difficulty and style of language. Some editing was done in an attempt to eliminate unnecessary technical terms and to restrict footnote references to only those which could reasonably be expected to be found in university or good public libraries. It is anticipated that those who wish to make in-depth studies of specific topics will go to the original sources.

The editors wish to thank all of the authors and publishers whose kindness in giving permission to publish papers made this book possible. We wish particularly to thank those authors who wrote new papers and those who substantially revised their papers (or permitted us to edit them severely) so that they would better suit the purposes of this volume. We also thank Gary Brannon and Norm Adam who prepared original artwork for the new papers and redrew all the figures for the reprinted papers.

Ralph R. Krueger
Bruce Mitchell
August, 1976
Waterloo, Ontario

Canadian Resource Management: An Overview

Historical Background

From the earliest days, Canada's economic and political development has depended to a considerable degree on the exploitation of renewable resources, which, if managed wisely, will continue to be of use to man indefinitely. Thus it is not surprising to discover that the concern for how Canada should manage its renewable resources is not new. There has been dialogue and debate about the wise use and conservation of resources for almost a century.[1] However, perhaps it is surprising to learn that early in this century some of the same basic arguments were presented by conservationists as are being presented by environmentalists in the 1970s.

In the first thirty years or so after Confederation, the major thrust of government was to forge and develop a unified nation. One means for achieving this was the building of transportation facilities in order to develop natural resources on what seemed an ever expanding frontier. There seemed little need to be concerned with conservation when the natural resources appeared to be inexhaustible. As historian R. C. Brown has said, this resource development policy was based on the "doctrine of usefulness".[2] Even though there have been major resource management policy changes over the years, vestiges of this doctrine (which may also be termed the short-run economic perspective), combined with a belief of unlimited natural resources, remain even today in the public attitude and in governmental and private resource development decisions.

Although there may have been a few conservationist voices crying out in the wilderness before the turn of the century, the Conservation Movement did not have much impact on resource development policy until the first decade of the twentieth century.[3] Starting in 1906, there was a series of Canadian Forestry Conventions which brought together professional resource managers, government personnel and conservationists. The prime concern of these conferences was forest management policies and practices, but the discussions invariably included other renewable resources such as water, soils, fish and wildlife, and thus the conservationists were provided with a forum in which to advocate co-ordinated resource use policies and introduce preservation themes.

The North American Conservation Conference in Washington, 1909, injected new life and enthusiasm into the Conservation Movement in Canada. This conference, attended by delegates from the United States,

Mexico and Canada drew up a "Declaration of Principles" covering a wide range of resource development and conservation topics. Among other things, the declaration called for legislation to preserve and protect wildlife, to prevent soil erosion and water pollution, and generally to manage renewable resources in such a way as to ensure their continued productivity in the future. The conference also called for the establishment of a Commission of Conservation in each of the participating countries and the convening of a world-wide international conservation conference. In making the latter recommendation, the delegates of the Conservation Conference of 1909 were obviously ahead of their time; it did not occur until the United Nations Conference on the Human Environment held in Stockholm in 1972.

The Canadian government was greatly influenced by the North American Conservation Conference and established a Commission of Conservation almost immediately. The detailed story of the Commission of Conservation, its objectives, successes, failures and political problems that led to its demise in 1921 has been told elsewhere, and will not be retold here.[4] However, its significance to the evolution of resource management policies in Canada should be pointed out. The Commission conducted and commissioned research which provided much needed information about Canada's renewable and non-renewable resources. The Commission provided an important national forum for the discussion of natural resource policy and management. The concepts of coordinated management of groups of resources, multiple-purpose resource use, the integration of resource management with urban and regional planning, the impact of management of resources on public health through pollution effects, and the idea that development and conservation are not necessarily conflicting activities, were formulated and propagated across the country. Many ideas picked up and developed later by academics and resource managers, and many programs initiated later by governments and private enterprises, had their origin in the various activities of the short-lived Conservation Commission.

Accompanying the abolition of the Commission of Conservation, was a rapid decline in public and governmental interest in a comprehensive approach to managing resources. During the 1920s the concern went back to specific resource problems such as forest fires. In the economic depression period of the 1930s the federal and provincial governments were most concerned with using resources to stimulate the economy and combat unemployment. For example, in 1935, the *Prairie Farm Rehabilitation Act* (PFRA) was passed to assist the rural economy of the Prairie Provinces which had been beset with both economic depression and serious drought. Funds were made available for projects such as water supply for livestock and irrigation, the planting of shelter belts, and the encouragement of farm practices that would reduce wind erosion. Even though it became evident that resources-oriented programs did relatively little to help the poor in economically depressed regions, similar programs were initiated in the following decades. The *Maritime Marshland Reclamation Act* (MMRA), passed in 1948, was designed to reclaim some 80,000 acres of saltwater marshland bordering the Bay of Fundy. MMRA did little, if anything for the economy of the Maritimes (the agricultural land was not worth what it cost to reclaim it) but it did have a major impact on the natural environment. In 1961, the *Agricultural Rehabilitation and Development Act* (ARDA) provided for joint federal-provincial agreements across the whole nation by which the greater efficiency in the use of land and water resources was encouraged with the ultimate goal of alleviating regional economic disparities.[5] In resource management terms, the significance of PFRA, MMRA, and ARDA is that they expressed a basic philosophy that an economy of a depressed region could be stimulated by more efficient use of its renewable resources.

During the two decades following 1939, the pervading national resource development policy was again based on the "doctrine of usefulness". During World War II, short-run efficiency of resource exploitation was most important. After the war, the major national concern was how could Canada's vast resources be developed so as to create employment for returning soldiers and avert the anticipated economic depression. Although the Dominion-Provincial Conference on Reconstruction in 1945 considered conservation topics, the focus was on resource development policies that would ensure continued economic growth in the future. At the Reconstruction Conference and during the balance of the 1940s and 1950s, pressing forward with economic growth was the paramount national issue. Pleas from a few conservationists for coordinated resource management, for preservation of agricultural land, for pollution control measures went largely unheeded as Canada rapidly became an industrialized nation with one of the highest standards of living in the world.

Although the emphasis of the discussion at the Resources for Tomorrow Conference, 1961, was still on the importance of Canada's renewable resources for economic growth and prosperity, in some ways this conference marked the beginning of a new environmental concern in Canada. Some of the issues of the days of the Commission of Conservation were revived and other new environmental concerns were raised. There were warnings of massive air and water pollution, and the loss of prime agricultural land to urban uses. There were criticisms of the lack of recreational resources for large metropolitan areas and the general deterioration of the environmental quality of the human environment due to unplanned sprawling of urban growth.[6]

One tangible result of the Resources for Tomorrow Conference was the creation of the Canadian Council of Resource Ministers (CCRM) which included the federal and provincial cabinet ministers most responsible for resource management policies. Later, in response to a growing public concern about the deteriorating quality of our environment, and the establishment of a federal and several provincial government Departments of Environment, the name was changed to Council of Resource and Environment Ministers (CCREM). This Council has facilitated the exchange of ideas and some co-ordination of resource and environmental policies among the federal and provincial governments.

In 1966, CCRM sponsored a national conference on Pollution and Our Environment. Again a set of background papers was prepared.[7] This conference initiated dialogue among the major actors in the pollution drama: industry, government, researchers, and the concerned public. After the conference, a new public awareness of the magnitude and seriousness of pollution problems grew to the point where they could not be ignored. Organizations such as "Pollution Probe" sprang up across the country; books were published on pollution and general problems of environmental degradation;[8] university environmental research increased and university courses on pollution and environmental problems multiplied; and the news media carried stories on pollution until the public was saturated with the topic.

In response to this wave of interest, the federal and provincial governments introduced much new anti-pollution legislation, new programs were introduced under existing legislation, and industries began pollution-control programs on their own initiative. The federal government, for example, passed both the *Canada Water Act* and the *Clean Air Act* in 1971.[9]

The crest of the wave of public clamour over pollution reached its peak some time during 1970 or 1971. In the early seventies, the emphasis shifted to broader environmental issues, including the rate of population and economic growth, planned obsolescence in consumers' goods, the ecological and social impacts of large dams, petroleum exploration, oil pipelines, highways and other public works, and aboriginal rights and land claims. In addition, citizens' action groups across the country began insisting on greater public participation in the decision making related to the environment.

In response to this new environmental thrust, CCREM sponsored another national conference in 1973 on Man and Resources. The theme of this conference focussed on "the concept of integrated resource use with the view of achieving the best possible balance between the social and economic demands and the ecological implications in the wise use of natural resources."[10] Except for the word "ecological", this statement would not have been out of place in the old days of the Commission of Conservation. Public participation was encouraged in this conference.

Two years in advance, local, regional and national workshops were arranged to which the public was invited to assist in identifying problems and suggesting alternative solutions. It is estimated that some 15,000 Canadians "from all walks of life" actively participated in the planning of the conference. The Conference Report indicates the extremely wide range of topics discussed.[11] The spectrum of suggested solutions was even broader. In fact, it may be that the conference went off in so many directions and had such widespread participation that it lost the focus required to achieve concrete results.

In the mid-seventies, national environmental dialogue concentrated on northern development, including the environmental impacts of water and mineral resource development projects and native land claims, and the preservation of prime farmland. The other environmental degradation topics were still of concern, and from time to time one specific problem, such as mercury pollution, would arise as a major national issue, but on the whole they were not so much in the public eye. In fact, other pressing national problems such as inflation, unemployment and possible energy shortages tended to push environmental issues into the background as far as the general public was concerned.

In addition to these activities within the country, Canada has also been active in international conferences related to environmental problems. When the Canadian government requested submissions to assist it in preparing a statement for the United Nations Conference on the Human Environment, Stockholm, 1972, it received over 500 briefs from concerned organizations across the country.[12] Canada also made significant contributions to three other international conferences concerned with renewable resources which were held in 1974: the World Food Conference, Rome, the World Population Conference, Bucharist, and the Law of the Sea Conference, which began in Caracus. Furthermore, during 1976 Canada hosted "Habitat", the Conference on Human Settlement, in Vancouver.

Emanating from all of the above-mentioned dialogue has been a stream of policies, legislation, programs and ringing declarations of intent. But the implementation of legislation and intentions is a different matter. The problems are complex. Different levels of government, various government agencies, and private enterprise seem to be heading in many different and often conflicting directions in the management of our renewable resources. There is undoubtedly a growing public clamour for a higher quality environment, for a clean-up of pollution, for preservation of certain natural environments, and for social and ecological considerations in resource development. However, the same public insists on a continued high rate of economic growth and an ever increasing "standard of living". Satisfying these latter goals usually means increased resource consumption, a short-run economic perspective in the use of resources, and the ignoring of environmental costs.

Among the public and professional resource managers, and the decision makers, there seems to be no clear priorities in goals and objectives, and no generally accepted policy and decision-making framework to assist in making trade-offs among conflicting objectives. Moreover, even the basic inventories and resource capability studies are far from complete.

Resource Management Approaches

Resource management is a complex decision-making process ideally involving inventory, assessment, goal formulation, policies, programs, legislation, administration and managerial strategies. The number and complexity of the considerations which must be incorporated in resource management is illustrated in the framework provided in Figure 1. Knowledge is required about individual aspects as well as regarding the manner in which they interact. For a given resource management problem, this framework helps to identify areas in which understanding is needed as well as where information is either adequate, inadequate or totally lacking.

Although this framework is only one way of looking at the management of resources, it does emphasize the array and difficulty of considerations involved in reaching decisions. For example, even for one specific resource (land, water, forestry, fisheries, wildlife), to devlop a thorough grasp of only one perspective, time period or spatial scale can be a monumental job. Thus, this framework is humbling to those of us who are critical of current management. We begin to realize the difficulty and complexity of making resource-related decisions.

Those in management positions do not have the luxury of studying and contemplating forever before making decisions. Conflicting demands for the use of resources increase, problems occur, issues arise and action must be taken. Even no action is an alternative and may represent a conscious decision. In some cases there are so many gaps in the information base that resource management becomes a matter of "muddling through", hoping that the results of mistakes will not be too devastating. In other cases, governments consciously ignore the information base available and make decisions on the basis of how they perceive the electors' preferences. If constructively critical contributions are to be made in resource management, a need exists for a sound information base, a systematic approach to decision making, an informed public, and adequate communication between the public(s) and those who are responsible for resource policies, programs and projects.

The organization of the sections in this reader is based upon the general considerations discussed above. Obviously, to incorporate all of the considerations shown in Figure 1 would take numerous volumes to

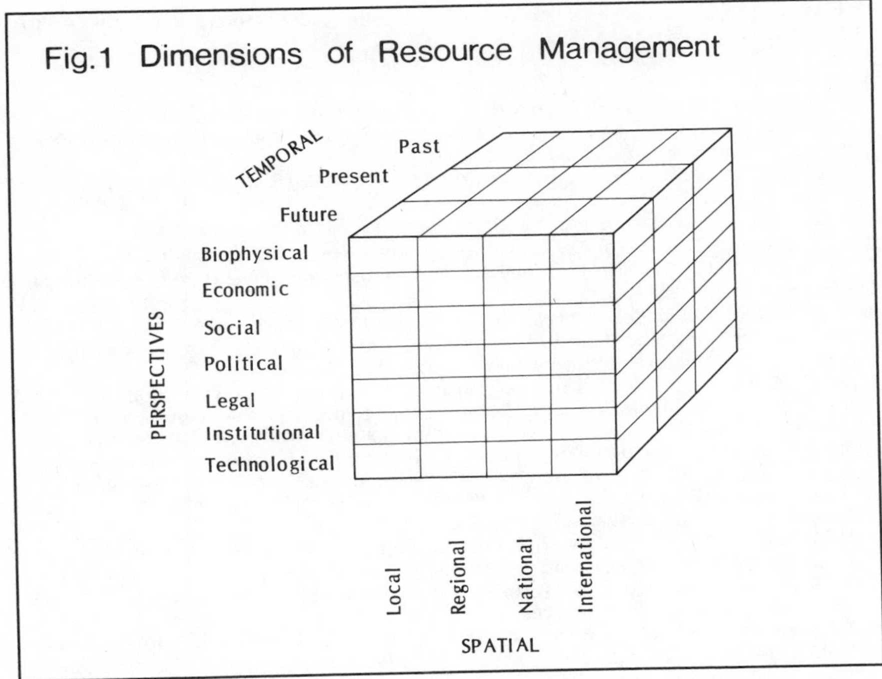

Fig. 1 Dimensions of Resource Management

cover the material in depth. As a result, the editors have created sections and chosen specific articles to illustrate many, but not all, of the considerations. In brief, the objectives have been to clarify and elaborate upon some of the perspectives crucial for resource management; to identify some of the questions which must be addressed when making assessments; to outline some of the characteristics and processes associated with policy and decision making; and, to illustrate these perspectives, assessment ideas and policy concerns with specific examples from Canadian land and water resources. One or more books clearly would be needed to handle each of these aspects in depth. However, a major goal is to create greater awareness of some of the perspectives, concepts, ideas and approaches which are important in resource management. It is hoped that this framework and the empirical studies will stimulate the reader to further thinking an inquiry.

NOTES

1. Because of the great variety of definitions and interpretations of the terms "wise-use", "conservation" and "resource management", no attempt has been made here to define them. For a discussion of these and other environmental terms, as well as a

history of the "Conservation Movement" in North America, the reader is referred to the following books:

W. L. Thomas (ed.) *Man's Role in Changing the Face of the Earth,* Chicago, University of Chicago Press, 1956.

H. Jarrett, *Perspectives on Conservation,* Baltimore, John Hopkins, 1958.

I. Burton and R. W. Kates (eds.) *Readings in Resource Management and Conservation,* Chicago, University of Chicago Press, 1965.

R. Nash (ed.) *The American Environment: Readings in the History of Conservation,* New York, Addison Wesley, 1968.

T. O'Riordan, *Perspectives on Resource Management,* London, Pion, 1971.

2. R. C. Brown, "The Doctrine of Usefulness: Natural Resource and National Park Policy in Canada, 1887-1914", in J. G. Nelson (ed.) *Canadian Parks in Perspective,* Montreal, Harvest House, 1969, pp. 46-62.
3. T. L. Burton, *Natural Resource Policy in Canada*, Toronto, McClelland and Stewart, 1972. See Chapter One, "The Historical Perspective" which provides a short but very useful history of the Conservation Movement in Canada.
4. A. H. Armstrong, "Thomas Adams and the Commission of Conservation" in L. O. Gertler (ed.) *Planning the Canadian Environment,* Montreal Harvest House, 1968.

   C. R. Smith and D. R. Witty, "Conservation, Resources and Environment, an exposition and critical evaluation of the Commission of Conservation, Canada", *Plan Canada,* Vol. 11, No. 1, 1970, pp. 55-71; C. R. Smith and D. R. Witty, "Conservation, Resources and Environment, A Commission of Conservation, Canada, Part 2", *Plan Canada,* Vol 11, No. 3, 1972, pp. 199-216.
5. R. R. Krueger, R. M. Irving and C. Vincent, *Regional Patterns: Disparities and Development,* Canada Studies Foundation and the Canadian Association of Geographers, 1975. Distributed by McClelland and Stewart, Toronto. See particularly pp. 17-24 and accompanying footnote references.
6. *Resources for Tomorrow Conference Background Papers,* Vol. 1 and 2 and Supplementary Volumes, and *Resources for Tomorrow Conference Proceedings,* Queen's Printer, Ottawa, 1961. A selection of some of the background papers appears in R. R. Krueger, *et al.* (eds.) *Regional and Resource Planning in Canada,* Toronto, Holt, Rinehart and Winston, 1963, (rev. ed. 1970).
7. *Pollution and Our Environment Conference Background Papers and Proceedings,* Vol. 1 to 3, Ottawa, Queen's Printer, 1966. A selection of some of the background papers appears in A. de Vos, *et al.* (eds.) *The Pollution Reader*, Montreal, Harvest House, 1968.
8. For example, two books on pollution and environmental problems were produced by one publisher in one year: R. O. Brinkhurst and D. A. Chant, *This Good Good Earth: Our Fight for Survival,* and R. M. Irving and G. B. Priddle (eds.), *Crisis: Readings in Environmental Issues and Strategies,* Toronto, Macmillan of Canada, 1971.
9. For a review of federal government environmental legislation and programs up to 1971 see E. R. Tinney and J. G. N. Parkes, "The Federal Government and Environmental Quality" in *Readings in Canadian Geography,* ed. by R. M. Irving, Holt, Rinehart and Winston, Toronto, rev. ed., 1972, pp. 344-358.
10. C. de Laet, in the Preface to *Man and Resources Reader,* Montreal, Canadian Council of Resource and Environmental Ministers, 1972.
11. *Man and Resources Conference Proceedings,* Montreal, Canadian Council of Resource and Environmental Ministers, 1974
12. *Conference on the Human Environment.* A Report on Canada's preparations for and participation in the United Nations Conference on the Human Environment, Stockholm, Sweden, June, 1972, Ottawa, Information Canada, 1972. This document includes the "Declaration of the United Nations Conference on the Human Environment". Many of the principles enunciated sound similar to principles expressed by the conservationists early in this century.

    Canada and the Human Environment. A contribution by the Government of Canada to the United Nations Conference on the Human Environment, Stockholm, Sweden, June, 1972. Ottawa, Information Canada, 1972.

Section I
Perspectives

Introduction

Before discussing different resource management perspectives,it is useful to clarify the meaning of the word resource.

In his classic book *World Resources and Industries*, Zimmermann provides a succinct functional definition which states that "resources are not, they become".[1] Zimmermann cites the example of how rubber trees were not a resource until the process of vulcanization was discovered in 1839. About a century later, the development of synthetic rubber greatly reduced the value of rubber trees as a resource. Another example is provided by the scavenger fish carp which is a valuable food resource in some parts of the world but is not consumed in Canada because of different perceptions and tastes. Before resource inventory and assessment is conducted, it is imperative that what is being counted and evaluated be defined.

Even after the nature of the resource is defined, its magnitude and value may be subject to different interpretations depending upon the assumptions we make. To illustrate, when assessing the potential of a hydroelectric project, the amount of power to be generated will depend upon technological, economic, legal and political assumptions. As Figure 1 shows, a site may have the physical potential of 100 kilowatts. However available technology might only be capable of tapping 80 kw, and economic feasibility could further reduce the potential to 60 kw. Legal and political matters (land claims, disruption to wildlife habitat) might reduce the potential even further. If an advocate of the project is thinking in terms of that which is technologically available, while an opponent perceives the project in light of what is legally feasible, two different magnitudes of the resource are being assessed. Communications often falter, or disagreements occur, because individuals are discussing a resource with different perceptions of its basic nature or the value of its magnitude.

The papers in this section present different perspectives or viewpoints basic to the understanding of resource management. The chosen perspectives were influenced by Firey's comment that at least three broad groupings of knowledge exist about natural resources. In his words,

> The first of them takes the physical habitat as its point of departure, the second starts with the culture of the human being; the third begins with the attribute of scarcity which attaches to human activities. These three approaches may be called the ecological, the ethnological and the economic.... [2]

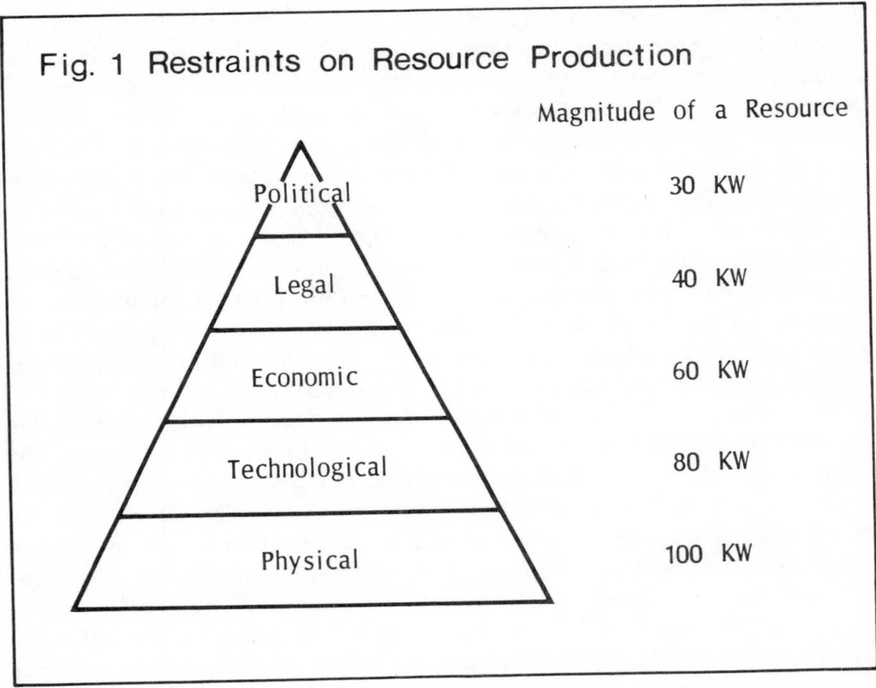

Fig. 1 Restraints on Resource Production

Pearse takes a critical look at Canadian resource policy from an economist's perspective. He illustrates how Canadian policies usually fail to ensure that our endowment of natural wealth is used to our best advantage. His touchstone is the welfare of Canadians generally. He proposes economic rules such as "land ... should go to whichever use yields the most value to society." The knotty problem of using such a rule is how to define and measure the value to society. Pearse asks, "What is the value to us of a wilderness park, a pleasing landscape, a sports fish, a game area, or bathing beaches? And how do we measure the loss we suffer from a polluted stream, the unpleasant smell of a pulp mill, or the flooding of wildlife habitat by dams?" These are real social and environmental benefits and costs, and must not be ignored in decision making just because they are extremely difficult to measure. In papers found in later sections of this book Sewell elaborates on the problems of implementing benefit-cost studies and Day provides a case study that illustrates some of the pitfalls in their use.

Although Pearse argues effectively for considering social values in resource development, his basic decision-making perspective is an economic one, and he admits that "there is a dangerous tendency to regard benefits that generate no revenues as valueless." Pajestka, on the other hand, puts social benefits first, arguing that economic benefits flow from improved social welfare. For example, he states that improved health care and better education are not only justified social aims, but also improve the capacities and qualifications of labour which are required for economic progress. "Since the human factor is of decisive importance for increasing the economic efficiency of each society, it is right that the transformation of man... should become the point of concentration in any development strategy." It is often argued that social and economic objectives are contradictory. Pajestka reasons that social objectives can be integrated with economic objectives and that both these sets of aims can be mutually supportive. Of the more empirical studies that follow later in the book, Usher illustrates this social perspective most effectively as he pleads for considering first and foremost the social impact on natives of any resource development in the North.

The paper by Odum presents the holistic view of the ecologist. He states that the success of managing our resources depends upon the degree to which the whole environment is considered in formulating strategy. Society lacks an effective control mechanism by which negative feedback signals can be received and acted on before there is serious environmental damage resulting from one particular resource management thrust. Academic, professional and government agencies are so hopelessly fragmented that there is no group that speaks or acts for the whole environment. Odum provides us with a planning model which is based on ecological principles and which uses as a starting point "the most important of all considerations, maintenance of the quality of life itself." Since the environment is our living space as well as our food and fibre supply depot, its waste purification, climate control and recreational and esthetic capabilities are as important as its capacity to yield consumable products.

Leopold effectively shows the relationships between ecology and ethics. That his statement is as relevant today as when it was written in 1949 is a commentary on how slow society has been in evolving a code of ethics relating to the land.

Leopold writes with such simplicity and yet with such powerful eloquence that paraphrasing does not do him justice. He says:

> All ethics so far evolved rest upon a single premise; that the individual is a member of a community of interdependent parts. His instincts prompt him to compete for his place in the community, but his ethics prompt him also to co-operate (perhaps in order that there may be a place to compete for). The land ethic simply enlarges the boundaries of the community to include soils, waters, plants, and animals, or collectively: the land.

Leopold complains about the tendency to use only economic criteria in making resource management decisions. "When one of these non-economic categories of the environment is threatened, and if we happen to love it, we invent subterfuges to give it economic importance." Should not, for example, biotic communities such as marshes, bogs or dunes be permitted to exist as a matter of biotic right, regardless of the presence or absence of economic advantage to man? "To sum up: a system of conservation based solely on economic self-interest is hopelessly one-sided."

In a report entitled *It Is Not Too Late – Yet,*[3] the Science Council of Canada states that, with the current social attitude that "growth for growth's sake is essential," we are creating environmental problems faster that we are solving them. If "it is not too late — yet," some of the papers in the following sections indicate that, in some cases, we have reached the eleventh hour.

NOTES

1. W. Firey *Man, Mind and Land,* Glencoe, Ill., Free Press, 1960, p. 20.
2. Erich W. Zimmermann, *Introduction to World Resources* ed. by Henry L. Hunker, New York, Harper and Row, 1964. See particularly Chapter 1, "Meaning and Nature of Resources." Zimmermann's original book, *World Resources and Industries,* was first published in 1933.
3. *It Is Not Too Late – Yet,* Ottawa, Science Council of Canada Report #16, 1972. A large portion of this report has been reprinted in *Protecting the Environment,* ed. by O. P. Dwivedi, Toronto, Copp Clark, 1974, pp. 21-60.

1
Natural Resource Policies: An Economist's Critique

*P. H. Pearse**

A conspicuous feature of Canadian economic development has been the consistently dominant position of natural resource industries throughout our history. It has been a succession of staple exports — fish, furs, wheat, minerals, timber — that has rapidly made us one of the richest nations. Indeed, natural resource exploitation still plays a more dominant role in our economy than in that of almost any other advanced country.

Our unique economic orientation toward natural resources means that government policies directed at their management and development are especially important. For the most part, our constitution vests responsibility for natural resources in governments of the provinces, which means that Canada's economic prosperity and growth depends very substantially on the natural resource policies formulated in provincial capitals.

We have two special reasons for concern about natural resource policies — each reinforcing the relevance of the other: the great significance of resources in our economy, and the omnipresent role of the government as landlord and manager. This paper takes a critical look at natural resource policies from an economist's point of view.[1] I intend to try to explain how our policies often fail to ensure that our endowment of natural wealth is used to our best advantage, how they lead in certain cases to waste, and where they are sometimes inconsistent.[2]

My touchstone will be the welfare of the people of Canada in the aggregate. I assume that the objective is to manage our endowment of natural resources in a way that will ensure their maximum contribution to the welfare of Canadians generally. Thus, I shall regard any measure that prevents or obstructs this optimum use of resources as grounds for criticism.

---

*Peter H. Pearse is Professor of Economics at the University of British Columbia in Vancouver. This paper is an edited and updated version of an earlier study, "Natural Resource Policies in British Columbia: An Economist's Critique," *Exploiting Our Economic Potential: Public Policy and the British Columbia Economy,* edited by R. Shearer, Toronto, Holt, Rinehart and Winston, 1968, pp. 45-57.

Rules for Efficient Resource Use

Before turning to a critique of policies, it will be helpful to set the stage by outlining briefly the general principles that must be followed to ensure best use of resources. What general rules must be followed if each parcel of every natural resource — land, water, forests, etc. — is to be allocated to its highest and best use?

RULE 1: COMPARISON OF ALTERNATIVE USES

The first rule is that the potential benefits that the resources will yield under alternative possible uses must be compared without bias, and the resources must be allocated (in the first instance, at least) to that use yielding the greatest benefit. For example, if a parcel of land can be used for either agricultural or forestry purposes, it should go to whichever of these uses yields the most value to society. This rule is almost obvious, but I shall try to point out later how we often fail to make an unbiased comparison and so misallocate land, water, and other resources. Misallocation means, of course, that we reduce the contribution of the resources to our welfare.

It is worth noting, in connection with this first rule, that the best use for most of our resources is no use at all. The proportion of our natural resources that are worthless to us is, of course, diminishing as we push back the frontier and use up the more accessible supplies. Technological progress makes previously inaccessible resources merchantable, and for other reasons environmental and recreational values are expanding. But it remains true that most of our physical inventory of land, water, forests, minerals and fish cannot be developed to our advantage. Wherever the cost of developing and exploiting a resource exceeds the value of its yield, exploitation involves us in an economic loss. There is no gain from using resources simply because they are there; although some of our policies associate unused resources with waste.

RULE 2: MULTIPLE USE OF VERSATILE RESOURCES

The second rule is that, if two or more simultaneous uses of a resource will yield a greater benefit than one use alone, then the resource must be used on a multiple-use basis. In other words, the primary use should give way to other uses to the extent that the net benefit from these other uses exceeds the sacrifice in the primary use. For example, we might find, following Rule 1, that the best use of a river is in hydroelectric generation, but this interferes with fish runs. We should then examine what modifications of the dams might be undertaken to accommodate the fish, and sacrifice hydro values to the extent that this produces a greater value in fish. Later, I shall point out that, by allocating resources to a single exclusive use, we often forego a greater benefit that might be gained through some combination of uses.

RULE 3: INTENSITY OF RESOURCE DEVELOPMENT

Third, the intensity of development of a resource, that is, the amount of labour and capital that is applied to it, should be increased only so long as spending more on the resource yields a net return. For example, the quality of timber that should be extracted from a forest should be decided by considering the lowest quality of logs that can be harvested and still yield a return on the operation. To remove poorer timber and incur a loss involves a waste of labour and capital. Similarly, if we require all ore in a mine above a certain standard of quality to be removed, and this means removing some ore at a loss, we force a waste by using labour and equipment where its yield is negative. Obviously, the best economic standard of utilization will vary widely in different situations, depending on costs and returns; and so arbitrary standards fixed by legislation for all situations will result in waste of the natural resource in some, and of labour and capital in others.

RULE 4: MAXIMIZE NET RETURNS OVER TIME

As a fourth rule, the rate at which resources should be used up must be determined with reference to expected changes in costs and values so that the resources will yield a maximum net value over time. There are well-established economic criteria for maximizing values through future time, which need not be described here. It is sufficient to make the point that, if we fix rates of exploitation on purely technical or biological grounds, as we often do, we cannot expect to gain maximum potential value because costs and prices of the product will certainly vary through time.

PROBLEMS OF MEASUREMENT

Before leaving these criteria for best management, we must acknowledge one major difficulty in implementing these four rules. This is the problem of measurement. Application of the rules involves measuring the costs and values involved. In many cases, if not in most, the market supplies us with figures we need. We can measure benefits in terms of the price of harvested timber, fish, minerals, and hydroelectricity. The costs are reflected in the costs of labour and capital required for development and exploitation. The objective is to maximize the difference between benefits and costs. But some costs and benefits to society are not measured by the market. What is the value to us of a wilderness park, a pleasing landscape, a sports fish, a game area, or bathing beaches? And how do we measure the loss we suffer from a polluted stream, the unpleasant smell of a pulp mill, or the flooding of wildlife habitat by dams? These are real social benefits and costs, but they are exceedingly difficult to quantify. Yet, to ignore them may well lead us to wrong decisions.

Recent research has helped to provide methods of estimating such non-priced costs and values, but the problem is by no means solved. The essential point to be made here is that all costs and benefits must be considered, whether priced or not. Market prices should be used whenever available, but they must be tempered or modified, at least subjectively, by relevant social costs and values that are not reflected in markets. There is a dangerous (but perhaps natural) tendency to regard benefits that generate no revenues as valueless.

Conflicting Ideals

Provincial governments must design economic policies within the framework of important external constraints. Much depends upon what happens outside each province — in Canada as a whole, and in foreign markets — and there are some economic forces, such as the free movement of people and products between provinces and external trade conditions, that governments of provinces are not free to manipulate. It is within this context that each provincial government must act. Within its limited scope for policy, it must do what it can to create a healthy economic atmosphere for efficient development and use of resources and see to it that resources are used in ways that will contribute to the quality of life in the province.

I can now turn to inconsistencies in our policies in pursuing these objectives. Some confusion can be traced to a conflict among three schools of thought on natural resource development, all of which are deeply entrenched in our traditions and imprinted in our policies. These schools of thought can be identified as the "conservationists", the "promoters", and the "technologists". They conflict because the conservationists advocate restraint and preservation, while the promotors press for greater efforts toward development and exploitation in the interests of economic growth. While these two schools both believe that their conflicting approaches are in the best interests of society, the technologists are primarily interested in the resources for their own sake.

The conservation ethic is a legacy of the conservation movement that was sweeping the United States at the time Canadian resource policies were first being formulated. It is concerned with the apparent despoliation of our bounty of natural resources under the pressure of expansion. But conservationists are a mixed bag by any standards, and the term conservation can apply to almost anything. Aesthetes use it to mean complete preservation. At the other extreme, oilmen use it to imply avoiding physical waste in recovery — that is, full use. To agriculturalists, it means rehabilitating the land, and so on. William Howard Taft once said that everyone is in favour of conservation, no matter what it means: and so it is perhaps not surprising that advocates of almost any policy use the word to describe their proposals. Often, it is meant to describe good management generally, but sometimes, the goodness defies logic. One favourite, for example, is that conservation is the use of natural resources for the greatest good of the greatest number for the longest time. As more than one commentator has observed, this is as illogical as setting out to distribute a bag of candy among children in such a way as to maximize simulataneously the amount of candy received by each child, the number of children who receive candy, and the length of time the candy will last.

But there is one consistent thread among conservationists which deserves attention. This is the conviction that private industry tends to exploit natural resources wastefully, or too fast. Conservationists therefore conclude that it is in the interests of society for governments to impose regulations and controls to enforce restraint and prudence on the part of private industries involved in natural resource exploitation.

The promoters are led to the opposite conclusion. This group sees natural resource exploitation as the key to growth. Governments, far from imposing restraints, are enjoined to subsidize development by expenditures on railroads, highways, exploration, and power and communications, in order to open up the frontier and otherwise to unlock the doors to nature's bounty. Primary industries deserve special concessions to encourage them to expand our primary industrial base. Unlike conservationists, promoters tend to have confidence in private business as a means of advancing the social interest, and so the proper role of government is to assist entrepreneurial activity. It is this school that advocates public programs to open up the North, to build roads to resources, and to provide tax concessions and other incentives to resource industries. At the extreme, development becomes an end in itself, almost regardless of cost.

These first two schools conflict directly. The third — the technologists — cuts across the other two. Technologists focus their interest on resources themselves, and the policies they advocate tend to be more in the interests of the resources than in the people who own or enjoy them. They set themselves technical or administrative goals for management, without much reference to economic and social considerations, and they often implicitly assume that these will best serve the social welfare. I refer to such goals as obtaining the maximum physical growth of timber or fish, and an equal annual harvest, without reference to whether these represent the most desirable systems on economic or social grounds.

These three schools have had a powerful influence on Canadian natural resource policies. The conservationists are widely dispersed and make themselves heard through organizations of naturalists, outdoor clubs, sportsmen, and aesthetes. The promoters are concentrated in industrial, financial, and promotional enterprises. The technologists consist of professional groups of biologists, engineers, foresters, and agriculturalists in government and private enterprises. Needless to say, the lines of demarcation between these groups cannot be clearly drawn; technical people, for example, sometimes advocate conservationist policies and sometimes policies more often associated with those of the promoters. But I think it is useful to identify conflicting forces in this way and to examine their varying effects on our policies.

Shortcomings of Present Policies

What are the results of these conflicting interests on natural resource policies? In particular, we are interested in effects that prevent our obtaining a maximum *value* from our resource endowment. I shall now attempt to identify a number of these perverse effects with reference to policies toward specific resources.

FAILURE TO PUT RESOURCES TO THEIR BEST USE

We observed earlier that, in order to get the most benefit from any natural resource, its alternative uses must be weighed against each other in an unbiased way, and the resource must be allocated to the use that yields the greatest benefit. Our complicated methods of public resource administration often prevent this choice of the best use. Some uses are arbitrarily assigned preference, and often subtle forms of subsidies to certain activities distort the apparent relative returns.

The most obvious case in point is our treatment of agriculture. Relevant provincial departments almost invariably give preference to agricultural use of rural land. Farmers have typically been given preference in the sale of public land, and it has often been sold at nominal prices. Little attempt has been made to weigh the potential productivity of land under agriculture against its potential yield in other uses and property and income tax preferences to farming distort comparisons. As a result, throughout rural areas, large tracts of land are under marginal agricultural use, much of which would be more productive in other uses, such as forestry, recreation, and other forms of development.

In addition, our agricultural policies distort economic activity in favour of farming and provide incentives for expansion of agriculture. Farmers receive, in addition to special land purchasing rights, a variety of fiscal concessions, special credit facilities, technical assistance, marketing protection (sometimes euphemistically referred to as "supply management"), certain direct subsidies on agricultural products, and other privileges and priorities not available to other industries. Provincial legislation relating to forests, water, game, trespass, motor vehicles, and so on, all provide special privileges to farmers. The impact of all these provisions is difficult to measure, but it is undoubtedly substantial. They all tend to cause too much land, as well as other resources, to be allocated to agricultural use relative to alternative uses. In other words, our rural land is often not being used in the most productive way.

Water offers another example. How much water should be allocated to different uses, to generate the greatest aggregate benefit? To most people this question is unfamiliar, evoking responses that, while not incorrect, simply obscure the problem. For example, it is often suggested that the water's indispensibility to human life offers a principle that might guide its allocation; or that factory uses should prevail over farming uses because industry provides more employment. These ideas are not helpful, because policy questions rarely involve all-or-nothing choices, but rather decisions about possible gains from allocating a little more of a resource to one use at the expense of another.[3]

Water resource agencies often allocate water use according to some arbitrary ranking of priorities that bears no relevance to water's value in alternative uses. In Ontario, the most conspicuous shortcoming of water allocation policy is its bias in the treatment of certain uses and users without reference to the social values served. Ordinary users, municipalities and Ontario Hydro can use water with relative impunity, regardless of the value that it could contribute in other activities. The regulatory authorities give priority to established users almost without exception. Beyond this they give preference to domestic and livestock uses over municipal, commercial and industrial purposes, and tend to accord these higher priority than recreational and aesthetic uses. The social cost is manifest not so much in the misuses of water as in more subtle misallocations of land and capital as users select locations that are otherwise less suitable from the point of land use, markets and transportation facilities.[4]

In a similar manner, resources are assigned to forestry, to parks, and to other uses without due attention to alternatives. A variety of fiscal preferences is available to other specific industries, such as the depletion allowances for mining enterprises, and so on. All these arrangements have the effect of distorting resource use patterns by interfering with our ability to compare alternative values either through market processes or through government discretion.

After resources have been assigned to particular uses in this unsystematic way, they are typically placed under the jurisdiction of departments and agencies that are exclusively concerned with those uses: a Forest Service in the case of forest land, a Parks Branch in the case of parks, a Department of Agriculture in the case of farmland, and so on. These agencies, understandably, see themselves as guardians of the resource for the assigned uses. But their special interests create an obstacle to secondary users.

Another precept for efficient resource use, noted earlier, is that secondary or tertiary uses should be allowed to encroach on the primary use to the extent that they produce benefts in excess of the loss to the primary use. But, under our single-minded administrative agencies, secondary uses often do not receive unbiased consideration. A Forest Service, for example, is primarily concerned with timber production on the forest land under its jurisdiction. There is a built-in bias against other uses, such as recreation, which might well interfere with forestry objectives. Foresters usually agree with the principle of multiple use, but they interpret it to mean that recreation, for example, should be allowed so long as it doesn't interfere with timber production. This, of course, is not adequate, because our second rule is that the alternative use should be allowed to interfere so long as recreational gains exceed forestry losses. These considerations are particularly important in planning the location of development and access roads, as well as methods of exploitation.

Technologists concerned with the primary use adopt the objective of attaining technical goals in the development of the primary resource, and promoters of the primary-resource industry are interested in maximizing the returns from the primary use. The conservationists become concerned mostly about whether the primary exploiters are exploiting wastefully or too fast. But there is little analysis directed toward improving the established pattern of uses and the balance between them.

The distortions and costs that result from misallocation of resources between uses increase with the passage of time. Efficient use requires a steady response to changing economic and social conditions that continuously alter the optimum pattern. Our policies of assigning land and resources to particular uses, so popular among planners, tend to obstruct this required flexibility.

FAILURE TO ENCOURAGE ECONOMICALLY EFFICIENT USE

Once a decision is made to use a resource for a certain purpose, it is in the interests of everyone that the exploitation take place as efficiently as possible, and this means minimizing costs relative to the value of output. The desirability of economic efficiency of this kind is most obvious in the case of commercial activities. It should be emphasized that economic efficiency is not the only goal sought by governments nor the only problem susceptible to economic analysis. Other valid objectives may be development of resources to promote certain kinds of activity, or to benefit certain groups in preference to others, or to favour certain areas. However, analysis of the efficacy of pursuing such other goals, implicitly or explicitly, requires evaluation of the benefits and costs in any event. I believe that governments frequently involve other policy objectives without sufficient awareness of the economic costs involved.

Many of our present policies prevent private industries from achieving the possible levels of economic efficiency and, hence, the value of our resources is diminished. A dramatic example is found in the administration of commercial fisheries.

To appreciate the problems involved, it is necessary to understand the nature of common-property resources, which are those characterized by lack of exclusive ownership rights, the inability of individual users to control rates of exploitation, and the absence of incentives to conserve the resource. Thus, a salmon is not owned by any particular fisherman, he cannot determine whether the fish is caught or left, nor does he have any incentive to consider saving it if it will be worth more later. Furthermore, as long as there is profit to be earned, new fishermen continue to enter the industry. To increase his share of the catch, each fisherman tends to invest in more sophisticated equipment. The outcome is too many fishermen chasing a relatively constant or depleting number of fish with ever more costly equipment. The result is not conducive to efficiency.

Until recently, the west coast salmon fishery (Canada's most valuable fishery) was controlled by federal restrictions on fishing time, gear and fishing methods. Inefficient fishing was made compulsory as individual fishermen spent increasing amounts of money in order to improve their share of the catch before time or quota limits were reached. The outcome was an industry characterized by too many fishermen with over-capitalized boats earning relatively low incomes.[5] The potential enormous net value of the salmon resource was dissipated in unnecessary production costs.

In 1968 the federal Fisheries Minister announced a program to tackle these problems. Licences were introduced in order to restrict the number of fishermen, and the government later offered to purchase boats in order to reduce the fleet size. By 1976 the fleet had been reduced to less than 5,000 vessels from over 8,000 in 1969.

The primary purpose of the salmon licensing program was to improve the economic performance of the fishery and to enhance the incomes of fishermen by eliminating excess fleet capacity. Economic efficiency requires, of course, that the catch be taken not by the "most productive" fishing vessels, but rather by those that can harvest at lowest real cost.[6] The fleet reduction program clearly has the effect of excluding first the casual, part-time, recreational and other low output fishermen. Insofar as the fishing boats that show low earnings are those that involve the lowest opportunity cost of fishing effort, the program distorts in favour of high cost fishing. At the same time capitalization in the fleet has actually increased, as the larger vessels remaining are rebuilt and re-equipped to increase their share of the harvest.

The distribution of costs and benefits must also be examined. The adverse effects of the program are felt most by the casual, part-time and low-income fishermen, while the major private benefits accrue to owners of licensed vessels. In spite of the objective of enhancing the meagre incomes of fishermen, those who will gain least are likely to include those with the lowest incomes and fewest employment alternatives.

In other industries, standards of utilization and management are imposed on technological grounds without reference to economic efficiency. The annual harvest of biological resources such as timber and fish is typically regulated according to technological criteria and is not responsive to economic variables. In both these industries, the goal of management is a purely technological one, namely to achieve a regime in which the maximum sustainable amount of the resource can be harvested each year.

But the goal of maximum sustained physical yield contains no economic logic. It does not take an economist to understand that more value could be gained by exploiting more when values are high and less when values are low, though economists have the analytical tools to provide criteria for the best adjustment to changing conditions. In some cases it would never be to our benefit to harvest the maximum sustainable yield, and in others, it would be in our interests to harvest more.

Maximum sustained yield frustrates economic efficiency by imposing an inflexible rate of production, but the concept of maximum yield is indeterminate in any event. It is always possible to increase yield or recovery by spending more in the growing or harvesting processes, and we should do so as long as the benefits exceed the costs. But such criteria are seldom applied: the age to which timber is planned to be grown is typically fixed at the age that will maximize the volume growth of wood. This calculation, it turns out, is a critical one because, having accepted the objective of converting the forests to a perfectly regulated sustained-yield regime, the age at which we expect to harvest second crops determines how fast we remove our stock of virgin timber. It also happens that the age to which trees must be grown to maximize physical growth is considerably greater than the age that will yield most value. The result is that we have adopted a growing age that is considerably too long, which, in turn, limits our present rate of harvest to a level well below an economically efficient rate. Nor are there compelling silvicultural or environmental reasons for these artificial growing periods. This series of technological constraints has serious economic consequences, for it is likely that the forest industry is too small to maximize the value of potential timber production, being constrained below its optimum size by technological goals of management.

All these policies are the result of the influence of technologists in pressing technical goals of resource management, such as maximum physical production and steady yields. They reflect a preoccupation with manipulating resources to achieve contrived regimes that concede little to their contribution to society at large, although this is the basic purpose of resource use and development.

FAILURE TO CONSIDER ALTERNATIVES

My third criticism is that, in seeking sources of supply of some product, we often fail to consider the alternatives with a view toward selecting the most advantageous. The need to consider all alternatives is an obvious requirement that needs no explanation, but our present approach of selecting sites for hydro developments and parks, for example, is to examine a particular proposal in isolation. Similarly, we are currently in danger of accepting proposals to develop very costly supplies of natural gas in the arctic and off-shore without rigorous analysis of the alternatives of reducing exports and increasing production in established regions.

It is not sufficient to demonstrate that a particular proposal is economically feasible or socially desirable when there are many others that are also feasible. We must make an effort to select the best. Instead, we often make a decision about a project on its particular merits alone, rather than by comparing the relative merits of alternatives. The history of expensive water-resource development in the United States is characterized by this failure to consider alternatives and we have witnessed the same thing in the preoccupation of Canadian decision makers, at one time or another, with the Columbia River proposals, the Peace River development and the James Bay project. Equally serious, projects are often considered on a take-it-or-leave-it basis with little attention to modifications to the design and scale that would enhance benefits relative to costs.

FAILURE TO CONSIDER NON-PRICED BENEFITS AND COSTS

Finally, present policies typically fail to respond adequately to values and costs that are not registered in the market place. With respect to most of the shortcomings of policy mentioned earlier, the available technical and economic information and tools of analysis are sufficient to prescribe solutions — at least as adequately as we can for most other economic problems. But, where the market does not demonstrate society's costs and values, the analyst lacks important data needed for identifying best choices. This is particularly common and important in natural resource management. Where mining development conflicts with recreational use, we need to compare relative values, but while the industrial value of the minerals is known rather accurately, the value of recreation is not easily quantifiable. Such values as outdoor recreation, fish and wildlife, and the amenity and quality of the environment are often affected by various forms of resource use, but their value cannot be measured in precise dollar terms for comparison with the commercial activity. But this does not justify ignoring them. Such values must be identified and considered — if only subjectively — in making decisions.

I suspect that there are two major reasons for the fact that non-marketed values are often given short shrift by decision makers. The first is simply that, if one activity yields revenues and another does not, the obvious worth of the former is difficult to subjugate to the nebulous claims of the latter. The second reason, which complements the first, is an out-of-date conviction that our resources are so vast that conflicts between uses need not arise. Thus, if a mining company wishes to develop mineral resources in a recreational area, the recreational values are considered expendable because plenty of other untouched areas exist. But we can no longer blandly assume that conflicts need not be rationalized, and until we realize this, our arbitrary decisions will obviously result in some resources being wrongly used. Indeed, a major justification for retention of public ownership of land and resources is the opportunity it affords to accommodate values that private owners would ignore.

Directions for Reform

Our natural resource policies generally are alarmingly devoid of economic logic. Indeed, economists have hitherto had very little influence on natural resource policies compared to other areas of public policy; nor, until recently, have they given much systematic attention to natural resource matters. This is not to say that the objectives of resource policies ought to be purely economic, or that economists have any special expertise in prescribing what the goals of society ought to be. The realm of the economist is in the process of making social choices — in demonstrating the implications of alternative actions. Given the objectives of social policy, the economist can analyse the alternative ways of pursuing those objectives, and help identify the most effective means of achieving them.

Our natural resources are capable of yielding a variety of products and services that contribute to our economic and social welfare, and our policies should aim at realizing their potential without waste. Yet, as I have tried to point out, our current policies are often inconsistent with this goal because they fail to incorporate even some of the most basic economic principles of social choice.

Any attempt to rationalize natural resource policies will be fraught with political reaction. Deeply vested and vociferous interests — not only the three schools referred to earlier, but also particular groups of resource users — will resist substantial changes. But, while the emotional and political obstacles will retard the pace of reform, the direction of improvement is clear enough.

As a first step, we should attempt to remove the barriers to coordinated land and resource-use planning. Decisions about how resources are to be used should be made through unbiased institutional arrangements using well-established economic criteria. Only then can we be sure that resources would be put to the use or uses that can reasonably be expected to contribute most to our welfare.

Second, resource-use planners, and the managers of public resources must pay attention to the implications of their decisions for the economic efficiency of the industry rather than concentrate exclusively on the technical aspects of the resources. The folly of concentrating on technical goals at the expense of economic efficiency has already been discussed. The value to us of our industrial resources depends upon costs of production, and so it is the government's role, as landlord and manager, to ensure that the production efficiency that private producers are capable of attaining is taken advantage of and is stimulated.

It is characteristic of our resource management that technological expertise has far outspaced policy. While it is true that most foresters, geologists, biologists, and so on are quick to assert that they still have much to learn about natural resources, it is also true that the major obstacle to improved management is seldom the limitations of scientific or technical knowledge: it is the policy framework within which the experts must work. Indeed, management policies are so out of date in relation to the state of scientific and technical knowledge that many experts have lost interest in the broad issues of policy.

This situation means that we are unable to take advantage of the great scientific advances in natural resource fields. What is the use, for example, of the startling new possibilities in the production and management of fisheries if the potential value of increased harvests will be dissipated by poor management policies? And what of the impressive new technical possibilities for catching fish, whose use we cannot allow precisely because they are so efficient? How can one get excited about developing new and better forest crops when we fail to take full advantage of what we already have and will probably manage the new crops in the same way? Economic efficiency in our resource industries does not get much attention by government at the level of managing the resources themselves; it is much more conspicuous at the processing, refining, and manufacturing levels where producers are less constrained by perverse public controls. And it is at these secondary levels also that the great scientific innovations have been used to advantage.

A third direction of reform would be to temper the technological orientation of resource management agencies by forcing them to consider the economic implications of their procedures and controls. The problem obviously has much to do with the training of technologists, which tends to be exclusively oriented toward the specific resources. It therefore appears desirable to introduce into professional education programs some of the principles of social choice.

Finally, decision makers must begin to take more serious and systematic account of values that do not yield monetary returns. As our society expands and grows richer and industrial technology advances, the non-industrial benefits of our natural environment can be expected to increase in relative value. While technological advance tends to free us from dependence on particular natural resources, growth in income and leisure time increases our demands on resources for recreational and aesthetic purposes. These considerations are especially crucial when irreversible decisions are at stake which foreclose options in the future.

But whatever policy we adopt, we must face squarely the problem of making judgements of value in the absence of prices. Researchers elsewhere have made a small start on this important problem, but for some time to come, it will be necessary to resort frequently to subjective evaluations. But while the academician's trite defence that much more research is needed is particularly apt in this connection, we should, nevertheless, use the best methods that are already available to us to ensure that all important social values are considered.

NOTES

1. For other economists' viewpoints concerning management of natural resources see F. O. Sargent, "A resource economist views a natural area," *Journal of Soil and Water Conservation*, Vol. 24, No. 1, January-February, 1969, pp. 8-11; T. L. Burton, *Natural Resource, Policy in Canada*, Toronto, McClelland and Stewart, 1972; and, papers by Crabbé, Scott and Dales in *Natural resource development in Canada: multidisciplinary seminar*, edited by P. Crabbé, and I.M. Spry, Social Science Studies No. 8, Ottawa, University of Ottawa Press, 1973, pp. 99-126.
2. An earlier article considering similar aspects is P. H. Pearse, "Public management and mismanagement of natural resources in Canada," *Queen's Quarterly*, Vol 73, No. 1, Spring 1966, pp. 86-99.
3. R. S. Campbell, P. H. Pearse, A. Scott and M. Uzelac, "Water management in Ontario — an economic evaluation of public policy," *Osgoode Hall Law Journal*, Vol. 12, No. 3, December 1974, p. 477.
4. *Ibid.*, pp. 477-478.
5. B. A. Campbell, "Salmon licence control: the first three phases," *Western Fisheries*, Vol. 84, July 1972, pp. 13-35.
6. P. H. Pearse, "Rationalization of Canada's West Coast salmon fishery: an economic evaluation," *Economic aspects of fish production*, Paris, Organization for Economic Cooperation and Development, 1972, p. 192.

2
The Social Dimensions of Resource Development

*Jozef Pajestka**

The process of resource development does not only consist of a series of algebraic relations between the increase of national income, investments, exports, imports, etc. Economic factors are powerfully influenced by social considerations; they also have weighty social consequences. Changes in the rate of expansion, in investment capacity, in the introduction of new technological processes and the like are, to a major degree, the result of modifications in the economic behaviour of man. Therefore, the development process must be viewed as a process in which progress results from changes in man's behaviour. And because it is a social phenomenon, conditioned by interhuman relations and by socio-economic institutions, the development process must be seen in a special light and certain factors must be taken into account in working out a strategy for development. Thus, such a strategy, must reckon with social development forces, social development objectives, social and institutional solutions likely to contribute to increased economic efficiency. To put it more precisely, *these social aspects must constitute the absolutely indispensable, integral element of any resource development strategy.* They are particularly essential for developing areas for which significant socio-institutional changes represent the most basic factor for modernizing their economy.

General Guidelines for a Strategy of Socio-economic Change

The development strategy is always conditioned by existing structures and by factors which are both internal (economic, social, political) and external. Therefore it is pointless to try to formulate universal strategic rules which would be valid for every area. Whatever is mature or, shall we say, socially and economically feasible and desirable at some particular stage of development may no longer be so, or may acquire different

---

* Jozef Pajestka is Director of the Institute of Planning, Poland, and Professor of Economics at the University of Warsaw. This paper is based upon exerpts from J. Pajestka, *The social dimensions of development*, New York, United Nations Centre for Economic and Social Information, Executive Briefing Paper 3, 1970, pp 13-17, 18-19, 23-25.

dimensions, in a future stage of development. Thus, solutions for different developmental stages in a given area cannot be universal.

I would now like to discuss certain aspects of the development strategy, placing the main emphasis on the human factor and its social conditioning. However weighty they may be, these are precisely the aspects most commonly underestimated. And they can be of wide application as general guidelines for action tending to quicken the pace of progress. Their practical use, however, always requires careful confrontation with the existing, concrete circumstances in a given area.

The following reasoning, as well as the solutions proposed in regard to a strategy, are concerned chiefly with quality rather than quantity. They provide certain guidelines for a development policy without quantitative models for developmental interdependence. Experience has shown, however, that it is precisely the qualitative concepts which are of key significance in the formulation of a development policy. We can speak of their consistency and of the socio-economic rationality, although they need not be expressed in figures. Of course, concrete programs of action designed to implement a well-defined strategy must be formulated in a more operational way and, to a large extent, in a quantitative way also.

Economic efficiency depends primarily on human qualities, a capacity for rational action, innovative ability, energy, etc. Not only is the contribution of each individual of concern, but the way it expresses itself in the social structure, where it acquires a new dimension and different values, is also important. This is the starting point for the multitude of undertakings related to a development strategy. We then reach rather basic conclusions which help chiefly to understand the range and type of development undertakings and to formulate the objectives of a development policy.

The distinction between economic and social objectives of development policy is widespread. Economic objectives are generally meant to include increases in the growth rate through a rise of the production potential (e.g. by way of capital investment); the expansion of exports, etc. Social aims comprise improved living standards for the widest social masses, education, health care and the like, increased employment opportunities and a more equitable distribution of income and of social opportunities. It is often argued that these objectives compete with one another and that they are mutually contradictory. Theory and practice are often based on the thesis that the implementation of social aims interferes with the achievement of a high rate of economic development.

There is no doubt that we face here a very complex and difficult problem, and that we would be ill-advised to try to formulate absolute principles of general application. Therefore, we must reject *a priori* arguments designed to show either the necessary contradiction of these objectives or their natural and total conformity with one another. Instead, we should like to demonstrate that the social objectives can be integrated with the economic ones and that both these sets of aims can be mutually supportive, resulting in a feed-back most advantageous to overall progress. This is not a purely theoretical argument; it is imbedded in reality and essential to any development strategy.

So then, improved health care, better education for the people, increased production and a wider spread of skills, knowledge and culture are not only justified social aims; they also improve physical capability, the capacities and qualifications of man, all of which are of the utmost importance whenever economic progress is concerned. Similarly, the greatest possible involvement of all those able to work, in productive activities or in any other socially useful action, is not only a social objective. It can also have significant economic effects and help to raise man's abilities. A policy which promotes equal social opportunities for all individuals has favourable economic effects, since it permits a fuller utilization of enormous human resources and talents. In general, one can say that it is by coupling skilfully the two problems *development for whom* and *development through whom* that economic and social objectives become integrated with the most favourable effect on overall socio-economic progress.

Of course, all this belongs to the realm of the potential. Its realization is a tremendous and extremely difficult task. For instance, there is no guarantee whatever that an increase in budgetary outlays for social purposes will produce any or all the economic effects already mentioned. In order actually to integrate social and economic purposes and to ensure that outlays for social undertakings are economically fruitful, the entire development policy has to be directed to this end, both in terms of the economic solutions it proposes as well as in regard to social and institutional changes.

In the light of the preceding remarks, we are able to formulate the following general conclusions:

1. Since the human factor is of decisive importance for increasing the economic efficiency of each society, it is right that *the transformation of man – of his behaviour, and of his socio-productive features – should become the point of concentration in any development strategy* designed for the areas.
2. This approach opens up the *possibility of harmonizing social and economic development objectives;* the achievement of this harmonization should be one of the main objectives of any development policy.
3. A development strategy oriented towards the transformation of men cannot be implemented only by increasing social outlays and by calling for change. It must assume the form of an *integrated action program covering the whole field and all factors affecting man.* The importance and the nature of the changes required by such a program, within existing stan-

dards of law and usage, relationships resulting from property ownership, various socio-economic institutions, the organization of social activity, training programs, etc., will be commensurate and proportionate to the rigidity of the existing structures, relationships and traditions impeding the development process and hindering the growth of economic efficiency. The scope of these changes must also depend on the extent of the ambitions and aspirations of the area. The choice of those who are able to elaborate and consequently implement such programs of action is of course a political question which must be left open; an appropriate solution must be worked out by each of the areas determined to assume responsibility for its destiny.

These arguments and observations also have direct implications for the scope of undertakings to be covered by the development policy. They boil down to the postulate that *the scope of undertakings resulting from a development policy, which also means the range of active socio-economic changes, covers the entire economy and the entire society.* If the increase in a society's economic efficiency is indeed to be achieved by raising the activity, qualifications, ability and enterpreneurship of man, the economic effects of the development policy will depend on the extent of the changes undergone by that society and on the degree to which it acquires new socio-economic features.

Convincing as this argument may be — and it would indeed be difficult to put forward any counterargument of similar weight — the postulate is clearly contrary to the actual development policies in most areas. It is also contrary to the more influential patterns of economic thinking on which an understanding of the development process is based, and which is almost universally applied in planning.

In economic analyses, the rate of development is rather a function of investment and of import capacity than of the human factor and of human ability in raising economic efficienty. The rate of development to be achieved is very often defined as a result of algebraic operations, performed by means of a few economic variables, while the main determinant of this rate is an assumed scarcity of investment means. Man appears here chiefly as a scant "qualification factor". Consequently, the range of people covered by the development process is determined by the range of feasible capital investments. As a result, a major part of society remains beyond the compass of the development strategy.

No doubt, one can express doubts as to the realism of a postulate which assumes massive change in man's behaviour as well as the involvement of all segments of society in development. But let us be quite clear, the question is not only one of the changes which transform man's environment by way of large investment undertakings, thereby bringing changes to his economic efficiency. The question also has to do with all other possible changes which are available to a given society as well as with policies which have a positive influence on the activity and economic efficiency of people. I claim that this postulate is a highly realistic one. Its implementation must be left to the reformers of each and every area, since they are more familiar with the conditions, possibilities and aspirations of the area to which they belong.

The implementation of a strategy capable of imparting social dynamism through a wide range of socio-institutional transformations has certain economic implications, some of which call for consideration in this paper. In particular, one of the main objectives is to ensure consistency between the social development strategy and the basic economic solutions.

Greater Social Justice As a Goal of Development Strategy

The sort of strategy which has just been proposed is a strategy of engineered social change on a scale involving the whole of society. Though it is being engineered and guided, it cannot produce its effects without popular support and in the absence of active social co-participation. This type of support and co-participation requires a development policy from which the various levels of society can benefit. As previously indicated, a link is essential between the "development through whom" and the "development for whom" concepts.

This simply means that social justice must preside over the distribution of the benefits resulting from a development strategy and this requires that the strategy itself must be a just one devised in the light of mankind's historical experience. Greater social justice is not only a properly recognized objective pursued by man since the dawn of history, it can also be a means of importing additional dynamism to social development. However, this remains more of a possibility than absolute truth, and its implementation is a proper objective of social development.

In the context of a general development strategy, social justice is indeed an indispensable condition; it is not, however, a sufficient condition for imparting dynamism to socio-economic development. Justice is not a substitute for efficiency and development dynamics. With a development policy devoid of the appropriate organizational, economical and other measures, one might have greater justice but not necessarily greater progress. We are faced here with the old and very fundamental dilemma: does greater social justice contribute to an increase in economic efficiency or does it impede it? This is, by no means, a theoretical question. It is the conceptual focal point on the basis of which various strategies for socio-economic development are devised.

The present growth process of many areas indicates considerable and increasing differences in the living standards of various social classes, groups, regions, etc. This process leaves in its train, or in some cases even creates, large areas of stagnation, degradation, poverty and hunger; it excludes large segments of society from the development process and relegates other social groups to the periphery of progress.

It is often argued that these differences are unavoidable. Supposedly, the transition from a traditional to a more sophisticated economy must be characterized by growing economic differences, particularly in the earlier stages of this transition. The reason for this is that development initially takes place in certain areas only, temporarily leaving aside some others. These areas are either those suitable for profitable crops or rich in mineral resources, or again certain sectors particularly attractive to industry. A similar argument is applied *mutatis mutandis* to certain social groups. Finally, it is claimed that sizable differences in incomes provide a powerful incentive, that great fortunes contribute to savings and, consequently, to investment. These and other arguments of a general nature are given as reasons explaining the important and growing differences now observable within developing countries.

The type of development characterized by great disparities and social injustice is undoubtedly a fact, and one which occurs on a very large scale. Facts, however, are no justification for necessity, nor do they prove that no alternative exists. Theoretical arguments, which generalize these facts, are unable to show that development based on greater justice is either impossible or that it would be less dynamic.

On the other hand, it is sometimes argued that greater social justice is such an important social objective that it is worth sacrificing, for its sake, a higher rate of economic growth. One could agree with this; in fact, an option is sometimes available between the rate of growth and other important socio-economic objectives. Nevertheless, it should not be too easily taken for granted that greater social justice results, as a rule, in reduction in economic efficiency and, thereby, in a lower rate of growth. This contention has never been demonstrated through experience.

3
Air-Land-Water — An Ecological Whole

*Eugene P. Odum**

Successfully manipulating the environment for the long-term benefit of man depends on the degree to which the whole environment is considered in formulating the strategy. In other words, most of our failures can be traced to shortsighted action that considered only the benefits to a part of the landscape rather than to the whole or to a lack of understanding of the entire chain of events that must follow any large-scale manipulation of the landscape.

In our agricultural zeal to increase crop yields we have either poured too much fertilizer and insecticides on the land or the techniques of application have been so inefficient that large quantities of these substances have leached into our waterways causing fish kills, serious reduction in water quality (i.e. eutrophication), and, as is now apparent, even endangering human health. Likewise, in our industrial zeal to produce more efficient detergents and other chemicals for "better living" in the city, we have created still other kinds of country-wide air, water, and soil pollution because the elementary necessity for degradation and recycling in the environment was not considered in the product design.

We must not forget that man is part and not apart from his environment. Whatever we put into or take away from our environment on any large scale will sooner or later directly affect all of us. This, then, is what we mean when we speak of the ecological whole or, in technical language, the ecosystem.

A "Good Thing"

Mankind has suffered so long from not having enough that it is hard for all of us to realize that having too much of a "good thing" can be equally serious. Concrete is a "good thing", but not if we cover up too much of our productive land, not to mention our scenic land, with it. As the human population approaches the saturation level, we must begin to

---

*Eugene P. Odum is the Alumni Foundation professor of zoology and director of the Institute of Ecology at the University of Georgia in Athens. This paper is an abbreviated version of an article by the same title that appeared in the *Journal of Soil and Water Conservation,* Vol. 24, No. 1, Jan. — Feb. 1969, pp. 4-7.

adjust to the steady-state situation where too much of a "good thing" can be as damaging as too little. Society currently lacks an effective control mechanism by which negative feedback signals can be received and acted on before there is a serious overshoot in environmental manipulations. Academic, professional and governmental departments and agencies are so hopelessly fragmented into technical specialities and special interest groups that there is no group that speaks or acts for the whole environment. For example, the building of large water impoundments is rapidly becoming an exercise of engineering skill as an end in itself rather than, as it should be, a part of an integrated plan for the whole landscape. Politically powerful but narrowly mission-oriented agencies in our government are putting on the drawing boards plans to dam up just about every river and stream in North America.

As individuals, we readily recognize that we can easily inundate too much of the landscape at the expense of other needed land uses. We also recognize that sedimentation and atomic power are making many of the large, existing impoundments obsolete before our tax dollars have half paid for them. Organized society, however, is finding it difficult to determine how and when to apply the brakes. How, then, can environmental science (i.e. our understanding of the ecosystem) control environmental technology (i.e. our manipulative skills with bulldozers and concrete)? The answer, of course, is two-fold: (1) we must have a body of sound theory on which to base land management strategy, and (2) we must have organizations capable of educating and maintaining the confidence of the public at-large so that governments can act for the benefit of the whole.

Ecosystem Development

Ecosystems undergo orderly development as do individual organisms because the biotic components are capable of modifying and controlling the physical environment to varying degrees. This process of change is commonly called "ecological succession", but I prefer to term it "ecosystem development" in order to emphasize the positive rather than the negative aspects.

Table 1 summarizes the major changes that occur in the development of an ecosystem, irrespective of the physiographic site or the climatic region. Trends are emphasized by contrasting the situation in early development with that at maturity. This table, in essence, contrasts "young nature" with "mature nature" and lays the foundation for an ecological solution to the growing conflicts between man and nature.

As shown in Table 1, youthful types of ecosystems, such as agricultural crops or the early stages of forest development, have characteristics that contrast to those of "adult" systems, such as mature forests or climax prairies, for example:

TABLE 1
Trends in the Ecological Development of Landscapes

Ecosystem Attribute	Developmental Stages	Mature Stages
Gross primary productivity (total photosynthesis)	Increasing	Stabilized at moderate level
Net primary productivity (yield)	High	Low
Standing crop (biomass)	Low	High
Ratio growth to maintenance (production/respiration)	Unbalanced	Balanced
Ratio biomass to energy flow (growth + maintenance)	Low	High
Utilization of primary production by heterotrophy (animals & man)	Predominantly via linear grazing food chains	Predominantly web-like detritus food chains
Diversity	Low	High
Nutrients	Inorganic (extrabiotic)	Organic (intrabiotic)
Mineral cycles	Open	Closed
Selection pressure	For rapidly growing species adapted to low density	For slow growing species adapted to equilibral density
Stability (resistance to outside perturbations)	Low	High

1. High net productivity that is available for harvest or storage.
2. Relatively small standing crop at any one time with a consequent low ratio between biomass and productivity.
3. Unbalanced metabolism with an excess of production over utilization.
4. Linear grazing food chains (i.e. grass-cow-man) in contrast to complex web-like energy flows involving animal-microbial detritus utilization that characterize older systems.
5. Low biotic diversity (for example, few species but large numbers of individuals).
6. Rapid one-way flux of inorganic nutrients in contrast to recycling and retention within the organic structure.
7. Selection for species with high birth rates, rapid growth rates, and simple life histories.

These attributes combine to produce a general lack of stability in that young systems represent transient states that will change unless stabilized by outside forces. They are also more easily disrupted by drought, storms, disease, or other perturbations.

These contrasts underline the basic conflict between the strategy of man and nature. For example, the goal of agriculture or intensive forestry, as now generally practised, is to achieve high rates of production of readily harvestable products with little standing crop left to accumulate on the landscape or, in other words, a high production/biomass efficiency. Nature's strategy, on the other hand, as seen in the outcome of the ecosystem development process, is dircted towards the reverse efficiency, namely, a high biomass/production ratio. The natural strategy of maximum protection (i.e. optimizing for the support of a complex living structure that buffers the physical environment) conflicts with man's goal of maximum production (i.e. maximizing for high efficiency in production). Since the environment is our living space as well as a supply depot for food and fibre, its gas exchange, waste purification and climate control, recreational and esthetic capabilities are as vitally important in the long run as its capacity to yield consumable products. Many of these "productive" or "living space" functions are best provided by the more stable or mature-type ecosystems. It is clear, then, that we must have both "productive" and "protective" landscapes in reasonable balance in order to safeguard the gaseous, water, and mineral cycles on which life itself depends.

Compartment Model for Planning

The relevance of ecosystem development to landscape planning can be summarized by the following pairs of contrasting words: production-protection, growth-stability, quantity-quality. Since one cannot have

Fig. 1 A Compartment Model for Landscape Planning Based on Ecological Theory

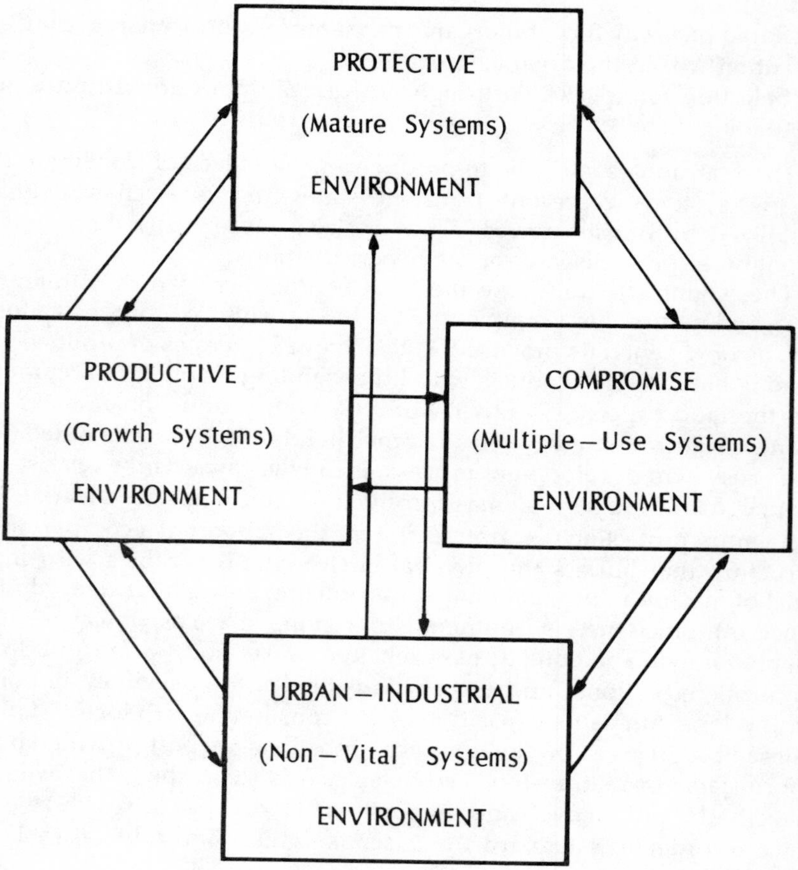

PROTECTIVE
(Mature Systems)
ENVIRONMENT

PRODUCTIVE
(Growth Systems)
ENVIRONMENT

COMPROMISE
(Multiple – Use Systems)
ENVIRONMENT

URBAN – INDUSTRIAL
(Non – Vital Systems)
ENVIRONMENT

both extremes at the same time and place on the landscape, a choice must be made. We can compromise so as to provide moderate quality, protection, and yield on all the landscape, or we can deliberately plan to compartmentalize the landscape so as to simultaneously maintain highly productive and predominantly protective ecosystem-types as separate units subject to contrasting management strategies. Since we do not yet fully understand exactly how energy flows and material cycles interact to produce the homeostasis so necessary for survival, it would seem prudent to work hard at both solutions.

Figure 1 is a simple compartment model that provides a starting point for land-use planning based on the most important of all considerations, maintenance of the quality of life itself. Four basic types of environments, each representing a system type, are indicated (1) productive (cropland), (2) protective (watershed, forest), (3) compromised (rivers and lakes), and (4) urban-industrial. The latter is designated "non-vital" from the biological viewpoint since little or no food, oxygen, or other physiological necessities are produced on the concrete- and ashphalt-covered surface. Urban-industrial systems are also "fuel-powered" in contrast with the other three components which are "solar-powered". It is important to recognize this difference when assessing the impact of one system on another.

Knowing the transfer coefficients defining the flow of energy and the movement of materials and organisms (including man) between compartments, it should be possible through analog computer manipulation to determine rational limits for the size and capacity of each compartment. By continually refining the transfer coefficients on the bases of real world data and by adjusting the relative size of compartments in a simulation procedure, it would be possible to determine objectively the limits that must eventually be imposed on each compartment (be it urban sprawl or intensive agriculture) in order to maintain regional and global balances in vital energy and material exchanges. A system analysis procedure provides at least one approach to the solution of the basic problem previously mentioned, namely, how to determine when we are getting too much of a "good thing".

Management strategy for the strictly productive or the predominantly protective landscapes is fairly clear cut, but management of that part of our landscape that must be compromised is more difficult and challenging. The zone around our large cities, our large rivers and lakes, areas containing valuable minerals, and our estuaries are examples of landscapes that must always be considered in the multiple-use category.

Implementing any kind of compartmental plan and establishing legal means to monitor multiple-use areas so as to avoid too much of any one use requires some form of landscape zoning and use restriction procedure. While the principle of zoning in cities is universally accepted, the procedures now followed do not work very well because zoning restrictions are too easily overturned by short-term economic and population pressures. Zoning the landscape requires a whole new order of thinking and many legal reforms, but we must begin to plan for this eventually.

4
The Land Ethic*

Aldo Leopold

The Ethical Sequence

This extension of ethics, so far studied only by philosophers, is actually a process in ecological evolution. Its sequences may be described in ecological as well as in philosophical terms. An ethic, ecologically, is a limitation on freedom of action in the struggle for existence. An ethic, philosophically, is a differentation of social from anti-social conduct. These are two definitions of one thing. The thing has its origin in the tendency of interdependent individuals or groups to evolve modes of co-operation. The ecologist calls these symbioses. Politics and economics are advanced symbioses in which the original free-for-all competition has been replaced, in part, by co-operative mechanisms with an ethical content.

The complexity of co-operative mechanisms has increased with population density, and with the efficiency of tools. It was simpler, for example, to define the anti-social uses of sticks and stones in the days of the mastodons than of bullets and billboards in the age of motors.

The first ethics dealt with the relation between individuals; the Mosiac Decalogue is an example. Later accretions dealt with the relation between the individual and society. The Golden Rule tries to integrate the individual to society; democracy tries to integrate social organization to the individual.

There is as yet no ethic dealing with man's relation to land and to the animals and plants which grow upon it. Land, like Odysseus' slave-girls, is still property. The land-relation is still strictly economic, entailing privileges but not obligations.

The extension of ethics to this third element in human environment is, if I read the evidence correctly, an evolutionary possibility and an ecological necessity. It is the third step in a sequence. The first two have already been taken. Individual thinkers since the days of Ezekiel and

---

*From *A Sand County Almanac with other essays on conservation from Round River* by Aldo Leopold, p. 217–220, ©1949, 1953, 1966 by Oxford University Press Inc. Reprinted by permission.

Isaiah have asserted that the despoliation of land is not only inexpedient but wrong. Society, however, has not yet affirmed its belief. I regard the present conservation movement as the embryo of such an affirmation.

An ethic may be regarded as a mode of guidance for meeting ecological situations so new or intricate, or involving such deferred reactions, that the path of social expediency is not discernible to the average individual. Animal instincts are modes of guidance for the individual in meeting such situations. Ethics are possibly a kind of community instinct in-the-making.

The Community Concept

All ethics so far evolved rest upon a single premise: that the individual is a member of a community of interdependent parts. His instincts prompt him to compete for his place in the community, but his ethics prompt him also to co-operate (perhaps in order that there may be a place to compete for).

The land ethic simply enlarges the boundaries of the community to include soils, waters, plants, and animals, or collectively: the land.

This sounds simple: do we not already sing our love for the obligation to the land of the free and the home of the brave? Yes, but just what and whom do we love? Certainly not the soil, which we are sending helter-skelter downriver. Certainly not the waters, which we assume have no function except to turn turbines, float barges, and carry off sewage. Certainly not the plants, of which we exterminate whole communities without batting an eye. Certainly not the animals, of which we have already extirpated many of the largest and most beautiful species. A land ethic of course cannot prevent the alteration, management, and use of those "resources," but it does affirm their right to continued existence, and, at least in spots, their continued existence in a natural state.

In short, a land ethic changes the role of *Homo sapiens* from conqueror of the land-community to plain member and citizen of it. It implies respect for his fellow-members, and also respect for the community as such.

Section II
Assessment and Decision Making

Introduction

Once appreciation has been developed for the nature of the resource and different perspectives, it is feasible to consider matters arising in the section labelled Assessment and Decision Making. Resource management usually includes judgements about the adequacy or inadequacy of policies, programs and projects. In making such judgements, a number of matters must be considered. For example, what *criteria* are to be used in assessment? With the same evidence but different criteria two individuals could draw conflicting conclusions about the desirability of a project. For example, one person may like a project because it creates the largest amount of income relative to costs. Conversely, another person may object to the project because he feels that the income will go to people who already enjoy high earnings and low income people will not be affected. We see here that one person's concern with the *absolute* amount of benefits leads to a favourable assessment while another's concern with the *distribution* of benefits leads to a negative evaluation. The second person would advocate a different alternative with lesser revenue if that money went mainly to lower-income people.

Numerous other considerations arise. When should assessments be done? Who should do assessments? Who should make the final decision concerning the adequacy of a proposal? How are intangible aspects measured? These and other points are elaborated upon in the first paper in this section which covers environmental impact assessment.

Mitchell and Turkheim discuss the evolution of environmental impact assessment in Canada. They first identify the variety of interpretations given to environmental impact assessment and then briefly describe its development in Britain, the United States and Canada. The Canadian approach is seen to be conditioned partially by the attitudes and approaches in these other countries. The discussion then turns to seven basic issues which must be handled during assessments, issues which range from the content of assessment documents to who should have the right to finally approve or reject a proposed action. With this perspective established, the study critically describes the policy and practice of the federal and seven provincial governments concerning impact assessment. Different strategies are appearing and a variety of assessments has been conducted. The conclusion considers what opportunities and constraints are likely to arise during the years ahead to incorporate environmental assessments into management decisions.

Once assessment has been completed, either prior to or following completion of a proposal, decisions have to be made. The next three papers elaborate upon the nature of policy and decision making in resource management. Different models have been developed to account for how the policy and decision process *does* work, as well as to suggest how it *should* work. It is useful to be aware of the different processes involved. Knowing them, an individual can better appreciate past situations and can better anticipate future events. Later, the reader can contrast the studies in the Land and Water sections to determine how well those models which attempt to describe the real world actually account for what happens. Conversely, the reader can then attempt to explore ways in which the policy process can come closer to what other models suggest or prescribe what should occur. Where the models appear inadequate, the reader might venture to consider how he could improve them. The reader might also speculate why we frequently seem to "muddle through", and why there may or may not be a strong possibility of ever realizing a carefully orchestrated procedure characterized by calmness, rationality, and objectivity. He might consider the role of emotions, conflicts and politics in the process, and how these aspects might be studied and incorporated into the different models. Furthermore, he might think about how the different perspectives, which often create conflicting evidence and advice, may be built into decisions. As well, the role of different assessment techniques in policy and decision making needs to be considered relative to the other pressures and constraints that influence judgements and choices.

Sewell's paper touches upon a number of aspects common to assessment and decision making. He notes the fact that assessments are done does not guarantee decision makers will adopt their recommendations. Indeed, not accepting recommendations is shown to be a common occurrence. Sewell suggests that those preparing assessments should not be overly critical over apparent disregard for their work until they determine whether the research actually answers the key questions and provides relevant data.

Sewell then describes the ideal decision-making procedure which involves identification of goals, problem definition, establishing means and strategies, selecting alternatives, and monitoring decisions. For each stage, he describes reasons why the ideal often collapses and is not followed. Subsequently, he reviews evaluation procedures available to resource managers, commenting upon benefit-cost analysis, reviewing the role of perception and attitude studies in determining needs, and examining the goals-achievement matrix for weighing values in the presence of multiple goals and multiple strategies.

O'Riordan's study complements that of Sewell's by considering how environmental quality criteria may be plugged into decisions. He examines some of the basic dilemmas which arise in decision making: how to identify problems and alternative strategies, the relative roles of experts and the public(s), the impact of value-laden assumptions, and the spatial and temporal aspects of decisions. Having discussed these aspects, O'Riordan concludes that the ideal decision procedure is just that, an ideal. To better understand the way in which decisions actually occur, he offers a descriptive model which emphasizes group struggle, stress and conflict, rather than the rationality and systematic approach characterized by the ideal.

The final paper in this section focuses upon public involvement in the decision process. Hendee *et. al.* assume that public involvement is desirable, but emphasize that it is a means to an end (better decisions) rather than an end in itself. They feel that traditional ways of sounding public opinions (advisory boards, *ad hoc* committees, key contacts) are unsatisfactory. Alternative methods are explored. In so doing, they discuss how the resource manager can identify the public(s), how viewpoints may be obtained, and how information may be assessed and weighed. Furthermore, they identify controversial issues such as when the public should become involved in decision making, what the role of the public is relative to professionals, how representativeness and continuous public input are assured and so on. By the end of this paper both the general principles and practical issues of public involvement are discussed.

5
Environmental Impact Assessment: Principles, Practice and Canadian Experiences

*Bruce Mitchell and Richard Turkheim**

A range of definitions exists for environmental impact assessment (E.I.A.). Lucas and McCallum suggest that E.I.A. is an appraisal which identifies the chain effects of actions and their cumulative impact on the total environment network. They see E.I.A. as a "planning tool" and a "decision-making model" through which environmental considerations are incorporated into early planning stages[1]. Sager defines E.I.A. as the examination and quantification of any alterations to the environment (including man), or to any environmental component[2]. Expanding the above definition, E.I.A. may be conceived as

> . . . an activity designed to identify, predict, interpret and communicate information about the impact of an action on man's health and well-being (including the well-being of ecosystems on which man's survival depends).[3]

Regardless of the varied interpretations assigned to the term environmental impact assessment, it may be characterized overall as a legislative or policy-based concern for possible positive/negative, short/long term effects on our total environment attributable to proposed or existing projects, programs or policies of a public or private origin.

Background to Environmental Impact Assessment Policy and Practice

Canadian approaches towards environmental impact assessment have not developed in a vacuum; experiences in other countries have influenced their evolution. The practices in Britain and the United States are briefly examined here. They represent different approaches and incorporate ideas which Canadians either have consciously adopted or ignored.

During October 1970, a new Department of the Environment was created in Britain. The first Minister of the Environment was asked

---

*Bruce Mitchell is an Associate Professor, Geography Department, University of Waterloo. Richard Turkheim is a doctoral student in the Geography Department at the University of Waterloo. This paper was written specifically for this book.

whether his department had an equivalent to the E.I.A. required in the United States. Significantly, he replied that Britain did not, nor did he intend to have them. In his view, each government department was expected to "pursue high quality decisions in terms of the environment." He felt that the environmental assessment ". . . really makes a land fit for lawyers to live in with no great impact upon the environment itself."[4] Thus, the British approach has consciously avoided specific legislation or regulations requiring environmental assessments. Instead, government departments are expected to explicitly incorporate environmental considerations in everyday routine.

The United States' approach stands in sharp contrast. The National Environmental Policy Act of 1969 (NEPA) was signed into law on January 1, 1970. As well as establishing a Council on Environmental Quality, the legislation required federal departments to consider the environmental consequences of development. The key element of the Act, Section 102(2) (c), states that all agencies of the federal government shall

> include in every recommendation or report on proposals for legislation and other major Federal actions significantly affecting the quality of the human environment, a detailed statement by the responsible official on —
> (i) the environmental impact of the proposed action,
> (ii) any adverse environmental effects which cannot be avoided should the proposal be implemented,
> (iii) alternatives to the proposed action,
> (iv) the relationship between local short-term uses of man's environment and the maintenance and enhancement of long-term productivity, and
> (v) any irreversible and irretrievable commitments of resources which would be involved if the proposed action should be implemented.

A critical decision affecting NEPA occurred in 1971. The Atomic Energy Commission had decided that in submitting environmental impact statements for nuclear power plants it would exclude non-radiological environmental questions as well as only allow hearing boards to consider environmental issues identified by its staff. When this procedure was used for a proposed nuclear plant at Calvert Cliffs, Maryland, a citizen's group protested. The courts rejected the Atomic Energy Commission's procedure, and instructed it to create a new procedure which would reflect the spirit and intent of NEPA. With this decision, government agencies became aware that the courts intended to enforce the legislation. Furthermore, citizen's groups realized that NEPA could be used to require consideration of environmental factors. As White later observed, it is clear that "no federal legislation of recent years bears greater potential significance for the management of environment in the

United States than does Section 102 of the National Environmental Policy Act of 1969."[5]

The American approach, based upon legislation and the courts, has generated a large number of environmental impact statements. By June 1972, some 2,933 statements had been filed. By 1975, 7,100 statements had been completed of which 35 per cent dealt with roads, 23 per cent concerned watershed developments, 10 per cent related to parks, forest and timber, 7 per cent reviewed energy-related projects, 6 per cent studied airports, and 19 per cent covered other topics. Significantly, over 80 per cent of impact statements were accounted for by highways, watershed developments, power projects, airports, sewage treatment plants, and mineral extraction.

In Canada, at both the federal and provincial levels, the American experience was studied closely. While agreeing with the ultimate goal of environmental assessments, Canadian policy-makers began to consider alternative means to implement them. Consequently, many Canadian governments have avoided the creation of new legislation for environmental assessment because of the fear of generating an avalanche of assessments which would overwhelm the courts. The federal government is a good example. When explaining its adoption of an administrative rather than legalistic procedure, the Minister of the Environment stated to the House of Commons during 1974 that

> I hope, in the process, that we can avoid the delays and other pitfalls which a strictly legalistic approach would cause in this country. . . . We will not hold up important developments which are clean from an environmental point of view and, in contrast to the situation which has developed in the United States, we will not bring the environmental assessment process into disrepute. We will not be charged with blocking everything.[6]

Thus, as in numerous policies and procedures, Canadian governments have adhered to a position located midway between British and American practices. While procedures have been developed to require explicit consideration of environmental issues, considerable discretionary power has been left in the hands of elected representatives to decide which projects are assessed, who finally approves or disallows a project, and what role the public plays in the process.

Problematic Issues in the Assessment Process

Although much debated in every effort to establish environmental impact assessment procedures, no consensus exists for seven key questions. Which projects should be assessed? When should assessments be conducted? What should be the content of an environmental impact statement? Who should conduct the assessment? Who should decide whether an assessment has been done adequately? Who decides whether a project should be approved or stopped? What role should the public have in the process? Each of these issues must be considered when formulating E.I.A. policy on legislation.

Environmental Impact Assessment in Principle in Canada

During the fall of 1975 and the winter of 1976, a survey of E.I.A. procedures in use in all ten provinces and two federal government departments was conducted. Letters asking questions related to the seven questions were mailed to appropriate provincial departments and to two federal departments, Environment Canada and Indian and Northern Affairs. With the exception of one province which did not reply, overall response to the questions was good. E.I.A. descriptions in the following sections concentrate on the more complex and unique issues involved in selected provincial and federal approaches. As well, the overall nature of individual approaches to E.I.A. as well as major strengths and weaknesses are discussed (Table 1).

THE FEDERAL APPROACH

All federal departments, agencies and Crown corporations conduct E.I.A.'s on the basis of the Environmental Assessment and Review Process established in 1973, although it is continually being modified. Assessments are to be undertaken as early as possible in the planning process whenever projects are initiated or funded by the federal government or when federal property is involved. The procedure stipulates that all federal proponents conduct an "Initial Environmental Evaluation" of projects before any decision to commence them. At this early stage, those projects which are apt to have "significant" environmental effects[7] are referred to Environment Canada for an indepth review involving the appointment of a federal Environmental Assessment Panel, the preparation of environmental impact statement (E.I.S.) guidelines by the Panel and a review of the statement. All important in the process is the composition of the Panel. It usually is chaired by a senior Environment Canada official and includes several other Environment Canada personnel with relevant expertise and one representative from the proponent department. Although somewhat discretionary in operation, the process ensures that environmental planning should be incorporated into the development process from conceptual to operational stages. Theoretically, all federal projects are subjected to environmental scrutiny.

TABLE 1
Accepted Canadian Environmental Impact Assessment Principles

E.I.A. Issues	Nova Scotia	New Brunswick
E.I.A. terms of reference relative policy/legislation	ministerial policy Environmental Protection Act	legislation environmental assessment procedures policy
acceptance date	April 6, 1973	October 8, 1975
criteria determining which projects are assessed	"Individual judgement" of "departmental personnel" requesting the E.I.A.	"all major developments" considered by a provincial agency, department, or Crown corporation – there are 8 screening criteria
criteria determined by	Department of the Environment and Environment Canada	Department of the Environment
initial & final assessments	—	yes
final E.I.A. content —project description	—	yes
—environmental inventory	—	yes
—description of alternatives	—	yes
—description of impacts	—	yes
—irreversible or irreparable impacts given special notice	—	yes
—impact minimizing or mitigating measures described	—	yes
—monitoring program recommended or described	—	yes
—public/private proponent or its consultant prepare E.I.A.	yes	yes
—proponent pays the costs	yes	yes
when should final assessment be conducted	—	initial one concurrent with economic & engineering feasibility studies – final one in time so as to incorporate ameliorative measures into project design
who judges final assessment adequacy	Department of the Environment/Environment Canada	assessment review co-ordinated by Department of the Environment which circulates copies for comment to affected departments
who grants or refuses project approval	Minister of the Environment	Minister of the Environment
—appeal mechanism	none	yes
—to whom	—	Provincial Cabinet Committee on Economic Development
Public's role in E.I.A. —discretionary/mandatory	discretionary	discretionary
—hearings possible and agency responsible	yes, Environmental Control Council	yes, Department of the Environment
—preliminary or final report available for inspection	—	preliminary report only
—timing discretionary or objective	discretionary	discretionary
—input appended to E.I.S.	—	yes
—proponent/public liaison	—	—

E.I.A. Issues	Quebec	Ontario	Manitoba
E.I.A. terms of reference relative policy/legislation acceptance date	ministerial policy — —	legislation Bill 14, The Environmental Assessment Act, 1975 —	legislation Manitoba Environmental Assessment & Review Procedures November 12, 1975
criteria determining which projects are assessed criteria determined by	large government and private enterprise projects (no uniform approach at present) Lieutenant Governor-in-Council	any new major commercial or business activity; or proposal, plan, or program regarding such, plus any significant change of an activity Lt. Governor-in-Council but Minister of the Environment can exempt certain projects	all projects significantly affecting the environment re: air, water, and/or soil contamination are subject to a "Project Description" or preliminary assessment EARA determines if true environmental assessment required, with Minister's approval
initial & final assessments	—	—	yes
final E.I.A. content —project description	yes	yes	yes
—environmental inventory	yes	yes	—
—description of alternatives	yes	yes	yes
—description of impacts	yes	yes	yes
—irreversible or irreparable impacts given special notice	yes	—	yes
—impact minimizing or mitigating measures described	yes	yes	yes
—monitoring program recommended or described	—	—	yes
—public/private proponent or its consultant prepare E.I.A.	yes	yes	yes
—proponent pays the costs	yes	yes	yes
when should final assessment be conducted	before a choice is made to approve or reject a project	after a feasibility study but before any licence, permit, approval, permission, or consent required under any statute, regulation, or by-law is granted (follows the "rule of reason")	prior to any irrevocable decisions or commitments if a preliminary assessment – if an E.I.S., prior to finalization of project planning, design, construction, and operation
who judges final assessment adequacy	Director of Environmental Protection Services	Environmental Assessment Board with recommendations to the Minister of the Environment	EARA which forwards its recommendations to the Minister of Mines, Resources, and Environmental Management
who grants or refuses project approval	Director of Environmental Protection Services	Environmental Assessment Board with recommendations to the Minister of the Environment	The Manitoba Cabinet
—appeal mechanism —to whom	yes Quebec Municipal Commission	[only for Minister of the Environment within 28 days after Board's advisement]	none —
Public's role in E.I.A. —discretionary/mandatory	both	mandatory	discretionary
—hearings possible and agency responsible	yes, [Quebec Environmental Advisory Council hears those directly affected while Minister of the Environment or Lt. Gov.-in-Council may create *ad hoc* committee to hold public hearings]	yes, Environmental Assessment Board	yes, EARA and Clean Environment Commission
—preliminary or final report available for inspection		yes	yes
—timing discretionary or objective		discretionary	discretionary
—input appended to E.I.S.		yes	—
—proponent/public liaison		—	—

Alberta	British Columbia	Indian and Northern Affairs and Environment Canada
ministerial policy Land Surface Conservation and Reclamation Act 1973	legislation Environment and Land Use Act (Section 3) July 1, 1971	legislation Environmental Assessment and Review Process (EARP) December 20, 1973
any operation or activity resulting in a surface disturbance including those recommended by the public, elected representatives, and provincial agencies	3 types: 1. simple, cross-agency referral procedure; 2. small-scale, cross-agency studies; and, 3. large-scale, multi-stage assessments	all projects initiated or funded by the federal government or where federal property is required . . . only projects having significant impacts taken beyond IEE stage are referred to EC for an E.I.S.
Minister of the Environment with recommendations possible as listed above	Environment and Land Use Committee (ELUC)	initiating department with some Environment Canada screening
—	—	yes
yes	yes	yes
yes	yes	yes
—	yes	yes
yes	yes	yes
yes	—	—
yes	yes	yes
—	yes	—
yes	yes	yes
yes	yes	yes
prior to proponent applications for authorizations, licences, and permits	environmental impact studies undertaken before various permits, licences, and leases are issued	"as early in the planning process as possible"
Environmental Coordination Services (Dep't. of the Environment) distributes E.I.A. to government agencies for reviews & recommendations	ELUC judges assessment adequacy on basis of Secretariat's recommendations for large-scale projects	Environmental Assessment Panel judges adequacy of assessment reports for major projects
Cabinet Committee advises proponent to proceed to "permitting" stage	ELUC grants approval of large-scale projects	Ministers of the Departments involved
none	yes	yes
—	Provincial Cabinet	Federal Cabinet
discretionary	discretionary	discretionary
—	yes, [ELUC holds meetings for major developments; various agencies hold meetings at ends of stages 1 and 2; regulatory agencies hold meetings at end of stage 3 re. licences	yes, Environmental Assessment Panel
yes		final report only
discretionary		discretionary
yes	—	—
yes	—	—

In addition to the basic E.I.A. content requirements (Table 1), federal environmental impact statements must contain a description of the need for the project, the reasons for specific site and project selection, and a description and discussion of residual environmental effects. As explained by the Panel Chairman, the last point presents a difficulty in that it requires criteria to be established against which Panel members may evaluate residual effects.

The decision-making process is complex. The responsibility for screening all projects or programs for probable environmental effects rests with the initiating department in consultation with Environmental Canada when necessary. If it is decided to submit a project to the formal assessment procedure, a Panel is convened which establishes guidelines relevant to the project at hand. Once the completed assessment is submitted to the Panel, they review it for adequacy and then render advice (proceed, proceed with conditions, do not proceed) to the Ministers involved, who have the final say regarding project approval. In cases of inter-ministerial disagreement, the matter is resolved by Cabinet.

With respect to public participation, the issue partially is clouded by discretionary ministerial power. For example, the policy directs the Panel Chairman, unless specifically constrained, to make the E.I.S. available through publication and to obtain public reaction to it. However, as clear and forthright as this policy appears, there is the catch that such actions must be sanctioned by the Minister of the Environment and the Minister of the proponent department. Comments by senior officials give some indication about the status of public participation. One official stated that effort is given to striking a balance between the error of no public input and that of initiating a long and costly process that may be out of proportion with the scope of a project. Another stated that obtaining public opinion is not done effectively. He suggested that public participation is an art still to be mastered by resource managers.

THE PROVINCIAL APPROACHES

Nova Scotia – The concept and implementation of E.I.A.'s is almost completely "in-house"; the combined decisions of the Nova Scotia Department of the Environment and Environment Canada in Ottawa fully dominate the process. Additionally, the process is grounded in "permit-required" legislation rather than E.I.A. legislation, per se.

The Environment Protection Act (1973) authorizes the formation of an Environmental Control Council and its Executive Committee which is responsible for reviewing information relevant to the authorization of a waste management permit, and for advising the Department of the Environment which carries out E.I.A.'s. The Department of Environment assesses each project to ensure that pollution abatement facilities are sound and makes a recommendation to the Minister of the Environment. For industrial and municipal projects, a similar permit system is followed. While the completed application form is forwarded to the Council for consideration, the Department of the Environment evaluates the proposal, carries out an engineering study, and co-ordinates inputs from other departments and interested parties. Once satisfied with project standards, the completed application is forwarded along with the review and recommendations to the Council and the Minister.

No specific requirements exist with regard to timing the implementation of E.I.A.'s, which projects are assessed, or what the assessment contents should be. Although environmental associations or concerned citizen groups can make suggestions to the guidelines which are developed jointly by the Department of the Environment and Environment Canada, this flexibility from one project assessment to the next also invites inconsistency of assessment quality. This factor mitigates against the development of a uniform body of E.I.A.'s suitable for comparative analyses and cross-referencing.

The decision-making process lacks visibility. Not only do the Department of Environment and Environment Canada determine which projects are assessed, but they also decide whether an assessment document is adequate. Further, these two public agencies then make positive or negative recommendations to the Minister of the Environment concerning project approval.

The opportunity for public input can be described as moderately favourable. The Council is usually composed of members from health, legal, and engineering professions; industry and labour, municipalities, agriculture, conservation, or ecology groups; university or academic communities; and forestry or fisheries. Additionally, public concern may sometimes be sufficient to result in public hearings conductd by the Council.

New Brunswick — New Brunswick follows an environmental assessment procedure through its Department of the Environment under an order-in-council passed in 1975. All major provincial agency, department, or Crown corporation developments are subject to E.I.A.'s, guidelines which are determined by the Department of the Environment. Although this matter seems clear cut, the department actually screens projects to determine which ones will be assessed. During screening, the following questions are posed

1. Will the natural, physical or aesthetic environment be significantly altered;
2. Will there be significant social or economic effects on a community or region;

3. Will large amounts of non-renewable resources be committed;
4. Do the uses of provincial resources pre-empt other uses or potential uses;
5. Will unique, rare or endangered environmental features be affected;
6. Is the proposed undertaking a part of a larger planned project;
7. Will major revisions in services such as water supply and highways be required;
8. Will there be significant third party costs or benefits?

Exactly who determines what is significant or major and what is a larger amount is not specified.

All E.I.A.'s are to be conducted "prior to a decision on implementation of the project." In reality, however, there are two phases. An initial assessment is carried out concurrently with economic, engineering and other feasibility studies related to a specific project or its alternatives. Once a project passes this stage, a detailed assessment is completed so that ameliorative measures may be incorporated into project design.

Once the department has determined which projects are to be assessed, and an E.I.S. has been prepared according to their guidelines, the department reviews the study, allowing time for other departments to review relevant parts. Decision alternatives range from acceptance, acceptance with revisions, to unresolvable. In the latter case, this issue is presented to the Cabinet Committee on Economic Development for a decision. Ultimate approval power rests with the Provincial Cabinet.

The Department of the Environment has discretionary power regarding public participation. Although a proponent must release its initial assessment to the public through the Department of the Environment, it is unclear as to whether the department is obliged to hold public meetings. Considering the detailed assessment reports, it is unlikely that much public input will be generated towards them as the proponent is directly responsible for public involvement at this stage. It is unlikely that concerned individuals will have an opportunity to comment upon probable impacts, their severity, or the value of remedial measures.

Quebec – E.I.A.'s are conducted as a matter of ministerial policy. The Director of Environmental Protection Services can demand an impact study to accompany an application for a project authorization permit. Although the government is investigating ways of standardizing the method by which projects are selected for examination, current practice stipulates that large government and private projects such as dams, major highways, industrial complexes, transmission lines, and large ports are assessment targets. The Cabinet plays a large role because it determines which projects require an authorization permit before proceeding. Additionally, it decides on tolerable emission, discharge, and other contaminant levels which may be released into the environment.

With respect to content, project goals and objectives are explained along with the general project description. The existing environment description provides a reference base from which to evaluate impacts, paying special attention to the rarity, sensitivity, variety, and evolution of environmental components involved. Project alternatives are described so that a comparative evaluation of costs, benefits, and risks is possible. Finally, a judgement is made regarding the local, regional, national, or international scale of impact. Once an assessment is completed, it is forwarded to the Director of Environmental Protection Services who decides on its adequacy and also whether the project will be approved or stopped.

Although firm implementation procedures for public involvement are not crystallized, numerous opportunities exist for the public to make its opinions known. The Quebec Environmental Advisory Council, created in 1973, receives and listens to individual and group requests and suggestions related to environmental quality, and advises the Minister of the Environment on such matters. In turn, the Minister makes recommendations to the Cabinet. Further, the Council is obligated to grant public audiences for a period of one year from the date of proposal submission to those individuals who are directly affected by the project. Public opinion may also be sought through the establishment of a parliamentary commission and an *ad hoc* committee to hold public hearings. Furthermore, any person or municipality may appeal a decision by the Director to the Quebec Municipal Commission.

Two major shortcomings are evident in Quebec's procedure. First stipulations regarding the timing of E.I.A.'s are not specific. As such, project conception could pass well beyond the economic and engineering feasibility stages before an assessment is implemented. Second, there is a distinct need to more clearly define the respective responsibilities of the Director, Minister and Cabinet regarding authorization of developments.

Ontario – E.I.A.'s are conducted under terms stipulated in the Environmental Assessment Act, 1975. After the Act was proclaimed in October 1976, any proposals, plans or programs of any provincial departments or agencies became susceptible to E.I.A.'s. At a later date, to be established by Cabinet, municipal and private sector projects will be examined. The Cabinet and the Minister of the Environment are empowered to further designate or exempt any activities or proposals from the Act.

Aside from content requirements as outlined in Table 1, emphasis is placed on describing the purpose and rationale of the undertaking and its alternatives. Additionally, the Act demands that an evaluation of environmental advantages and disadvantages of the undertaking, the alternative methods of carrying out the undertaking, and the alternatives to the undertaking be included.

Upon completion, the assessment is submitted to the Minister of the Environment who refers it to the Environmental Assessment Board which was appointed in April 1976 and which determines its adequacy and makes a recommendation to the Minister. After a review has been prepared and the public has been given an opportunity to participate, the Board makes a recommendation to the Minister regarding whether to grant outright approval, approval with conditions, or outright refusal. The Minister has 28 days after receipt of the Board's decision to vary the whole or any part of the decision or else require the Board to reconsider its decision.

Concerning the status of public participation, each assessment and its review are to be available for public inspection. Any person may examine the asssessment and its review within 30 days after they become available. Written submissions to the Minister may be made regarding the undertaking, its assessment, and the review. Furthermore, individuals may write the Minister and request a hearing by the Board regarding the project, its assessment, and the review. This hearing occurs unless the Minister

> . . . .in his absolute discretion . . .considers that the requirement is frivolous or vexatious or that a hearing is unnecessary or may cause undue delay.[8]

The Minister also has power to withold disclosure if, in his judgement, it is in the public interest to do so.

Ontario's procedure can be criticized on several accounts. Although it attempts to avoid an avalanche of paper in the provincial courts, the Act may have ridden the pendulum too far in the opposite direction, having given the Minister discretionary powers that are too broad, while denying the Board any decision-making powers. For instance, the Minister may exempt projects from assessment, disallow public hearings, stop information disclosures, and make the final decision on project approval. Of further concern is the vagueness of the timing issue. When will regulations be made to bring public and private sectors alike under the Act? Other problem issues centre around the failure of the Act to provide financial support for citizen's groups which wish to become involved and to omit court appeal and/or judicial review of ministerial decisions.

Manitoba – The Manitoba procedure, given Cabinet approval in 1975, requires environmental assessment of all government projects significantly altering or affecting the environment. Every proponent must submit a "project description" to the Environmental Assessment and Review Agency prior to making any irrevocable commitments respecting proposed provincial undertakings. Also, a proponent may have to complete a detailed assessment of the project, if it will have significant effects, and submit the assessment for review. The E.I.A. must be completed in sufficient time to allow incorporation of all its recommendations into project planning, design, construction and operation stages as conditionally or unconditionally approved by Cabinet. Further, the proponent must conduct post-operational studies to appraise the accuracy of predictions made in the original E.I.A. and he must take necessary steps to minimize or mitigate any unforeseen impairments.

In addition to the standard requirements of a description of the project, its alternatives, the need and rationale for it, and providing information on anticipated wastes, the preliminary assessment must contain a description of transport requirements affecting air, water, and/or soil contamination, plus a description of the administration and managerial structure for all proposed project aspects. For a full-scale assessment, the Agency has developed four sets of guidelines, one for each area of concern in the assessment: probable and direct environmental impacts of a proposed project, probable adverse effects which cannot be avoided, alternatives, and the relationship between local short-term uses of the environment and the maintenance and enhancement of long-term productivity.

Aside from information normally contained in such detailed assessments, there are also more unique, far-sighted requirements. The time frame in which impacts are expected is to be detailed. The description of implications and reasons why the proposed action should be accepted must be provided. Another stipulation requests the specification of the basis upon which acceptable adverse-effects levels are deemed adequate. The alternatives analysis must be structured so as to enable comparisons of environmental benefit or damage. The proponent must weigh the desirability of the proposed action against the foreclosures of future options or needs.

Decision-making powers are evenly distributed. The "project description" is evaluated by the Agency which decides if project effects are sufficiently serious to warrant a detailed assessment. This decision, however, requires the approval of the Minister of Mines, Resources and Environmental Management. The Agency also evaluates the adequacy of any E.I.S.'s that are submitted and forwards recommendations to the Minister. Final decisions to permit, modify or disallow proposals rest with the Cabinet. No appeal mechanism exists.

Public participation opportunities are virtually identical to those found in Ontario. Any E.I.S. and its review may be inspected by the public and any person may make a submission within 15 days to the Minister.

Public hearings may be initiated by the Minister through the Agency or the Clean Environment Commission prior to any Cabinet decision. Additionally, the proponent has the opportunity to introduce citizen involvement in the initial stages of the enviromental assessment.

Alberta – E.I.A.'s are conducted at the Minister of the Environment's discretion under authority granted to him by the Land Surface Conservation and Reclamation Act, 1973. Overall, the purpose is to provide comprehensive information to facilitate the early identification and resolution of potentially significant, adverse environmental affects of proposed resource developments. The Minister may order a proponent to prepare an E.I.A. if he feels that the project will "result or is likely to result in surface disturbance." Further, the public, elected local or provincial representatives, the Department of the Environment or other government department and agencies may recommend to the Minister that an E.I.A. be requested of a certain project. The fact that so many parties have the opportunity to request an E.I.A. is perhaps one reason why 17 had been completed up to the end of January 1976.

Once an assessment is requested, the subsequent review process becomes complex and lengthy. A draft assessment is submitted to the Department of the Environment for distribution to all concerned government departments and agencies. Once appropriate changes have been made, a final E.I.A. is prepared and copies are once again distributed to all previously involved parties. Their reviews and recommendations are forwarded to the Minister of the Environment and appropriate departments. Once the report plus each agency's comments have been reviewed by the Minister, they are referred to the appropriate Cabinet Committee. This committee then advises the proponent to proceed to the permitting stage, if everything is in order. At the permitting stage, the proponent prepares detailed plans required to support applications for approvals submitted under various statutes that apply to the proposal. Government departments and agencies with specific statutory responsibilities review each application for conformity with existing government policies and standards. If the proposal meets all the requirements under existing laws, the project may proceed.

Despite lofty ideals regarding the frequency and style of proponent-public interaction, the participatory level is likely much lower. Project proponents are urged to include the public in the process through informal meetings so as to gain their support before presentation to government. As the assessment progresses, the public should be kept informed of specific areas being addressed. Additionally, the proponent should ensure that the public has had opportunity to review the completed E.I.S. and to express their views about its findings. Finally, specific public views should be incorporated as an integral part of the final report submitted to the government.

Noteworthy in Alberta's process is the high degree of interaction fostered between proponents and relevant government agencies. First, the assessment review process provides for interdepartmental and multidisciplinary review. Second, the process provides for the review of the report and government agency recommendations by elected representatives. Third, is the concept of the "permitting stage". This means that because an individual project is environmentally sound does not necessarily mean that other departments operating under other legislation have to accept the proposal. The proponent must prove that the project satisfies all other requirements and standards even though environmental approval has been granted.

British Columbia – E.I.A.'s are conducted by technical committees appointed by the Environment and Land Use Committee which in turn gains its authority from the Environmental and Land Use Act, 1971. Three assessment levels exist, each of which has its own criteria: a simple cross-agency referral procedure such as in the case of timber harvest permits; small-scale, cross-agency studies for projects such as marinas and ski developments; large-scale, multi-stage assessments for major power projects, and industrial and port sites. In all cases where doubt may exist as to a proper review classification for a project, the Committee makes the final decision. In terms of timing, preliminary impact studies must be undertaken before various permits, licences and leases allowing project go-ahead are issued. British Columbia claims an integrative approach to resource planning, since E.I.A.'s are built into the planning process through the early interchange of ideas and data between the appropriate proponent agencies and the Committee, the latter comprised of members from the provincial Cabinet.

A multi-stage decision procedure has been developed for large-scale projects. The first stage involves a project description, an environmental inventory, and the selection of a preferred alternative. Stage two is represented by the preparation of a detailed E.I.S.. To aid in decision making at this stage, a Special Projects Unit has been working to formulate broad regional assessment guidelines so that a comprehensive and comparative array of information can be developed for a number of alternative projects. A preferred project design is selected for final design in stage three. Site specific impacts and possible compensatory or mitigatory measures are identified at this stage. Rehabilitation efforts are monitored during and following project construction.

Specific guidelines for undertaking E.I.S.'s are being developed by the Committee's Secretariat. These will amplify and integrate earlier draft manuals specifying analysis guidelines for social, economic and environmental impacts. Use of such guidelines should ensure greater consistency for assessment procedure.

The Committee decides which projects will be assessed and determines assessment adequacy based upon recommendations from its Secretariat which reviews each E.I.S. in conjunction with other government agencies. For large-scale projects, the Committee also decides on project approval or denial with the provision of appeal to the Cabinet. For small-scale assessments, the entire process may be co-ordinated by line agencies, such as the Department of Land and Water Resources or the Department of Mines, without any input from the Secretariat.

Three different discretionary mechanisms are available for providing the public with access to the process. First, the Committee may hold public meetings to debate major developments and educate the public. Second, various agencies may hold general public meetings at the conclusion of either Stage 1 or Stage 2 of the assessment procedure. Finally, regulatory agencies have the discretionary power to hold public hearings at the conclusion of Stage 3, but prior to granting licences or permits.

Environmental Impact Assessment in Practice in Canada

The previous section outlines Canadian policies concerning E.I.A.'s. The evidence indicates that considerable progress has occurred since 1970 when no government had a specific mechanism for conducting assessments. Indeed, numerous assessments have been completed. Some of these have been done by provincial governments, some by the federal government, and some have been joint federal-provincial exercises. On the other hand, not all obstacles have been overcome. For example, after surveying the record of environmental assessment in Canada, Lash *et al.* commented that

> When studies have been conducted on the effects of projects, they have not been systematic. Frequently they have been perfunctory, commonly they have been fragmentary, and, almost invariably, they have been set in motion too late in the process of project conception and design. In many instances, the decision to make environmental studies has come *after* the decision to undertake the project, and the subsequent investigations have then been so poorly co-ordinated that what little has been done has nevertheless managed to result in duplication.[9]

To determine the validity of this type of criticism, a brief review of selected resource developments is presented. Several categories are identified. First are projects which had no E.I.A. but had subsequent significant environmental problems. Second are projects for which assessments were conducted after initially deciding to proceed with the project. The third type includes projects which had E.I.A.'s done prior to a decision to proceed. The final category represents projects which had assessments prior to a go-ahead decision as well as follow-up monitoring after project completion.

The first category represents the type of situation which led to the establishment of E.I.A. procedures. Perhaps one of the best known examples is the W.A.C. Bennet Dam on the Peace River. Designed and constructed without any studies of its potential environmental impact, the structure was completed in 1967 and the reservoir began filling in 1968. Once the dam became operational, significant environmental impacts resulted, although these were over 700 miles downstream in Alberta's Peace-Athabasca Delta. The ecology of this delta depended upon annual spring flooding. W.A.C. Bennet Dam reduced the water flow and altered the natural hydrologic conditions upon which vegetation, wildlife and native Indians had become dependent. In 1970 a report brought these changes to light, and the next year the Canadian, B.C. and Alberta governments appointed a study team to analyze the problem. Remedial work was completed to reduce the impact of the reservoir. Nevertheless, if impact studies had been conducted prior to construction the opportunity to reduce negative effects would have been greater.

The second type of project is now more common. For example, in April 1971 the Quebec government announced details of the James Bay Project. However, it was not until August 1971 that a joint federal-provincial investigation of environmental consequences of the development was initiated with a report submitted during December 1971, less than one-half year later.

Other projects fit the same pattern. The federal Cabinet gave approval-in-principle during July 1973 for offshore drilling in the Beaufort Sea of the Western Arctic, and simultaneously ordered a crash environmental study. Later, in April 1976, the Cabinet authorized two exploratory well drillings offshore from Tuktoyaktuk, even though knowledge about possible environmental problems of Arctic offshore drilling was incomplete.[10] The Nanisivik Mine at Strathcona Sound is another example. This lead and zinc mine, approved by the federal government in June 1974, received authorization before environmental studies were undertaken. Although subsequent investigations of two tailings disposal alternatives indicate that substantial problems may arise, an alternative still may be found. But, because the project has government support and is under construction, "there is practically no chance that there will be any serious examination of the possibility that none of the alternatives is actually environmentally acceptable."[11] In justifying its decision, the Department of Indian and Northern Affairs stated that an E.I.A. was not required before project approval in 1974 because Environment Canada by that time had not established standard procedures for such assessments.

On the other hand, there is an increasing number of projects which are having E.I.A.'s done prior to the decision to proceed. Considerable effort has been made to determine the environmental, economic and social consequences of gas and oil pipelines from the Mackenzie Delta.[12] These inquiries have ranged from industry and government studies to the well-publicized Berger Inquiry. In more settled parts of Canada, Ontario Hydro has been studying the environmental impact on proposed power corridors. At the local scale, the Regional Municipality of Waterloo in Ontario has designated "environmentally sensitive areas" for incorporation into its official plan which guides future development, and in July 1976 the Regional Council became the first local government in Ontario to require a developer to prepare an E.I.A. for a proposed subdivision.

Given the relative newness of E.I.A.'s, examples could not be found which fall within the fourth category. It appears that there are few, if any, projects for which assessments were done prior to the decision to undertake the project and then were followed up with monitoring. From an enviornmental viewpoint, this situation is not desirable. In the future, if provinces such as Manitoba are successful in implementing their stated policies, more follow-up assessments may be seen.

Prospects and Needs

E.I.A. policy and practice in Canada and elsewhere provide background for several observations. Developments usually create more than one type of disturbance to the environment. In addition, more than one phase of development occurs. Typical phases are pre-construction, construction, operation and abandonment/reclamation. For each type and at each phase, the nature and magnitude of environmental impact may be different, requiring different assessment procedures. It is particularly important to remember that impact is not confined to construction and operation phases. For some projects the most significant impact may occur after abandonment.

Given the different types and timings of impacts, it is clear that the numerous questions of who, what, and when addressed earlier in this paper still remain to be assessed and answered satisfactorily. Not only will responses vary at the more local scale because of differences in projects, locales, and government levels; but, also at broader scales due to such aspects as social demands, form of government, and state of technological or economic advancement.

Even after these general strategic questions are addressed, other more specific ones need to be considered. For example, how are possible impacts to be identified, when understanding of ecosystem interrelationships is still imperfect? What indicators are available to signify environmental damage? How adequate are present standards in reflecting critical thresholds beyond which irreparable damage may occur? Assuming that impacts can be identified and measured, how are they to be weighted and valued? As Sorenson notes

> . . . no matter how much information or how many procedures are brought to bear in impact assessment, there will always be irreconcilable differences in values which can only be resolved in the political arena.[13]

What extra development time and costs are necessitated in conducting E.I.A.'s? What is the cost of not doing assessments? What relationship will environmental assessment policies, legislation and regulations have with other policies, laws and regulations? Most governments already have extensive regulations for land and water use, pollution control, and economic development. The role of E.I.A.'s relative to these other considerations will have to be clarified. And finally, to what extent will the stated policies actually be translated into action? Only the passage of time will indicate whether the emergence of environmental impact assessment procedures will have a substantial influence upon the manner in which decisions are made.

NOTES

1. A. R. Lucas and S. K. McCallum, "Looking at environmental impact assessment", *Environmental management and public participation,* edited by P. S. Elder, Toronto, Canadian Environmental Law Association and the Canadian Environmental Law Research Foundation, 1975, p. 306.
2. P. Sager, "Conceptualizing environmental impact", *Environmental impact analysis: philosophy and methods,* edited by R. B. Ditton and T. I. Goodale, Madison, University of Wisconsin Press, 1972, p. 79.
3. R. E. Munn, editor, *Environmental impact assessment: principles and procedures,* Toronto, Workshop on Impact Studies in the Environment, Scientific Committee on Problems of the Environment, 1975, p. 12. An action is defined as any engineering project, legislative proposal, policy, program or operational procedure with environmental implications.
4. S.. Lindsay, "Conversation with Britain's Environmental Chief", *Saturday Review,* Vol. 55, January 1, 1972, p. 70.
5. G. F. White, "Environmental impact assessments", *Professional Geographer,* Vol. 24, No. 4, November 1972, p. 70.
6. Canada, House of Commons, *Debates,* 2nd Session, 29th Parliament, Vol. 1, 1974, Hon. J. Davis, p. 499. For further comments, see B. Mitchell, "Environmental impact assessment: Canadian approaches", *Area,* Vol. 8, No. 2, 1976, pp. 127-131.
7. Significant environmental effects are not defined anywhere in the federal policy, but rather the expression is developing its own definition by practice. As expressed by one Environment Canada official, environmental effects may be considered significant when they arouse concern among the public or among the professional community. This definitional problem highlights the overall "discretionary" federal approach to environmental impact assessment.

8. Ontario, *Environmental Assessment Act 1975*, Section 12, Subsection 2(b).
9. T. J. F. Lash, D. E. L. Maasland, G. Filteau and P. A. Larkin, "On doing things differently: an environmental impact assessment of major projects", *Issues in Canadian Science Policy*, Ottawa, Information Canada, September 1974, pp. 9-10.
10. D. H. Pimlott, "The hazardous search for oil and gas in Arctic waters", *Nature Canada*, Vol. 3, No. 4, October/December 1974, pp. 20-28.
11. "Nanisivik", *Northern Perspectives*, Vol. 4, No. 2, 1976, p. 2.
12. E. B. Peterson, "Environmental considerations in Northern resource development", *The Mackenzie pipeline: Arctic gas and Canadian energy policy*, edited by P. H. Pearse, Toronto, McClelland and Stewart, 1974, pp. 115-142.
13. J. C. Sorenson, "Some procedures and programs for environmental impact assessment", *Environmental impact analysis: philosophy and methods*, edited by R. B. Ditton and T. I. Goodale, Madison, University of Wisconsin Press, 1972, p. 104.

6

Broadening the Approach to Evaluation in Resources Management Decision Making

*W. R. Derrick Sewell**

In May 1968, the British government appointed a Royal Commission charged with the responsibility to recommend a location for a third London airport. After what was probably the most extensive analysis of a public project ever undertaken in the U. K., the Commission concluded that the most advantageous site was at Cublington in Buckinghamshire. The government, however, has decided to build the airport at Foulness in the Thames estuary, at a cost of almost 200 million pounds more than that estimated for Cublington.

In British Columbia, following a disastrous flood on the Fraser River in 1948, an engineering board was established to study the problem and recommend solutions. In its Final Report, published in 1963, the Fraser River Board stressed the urgency of taking immediate action. It noted that the existing dyking system was inadequate, and recommended the construction of a multiple-purpose scheme of upstream storage. More than a decade later, little action has been taken, other than the repair of some of the existing dykes. The flood threat remains.

The foregoing experiences raise some important questions about the role of evaluations in the decision-making process, and about the ability of such studies to provide the data that are required for sound decisions. A cynical reaction to the experience relating to the Royal Commission report and the recommendations concerning flood control on the Fraser River might be that the outcomes of such enquiries have little influence on decisions and therefore the former are a waste of time. The evidence is, however, that decision makers usually attach considerable importance to the findings of these investigations, even though they may choose not to accept all the recommendations that are based upon them.

The more serious problem is the nature and adequacy of the information which the evaluations provide. The abandonment of the Spadina

*W. R. Derrick Sewell is a professor in the departments of geography and economics at the University of Victoria in Victoria, B.C. This paper is a revised version of an article with the same title in the *Journal of Environmental Management*, Vol. 1, No. 1, January 1973, pp. 33-60. The original version contains an extensive bibliography which may be of use to readers in this field.

expressway in Toronto after some $65 million had been spent on it, the costly delay in the Nelson River Diversion Scheme in Manitoba, and the failure of the South Saskatchewan River Development scheme to yield the benefits claimed for it by the promotors suggest that some important questions may not have been asked. Had they been posed and satisfactorily answered, the decision makers would have been able to detect, for example, changes in the public's view about the desirability of the projects, shifts in values placed upon the preservation of certain environmental attributes, or preferences for one way of life (such as dry farming) versus other ways of life (such as irrigation farming).

The task of evaluation in resources management decision making is clearly becoming increasingly complex. No longer is it a simple matter of estimating costs of construction and weighing them against anticipated revenues. No longer is it a matter of assessing only the local on-site impacts. More and more it is becoming necessary to consider proposals for resource development in terms of their broad social, environmental and institutional consequences, as well as their economic and financial effects. More and more the region or the nation rather than the local area is the appropriate areal unit for evaluation.

Given this change in focus, it is pertinent to ask if present procedures for evaluation are adequate to meet the challenge and, if they are not, in what ways they need to be improved? More specifically, in what ways might geographical and other social science research assist in improving them? The answers to these questions might best be found through an examination of the decision-making process on the one hand, and of techniques of evaluation on the other.

The Decision-making Process

The decision-making process may be thought of as a series of interconnected elements or steps, leading from the recognition of a problem and the identification of potential solutions to the selection and adoption of an appropriate strategy. Ideally, the various steps follow in sequence and there is feed-back amongst particular elements. Sometimes only one person, or a single group of people, is involved in the various steps. More often, however, different groups play particular roles at various stages in the process.

Figure 1 describes the basic elements in an idealized planning and policy-making process. The process begins with a statement of the goals sought and is followed by the identification of the specific problems to be solved, and the delineation of the planning or policy-making context in which the analysis is to be undertaken. It continues with a delineation of potential solutions, formulation of alternative sets of strategies, and the evaluation of each of these sets. It reaches a final stage with the selection of an optimal solution or set of strategies. Hindsight reviews of

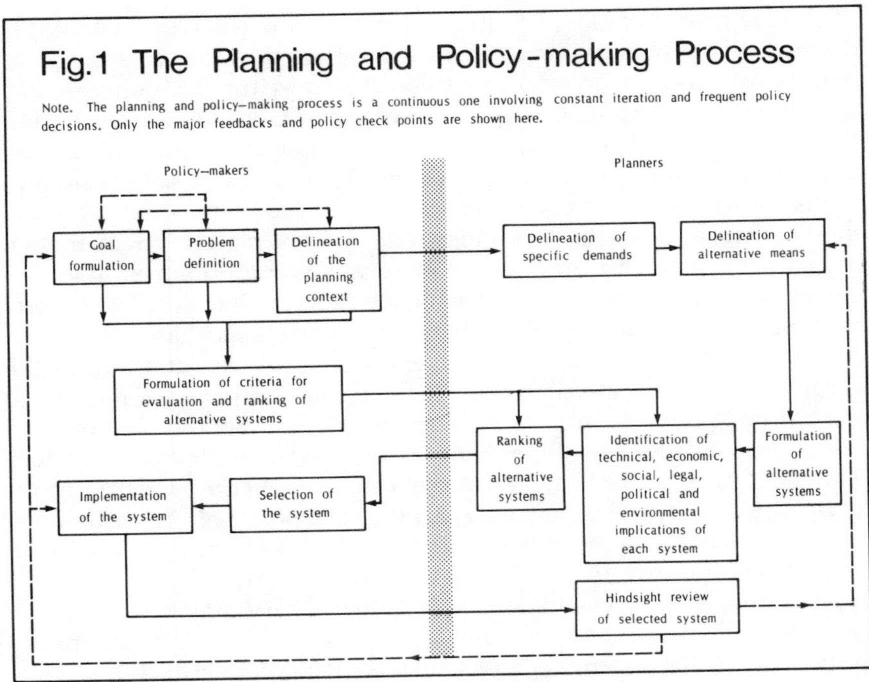

experience with the selected solution provide an input into future planning and policy-making processes.

STATEMENTS OF GOALS

Goals might include one or more of the following broad social objectives: (a) increasing national or regional income, (b) redistributing income among regions, (c) redistributing income among social groups, (d) improving environmental quality.

Sometimes goals are set out in a formal statement of government policy. More often, however, goals are implicit rather than explicit, and even when they are stated they are more expressions of means than of ends. For example, typical objectives stated in water resources plans in North America are "increasing irrigated acreage", "providing hydroelectric power", or "furnishing low cost water transport". Satisfactory appraisal of such plans, of course, is possible only if it is known *for what purpose* such goods and services are to be provided. Is it to facilitate an increase in national income, or a transfer of income from the rich to the poor? Is it to stimulate the growth of a lagging region? Only with answers to these questions would it be possible to determine whether a given plan represented the best means of attaining a given end or purpose.

Ideally, goals should be formulated through extensive, rational discussion between the various groups involved in decision making, as well as with those who are likely to be affectd by the decisions. Generally, however, it seems that goals evolve not from logical debate but from an admixture of historical precedent, political opportunism, and assumptions about public attitudes. Usually there is little or no attempt to discover what the public wants or would like to have. Politicians and their technical advisors, it seems, tend to rely mainly on their own judgements as to the latter rather than canvassing public opinion in a systematic way. A possible consequence may be that decision makers will misperceive the goals which the public expects them to pursue. Another may be that decision makers will fail to detect shifts in the relative importance attached to particular goals. Experience relating to the South Saskatchewan project seems to suggest that the promotors of the scheme misperceived the goals of the people in the Prairie region. The costly delays in the construction of electric power projects in various parts of North America may be a result of a general shift in the relative importance attached to continuous economic growth as compared with attempts to improve the quality of the environment.

A prerequisite in evaluation of resources management projects or policies is then a clear statement of the goals to be pursued, and an indication of the extent to which that statement reflects the relative importance which the public currently attaches to particular aims and objectives.

IDENTIFICATION OF PROBLEMS AND NEEDS

The next step in the planning and policy-making process is the identification of specific resources management problems to be solved, and the estimation of demands for the goods and services which the development of resources projects would provide. Here it is necessary to do more than merely state that "there is a major flood problem in the West," or "the level of water quality in the River Trent has reached intolerable proportions," or that "requirements for electric power in the London area will double by 1985." Faced with a growing number of claims on the public purse and with an increasing number of conflicts in the use of particular resources, decision makers must know *how* serious problems are, not only in terms of their physical magnitude but also in terms of their impact upon human activity and social relationships. They must also have some indication of the willingness of the public to pay for the benefits which resources development projects would provide. Thus, it is essential to have good estimates of the losses that would occur with given magnitudes and frequencies of floods, taking into account various assumptions about human behaviour, with and without the provision of flood control. Similarly, the determination of appropriate policies for water quality improvement requires estimates of the economic and social impact of various levels of water quality, and indications of how much those who are affected would be willing to give up in order to secure an improvement.

Unfortunately, the problem identification and demand estimation phase of the planning and policy-making process is often weak. In many instances, little time or effort is devoted to it, and in some cases it is undertaken almost as an afterthought. Sometimes the data produced are used to justify decisions which have already been made rather than to evaluate whether the project involved is the best possible means or whether in fact any project is required at all. Some of the greatest deficiencies in this connection have occurred in water resources planning. In certain instances, several years have been devoted to the planning of dams and diversion structures, with millions of dollars allocated to site investigations and project designs, but only a few months (generally towards the end of the study) and a tiny proportion of the costs of the investigation allocated to studies of the need for the project.

The lack of attention to demand estimates in resources management policy making results in part from the fact that planning in this connection has been largely in the hands of the engineering profession and has involved relatively few social scientists. The training and experiences, as well as the professional interests of the former, are more in the area of supply than demand.[1] Social scientists for their part, however, have been slow in pointing out this deficiency and in developing satisfactory methodologies for demand estimation. Although some advances have been made in the latter connection in the past few years, many of the techniques presently in use permit little more than educated guesses about public preferences.[2] In many instances, the estimates are mere extrapolations of past experience. The underlying assumptions therefore are that preference patterns will remain unchanged, that price will have no effect on consumption, and that no innovations will be adopted which will reduce per capita usage. Past experience clearly shows, however, that such assumptions are not valid. People do substitute one form of energy for another and they do engage in new forms of outdoor recreation. Price does tend to affect the demand for goods and services such as domestic water supply, or outdoor recreation. And there is evidence that resource scarcities stimulate the adoption of resource conserving techniques, such as recycling and waste water treatment.

IDENTIFICATION OF ALTERNATIVE MEANS AND STRATEGIES

There are usually several possible alternative ways of dealing with a given resources management problem or of providing the goods and services which a resources development project would supply. Often the range of choice is quite wide. White has shown, for example, that there are at least seven major alternative ways of dealing with flood problems.[3] Empirical studies have shown, however, that only a few of these possibilities are actually considered by policy makers concerned with flood problems because of various institutional constraints, professional biases, and other factors. Similarly, narrow ranges of choice also seem to characterize decision making in other fields of resource management, such as the use of arid lands, the provision of outdoor recreation opportunities, and the management of atmospheric quality.

In resources management generally, there seems to be a strong bias towards construction, punitive legislation, and the provision of financial aid even though there may be empirical evidence that other kinds of strategies would be more efficient. Water utilities, for example, appear to concentrate upon reservoir and aqueduct construction as a means for solving water shortages rather than encouraging more efficient use through regulating use or raising the price of water.

The typical approach to water quality management has been to fine offenders and in some cases to provide financial assistance for the construction of treatment plants. Little attention has been given to such strategies as the provision of economic incentives (like effluent discharge fees), research or public involvement. Experience in the Genossenschaften in West Germany and more recently in the River Basin Agencies in France suggests that economic incentives may be more effective in controlling pollution than sole reliance on punitive legislation, and the results of experiments in public participation in the United States and France suggest that the latter strategy has merits, not only in identifying the nature of the problem, but also in developing support for the implementation of policies.

The range of choice has also been limited by the tendency to concentrate on only one part of a resources management system. This has been especially so in the search for solutions to the pollution problem. Almost always the focus of attention has been on handling effluents after they have been generated: comparatively little effort has been devoted towards the reduction of residuals by altering the production process or the mix of raw materials used in it.

EVALUATION OF ALTERNATIVE STRATEGIES

Given the nature of the problem to be solved, and a set of alternative strategies, on what basis might a choice be made? In the past, selection has been based largely upon the application of a few simple criteria, such as (a) is the strategy technically possible? (b) is it legally permissible? (c) is it financially viable? Today, however, the task of evaluation is much more demanding. As noted earlier, considerations of overall economic impact, social consequences, ecological impacts, and political effects have to be weighed as well. Table 1 lists considerations that might be taken into account in evaluating alternative strategies for air quality management. The feasibility of measuring the various parameters, of course, varies considerably, being greatest with the physical aspects and most difficult with those relating to behaviour and institutions.

TABLE 1

Elements of Indices for the Evaluation of Management Strategies

I *Physical and ecological impacts*
1 Time and spatial pattern of gaseous residuals generated.
2 Time and spatial pattern of gaseous residuals discharged.
3 Time and spatial pattern of ambient air concentrations.
4 Time and spatial pattern of solid and liquid residuals generated and discharged in the process of handling the gaseous residuals.
5 Physical impacts upon various physical, natural, and human systems, i.e. distributional effects.

II *Economic impacts*
1 Impacts upon costs of operations of residuals generators over time.
2 Impacts upon damages sustained by receptors over time, where reduced damages comprise the benefits from implementation of the strategy.
3 Indirect impacts upon income, employment, and their distributions, e.g. trade balance, and international competitive position, interregional distribution of industry.

III *Timing considerations*
1 Time required to put the strategy into operation.
2 Time required to obtain first results and/or benefits.

IV *Administrative considerations*
1 Simplicity of administration.
2 Costs of administration, e.g. manpower, instrumentation.
3 Flexibility, e.g. in relation to improving the system of management, to changing the system in response to changed conditions and objectives.

V *Legal considerations*
1 Constitutional constraints.
2 Nature and extent of legal precedents.

VI *Political considerations*
1 Politicians' perceived urgency of the air-quality management problem in relation to other problems of society.
2 Professionals' perceived urgency of the air-quality problem.
3 Public's perceived urgency of air-quality problem.
4 Politicians' perceived impact of the strategy upon various political groups.
5 Impact upon federal-provincial relations.
6 Impact upon local-provincial relations.
7 Degree of coincidence of areal scope of strategy with existing political jurisdictions.

VII *Public responsiveness*
1 Extent of coincidence of the proposed strategy with notions of the public about such matters as equity, efficiency and adequacy of this strategy to deal with the problem.

SELECTION OF AN ALTERNATIVE

Based on the information provided by the formal evaluation process described above, as well as various extraneous factors, decision makers select an alternative which they believe is in the public interest, and which they feel is the best way of dealing with the problem in question. Means are then provided to implement the decision in the form of legislative enactments, provision of funds and/or administrative readjustments.

Generally this is the final step in the policy-making process. If it solves the problem, the public will be satisfied and the stress which brought it to the decision maker's attention will be relieved. If it does not, further crises will occur and the demands for more appropriate action will grow.[4]

HINDSIGHT REVIEWS

An extremely valuable but generally neglected step in the policy-making process is the monitoring of experience in implementing projects and policies with a view to determining the extent to which they succeed in attaining the goals set for them, and the degree to which they result in unpredicted consequences. Studies of agricultural readjustment programs in Canada have shown, for example, that subsidies to farmers have not succeeded either in improving the lot of the average farmer, or in promoting major changes in the types of farming undertaken.[5]

While it is clear that valuable insights could be gained from hindsight reviews, resources planning and management agencies have generally been very reluctant to undertake them. The reasons may be rooted in a fear that the findings of such evaluations might result in criticism of the management agency or its personnel. Politicians may also be reluctant to agree to such evaluations for similar reasons. There is no doubt, however, that they could furnish one of the most useful of all inputs into the policy-making process. It is important of course to ensure that they are undertaken by an independent agency, such as a Royal Commission or a Treasury Board, and that the latter is given the facts it requires for an impartial assessment.

Evaluation Techniques

During the past two decades, numerous techniques have been devised for assessing the merits of alternative resource management strategies.

An overview of the experience to date in the development and application of various techniques suggests the following four broad conclusions:

1. Of the various techniques devised so far, benefit-cost analysis appears to have been the most widely used, the most comprehensive in coverage, and the most severely criticized in its applications.

2. There have been several attempts in recent years to broaden the scope of various techniques of analysis by taking into account several goals rather than just one, by attempting to trace impacts beyond first round or direct effects, and by building various alternative constraints specifically into the evaluation.
3. Much remains to be learned about the ways in which people perceive problems and solutions, and the values they place upon various resources and resource uses and their attitudes as to the locus of responsibility for initiating action. Without this knowledge it is difficult to determine what the public wants or how it will respond to what is provided.
4. There is a growing desire to include assessments of environmental impacts in evaluations of resource management policies and programs, but great uncertainty as to how this can best be accomplished.

BENEFIT-COST ANALYSIS

Benefit-cost analysis is perhaps the best known and most widely adopted technique of evaluation. Developed mainly in the United States, first by engineers and more recently by economists, it was used initially for the evaluation of water resources development projects, particularly those concerned with navigation or flood control. Its applications are now very wide, embracing policies relating to the management of different types of resources, highway construction, education, mental health and many other problems of public concern. It is used not only by government agencies but also by industry. In the United States, it has become institutionalized in the federal government's procedures for reviewing proposals for public investment in resources management. It is also widely used in Canada.

The popularity of benefit-cost analysis stems partly from the fact that its objectives are fairly easily understood, and partly from the relative ease with which it can be applied to different types of situations. It is especially useful as a technique in situations where (a) the choice is to be made within a single resource context, (b) the benefits and the costs are fairly easily recognized and measured, and (c) the scale is comprehensible (the local area, region, or other basis rather than the nation).

Like any technique of evaluation, benefit-cost analysis is not a panacea. It does not provide answers to all the questions that might be posed in an evaluation of a resources management policy or proposal. It has in fact a number of limitations stemming in part from its conceptual underpinnings, and in part from difficulties in measuring benefits and costs, and from problems dealing with external effects, time, risk and uncertainty. In addition, there are the difficulties of taking such considerations as income redistribution, regional economic development, and environmental modification into account.

Broadening the Scope of the Evaluation

In recent years, numerous improvements in using benefit-cost analysis have been proposed.[6] Traditional benefit-cost analysis has assumed a single goal of public policy, that of increasing national income. However, it is now recognized that other important objectives exist for public policy, notably regional economic development, improvement of environmental quality, and improvement of social well-being (such as in income redistribution, protection of life, and national security). It is suggested that lists of beneficial and adverse factors relating to each of these objectives should be determined for each proposed plan or policy rather than concentrating only upon the objective of increasing national income.

The consideration of objectives in addition to that of national economic development is desirable since such a procedure recognizes that plans and policies generally aim to achieve several goals simultaneously, or at least to attain a particular goal subject to one or more constraints. A potential danger arises, however. If these multiple objectives are considered at a regional rather than a national level, benefit-cost would be robbed of one of its principal means of determining relative merits of proposed plans or projects. Unless a national perspective is maintained, some feel that there is a danger of funds being shifted from more economic to less economic activities.

Improving the Measurement of Benefits

Three possible approaches for calculating the benefits to be derived from a project have been developed: (i) willingness to pay, (ii) change in net income, (iii) costing the most likely alternative. Each one of these approaches has weaknesses as a means of assessing benefits.

Economists have long argued that the value of goods and services is indicated by the consumer's willingness to pay for them. While this criterion does show that there is a demand for the goods and services, it is an insufficient measure of the value. One would also need to know what was the cheapest means of providing the goods and services in order to appraise the merits of alternative ways of producing the latter. Similarly, the change in net income may not provide a satisfactory measure of the benefits derived, particularly where subsidies are involved. Only if the latter are subtracted from the income derived is it possible to weigh the benefits of alternative strategies. Finally, the cost of the cheapest alternative is not by itself a satisfactory measure of benefits. It is necessary to know also whether the value society places on the output of the cheapest alternative exceeds the cost of providing it.

Two questions, therefore, need to be posed in appraising the validity of estimates of benefits. First, do the benefits exceed the costs? And second, what is the least-cost means of providing the benefits?

Incorporating Environmental Impacts

The attempt to incorporate environmental impacts specifically into project evaluation has considerable merit. Information is needed regarding the nature and magnitude of these effects. Ideally, the procedures should reflect the opportunity costs of using a resource for one purpose rather than another, such as hydro-power generation rather than sport fishing.

Specific statements are needed about such factors as (a) the extent to which a given strategy would lead to an irreversible change in the environment, (b) the importance of keeping options open, and (c) the non-reproducibility of natural environments. Without such statements, it is certain that such considerations will be ignored. And these perhaps provide the major motivation for taking environmental impacts into account.

Interest Rates

The most controversial aspect of benefit-cost analysis in North America is the interest rate selected for discounting benefits and costs. Various economists have suggested that the low rates used by government have led to gross misallocations of capital, since they have been far below actual costs of borrowing money. Fox and Hirfindahl have shown, for example, that in 1962 if market rates had been used instead of the "administrative rate" of 2.6%, less than 80% of the projects submitted to the U.S. government in that year for funding would have had a benefit-cost ratio in excess of unity.[7]

The U.S. Water Resources Council suggests the use of a seven per cent rate of interest for discounting purposes. This is considerably higher than rates used in the past, and no doubt will placate some critics. There will be others, however, who will claim that even this rate is too low, for at least two reasons: first, it is below what the private sector would demand as a return for investment in ventures of comparable risk; and second, it tends to favour development over preservation, and in the case of irreplaceable assets, this does not fully reflect the social cost involved.

Taking Account of Regional Economic Development

It has long been suggested that the impact of resources development projects and policies on regional economic development should be identified and measured as an integral part of the evaluation. There are, however, substantial difficulties in tracing such impacts. First, although it may be possible to trace the positive effects within a region, it may not be possible to determine whether these are offset by losses elsewhere. Second, it is an open question as to how far resource development, and especially water resource development, stimulates economic growth, and third, it is not certain that investment in water resources projects is more efficient than investment in other means of stimulating such growth.

The Role of Public Participation

The logical extension of broadening the perspective of the evaluation of resources management projects and policies is to determine more accurately what the public wants and how it is likely to react to what is provided. As noted earlier, there may be major gaps between what the planner or policy maker perceives as important and what the public feels is significant. At present, planners and policy makers rely mainly upon public opinion polls, the ballot box and the referendum, and public hearings for indications of public views. However, such means do not always yield very accurate assessments of such views. Public opinion polls may reflect only the individual's reaction to a question and not his true preference. They provide no information as to strength of preferences or as to how an individual would react if faced with an actual choice. The ballot box has the disadvantage that it usually calls for views upon a collection of issues rather than just one. Like the referendum, it canvasses only those who turn up to vote: sometimes this is as little as 20% of the electorate, and an even smaller proportion of the total population. In the future, a number of possibilities for obtaining public views might be considered, including (i) studies of perceptions and attitudes, undertaken on an *ad hoc* or continuous basis, and (ii) involvement of segments of the public in actual planning and policy making.

Among the indirect means of tapping views, studies of perceptions and attitudes offer much promise. This method has already been used in water resources planning in the United States, particularly in connection with flood plain management, and the establishment of air pollution control regulations. Like other methods of assessing public views, studies of perceptions and attitudes have limitations, stemming from problems of soliciting information, the availability of skilled personnel to undertake the studies, and the tendency of views to change over time. Many of these problems, however, can be overcome by skilful organization and by well-structured and skilfully administered interviews.

Another attractive technique is the game simulation approach in which the actors assume the apparent roles of participants and act out a problem according to certain specified inputs or rules. It provides the participants with an opportunity not only to isolate the problems which they believe confront those whose role they are playing, but also gain a sense of appreciation of the way in which decisions are actually arrived at. Game simulations can be used to furnish reflections of public views on such questions as: what is the best use of a given parcel of land?

Should the Fraser River be used for the maintenance of salmon runs or the development of hydro-electric power? What position should British Columbia take on proposals to ship oil from Alaska to the State of Washington along the B.C. coast? Where is the most appropriate location for a new airport?

More specifically, such simulations, if carefully structured, make it possible to

(a) explore each range of alternatives, allowing particularly for the influence of chance/random elements,
(b) explore the role(s) of participants, and especially their perceptions and attitudes and group behaviour,
(c) examine those features of decision making that are difficult to quantify, such as views about environmental quality,
(d) examine those procedures which are conducive to conflict resolution through bargaining.

The technique has been little used to date, but applications to resources management questions by geographers in the U.K., the United States, and in Canada have emphasised its value as a tool for planning and policy making.[8] Its potential applications, beyond those explored to date, merit serious consideration by planners and policy makers.

OTHER TECHNIQUES OF EVALUATION

Besides improvements in benefit-cost analysis, a number of other techniques of evaluation have been developed in the past decade or so. These include systems analysis, engineering economic analysis, and the goals-achievement matrix. Brief comments on the latter technique are offered here. Discussions of the other techniques appear in the rapidly growing literature on the subject.

The Goals-achievement Matrix

In a resources management decision-making situation, policy makers try to pursue several objectives simultaneously. Typically, too, the attainment of any objective (or set of objectives) is accomplished by a combination of strategies rather than by just one. The problem is further complicated by the fact that differing relative importance is attached to particular goals on the one hand, and to particular kinds of strategy on the other. In addition, the incidence of the benefits and costs of given strategies may vary considerably among different groups in the community. Finally, not all benefits and costs can be expressed in monetary terms. Lichfield[9] and Hill[10] have developed an ingenious technique for taking into account multiple objectives, multiple strategies, varying weights, differing social impacts, and effects which are not readily expressed in monetary terms. It is described as the goals-achievement matrix.

For every plan that is proposed a goals-achievement matrix may be drawn up. The set of goals is known and a relative value is established for each goal. The objectives are defined in operational rather than in abstract terms. The consequences of each course of action for each social group are worked out and weights are established for each of the latter. The product of the analysis is shown in Table 2.

TABLE 2
The Goals-achievement Matrix

Goal description:	I			II		
Relative weight:	2			3		
Incidence	Rel. wt.	Costs	Ben.	Rel. wt.	Costs	Ben.
Group *a*	1	A	D	5	E	—
Group *b*	3	H		4	—	R
Group *c*	1	L	J	3	—	S
Group *d*	2	—		2		—
Group *e*	1	—	K	1	T	U

Goal description:	III			IV		
Relative weight:	5			4		
Incidence	Rel. wt.	Costs	Ben.	Rel. wt.	Costs	Ben.
Group *a*	1		N	1	Q	R
Group *b*	2		—	2	S	T
Group *c*	3	M	—	1	V	W
Group *d*	4		—	2	—	—
Group *e*	5		P	1	—	—

In the Table, I, II, III and IV are the descriptions of the goals. Each has a weight, 1, 2, 3, . . . previously determined. Various social groups, *a, b, c, d* . . . are identified as being affected by the course of action, and a relative weight is determined for each group, either for single goals, or for all goals taken together. The costs and benefits of each course of action are assigned the letters A, B, C . . . and these may be defined in either monetary or non-monetary units or in terms of qualitative statements.

For certain of the goals, it is possible to draw up a summation of the benefits and costs which is meaningful and useful. This will be the case when all the costs and benefits can be quantified. When this can be done, comparison can readily be made among competing alternative plans and between the pursuit of different objectives. Operationally, comparisons would be made between several matrices similar to that in Table 2.

There are a variety of possible uses for the technique, such as decisions relating to the use of the resources of a given river basin, the improvement of water quality, the development of outdoor recreational opportunities, or the rescue of a declining region.

Although the technique has some problems of application — such as those of interaction among objectives, and difficulties where a project serves several sectors — it can be a most useful device for assessing the relative merits of alternative plans. It is particularly valuable where the number of objectives is limited, the number of alternative plans is not large, where the impacts can be quantified in comparable terms, and where weights can be objectively assigned to goals, strategies, and different social groups.

The Potential Contribution of Research

The foregoing review has indicated that although the perspective in resources management evaluations has broadened considerably in the past decade, and although techniques of measurement are now much more sophisticated, policy makers still lack the kinds of information they need to make sound decisions. Research, especially in the social sciences, could make an important contribution towards remedying this deficiency. Studies in five areas in particular are urgently required.

(i) The identification of the nature and magnitude of resources problems, and the demands for resources-related goods and services. These include the assessment of natural and man-made hazards, and the demands for goods and services derived from water resources, forests, fisheries, mineral deposits, the atmosphere and agricultural lands.

(ii) Delineation of alternative strategies for dealing with resources problems and for supplying resources-related goods and services. In particular, studies are needed of potential alterations in patterns of human behaviour as well as those accomplished through alterations in the physical environment (as in the construction of dams, power plants, or factories).

(iii) Examinations of past performance of particular kinds of strategies, such as subsidies in agriculture, flood control works, reforestation, creation of wilderness reserves, and so on.

(iv) Examination of alternative ways of identifying public views including studies of perceptions and attitudes, experience of direct involvement in the planning and policy-making processes, and the use of simulation games.

(v) The refinement of existing techniques of evaluation and the development of new ones to take into account multiple objectives, multiple strategies, and intangible as well as tangible values.

Three broad conclusions may be drawn. First, the range of topics for study is very wide, involving research in both the physical and the social sciences. Much of it, however, requires experience in a specialized area within particular disciplines. The opportunities, as well as the needs, are particularly great for researchers with sound backgrounds in economics, psychology, and ecology; individuals with an understanding of quantitative techniques; and workers with a bent for sophisticated field research. Second, much of the most rewarding research will require co-operative efforts from people in a wide variety of disciplines. Fruitful ventures might be anticipated, for example, from geographers, and economists working together on the assessment of national or regional demands for particular resource-related goods and services, or between geographers and various natural scientists in the assessment of natural hazards. In addition, inter-disciplinary approaches involving psychologists, sociologists, political scientists, and geographers seem particularly appropriate to the study of problems such as public participation in policy making, and in undertaking hindsight reviews of project or policy effectiveness. Third, while some of the research can build upon what is already known, there are certain areas where real pioneering work is required: application of existing concepts or techniques may be either difficult or inappropriate. One such area relates to the evaluation of intangibles — those components of environmental appreciation, entailing either observation or physical exploitation, which are not directly quantifiable, or if quantifiable, cannot be valued by the market mechanism. Another area concerns externalities — the indirect, often unintended effects of resource development. Much of the current public concern about the environment is rooted in these two problems. Unfortunately, present techniques of evaluation do not deal with them satisfactorily. The social returns to successful research efforts in this connection, therefore, will be especially high.

NOTES

1. W. R. D. Sewell, "Environmental perceptions and attitudes of engineers and public health officials", *Environment and Behavior*, Vol. 3, No. 1, March 1971, pp. 23-59.
2. W. R. D. Sewell and B. T. Bower, eds., *Forecasting the demands for water*, Ottawa, Queen's Printer, 1968. See also, T. R. Lee, *Approaches to water requirement forecasting: a Canadian Perspective*, Environment Canada Social Science Series No. 9, Burlington, Ontario, Canada Centre for Inland Waters, 1972; D. M. Tate and R. Robichaud, *Industrial water demand forecasting*, Environment Canada, Social Science Series No. 10, Ottawa, Inland Waters Directorate, Water Planning and Management Branch, 1973.
3. G. F. White, *Natural hazards: global, national and local*, New York, Oxford University Press, 1974.
4. R. Kasperson, "Environmental stress and the municipal political system," *The structure of political geography*, edited by R. Kasperson and J. Minghi, Chicago, Aldine Press, 1969, pp. 481-496.
5. H. Buckley and E. Tihanyi, *Canadian policies for rural adjustment*, Economic Council of Canada Special Study No. 7, Ottawa, Queen's Printer, 1967.
6. U.S. Water Resources Council, *Proposed principles and standards for planning water and related land resources*, Washington, D.C., U.S. Government Printing Office, 1972.
7. I. K. Fox and O. Hirfindahl, "Attainment of efficiency is satisfying demands for water resources", *American Economic Review*, Vol. 54, 1964, p. 198.
8. P. Gould, "Man against his environment: a game theoretic framework", *Annals of the Association of American Geographers*, Vol. 53, No. 3, September 1963, pp. 290-297; R. Walfrod, *Games in geography*, London, Longman, 1969; C. Wood, *Geographical games*, Western Geographical Series Vol. 6, Victoria, University of Victoria, Department of Geography, 1972.
9. N. Lichfield, "Economics in town planning", *Town Planning Review*, Vol. 39, No. 1, April 1968, pp. 5-20.
10. M. Hill, "A goals-achievement matrix for evaluating alternative plans", *Journal of the American Institute of Planners*, Vol. 34, No. 1, January, 1968, pp. 19-29.

7

Decision Making and Environmental Quality

*Timothy O'Riordan**

The incorporation of environmental quality criteria in enviromental management in recent years has led to the general recognition that the propositions underlying traditional decision processes are no longer valid, and indeed may lead (if they have not already led) to serious environmental misuse. Yet to incorporate such criteria fully into the decision process involves radical changes in the existing procedures so it does not appear likely that major innovations will come easily. Let us turn to the underlying propositions and examine them in the context of environmental quality issues.

1. *Problem identification and alternative solutions.*

In many environmental issues, once the problem has become sufficiently serious to be defined, it is too late. The side effects of DDT and other biocides, symptoms of lake eutrophication and delayed reactions to atmospheric toxicants are examples. The dilemma facing the political decision maker is to gain sufficient public support for what might prove to be a costly proposal in anticipation of any manifest consequences and when public information (and indeed expert information) may be scanty or at least contentious. An even more difficult dilemma is that a more suitable means of controlling an environmental problem may mean a change of public tastes or the control of traditional 'freedoms'. This is the message of Hardin's thought-provoking article, "The Tragedy of the Commons" in which he claims we are locked into a system of mutually enforced destruction of common property resources to the ultimate ruin of us all, unless we control individual actions by mutual sanction.[1] However, to get this message across in the absence of manifest crisis is not an easy task. Generally speaking, the implementation of solutions to counter environmental problems only begins when the problems are already manifest, and even then 'technological' as opposed to 'socio-economic' solutions are sought at least initially.

This dilemma is a very real one. To await a fundamental change in public tastes may take too long, yet a poorly defined technical solution

---

*Timothy O'Riordan is a Reader in the School of Environmental Science at the University of East Anglia in Norwich, England. This paper is an edited and updated version of pages 8 to 18 from a longer study entitled, "Decision making and environmental quality: an analysis of a water quality issue in the Shuswap and Okanagan Valleys, British Columbia," *Okanagan Water Decisions*, H. D. Foster, ed., Western Geographical Series, Vol. 4, Victoria, University of Victoria, Department of Geography, 1972, pp. 1-111.

may worsen the problem or create fresh difficulties. On the other hand, to do nothing while waiting for public preferences and/or better thought out technical solutions may allow the problem to worsen and restrict future options. This is to say nothing of the political repercussions created by the inconveniences that 'temporary' delay imposes. To quote from Meier:

> The cultural prohibitions and non-material values attached to pollution are especially significant for public policy where physical conditions, objective circumstances and hard facts are less influential over the short-to-middle run than sentiments and attitudes. Beliefs held tenaciously by educated people present the greatest hurdles to be overcome before major programs for the conservation of water and energy resources can be put into operation. The technologies for striking improvements in efficiency are at hand, but it is now clear that the beliefs of one splinter or another of the educated classes will be violated by taking such action. These tiny minorities do not have the power to promote alternative changes, but they often succeed in confusing the choice-making processes in a democratic society so as to effect a practical veto.[2]

2. *The role of expert advice vis à vis public opinion.*

Meier's comments lead us to the discussion of the confrontation between expert and 'lay' opinion. Many environmental problems are the result of inappropriate technical decisions made in the past. In all fairness it should be emphasised that many of the environmental side effects were not sufficiently known about or regarded as a matter of concern to be avoided, and to foresee all potential environmental side effects resulting from any given course of action is well nigh impossible given our current state of knowledge of ecological systems. However, even if the experts could foresee all the consequences, it is not theoretically their job to evaluate in social welfare terms the nature of such consequences. This has usually been the politician's responsibility, but it is difficult for any single individual or group of individuals to assess all the possible environmental consequences of various alternative proposals. Thus the public, in the form of increasingly numerous and articulate citizens' groups have appeared in the political decision-making forum with the intention of injecting their assessment of various environmental consequences *directly* into the decision process. In the past, such views were supposed to be conveyed to the political representative whose responsibility it was to bring these to the attention of the whole decision-making body. But this state of representative democracy is increasingly being overrun by a form of participatory democracy where direct public involvement and a transfer of power to the citizen is considered necessary.

However, such a shift will not come easily. Politicians who feel that it is their job to represent their constituents' interests feel somewhat offended if some of their constituents attempt to do their job for them.

This is particularly true where articulate citizens' groups seek to impose their morality on a political process to such a rigid extent that the traditional councils of bargaining, compromise and conciliation pass unheeded. Experts, who feel it is their job to provide the politician with the necessary sophisticated advice feel similarly offended when citizens' groups appear before them attempting to tell them how to do their job better. In essence then the professional resource manager sees himself being demoted from the role of policy maker to one of consultant.[3] Nevertheless, if the professional manager attempts to avoid the input of public opinion, he is determining societal norms by assuming powers over the allocation of public preferences and the distribution of social welfare impacts. Given existing information systems, such a situation is untenable; experts trained in highly specialised fields frequently exhibit complete lack of understanding of ecological and/or social side effects of their proposed actions. It seems that at present we are in a very interesting stage of transition between representative and participatory democracy and between 'rational' expert opinion and input of 'emotional' public feeling often supported by professional advocates.

3. *Assumptions upon which evaluation is based*.

The rising tide of environmental concern has brought with it a new set of values and associated objectives which cannot be subsumed under the criteria of efficiency and economic growth. It is now apparent that there are multiple objectives and multiple criteria against which to judge benefits and costs. Such objectives may include one or more of six terminal goals in various orders of priority: national security, environmental health, economic growth, equalisation of economic opportunity, equalisation of social welfare and political opportunity, environmental quality and ecological harmony. Traditionally, these goals have tended to be hierarchical in arrangement reflecting a priority predicated upon security, health and wealth. Goals associated with quality, equal opportunity and man-nature harmony tend to follow in sequence as society evolves and becomes more opulent, not because they are not relevant to security, health and wealth (as indeed they are), but because traditionally they have not seemed necessary to the attainment of these three major priorities. Indeed, it still seems difficult to suppress the current belief that until security, health and economic progress are attained in the most expedient manner, environmental side effects can be ignored.

Attempts are now being made to incorporate multiple objectives into resource management decisions. It is important to avoid the dangers of solving 'problems' to the neglect of other objectives.[4] Part of the reason why political conflict over environmental issues is so bitter and protracted is because the underlying values of the combatants are not clearly exposed. Indeed we have no formal institutional mechanism to clarify goals and to distinguish preferences. Until this process is drastically improved multiple objectives and multiple means are doomed to failure.

Not the least of these difficulties involves the formal inclusion of values into what was formerly largely a technical process. Values enter in two ways: the value systems of the various gainers and losers of each alternative solution, and the value systems of both the technical experts and the political decision makers who are specific actors in the process. In the first instance, namely the values of the affected constituents, conflicts in response will be apparent in relation to the degree of perceived impact, the socio-economic status of the individual, his sense of political efficacy, his understanding of the problem under review, his awareness of the social impact of the issue and his own sense of personal responsibility in attempting to alter the decision.[5] All this in turn will be reflected by the spatial incidence of project benefits and costs, the income distribution of the population affected, the degree of public information and awareness and the nature of formal and informal procedures for incorporating public opinion in the decision process.

One value gaining increasing prominence is that of the 'no growth' philosophy. Stability of populations and of economic activity are seen by a certain section of the North American population as a prerequisite for environmental quality and ecological harmony.[6] However, traditional decision-making criteria and legal arrangements have assumed that some degree of resource use was necessary and that resource management was based upon the attainment of wealth and social progress. To desire a steady state in biologic and economic systems is not necessarily incompatible with the concept of improving social welfare, but it certainly requires a reappraisal of existing decision criteria and legal guidelines. At issue here therefore is the very real question of how to identify and incorporate shifting and diverging values into a process that formerly was based on relatively simple objective functions.

The values of technical advisors and politicians also play a key role. The attitude-guiding nature of the value systems of technical experts can influence political decisions, distort the process of establishing suitable environmental standards, and assist in the interpretation of 'facts'. Value systems of expert advisors influence policy analysis in a number of very fundamental ways such as moral judgement, internal ideological conflict, the desire to maintain what is feasible rather than search for or promote radical solutions, and the interpretation of outcomes. Political decision makers are similarly influenced by their values, and by their visions. The values of political decision makers not only influence their own judgements, but permit them to interpret what the public wants or should want in terms of decision outcomes. Public reaction to environmental quality decisions may consequently be assessed more upon assumptions of what public opinion ought to be than upon its direct content. Subsequent interpretation of the nature and degree of public protest, particularly in cases where the decision maker genuinely believes (or has convinced himself) that he is acting in the public interest, may be seriously misjudged.

The above comments should not be taken to mean that values have heretofore not played a significant part in decision making, but merely to emphasise that the introduction of environmental quality issues into public policy making with their dependence upon non-measurable value-laden phenomena has greatly emphasised the part played by such values.

4. *Spatial and temporal impact of environmental decisions.*

At the purely political level, the introduction of environmental problems creates two more additional problems, both by now widely recognized but worth re-emphasising. One is the question of external effects impinging upon areas and groups beyond the boundaries of the decision-making unit. Sewage from one municipality damaging a beach in another administrative area is but one example. Various institutional mechanisms have been developed to overcome this class of problems, for example, regionalisation of the decision units, the establishment of provincial or national guidelines and improved legal remedies. But where the guidelines still fail to control all externalities, or where regionalisation is either rudimentary or inadequately enforced, the question remains that taxpayers and voters in other jurisdictions have no formal political weight in the decisions of the polluting municipality. Thus the impact of external effects, particularly those which are disaggregated and difficult to measure, is usually not properly incorporated in existing political decision-making procedures.

The second class of problems in the political sphere relates to the time scale of decision implementation. Solutions which involve short-term sacrifice (whether it be financial or in terms of loss of individual freedom) for uncertain long-term gains are not politically popular. Yet many solutions to environmental problems fall into this category, for example, paying for air pollution control devices on automobiles when smog is neither noticeable nor its effects clearly proven (or at least it only affects certain minority groups), or banning all biocides (with concomitant effects on the chemical industry) from use by the farmer and the home gardener when the side effects of such products have not clearly been identified. It is in these situations that the politician has to act *'pro bonum publicum'* and trust that he still straddles the credibility gap. Should he fail to do so, and a number of politicians now recognise that for many of the reasons cited above it is difficult to maintain public trust, it becomes increasingly difficult to legislate in a paternalistic fashion.

Summarizing the above discussion, the introduction of environmental issues into public sector decision making has placed great stresses upon traditional decision-making processes. Goals are multiple and internally inconsistent; as a result the nature and incidence of gainers and losers and costs and benefits both spatially and temporally vary depending upon the value framework of the analysis. Conflicts arise between expert opinion (which itself is not unified) and emotional but not necessarily uninformed non-technical citizen opinion. The political decision maker is caught in the centre of this conflict, guided by technical advice yet influenced by the rhetoric of his constituents. The degree of public participation is also a contentious issue: total involvement is impossible in practical terms yet even widespread involvement may seriously lengthen the decision-making process. Usually, however, the public is 'represented' by a small number of active citizens' groups each led by a very concerned and highly articulate minority. So the question of representation or participation is left unresolved. Finally, the issue of measurable versus incommensurable impact, particularly where side effects cross political boundaries and extend over time, remains thorny.

A Model of Decision Making and Environmental Quality

The emergence of these issues as having a major impact on the decision-making process leads to the reappraisal of the process itself. Figure 1 portrays a model based on the work of Wengert[7] and Kasperson[8] and it visualizes a decision process evolving from group struggle.[9] Stress (in the form of a manifest problem) is identified by an impacted or interest group, and if it is of sufficient magnitude (or if the

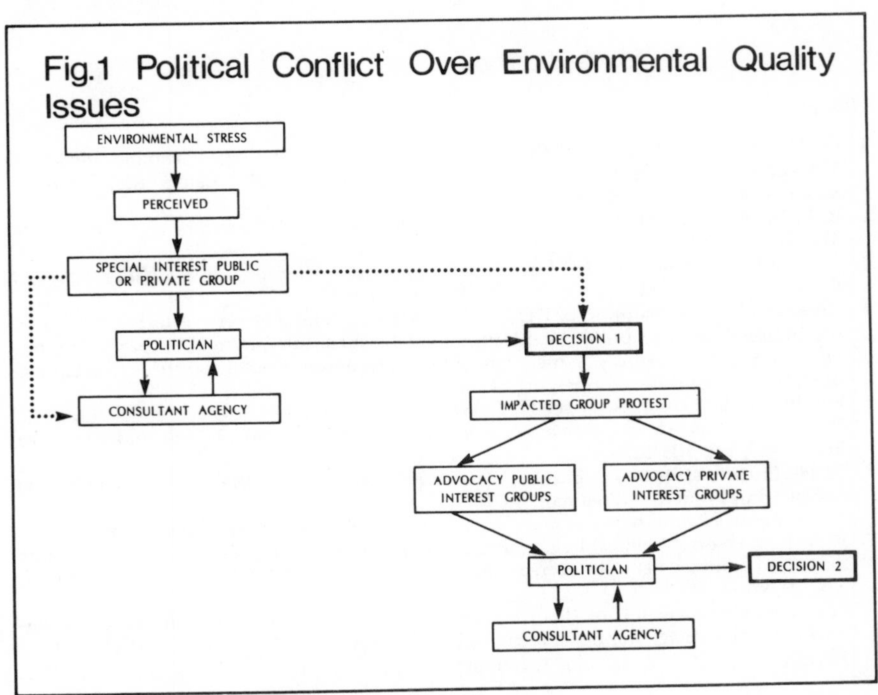

Fig.1 Political Conflict Over Environmental Quality Issues

affected group has sufficient political influence) it will be communicated directly to the decision maker (the politician) or to the responsible public agency. If the political 'noise' created by the issue and/or the group(s) involved is focussed sufficiently to create political stress upon the decision maker, he will seek expert advice from consultants or the appropriate administrative agency. Normally, fairly restricting terms of reference and cost ceilings are imposed, and the suggested solutions (usually few in number and narrow in perspective) are based upon the assumption of public preferences. Not infrequently the solution recommended by the expert advisor is adopted by the decision-making body, particularly if the issue involves fairly complex technical considerations. This is Decision 1 on the diagram and may be the final decision.

However, if this decision involves potential environmental side effects which have not been fully incorporated into the analysis, or at least not discussed publicly, subsequent protest by one or more groups acting either in their own self interest or in the purported advocacy for the general public interest may generate a second round of political stress on the decision maker. He may then seek to resolve this either by new studies, a public hearing or through referenda. The result may mean a second decision (Decision 2) which usually incorporates some degree of 'public opinion' however that may be defined.

NOTES

1. G. Hardin, "The tragedy of the commons", *Science*, Vol. 162, December 1968, pp. 1243-1248. This has been reprinted in A.C. Enthoven and A.M. Freeman eds., *Pollution, resources, and the environment*, New York, W. W. Norton, 1973, pp. 1-13.
2. R. L. Meier, "Insights into pollution," *Journal of the American Institute of Planners*, Vol. 37, 1971, p. 218.
3. G. Wandesforde-Smith, "The bureaucratic response to environmental politics," *Natural Resources Journal*, Vol. 11, No. 3, July 1971, pp. 479-488.
4. An example is the banning of DDT which, while lessening adverse effects on wildlife, has indirectly created public health problems. Its substitute in the U.S., parathion, has killed or blinded dozens of Americans, while in underdeveloped countries the removal of DDT may produce an upswing of malaria.
5. For an excellent discussion, see G. F. White, "Formation and role of public attitudes," *Environmental quality in a growing economy*, edited by H. Jarrett, Baltimore, Johns Hopkins, 1966, pp. 105-127.
6. P. H. Ehrlich and A. H. Ehrlich, *Population, resources, environment: issues in human ecology*, San Francisco, Freeman, 1970.
7. N. Wengert, *Natural resources and the political struggle*, New York, Doubleday, 1955.
8. R. E. Kasperson, "Political behavior and the decision-making process in the allocation of water resources between recreational and municipal use", *Natural Resources Journal*, Vol. 9, No. 2, 1969, pp. 176-211.
9. For an updated version of this diagram, see T. O'Riordan, "Policy making and environmental management: some thoughts on process and research issues", *Natural Resources Journal*, Vol. 16, No. 1, January 1976, pp. 177-196.

8
A Framework for Agency Use of Public Input in Resource Decision Making

*John C. Hendee, Roger N. Clark and George H. Stankey**

Public agencies have changed the way they make decisions about the use of natural resources. The stress now is on incorporating public input. The basic concept is that agencies serve the people — what do the people want?

The search for public participation is not new. Resource managers traditionally have turned to advisory boards, *ad hoc* committees, and contacts with key people. But some feel that past contacts often were selective, limited, and interest-group oriented, with a tendency to reflect the whims of industry, conservation organizations and local political figures.

The increasing tendency for citizens to challenge resource decisions at public meetings, in court cases, and through legislative proposals indicates that some segments of the public feel excluded from policy making. Many citizens feel left out of any policy or decision making and resort to protest as the only available means of being heard. As O'Riordan pointed out, "Though the majority might be 'silent', they are not necessarily indifferent. . . . That silence may be as much a function of political inefficacy and limited information as it may be to the holding of mild preferences."[1]

There is a growing body of literature about public participation — its policy implications and its significance as a research problem.[2] Our concern is how public participation is linked to resource management decision making.

The subtle complexities and influences surrounding public involvement impress us. Just how issues are defined; how public input is collected, analyzed, and evaluated; and how the resulting decisions are implemented are particularly important questions in dealing with these inherent complexities and influences.

---

*John C. Hendee is recreation research project leader and Roger N. Clark is a research social scientist at the Forest Service, Pacific Northwest Forest and Range Experiment Station of the U.S. Department of Agriculture in Seattle, Washington. George H. Stankey is a research social scientist at the Forest Service Intermountain Forest and Range Experiment Station, U.S. Department of Agriculture, at Missoula, Montana. This paper is an edited version of an article by the same title that appeared in the *Journal of Soil and Water Conservation*, Vol. 29, No. 2, March-April 1974, pp. 60-66.

As a basic structure for making use of public inputs in resource decision making, we propose the following framework.

A Means to an End

The major objective of public resource management is to provide people with a sustained flow of the benefits they desire. Some of these benefits are material, such as low-cost lumber for housing and adequate quantity and quality of water. Others are less tangible, such as people's happiness by virtue of the recreational opportunities and environmental quality they enjoy.

In devising programs to provide the desired mix of benefits, resource managers must consider many factors, technical as well as social-political. These include, among other things, resource inventory and capability data on soil, water, timber, forage, and scenery; legal and budgetary constraints; and potential economic impacts.

Public sentiment, expressed and gathered as citizens participate in decision processes, is a particularly important input because it helps identify the values that people attach to the alternative goods and services that resources might provide. Sentiment serves as a necessary guide to achieving more acceptable resource decisions. In addition, public participation in decision making is a source of satisfaction, meaning and identity for the citizens involved.

The overriding objective of public involvement must be to arrive at more acceptable resource management decisions. Public input is not an end in itself but a means to better decisions.

Five Processes in Decision Making

From the resource manager's perspective, public involvement has five integral processes: issue definition, collection, analysis, evaluation, and decision implementation. Problems requiring public involvement must first be defined. Then input must be collected, analyzed to see who said what, and evaluated to determine what it means and how it is important to the decision. Finally, the decision must be translated into a program of action.

If oversimplified, these processes might be viewed as subsequent stages. But this is not necessarilly true because all land use planning efforts take a variety of approaches and sequences in involving the public.

Figure 1 shows how these processes relate to public participation in a resource issue, how they relate to other decision factors, and how they combine in leading to a decision. It is important for resource managers to keep these processes separate. Mixing them can seriously affect the usefulness of public input.

ISSUE DEFINITION

This is the process or stage in resource planning during which mana-

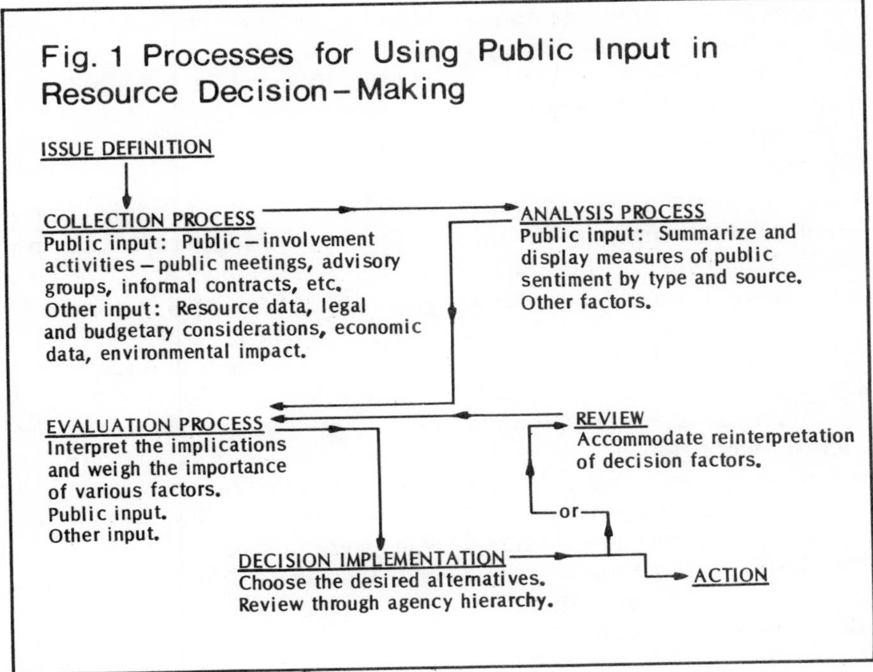

Fig. 1 Processes for Using Public Input in Resource Decision-Making

gers, working within legal, fiscal, political, resource capability, and environmental constraints, identify the range of alternatives that might require additional public input. The resource base is studied. Environmental and resource-capability data are integrated within broad legal and fiscal constaints. Viable management alternatives are identified.

Advice from key members of the public at this stage can assure that no interests or reasonable alternatives are overlooked. But major public input is yet to be collected, and managers must not become locked in to any one alternative.

COLLECTION

The collection process includes all the varied techniques that yield citizen input. The objective of the process is to secure the full range of views from all who are interested or affected. It often begins with efforts to inform the public about issues, alternatives, and consequences. It also includes efforts to solicit and record citizens' views about what courses of action they prefer.

A wide range of activities is involved. Advisory boards, *ad hoc* committees, public meetings, opinion leaders, professional contacts, workshops, letters, editorials, opinion polls, petitions and surveys are possible sources of public views.

There is no single, best way to obtain public input. All collection methods have advantages and weaknesses, and too much reliance on one can distort the range of input.

The input must be collected in a form that can be analyzed and evaluated. Collection methods should involve some record of the input to facilitate its use.

ANALYSIS

Analysis describes (summarizes and displays) the nature, content, and extent of public input so the input reflects public ideas, opinion, and values. Wherever possible, analysis should be systematic, objective, and quantitative. It should use processes that can be replicated by independent analysis.

Analysis should focus on questions about the content of input: What was said? By whom? Where did the input originate? How did it vary? How many people provided input? What views did they express? What interests were represented and what ones were not? What were the prevailing opinions and views about management alternatives, general issues, and specific areas? What reasons were given to support the views expressed? What additional issues were raised?

With this information, responsible managers can subjectively evaluate its meaning and implications. But it must be stressed that analysis merely describes public input. It makes no attempt to evaluate the importance of that input. Serious biases result when judgements of importance or "quality" are made in the process of analysis, thereby prematurely screening out certain kinds of input.

EVALUATION

Evaluation is the interpretation and weighing of all data collected and analyzed — relative to a decision or recommendation. The process is necessarily subjective. No set formula exists to guide it. But when the resource manager presents his decision, he should clearly state the relative importance he placed on the kinds of public input received and why.

For example, where local, regional, and national inputs differ, he should specify the importance attached to each in arriving at the decision and his criteria for such judgement. Likewise, he should clarify the importance he attached to factors other than public opinion (such as resource capability and legal and budgetary constraints).

It is in the evaluation process that resource managers serve most directly as para-politicians. Decision makers at several levels usually are involved. With a more accurate understanding of public opinion and values, coupled with the other decision factors, decision makers can be better para-politicians. They can justify decisions and recommendations both to the public and to the agency hierarchy. If each decision maker clearly states how he weighed the various public input and the relationship of this input to other factors, his judgement can be reviewed more easily by those who question his decision. In time, guidelines for evaluation will evolve from decisions that are accepted and those that are not.

DECISION IMPLEMENTATION

Here, decision makers must consider such processes as providing feedback to the public, providing review when necessary, and taking whatever steps are required to translate a decision into an action program. Successfully implementing a public resource decision is not a spontaneous event, particularly when there has been controversy.

It is important to give the public time to react. Reaction to a decision depends on what the public thought the agency would do. When that decision runs counter to public sentiment, untapped opinions can surface again. The "silent majority" suddenly can make itself heard.

Decision implementation should facilitate rather than stymie review when the decision or factors leading to it are seriously questioned. For example, subjective matters such as the importance placed on various factors and input in reaching a decision are legitimate matters for public review and debate. Patience, tolerance, and a good job on the previous processes are the manager's best assets at this stage.

Interdependence of Processes

Resource managers must understand the interdependence of the five decision-making processes. The way any one is conducted can dramatically affect the others. The ability of decision makers to evaluate data obtained from analysis will be greatly affected by the extent to which issues were defined at the outset of planning effort, the collection techniques used to tap public sentiment, and the analytical system used to describe and display public input. The ability to implement decisions, with public understanding and support, depends largely on the decision maker's ability to evaluate rationally the factors affecting the decision. Like the proverbial chain and its weakest link, the interdependence of the decision-making processes requires that each be designed rigorously and in full recognition of its relationship to the others.

Some Controversial Issues

Certain complexities, issues, and subtle implications are important to those who need to understand and use the framework we propose.

CRITERIA FOR EFFECTIVE PARTICIPATION

Many people welcome efforts by resource management agencies to secure public participation. Nevertheless, accusations still prevail that such efforts merely represent lip service.

Public involvement must become an explicit, visible part of decision making at the local, regional, and national levels. It must be a process that both administrators and the public expect and recognize as fundamental to decision making, just as resource inventories are recognized as a necessary and fundamental component. The range of public sentiment on any issue should be available for review by administrators and public groups alike.

Public involvement must also be traceable so that an independent second party can determine how input was collected, analyzed, and evaluated. For instance, the party might want to examine how public input influenced development of alternatives, decisions, and overall management direction. Administrators should be able to demonstrate how the input related to their decision. Decisions based on some intuitive "feel" for public sentiment are unacceptable because they are not susceptible to public review.

The demand for public scrutiny no doubt will lead to requests for formal inspection and review of how an agency used public input in making a decision. This pressure for accountability will require public agencies to develop systems for public-input analysis that are not only visible and traceable but also objective and reliable so that agency interpretation of public input can be validated by dependent observers.

PROFESSIONALISM AND PUBLIC INVOLVEMENT

Skilful handling of public participation requires considerable professional skill on the part of a resource manager. He must identify those issues and problems that have consequences significant enough to seek public knowledge, advice, and consent before taking action.

He must define a reasonable range of feasible alternatives within legal, fiscal, political, environmental, and resource limitations. The mark of a professional is that the constraints he imposes are genuine and do not reflect his prejudices.

He must define the probable consequences of each alternative and identify the trade-offs between them. He must clearly communicate this information to the public, face critical scrutiny and, using a variety of collection techniques, acquire public input.

He must analyze public input to identify public opinion and values from a variety of public comments that often are emotional in nature and not offered in resource management terms. He must learn the public's language.

He must evaluate the importance of public input in relation to other decision factors and devise resource programs balanced against all of them.

He must face the public with his recommendations and decision, explain how he arrived at them, defend them or, if conditions warrant, call for additional review of the decision factors and offer appropriate revisions.

He must then implement decisions through effective, efficient action programs under greater public scrutiny than ever before.

WHAT KIND OF INPUT IS BEST?

The public expresses its views in many forms, all of which are important in determining the balance of public sentiment. But whether input comes in letters, statements from public meetings, *ad hoc* committee reports, opinion polls, petitions, or some other from objective analysis requires that the input be recorded accurately.

To ensure effective use of public input, an enduring record should be kept. The input must be written or otherwise recorded if it is to be summarized objectively.

Open meetings and publicly solicited written input best exemplify the democratic tradition in which an agency opens its channels to public opinion and, in turn, commits itself to respond to public desires. Open meetings also help insure that segments of the public not represented through other channels have the chance to hear the issues and be heard.

Written inputs can be particularly significant. They represent a deliberate commitment to action on the part of respondents and are influenced less by the spontaneous atmosphere of public meetings — an environment that often precipitates oral input that differs from the more thoughtful, written input received later. The anonymity of written input also helps avoid the influence of peer-group pressure at meetings, which can be enormously intense in small, close-knit communities. Most importantly, written input is in a form that resource managers can thoughtfully study and analyze.

WEIGHING PUBLIC INPUT

Many things prompt public input. Employers urge employees to write letters. Students respond at the suggestion or request of teachers. Special-interest groups spur form letters, coupons, and signed petitions. Voluntary organizations and industrial groups file formal position statements on behalf of their members.

Both the philosophy underlying public involvement in decision making and the techniques used to secure input are important when combining and evaluating such diverse forms of input. The major question, of course, is: What importance should be attached to each when evaluating their implications for a pending decision?

Judging the importance of different kinds of public input is difficult and sometimes controversial. The task is necessarily subjective and must be done by officials within their political-administrative structure, as is the case with the assignment of priorities in other areas where differing demands compete.

But if the nature of all public input is clearly described as the result of traceable collection and analytical procedures, the proper weights to be assigned will soon become apparent from the degree to which decisions are accepted and from the review of unacceptable decisions. For example, public input can be summarized and displayed in the analytical process as so many letters, statements, petitions, etc., for or against a given alternative. In the evaluation process, administrators must weigh the relative importance of these factors when ruling for or against an alternative. If the data used are visible and traceable, the relative importance assigned either will be sanctioned by public acceptance of the decision or reassigned in any review leading to a reversal or modification of the decision.

Two important considerations must guide the weighing of public input: (a) It is the responsibility of decision makers — officially responsible line officers — and not their staffs or analysts; (b) effective evaluation depends on a previous analytical process that clearly describes the content of all input received.

Weighing Cannot Be Avoided

We have encountered a spectrum of attitudes among resource managers ranging from "we need formulas and guidelines telling us how to weigh various kinds of input" to suspicion and mistrust because "anyone seeking to systematize the handling of public input must advocate weighing it."

In no way can or should formulas guide the weighing of public input. But whenever a line officer makes a decision or recommendation in the evaluation process, he implicitly places varying degrees of importance on all the input he has. There is no way to escape this kind of weighing. For example, a decision favouring a resource development alternative might implicitly place more importance on local opinion than on urban response favouring a preservation alternative. Similarly, a decision contrary to numerous petition signatures implicitly discounts them in favour of other public input, evidence and/or criteria.

The point is that any time a decision is made, varying degrees of importance are implicitly or explicitly assigned to all available input. Debate over the importance assigned to various inputs is an appropriate matter for public concern, and the public involvement process should facilitate it. If resource managers are not accountable for how they use public input, their tendency to be responsible to it will be limited.

Direct Versus Indirect Input

One might argue that if an agency is to respond to all segments of society, then that agency should weigh equally all public expressions of sentiment regardless of their form or apparent motivation. But managers usually assign more importance to a personal letter than to each signature on a petition, form letter, or coupon.

Public input can be distinguished as "direct" — generated principally by the independent action of a citizen — and "indirect" — principally the result of group influences. Statements made at meetings and personal letters are direct input. Petitions, form letters, coupons, and questionnaires are indirect. Likewise, the positions of organized groups on behalf of "x" number of members should be identified in such a way that decision makers can evaluate their relative importance.

Assumptions and Judgements

How public input will be evaluated must be clarified because it will seriously affect the kind of input that will result. If indirect input will be considered less important than direct input, then administrators must let the public know so they can act accordingly.

A frequent complaint of citizen groups is that the rationale behind a decision is unclear. There is uncertainty about how public input and other factors were evaluated and related to one another.

We feel it is absolutely necessary that the importance attached to public input be indicated, as well as the relative value placed on such other factors as legal, fiscal, and political constraints; resource capability; environmental protection; etc. If the decision maker states what importance he will or must place on each factor, his judgement can more easily be reviewed by those who question his decision.

Quality Versus Quantity

Resource managers want "quality" input — defined from their perspective as well-reasoned, site- or issue-specific, and couched in appropriate management terminology. Such input is valuable, but too much emphasis on those quality attributes of input can restrict the quantity of input.

Whether well-reasoned and detailed or not, all input expresses values, and definition of these values is the overriding objective of public involvement. That citizens must support their opinions with reasons runs contrary to the intangible and emotional values that many people place on some renewable resources.

It can be difficult to articulate feelings and beliefs about resource development, wilderness, scenery, wildlife, environmental quality, or multiple use and much more difficult to cite reasons that fully explain them. Reasons offered in support of an opinion add depth and meaning to a citizen's input, but their absence should not detract from the fact that his statement represents an important expression of values.

There also is a hazard in trying to identify what constitutes quality or substantive input. Input that decision makers do not support or understand may be tossed out inadvertently or purposely. Their ideas of good or substantive reasons reflect "their" personal values or opinions. This can jeopardize credibility in public involvement, and it certainly can reduce the usefulness of public input as a means to better, more acceptable decisions.

An involved public will continue to express conflicting opinions about public resources management. The relative merits of these views, along with other considerations, must be examined so that decisions reflect the public's best long-term interests.

Therefore, it is dangerous to overstress substantive input at the expense of quantity of input. But it is just as dangerous to simply emphasize the number of opinions for or against an alternative. Both quality and quantity of input are important dimensions of public involvement. Both identify public values, preferences, and possible trade-offs.

Representativeness

Many people become concerned about the representativeness of public input. They are anxious to have the views of the full cross-section of the public on resource management issues. This is an admirable objective but a difficult one to achieve. Despite the best efforts to involve the public, not everyone will respond. Care must be taken in the collection process to assure that anyone wanting to give his opinion has the chance to do so. But resource managers cannot hide behind the "silent majority." It may also reflect a lack of information on the part of a potentially interested client.

Here it is useful to distinguish between *demographic representation* of sex, age, residence groups, etc., and *interest representation*. It is important to see that everyone known to be interested or affected has had an opportunity to make his views known. If groups known to be affected have not responded, there is a responsibility to solicit their views before making a decision.

This has important practical implications. If input is not obtained before the decision, it may come later when unsolicited interests feel they have been ignored or victimized.

Vote Counting

Another concern to resource managers and the public is "vote counting". Some professionals fear that public participation means abdicating responsibility and letting the public dictate a final decision. This is what voting usually means in a democracy. And the public appears equally confused. Are they voting or not?

Public input does not dictate the decision. It is useful and proper to determine the balance of opinion by questioning organizations and individuals, but the search is not for an either/or solution dictated by votes. The goal is an approximate measure of public opinion and values that can be weighed against other decision-making factors.

Tabulation of opinions is not new. Administrators in the past have defended decisions on the amount of support or opposition voiced. The concept of soliciting public input rests on the premise that public participation enables a more accurate measure of public opinion and values. The objective of counting input is to determine more systematically and objectively how all the various segments of the public and affected interests feel about the issue and why they feel as they do. This knowledge leads to decisions that are based on a better understanding of the balance of values expressed.

The balance of opinion about an issue should be supplemented with qualitative information, such as supporting reasons. Reasons given in support of various opinions hold significant clues to their meaning and provide additional information. They may indicate a unique feature that may be lost or how a minority interest would suffer if a particular decision is made. In such a situation the decision maker could logically decide to protect that feature whether or not the balance of opinion favoured that alternative. In the absence of such qualitative information, disastrous mistakes can be made simply by ruling in favour of the majority.

Continuing Input

Public input affecting resource management decisions generally is solicited during a critical period prior to the decision. However, many inputs precede or follow the formal gathering process, in some cases by several years. The balance of opinion can change as more people become involved, as more and better information is obtained, and as public attitudes shift in response to changing situations as decisions and management programs are implemented. It should be possible for managers to consider all input, even that which does not coincide with a special appeal for response.

It is essential, therefore, that the analysis of public sentiment reflect input made prior to any special appeal for response and that continuing input be recorded for subsequent retrieval when needed, for example, when significant shifts in opinion and values are suspected. Interested persons should not be required to resubmit their views time and again to coincide with administrative convenience.

The Need for Analysis

Techniques for analyzing and summarizing public input are particularly needed. This is important because evaluation of input depends on adequate data, clearly described and summarized. And this is no easy matter when thousands of public inputs are received.[3]

Systematic, objective, and reliable systems for analysis are needed to (a) efficiently summarize and display various kinds of public input using methods that can be validated by independent observers; (b) describe the extent and nature of public expression surrounding a given issue, i.e., all opinions supporting reasons; (c) reveal the sources of input by location of respondent and particular interest in the issues; (d) record both direct and indirect input; (e) provide for continuity in recording input before and after any formal period of collection and the ability to summarize input as needed; and (f) respond sensitively to general expressions of value as well as to specific management suggestions.

If analysis provides a clear summary of public input, the decision maker can evaluate its implications more effectively.

Conclusion

Failure to solicit public participation aggressively and innovatively — and respond to it — can result in the loss of agency stature, damaging public criticism of agency policies and programs, and continued antagonistic situations between the agency and some of its clientele. Public participation is unlikely to eliminate confrontations with polarized constituents, but it can bring out and focus the conflict well in advance of the deadline for making a decision.

Pressures to secure better public input are, in part, a response to the public's demands for a greater voice in land management. By increasing public participation in decision making, public agencies should avert disastrous mistakes and diminish *ex post facto* confrontations.

But the issue is a broader one. Public involvement provides a forum in which the public can effectively exert its rightful role as a goal-setting body. On the other hand, with a more accurate assessment of public desires, professional managers can better fulfill their role as achievers of those goals.

NOTES

1. T. O'Riordan, "Public opinion and environmental quality: a reappraisal", *Environment and Behaviour*, Vol. 3, No. 2, 1971, pp. 191-214.
2. In a Canadian context, see for example: J.A. Draper, ed., *Citizen participation in Canada*, Toronto, New Press, 1971; D. Draper, "Environmental interest groups and institutional arrangements in British Columbia water management issues", *Institutional arrangements for water management: Canadian experiences*, Publication Series No. 5, Waterloo, University of Waterloo, Department of Geography, 1975, pp. 119-170; W.R.D. Sewell and I. Burton, eds., *Perceptions and attitudes in resources management*, Ottawa, Information Canada, 1971.

   In a more general context, see: S.R. Arnstein, "A ladder of citizen participation", *Journal of the American Institute of Planners*, Vol. 35, July 1969, pp. 216-224; N. Wengert, "Public participation in water planning: a critique of theory, doctrine and practice", *Water Resources Bulletin*, Vol. 7, No. 1, February 1971, pp. 26-32; N. Wengert, "Environmental policy and political decisions: the reconciliation of facts, values and interests", *Politics and ecology*, edited by P.O. Foss, Belmont, Wadsworth, 1972, pp. 39-49.
3. Five methods of public input analysis that have been used by decision makers are described in J.C. Hendee, *et al.*, *Public involvement and the Forest Service: experience, effectiveness and suggested direction*, Washington, D.C., U.S. Dept. of Agriculture, Forest Service, 1973. A specially designed content analysis for public input analysis was developed and is described in R. Clark, G.H. Stankey and J.C. Hendee, *Codinvolve: a system for coding, summarizing, storing, retrieving and analyzing public input to resource decisions*, Portland, Pacific N.W. Forest and Range Experimental Station, 1974 as well as in R. Clark and G.H. Stankey "Analyzing public input to resource decisions: criteria, principles, and case examples of the CODINVOLVE system", *Natural Resources Journal*, Vol. 16, No. 1, January 1976, pp. 213-236.

Section III
Land

Introduction

In a country which has grown up with the myth that its land resources are virtually unlimited, it is not easy to arouse public (and consequently governmental) concern about the preservation of farmland and wilderness. The same can be said about the need for careful planning of our parklands and other recreational resources, and about the need to guard against social and environmental damage in developing resources in the vast territory of the Canadian Arctic. The papers in this section provide information about the quantity and quality of some of Canada's land resources as well as insights about the problems and issues related to their management.

Although the papers in this section concern specific resources and/or specific jurisdictions, they illustrate perspectives and decision-making approaches that have relevance to the management of a wide range of renewable resources across the country. They also suggest many questions which have general applicability, a few of which are presented below:

— Which perspective or combination of perspectives discussed in Section I is held by the different publics, by professional resource managers and by government decision makers? Do these perspectives remain the same for each specific resource?

— What range of resource assessment and decision-making processes (see Section II) have been used in managing Canada's land resources? To what degree have they followed theoretical models? To what degree have these processes been used as "window-dressing" with the real decisions being made on political grounds?

— How adequate is Canada's supply of various renewable resources? What has been happening to these resources? Do we have adequate inventorying and monitoring methods? Is the inventory information readily accessible in a form useful to the decision makers?

— What has been (and will be) the role of technology in creating new resources, and in making more productive use of current resources? Does the greater use of technology increase or decrease the impact on the quality of the environment?

— Will society's demand for a high quality environment decrease the supply of resources needed to maintain its current "standard of living"?

— How useful are our currently used types of benefit-cost and environmental impact studies? Do they accommodate the different resource management perspectives?

— To what degree should the public become involved in resource management decisions? How can public input be institutionalized? How can different and conflicting values and goals of various public groups be reconciled?
— What role should residents of a particular region have in determining the type and quality of the environment in which they live?
— What should the role of the federal government be when provincial or local governments permit wasteful or destructive use of a resource that is of long-run national benefit? (e.g., the urbanization of unique agricultural or recreational resources?)
— If the current owners of a resource are restricted in making certain profitable uses of their resource in the greater public interest, who should pay for losses of potential income?
— What role should scientists and resource management professionals play in evolving resource management policies and in resolving resource management problems?

The first three papers discuss the renewable resource of agricultural land: its supply, quality, and preservation. Nowland and McKeague first describe the Canada Land Inventory (CLI). They then identify the problems of carrying out a land capability inventory which could be coupled with productivity data, input costs and other economic data, so that evaluations could be made of alternative land uses under given management systems. According to CLI data, only eight per cent of Canada's land area is suitable for the production of field crops. Less than one per cent has the climate and soils suitable for the production of crops such as corn and tree fruits. Most of the best farmland (CLI Classes 1, 2 and 3) is in the Prairie Provinces where there are severe climatic limitations. Most of the potential new farmland in Canada has both marginal climate and soils. All the evidence points to the conclusion that Canada's agricultural resource base has very definite limits.

If the conclusions of the previous paper are valid, then the preservation of good agricultural land is of vital concern to Canada. Krueger rejects the short-run economic view that the "highest and best" use of land is determined adequately by the market-place mechanism. He argues that agricultural land around our cities not only produces food, but also provides open space and green area for the urbanites and is a valuable ecological resource in the metropolitan area. Moreover, the low density sprawl pattern of urban growth results in much greater costs of providing urban services and in a general deterioration of the human habitat. Therefore, it is in the long-run social, economic and environmental interests of society to preserve prime agricultural land in our urbanizing areas. He predicts that the Ontario attempts at saving farmland will fail if the current lack of leadership and commitment on the part of the provincial government continues. It is suggested that bolder action, such as the Land Commission Act in British Columbia, is required.

In his second paper, Krueger documents the on-going destruction of the Niagara fruitlands, Canada's most valuable horticultural resource. By 1976, alarming proportions of the best fruitlands had been urbanized and the Regional Municipality of Niagara made a decision not to alter urban growth patterns. By the turn of the century it appears that there will be insignificant tree fruit production in the Niagara Fruit Belt. This, despite the fact that the inventories and assessments were made and the decision-making mechanisms were in place. Sophisticated resource management decision-making models are of little use if elected governments at various levels lack the necessary leadership qualities.

According to Horton, the management of the unique natural resource known as the Niagara Escarpment is proceeding in a similar vein as the management of Ontario's farmlands. Public concern was expressed that this recreational and ecological resource would be destroyed by unplanned development; the provincial government conducted a thorough study of the resource, including alternate ways of rationalizing its use; and the legislative and decision-making machinery was established. However, the majority of local municipalities along the Niagara Escarpment were not in favour of strict land-use controls and were able to slow down the planning process. Then a set-back in a provincial election induced the provincial government to back off its resolve to preserve the Niagara Escarpment.

Once again it has been shown that all of the resource management theories and methods bear few results if resolve is lacking in our elected governments at various levels. Perhaps the real lesson to be learned is that if the public is really concerned about certain resource management issues, it must be forceful in expressing itself, including the way in which it votes at election time.

The theme of preserving wilderness areas is taken up by Nelson in his paper on the research needs and management of national parks and related reserves. In his review, he shows how little we really know about our national parks and wilderness reserves in terms of ecology, management strategies, attitudes and technology. He poses and discusses many provocative questions such as: What is wilderness and nature? At what point in time are human actions unnatural? To what degree should man interfere with the "natural" ecological processes in national parks? Is the major aim of our national park system to provide recreation and a "wilderness experience" for man or to preserve and protect "nature"? What are the impacts of large numbers of human visitors on various types of ecosystems? Why do we have no national parks representing the grasslands of the Prairie Provinces, the semi-arid valleys of British Columbia, the Barren Grounds of the Northwest Territories, or the taiga forests of Quebec and Ontario? In posing these questions, Nelson emphasizes the relevance of research to park management.

The last two papers discuss the environmental ramifications of developing resources in the Canadian North. Fuller comments on the need to do more research and to integrate existing and new information into a comprehensive resource inventory. This information must then be made public so that there can be adequate public comment before policies are evolved. Nor is it good enough to hold hearings in southern Canada; the people whose lives will be affected must have a voice in decisions concerning resource development in the North. (It is interesting to note that Mr. Justice Berger spent the largest proportion of his time on hearings in the North in his Mackenzie Valley Pipeline Inquiry.) The policies must be enforceable, which has not been the case in the past. Perhaps there is an administrative problem in having one Minister responsible for both promoting development and enforcing environmental regulations that tend to control or restrict development. Impact assessments should precede a decision on every major development. And last, but not least, policy should be designed to keep open as many options as possible for future generations.

While Fuller mentions the need to consider native land claims and other native interests in the North, Usher makes the native's interests and aspirations the focus of his paper. The native people of the Western Arctic do not view their land simply as a commodity to be exchanged for cash. They have experienced the boom and bust of white man's economy. Jobs come and go but the land is always there; it is the permanent basis of their welfare and security, and will not be lightly traded off.

The northern natives are also wary of the social impacts of white man's economic development. Large resource development projects tend to break up communities by drawing off the most able members, disrupt family life, and bring problems associated with alcohol, sex, drugs and racism. The influx of outsiders pushes up the prices of local goods and services which tends to offset increased wage benefits. Moreover, as white administrators and entrepreneurs start taking charge of almost every aspect of community life, the native people feel that they have become superfluous in their own land. Their special knowledge and experience of the northern environment are devalued.

In conclusion, Usher claims that the research of social scientists should not be totally objective and value-free. Evaluating the social and economic impact of some specific action is relatively meaningless unless it is done in the context of some larger vision of what society is or ought to be. Then Usher asks, "Must we, as scientists and professionals, always work within the confines of the 'reality' of the growth ethic, and keep our private regrets to ourselves"?

In his own research and consulting work in the North, Usher has provided us with an example worthy of emulation. He has not only done original and innovative research, but he has not kept his "regrets" to himself, and has assisted the northern natives in understanding the issues and in articulating their values.

9
Canada's Limited Agricultural Land Resource

*J. L. Nowland and J. A. McKeague**

The fact that Canada's resources of good agricultural land are limited has been known for decades and conservationists were pleading the case for preservation of prime agricultural land some thirty years ago. Public interest in land has increased markedly in the last few years due to increased concern about the environment and higher food prices. Many articles on agricultural land have appeared recently both in the daily papers and in technical publications. The purpose of this article is to summarize the information on land suitable for agriculture in Canada and to present a point of view on its use.

Effective planning for the use of Canada's land resources requires a reliable inventory of land. Information is available on most of the land area of Canada but it varies greatly in detail, quality and scope. Well over half of Canada's land resources are wildland: a combination of tundra, rock, muskeg and other land which, because of extreme climate, lack of soil or adverse soil conditions, is unsuitable for agriculture and productive forests (Figure 1). About 260 million hectares (ha),[1] nearly 30 per cent of the land area, is forest land that is not suitable for agriculture because of steep or broken topography, adverse climate, excessive stoniness or other adverse soil features.[2]

The 120 million hectares (13 per cent of the country) defined as potential agricultural land includes about 3/5 that is suitable for field crops and 2/5 suitable only for pasture; much of the latter is now forested. The 4 million ha (0.4 per cent) of the land occupied by cities, roads, etc. seems deceptively insignificant.

Kinds of Land Inventories

Obtaining a comprehensive inventory of Canada's land resources is a major task that remains incomplete. Such an inventory should include data on climate, geology, vegetation, soil, landform, water, wildlife and current land use of the area. Few surface feature inventories in Canada

*J. L. Nowland and J. A. McKeague are researchers at the Soil Research Institute, Central Experimental Farm, Ottawa. This is an expanded version of a paper entitled "How Much Land Do We Have?" by J. A. McKeague, *Agrologist*, Vol. 4, No. 4, 1975, pp. 10-12.

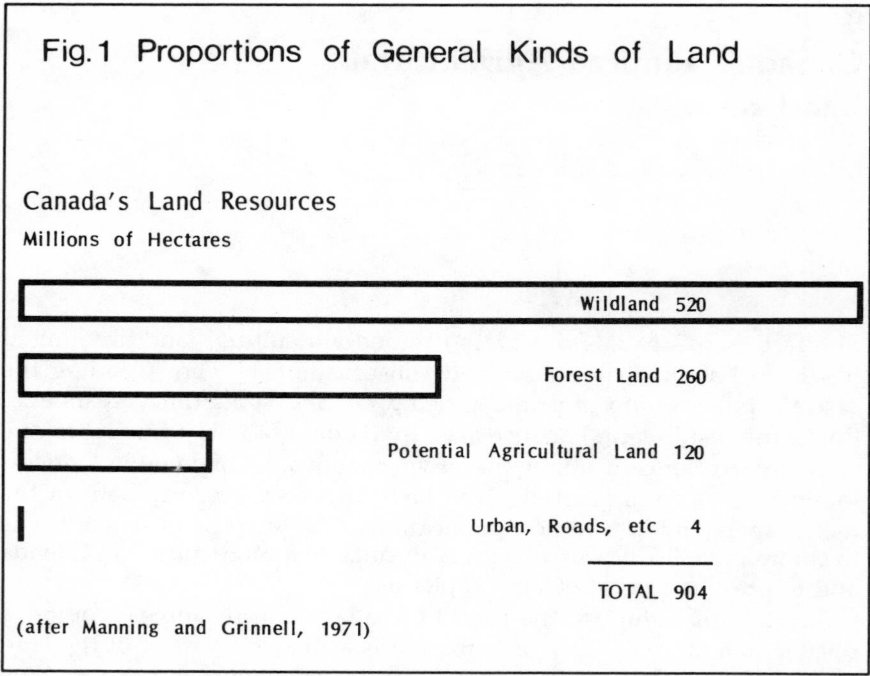

— surveys of surficial geology, soils, vegetation — have considered all aspects of land.

Soils surveys have been carried out as a co-operative undertaking of federal and provincial Departments of Agriculture and Soils Departments at universities, and co-ordinated through the Canada Soil Survey Committee. They have provided an extensive coverage of southern Canada and the published maps and reports include information on most aspects of land. However they give an exaggerated impression of the completeness of soils information as many of the surveys are out of date and maps and reports for several areas are out of print. For example, modern soil surveys (since 1950) have not been done of much of the prime agricultural area of southern Quebec and Ontario.

The Canada Land Inventory

After the mapping of soils, a second step is required to interpret the basic information in terms of capability of the soils for a variety of possible uses. The most comprehensive attempt in Canada to carry out this step was the Canada Land Inventory (CLI).[3] "Land" has broader connotations than the soil component alone, and both basic surveys and the various CLI interpretations considered the broader concept in varying degrees. The CLI interpreted information from the Canada Soil Survey and supported the Survey in carrying out inventories in unsurveyed areas within the 200 million ha of southern Canada that includes nearly all of the potential agricultural land. Systems were devised for rating the capability of the land for agriculture, forestry, recreation and wildlife. The project was started in 1963 and in 1976 was complete except for British Columbia and Newfoundland.

Seven capability classes for agriculture were defined in terms of severity of limitations for the production of field crops:

1. No limitations
2. Minor limitations
3. Moderate limitations
4. Severe limitations (marginal land)
5. Not suitable for field crops but suitable for hay or improved pasture
6. Suitable for grazing
7. Unsuitable for agriculture

Subclasses indicate the kinds of limitations: low temperatures, low water holding capacity, excess water, low fertility, stoniness, adverse topography, combination of adverse soil or climatic features. The distribution of soil capability classes for agriculture by province or region (Table 1) shows clearly the limited area of top quality soils in Canada: only 21.9 million ha or 2.4 per cent of the total land area is prime agricultural land (classes 1 and 2), and less than one-third of this area is climatically suitable for a very wide range of crops.

Crude productivity relationships among the soil capability classes have been demonstrated. Compared to a performance index of 1 for Class 1 land, Classes 2, 3 and 4 in Ontario have indices of 0.8, 0.64 and 0.49 respectively.[4] For Prairie soils, comparable indices were estimated to be 0.85, 0.7 and 0.5, based on Class 1 soils in that region. These indices have been used for a preliminary estimate of the ultimate land resource of the country in terms of "Class 1 equivalents", i.e., 2 ha of Class 4 soils, being thought of as equivalent to 1 ha of Class 1.[5] While this approach may have some merit in purely physical terms, the high costs of utilizing lower-class land mitigate against its substitution for higher-class land in the food production system.

The CLI information provides a useful general assessment of the capabilities of Canada's land resources for several possible uses but it is far from a complete inventory:

1. Productivities of soils of a given class or subclass in different regions are not necessarily the same. For example, Class 1 soils on the Prairies have a lower productive capacity and a narrower range of crops than Class 1 or 2 soils in southern Ontario.
2. It covers only about 20 per cent of the land area. Potential agricultural land is covered, excluding minor areas in the northern parts of the

TABLE 1

Areas in Soil Capability Classes by Regions and by Provinces (thousands ha)[1]

	CLI Capability Classes for Agriculture								
Location	1	%	2	%	3	%	4	%	5
Atlantic Provinces			611	2.5	2,561	10.4	2,544	10.4	2.352
Nfld.					5.5	.1	62	6	388
P.E.I.			261	45.9	157	27.6	23	4.0	98
N.S.			178	3.0	1,056	18.0	448	7.7	94
N.B.			173	2.4	1,343	18.5	2,011	27.7	1,772
Central Canada	2.263	3.7	3,336	5.3	4,660	7.3	5,732	9.1	3.546
Que.	14	.2	976	2.9	1,381	4.2	2,830	8.8	1,636
Ont.	2,249	7.4	2,360	7.7	3,279	10.8	2,902	9.5	1,910
Prairies	2,069	1.9	13,044	11.7	19,090	17.1	16,766	15.0	21,482
Man.	184	.8	2,556	10.7	2,561	10.7	2,573	10.8	2,250
Sask.	1,072	2.8	6,446	16.8	10,082	26.2	4,252	11.1	7,799
Alta.[2]	813	1.7	4,041	8.2	6,447	13.1	9,940	20.2	11,433
Canada[3]	4,332	2.2	16,991	8.5	26,312	13.2	25,042	12.6	27,379

Areas measured on 1: 250,000 scale maps of Soil Capability for Agriculture, Canada Land Inventory.

[1]The percentages are based upon the area of each province or region covered by CLI. To convert the percentage data for Canada to values based upon the total land area, multiply the percentage values by 0.22.

[2]For Alberta Class 1 area includes 105,100 ha of Irrigated soils, Class 2 area 144,000 ha, and Class 3 area 158,500 ha.

[3]Canada total does not include British Columbia; estimates for B.C. are: 600,000 ha in Classes 1 and 2, 1,400,000 in Class 3 and 2,600,000 in Class 4.

provinces and in some valleys of the Yukon and Northwest Territories (perhaps 2 million ha of Classes 4 and 5 land).

3. Organic soils, which account for about 10 per cent of the land area of Canada, are not rated. They constitute a most significant resource in most provinces and some of them are capable of sustaining enormous yields of vegetables.
4. The agricultural capability rating is for common field crops of the region. Many lower-class soils are highly suitable for forage crops, and certain specialty crops, such as tobacco and blueberries.

Requirements for a National Inventory

Regional productivity differences within CLI classes indicate a serious deficiency that points the way to the next phase in the evaluation of the national agricultural land resource. A typical problem is as follows. The local average spring wheat yield on Class 2 land on grain-beef cattle farms in the Lloydminster area of Saskatchewan was 1.5 tonnes/ha compared with an estimated 3.2 tonnes/ha on Class 2 land on mixed farms in

(Continued)

%	6	%	7	%	Organic soils	%	Water parks and urban areas	%	Total	%
9.6	2,903	11.9	9,350	38.2	3,695	15.1	442	1.8	24,458	100
3.6	2,891	26.8	3,742	34.7	3,460	2.1	226	2.1	10,775	100
17.3			28	4.8	28	9.5			568	100
1.6	6.1	9.1	3,895	66.4	137	2.3	48	.8	5,862	100
24.5	5.6	.1	1.686	23.2	96	1.3	168	2.3	7,261	100
5.6	1,201	1.9	34,887	55.3	3,422	5.4	4,057	6.4	63,104	100
5.0	8.9	9.1	21,851	66.8	1,268	3.9	2,633	8.2	32,598	100
6.3	1,192	3.9	13,036	42.5	2,154	7.7	1,423	4.7	30,504	100
19.3	10,025	9.0	6,308	5.7	13,199	11.8	9,630	8.6	11,612	100
9.4	2,162	9.1	1,254	5.3	5,113	21.4	5,192	21.8	23,844	100
20.3	4,065	10.6	284	.7	2,914	7.6	1,581	4.1	38,494	100
23.2	3,794	7.7	4,770	9.7	5,173	10.5	2,858	5.8	49,274	100
13.7	14,130	7.1	50,545	25.4	20,316	10.2	14,129	7.1	199,176	100

south-central Ontario. The input costs (1969) on the Saskatchewan farms amounted to $25/ha or $16/tonne, and in Ontario $85/ha or $26.50/tonne.[6] In Saskatchewan, productivity is sustained by summer-fallowing every second or third year, whereas the yields in Ontario may be realized year after year. Moreover the yields in Saskatchewan cannot approach Ontario levels by an equivalent or even threefold increase in inputs, whereas in good years better management in Ontario can result in yields of over 5 tonnes/ha.

In other words, Class 1 and 2 soils in the Prairie Provinces have a much lower productive capacity than Class 1 and 2 soils in Ontario. And they cannot be used for as wide a range of crops.

In terms of energy use and energy output in crop production, Ontario's higher production per hectare compared with the Prairies is achieved only with a much greater consumption of energy, in the form of fuel, electricity, the manufacture of farm equipment, seed, fertilizer and pesticides. While crop production everywhere is a net producer of energy, the ratio of energy outputs to inputs have been estimated at 4.8:1 for Ontario and 8.7:1 for Saskatchewan.[7]

The foregoing examples of regional productivity and energy differences on land rated similarly by CLI underline the need to consider the *versatility* of land for different crops and uses, the *costs* of overcoming the physical limitations recognized by CLI, the implications of varying *levels of management*, *competition* from other users, and *land suitability* not so much for individual crops, but rather for *systems* of farming, or *land utilization types*.

It can be seen that in the post-CLI era an adequate inventory of Canadian land resources requires a co-ordinated national system of mapping the major components of land at various scales with standards for indicating the climate, landform, soils, vegetation and land use. To date no such co-ordinated system has been developed by the agencies mapping land, although effective co-operation has been established between some of the groups involved. Also, a computer-based system of land evaluation is required for the interpretation of inventory data. Such a system should include data on all of the physical attributes of land, and on current land use, coupled with data on productivity, input costs and other economic data. This would make possible the evaluation of land-use alternatives and the prediction of food and fibre production under given management systems. A system of land evaluation for agriculture is now being developed by Agriculture Canada in co-operation with provincial agencies.

Agricultural Land

According to CLI data only 77 million ha (8 per cent) of Canada's land is suitable for the production of field crops and an additional 42 million ha (nearly 5 per cent) is suitable for pasture. This low proportion of agricultural land is due to climatic, topographic and soil restrictions. An estimated 35 per cent of Canada's land area has climatic conditions that would permit some agricultural development but nearly two-thirds of this area is eliminated by soil and topographic factors.

TABLE 2
Distribution of Good Agricultural Land by Regions and by Provinces

	Percentage of Canadian Total	
	Classes 1 and 2	Class 3
Martime Provinces[2]	*2.8*	*9.2*
Prince Edward Island	1.2	0.6
Nova Scotia	0.8	3.8
New Brunswick	0.8	4.8
Central Canada	*25.5*	*16.8*
Quebec	4.5	5.0
Ontario	21.0	11.8
Western Canada	*71.7*	*74.0*
Manitoba	12.5	9.2
Saskatchewan	34.3	36.4
Alberta	22.1	23.3
British Columbia	2.8	5.1
Total	100	100

1. Based on data from Table 1 of this paper.
2. Newfoundland has been excluded because of relatively insignificant areas of good agricultural land.

By far the largest proportion of prime agricultural land (Classes 1 and 2) is found in western Canada (Table 2). The provinces endowed with the most prime land are Saskatchewan (34% of Canadian total), Alberta (22%) and Ontario (21%). The same three provinces lead the country in amounts of Class 3 land.

The physical imperfections of our good and marginal quality cropland (Classes 1 to 4) vary from province to province. Thus in Ontario the chief problems are excessive soil moisture, low natural fertility, deficient soil moisture and undesirable subsoil structure, in that order. For the Atlantic Provinces they are low natural fertility, climatic problems, adverse subsoil structure and excessive stoniness. Alberta soils suffer most from poor soil structure, adverse topography, adverse climate (too cool or too dry) and deficient soil moisture, whereas in Saskatchewan deficient soil moisture affects over twice the area affected by the next four limitations combined — cool or dry climate, poor soil structure and adverse topography.

The total farmland area improved and unimproved in Canada increased by 35 per cent (47 to 63 million ha) between 1921 and 1971 but it decreased by 2.6 per cent during the last 5 years of that period. The overall increase was compounded of declines of 61 per cent and 28 per cent in the Atlantic Provinces and Quebec-Ontario, and by increases of 60 per cent in the Prairie Provinces and 180 per cent in British Columbia.

Potential New Farmland

Potential new cropland can be estimated by comparing the area of improved farmland with the area of land in CLI soil capability Classes 1 to 4. The greatest potential, 14.7 million ha, is in the Prairie region with 9.6 million ha of this in Alberta. Similar estimates for other regions show 5.2 million ha in the Atlantic Provinces, 2.6 million ha in Quebec and 4.7 million ha in Ontario — a total of about 27 million ha. There is also some potential new agricultural land in B.C., the Yukon and Northwest Territories (Figure 2).

This estimate of undeveloped cropland is optimistic. The majority of this land is marginal for field crops (Class 4) and nearly all of the remainder is Class 3 land. About half of the potential new farmland in the Atlantic Provinces consists of fragmented parcels too small to be developed economically. Much of the potential new land in the Prairie Provinces is too near the climatic frontier for many field crops. Most of the potential area in Quebec and Ontario is on soils that are marginal for agriculture and are now productive in forest. The costs of bringing Canada's potential new cropland under cultivation would be major and the productivity per unit of energy consumed would be much lower than that of good soils in climatically favourable areas. Even so, a considerable potential exists for the expansion of cropland in Canada and there is at least an equal potential for improved pastureland.

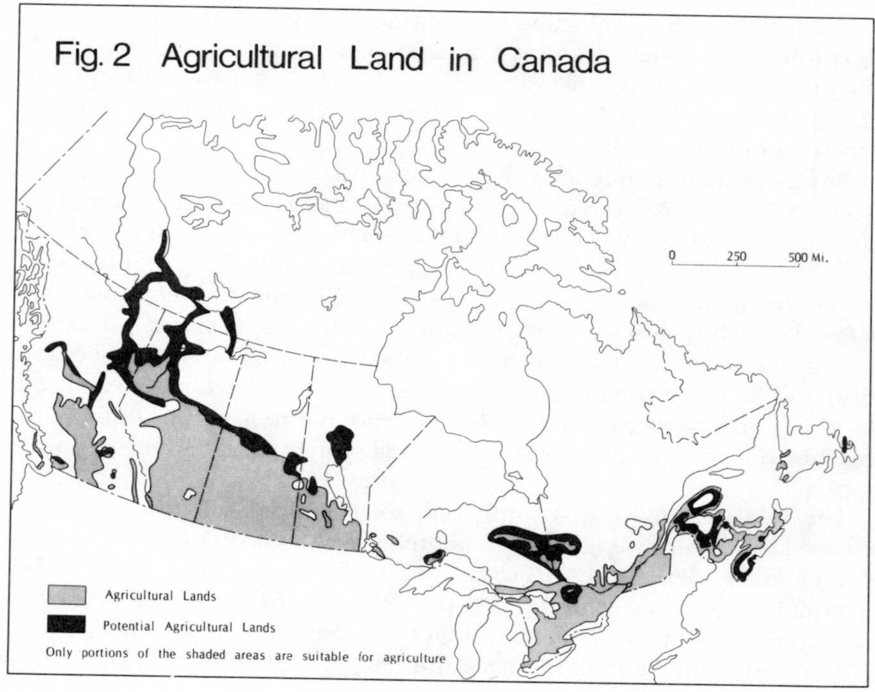

Losses of Agricultural Land

The reversion of marginal farmland to forest in eastern Canada has resulted in major decreases in the area farmed, but such land remains available for agricultural or other development if the need arises.

More critical is the permanent conversion of farmland to urban and industrial development. Accurate data on the rate of such losses are not available, but estimates of the area of land absorbed for every increase of 1000 in urban population vary from about 10 to 400 ha. The higher figure includes urban fringe land alienated from agriculture by land speculation and resulting high prices. If the value of 80 ha per 1000 increase of urban population is used, the projected permanent conversion of land to urban development in Quebec and Ontario between now and the year 2000 are 300,000 ha and 500,000 ha respectively.[8] More than half of this land would be good agricultural land (soil capability Classes 1 to 3) in climatically favourable areas. Around Montreal, for instance, 8700 ha of the best land in Quebec is being lost to agriculture each year.[9] Equally serious may be the loss of farmland to low-density rural housing, but no firm data are available. It appears that with the aid of modern highways, and despite fuel costs, this kind of extended urban impact spreads one hour's drive out from the cities.

Concern about urban and low-density rural encroachment on the limited area of choice farmland in the valleys of British Columbia was a factor leading to that province's Bill 42 which defined Agricultural Land Reserves. About 40,000 ha of B.C. farmland was lost to urban development between 1962 and 1972.

In Alberta, over 16,000 ha of prime land was gobbled up in the course of seven years by the cities of Edmonton and Calgary,[10] and there is evidence that smaller towns on the Prairies are consuming farmland at up to twice the rate, per unit population, of the big cities.

The areas mentioned may not seem impressive in relation to the total area of farmland in Canada and it is true that few hard data are available on the rates of loss of farmland. However, the picture is clear enough to provide the basis for rational choices.

It must be remembered that only tiny areas of Canada, less than one per cent, have climates and soils suitable for the production of corn and soft fruits. Most of these valuable parcels of land are in the path of rapid urban and industrial growth. Productive farmland close to the city is basic insurance against future events such as food shortages and high prices that would result from: doubling of the world's population by AD 2000; a decrease of even a degree or two in the mean annual temperature, or a series of dry years; increasingly high transportation costs due to energy shortages.

There may be no threat to Canada's ability to feed itself at some future time if there is willingness to pay the huge costs of developing marginal land. But there remains the possibility of some future world food supply role for Canada that might easily be coupled with domestic policies designed to keep remote and not-so-remote rural areas populated and enjoying an acceptable quality of life. This option becomes more constrained as farming needs for unique qualities in land are overidden by needs that can be satisfied and located elsewhere.

Because of its "greenbelt" character, farmland is also of immeasurable aesthetic value. City dwellers often drive for miles to experience an orchard in blossom and enjoy the rural scene.

Wildlife ecologists have persuaded us of the value of preserving the whooping crane and of the necessity of selecting pipeline routes that will not disturb the migration of the caribou. Surely it is not too much to expect that we recognize the necessity of preserving for agriculture the prime farmland close to cities such as Montreal, Toronto and Vancouver.

NOTES

1. One hectare equals approximately 2.47 acres.
2. G.A. Manning and H.R. Grinnell, *Forest Resources and Utilization in Canada to the Year 2000,* Canadian Forestry Service Publication No. 1304, Environment Canada, Ottawa, 1971.
3. *Soil Capability Classification for Agriculture,* Canada Land Inventory, Report No. 2, ARDA, Dept. of Forestry, Ottawa, 1965. See also "The Canada Land Inventory" in R.R. Krueger *et. al.* (eds.) *Regional and Resource Planning in Canada*, (rev. ed.) Holt, Rinehart and Winston, Toronto, 1970.
4. D.W. Hoffman, *The assessment of Soil Productivity for Agriculture,* ARDA Report No. 4, Ottawa, 1971.
5. J.A. Shields and J.L. Nowland, "Additional Land for Crop Production: Canada," *Proceedings of 30th Meeting of The Soil Conservation Society of America*, San Antonio, Texas, 1975, pp. 45-60.
6. N.N. Sorboe, "An Economic Analysis of Grain-Beef Cattle Farms in the Lloydminister Area, Saskatchewan," *Canadian Farm Economics*, 1972, Vol. 9, pp. 17-27.
7. C.G.E. Downing, "Energy and Agricultural Biomass Production and Utilization in Canada," *Proceedings of 7th National Agricultural Waste Management Conference,* Syracuse, N.Y., 1975, pp. 261-69.
8. J.L. Nowland, "The Agricultural Productivity of the Soils of Ontario and Quebec", Ottawa, Monograph No. 13, Research Branch, Canada Department of Agriculture, 1975.
9. L. Tardif, "La planification de l'aménagement et de l'utilisation des ressources", *Agriculture* (Quebec), Vol. 30, 1973, pp. 3-10.
10. P. Crown and S.S. Kocaoglu, "Land-Use Conflict in Alberta: Agriculture vs. Urban Development," Edmonton, University of Alberta, *Agricultural Bulletin* No. 25, pp. 3-5.

10
The Preservation of Agricultural Land in Canada

*Ralph R. Krueger**

Under current economic conditions and market-place mechanisms, the agricultural industry cannot compete favourably for land desired for urban development or related urban uses. When land with a farm use value of $500 an acre is priced at $5,000 an acre for urban purposes, agricultural use for that land can no longer be economically justified. A farmer with 200 acres, valued at $5,000 an acre, could earn $80,000 a year at a modest eight per cent interest rate, without making any labour input and with minimal risk and managerial input.

Some economists claim that this is the way things should be. The "highest and best" use of land is determined by the market-place mechanism. As long as the agricultural industry cannot afford to compete with the manufacturing industry for land, there must be a surplus supply of agricultural land and products. When the demand catches up with the supply, the agricultural industry will be able to compete, and farmers with good land will be able to resist selling for urban purposes. It is interesting to conjecture on the prices of food if this theoretical supply-demand balance were ever to occur. In this connection, it is interesting to note that no country where food is expensive has a high standard of living and a rich life in other respects. The most dangerous flaw in this short-run economic perspective is that by the time that the supply-demand balance is achieved there will be little good agricultural land left in Canada. Unfortunately the urbanization of agricultural land is irreversible.

Urban Demand for Space

With an increasing population and constantly increasing percentage of that population living in urban areas, there is an ever growing urban demand for space. The mobility afforded by the automobile has resulted in low density suburban developments with their increased spatial demands, as well as wide swaths of land for streets and expressways, and

---

*Ralph R. Krueger is a professor in the Department of Geography, Faculty of Environmental Studies, University of Waterloo. This paper was written specifically for this book.

large expanses of asphalt for parking. The more recent trends to higher density residential areas and the very beginnings of an emphasis on public transportation are not likely to reduce significantly the urban demand for space. More vociferous demand by the public is leading to greater amounts of private and public open space for both passive and active outdoor recreational activities within the city boundaries. Urbanites are also creating demand for space in the urban fringe: drive-in theatres, golf courses, riding stables, bridle paths, snowmobile courses, game farms, and so on. In addition to all of this, there is the demand for summer cottages, camping grounds, and other recreational facilities in areas remote from the cities.

The "city life space" or "urban field" is constantly expanding. Affluence and transportation technology have permitted it to expand as far as the Arctic regions of the continent as is witnessed by the hunting expeditions that are common to the Canadian North. Thus the urban demand for space is no longer restricted to the urban fringe. Nor is the impact restricted to agricultural resources only. And if current trends continue, in the future there will be an even greater urban demand for space across the entire country.

Urban Impact on Agriculture

In the large areas of the urban fringe and surrounding urban shadow, and even in the whole urban field,[1] farmers readily sell their land at high prices that reflect urban uses, not farm profits. These high land prices lead to farmers selling off parts of their farms, thus creating subeconomic units. Although, in some cases the farmer can rent back land from urbanites, often the land is held for speculative purposes, becomes derelict, grown over with weeds, and is of no use to either the rural or urban residents. In other cases, small holdings are farmed on a part-time basis, and as a result are usually less productive. The expectation of urban development within the near future discourages investments in farm improvements that would increase long-term productivity.

The influx of non-farm people to a rural municipality is accompanied by a greater demand for municipal services. Since residential developments do not pay sufficient taxes to defray the cost of their own services, the increased costs fall upon agricultural land. In addition, urbanization of a farm community brings with it the problems of pilfering, neighbour complaints about spraying and using noisy equipment, and the odours of livestock operations.

In total, it has been estimated that for every acre of land actually used for urban purposes, at least another two acres of land are sterilized for agricultural use.[2]

Needless destruction of agricultural land may be of little concern in a nation beset with farm surpluses. However, when one looks at the man/land ratio on the global scale and in the long run, it is apparent that it is only a matter of time until agricultural resources will be of concern even to such "bread baskets" as Canada. I concur with the conservationist view that future generations will condemn us for permitting the needless destruction of an irreplaceable renewable resource. As is indicated in another paper in this volume, the percentage of Canada's land area that is good agricultural land is extremely small.[3] More than two-thirds of the prime agricultural land (CLI Classes 1 and 2) is found in the Prairie Provinces where there are severe climatic limitations for many crops. Areas in Canada where a wide variety of crops can be grown (including specialty crops such as tender tree fruits, grapes, small fruits and vegetables, grain corn, and soya beans) are severely limited indeed. Unfortunately, it is in some of these limited areas where urbanization is occurring most rapidly.

At the Resources for Tomorrow Conference in 1961, A.D. Crerar forecast that if existing urban growth and patterns continued, by the year 2000 there would be insignificant agricultural production in the Lower Fraser Valley of British Columbia, the southern portion of the Ontario Peninsula, and the St. Lawrence Lowlands.[4] This forecast has been repeated many times, but has triggered little public concern despite the fact that the named areas include the best and most unique agricultural lands in all of Canada. Only in British Columbia, as will be discussed later in this paper, has any effective action been taken to preserve agricultural land from urban encroachment.

A recent detailed study by Maurice Yeates of urbanization in the Windsor to Quebec Axis[5] shows that by the year 2001 urban densities will be found in an almost continuous strip between Windsor and Hamilton and along the Lake Ontario shore and the north bank of the St. Lawrence River (Figure 1). Yeates' forecast is even more alarming when one considers that if current trends continue, all of the area shown as semi-urban will ultimately become urban, and the entire Windsor-Quebec Axis will be within the urban shadow. The Yeates study will likely raise as little public and governmental concern as did Crerar's forecast fourteen years earlier. It seems clear that something in addition to a concern for the loss of agricultural land will have to be used to rally sufficient public support for the action required to rationalize urban growth patterns.

The Costs of Urban Sprawl

Most citizens become concerned about land-use issues only when a particular problem directly affects them. Therefore, since our governments usually follow rather than lead public opinion, if urban growth is to be planned and urban sprawl controlled, it will be necessary to con-

Fig. 1 Windsor-Quebec Axis Population Densities in the Year 2001

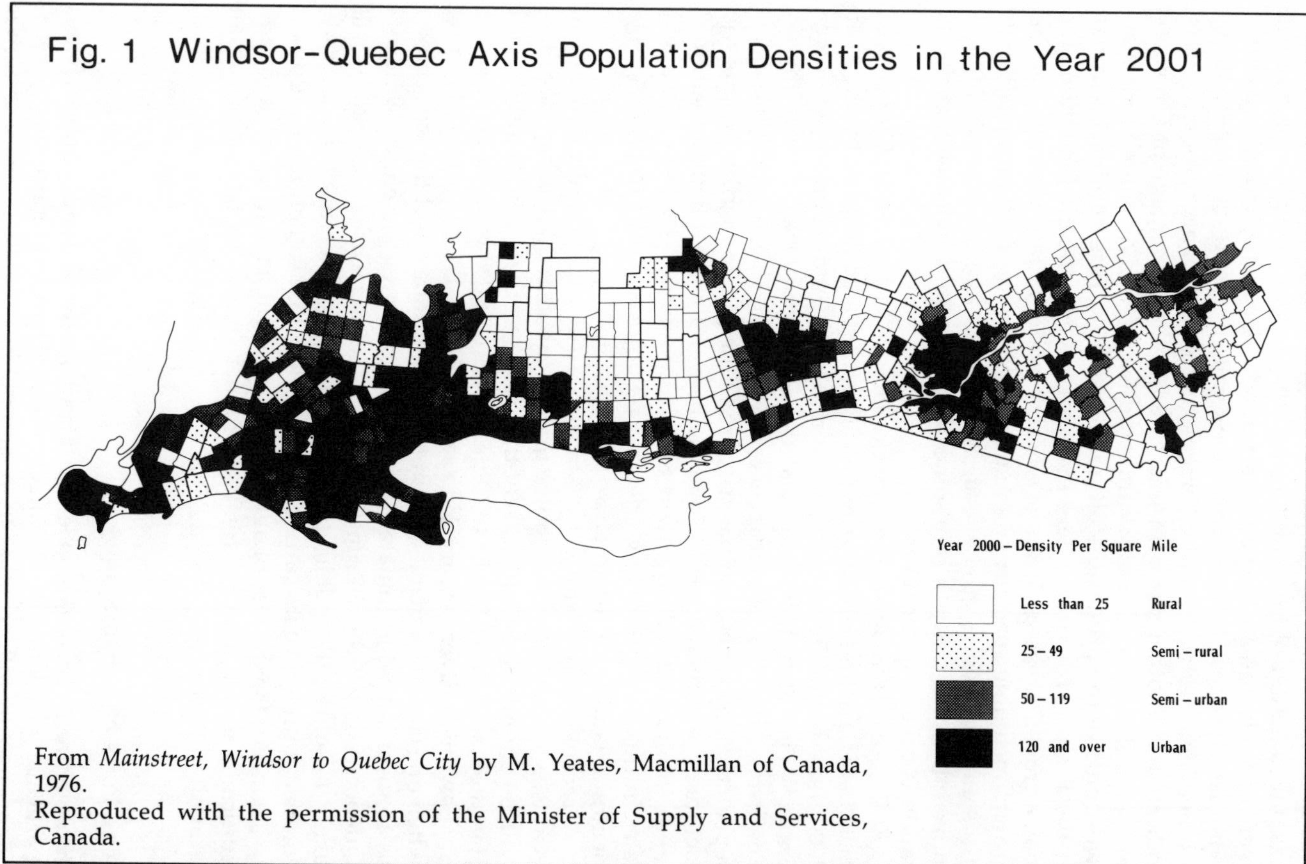

From *Mainstreet, Windsor to Quebec City* by M. Yeates, Macmillan of Canada, 1976.
Reproduced with the permission of the Minister of Supply and Services, Canada.

vince the electors that low density, scattered urban development is costly to them.

In studies in the Vancouver Metropolitan area, it was shown that the real costs of installing utilities and services in a typical urban sprawl area was *two-and-one-half times greater* than in a compact subdivision of normal density.[6] Some services, such as sewerage, were so uneconomic in a sprawl area that they could not be provided at all, even when they were necessary for health reasons. Low density development also increases the costs of providing services such as fire and police protection, and makes it virtually impossible to provide adequate public transit.

The general deterioration of the living environment is another cost of the urban sprawl pattern of growth. This contention has been stated forcefully in the following quotation from a Metropolitan Vancouver study.[7]

> . . . the bitterest consequences fall to the suburbanites themselves. The dusty gravel roads have no sidewalks or street lights. Small water mains run dry in the summer sprinkling season. Septic tanks cause health problems when yards and ditches flood with unabsorbed effluent. The distant fire brigade and the unreliable water supply give rise to high fire insurance rates. Parks are few, distant, and inadquately developed. The small schools are unable to provide a full range of educational opportunities. Shops are few and far between, and offer only limited variety. The bus service which could carry housewives, children, and older folks to better facilities is poor, frustrated by the sparse population that cannot be served economically. In short, the suburbanites find themselves isolated, forced to travel excessive distances each day to city jobs, major shops, and other facilities they cannot find locally. They are faced with an inadequate environment and hold little hope for change.

Scattered development in the rural-urban fringe promises people peaceful country living in a pleasant rural environment, at a low cost. The first few people to move have the promise fulfilled. But when thousands of others follow suit, the rural countryside itself is destroyed and the costs spiral. Hordes of commuters clog the highways, thus increasing the time spent on journey to work, and putting pressures on governments to build expressways that further carve up the countryside and entice urbanites to live even farther from the city.

Because the earliest developments occur in a rural municipality with inadequate planning controls, they are often poorly planned and when the city does catch up, rational community development is impossible. In brief, urban sprawl offers nothing of lasting value that contiguous urban development with planned community centres and adequate open space and services cannot offer in infinitely greater measure.

Land As an Open Space Resource

Land is not only a resource that can produce agriculture, forest, and wildlife crops; it also is a resource which supplies the physical and psychological space required by human populations. For too long, the countryside surrounding cities has been considered by urban developers and planners merely as a reservoir of space which eventually will be urbanized. On a zoning map, agricultural land is often labelled "H", meaning a Holding Zone.

Our thinking about the role of land around our cities must change. We must think of the land around our cities as part of the total space resources of the entire urban-centred region. Some of it can be designated for various urban land uses; some of it can be purchased as active and passive recreational parks; some, particularly scenic lands, can be protected by placing scenic easments on them; and some prime farmland can be left to produce food as well as to act as useful open space.

Farmland, with its quiltwork of fields of ever changing colours, its variety of house-types, barns, and fences, and its seasonal parade of farmwork activities, can provide a very satisfying element to the open space complex of a metropolitan region. Since the preservation of farmland as an open space resource is primarily for the benefit of the urbanites, then the economic cost of the preservation cannot be charged against the farmers alone. There are a number of methods available: acquisition of land by a public agency and lease-back arrangements to the farmers, purchase of development rights, assessment and taxation policies that relieve farmers of taxes on the land itself, and guaranteed farm income programs that provide farmers with reasonable recompense for their work of producing food, and managing the land as an open space resource.

Land As an Ecological Resource

It has long been known that there is an ecological relationship among landforms, soils, vegetation and the water table. However, by-and-large, this knowledge has not been much used by planners in plotting urban development strategies. Land-use capability has been little used by urban planners. City shape and form have been primarily determined by the economics of location and an almost complete disregard for the capability of the land. Housing subdivisions have been located on organic soils with cracked foundations as a result; swamps have been set aside as parkland which, when drained, lost all of their vegetation; expensive houses have been built in mature woodlots that could not survive the disturbance; houses on septic tanks have been permitted on impermeable clay soils; crucial water catchment areas have been built upon thus reducing the city's ground water supply; populations have been permitted to grow far beyond a stream's capability to assimilate the sewage effluent; sand and gravel deposits have been built upon (or the extractive industry completely prohibited) thus increasing costs of construction in the area; micro-climate differences have been completely ignored, resulting in increased air pollution hazards; and, more pertinent to this paper, urban development has been permitted on good agricultural land even when poor agricultural land was readily available.

In many cases, large blocks of farmland, complete with woodlots, swamps, streams, and cropland, can be an extremely valuable ecological resource in the metropolitan region. Agricultural land can provide catchment area for ground-water recharge, habitat for wildlife, as well as scenic open space for the urban inhabitants.

I hypothesize that if appropriate monetary values were placed on the costs of urban sprawl, and on the benefit of farmland as open space and as an ecological resource, then leaving land in agriculture could be justified on economic grounds, not to mention the social benefits that would result.

Because the preservation of agricultural land is dependent upon patterns of urban growth, the crucial decisions are usually made by urban planners and urban politicians. In order to rationalize the urban and rural competition for agricultural land, it would appear necessary to establish a framework of regional planning units with both urban and rural components. The planning process within these urban-centred regions would have inputs of both urban and rural viewpoints and hopefully would employ ecological principles in making the basic land-use decisions.[8] All of this planning must be done within an urban development strategy at the provincial level.

Need for a Viable Farm Economy

There is only space in this paper to treat farm economics very superficially. I merely wish to point out that the economics of farming must be considered in this whole issue of competition for land and environmental quality in our urban-centred regions. It is not true that all farmers have become captives of the idea that life in the city is superior. Some very capable and well-educated young people are planning to make a career out of farming, and many of these would like to remain relatively close to the city so that they could enjoy some urban amenities as well. However, to keep them on the farm, farming must be a viable business enterprise. Society cannot expect farmers to refuse to sell their land for high prices when they have difficulty making a comfortable living from the farm operation. Nor can society expect farmers to support provincial or local policies which would prevent them from selling their land to the highest bidder. The farmer is not the culprit; the economic system which places him in an unviable economic position is. Changing that economic system is a complex job which involves all levels of government from federal to local, and even with commitment at all levels, will take a long time to accomplish.

If we wait for adequate adjustments to be made in the economic system before trying to preserve agricultural land, there likely will be none left to preserve. It is indefensible to sacrifice a renewable resource which would produce in perpetuity in order to solve a current economic problem. In the long-run interests of society, action must be taken soon. Two different approaches being taken in Canada are briefly described in the balance of this paper.

Regional Planning in Ontario

In the latter part of the 1960s the government of Ontario committed itself to a program of regional planning and development in two policy statements under the catchy title of "Design for Development".[10] The major goals of these planning policies were increased economic development in the slow-growth regions of the province, and the restriction and control of growth in the highly urbanized areas. Among a number of objectives of the policies was the preservation of good agricultural land.

The proposed mechanisms to achieve the planning goals were basically twofold: (i) the reorganization of local municipalities into regional municipalities which would be required to create "Official Plans" to direct urban development and control uses of land and (ii) a provincial plan of development and provincial growth strategies for large regions (agglomerations of regional municipalities).

In the late 1960s and early 1970s a number of regional municipalities in the more urbanized areas of the province were formed and they began working on their "Official Plans". The regional municipalities have conducted thorough planning studies and comprehensive "Official Plans" were near completion in most regions by 1976. Although the regional municipalities have been able to hold back some premature urban development of agricultural land, generally they have not been able to prevent the continuous urbanization of good farmland. The political pressures from developers, farmers and real estate speculators have been too great to resist. Each local municipality is more concerned with getting its share of urban development than it is with preserving renewable resources.

The provincial government also backed down on its commitments. Because of some negative political feed-back, the government slowed down its program of local government reorganization. By the mid 1970s it was talking in terms of "restructured county government" and then only upon the request of the local municipalities. Neither have all counties been forced to become involved in land-use planning. As a result, planning at the county scale is still on a patchwork basis in southern Ontario, and the urban shadow keeps spreading further over the landscape.

Much of the provincial government planning effort has been concentrated in the broad region surrounding Metropolitan Toronto. In 1970, a concept plan for the Toronto-Centred Region was published. The objectives of the Toronto-Centred Region Concept were to discourage excessive growth in Metropolitan Toronto, structure new urban growth in well-defined centres separated by open space, and prevent urban sprawl from ruining the agricultural, recreational and other resources within the region. A broad zone around the urban and urbanizing area was designated primarily for agricultural uses. In this zone limited urban growth would be permitted only around existing town centres.

The main problem with the Toronto-Centred Region Concept was that it lacked the legislative base for and the methods of implementation. The regional and local governments within the Toronto-Centred Region did not all agree with the suggested growth strategy. The concept called for the development of growth centres beyond the agricultural zone to the north and east in order to help slow the growth in the highly urbanized lakeshore zone. However, the concept was not accompanied by studies to ascertain whether this would be economically feasible nor what social and environmental impact such growth centres would have. Also, there were no methods proposed to attract development to the proposed growth centres. Moreover, there was no provincial plan of development to provide a context for the Toronto-Centred Region Concept. By about 1974, it appeared from the comments by government spokesmen that the Ontario Government was not really committed to implementing the Toronto-Centred Region Concept. It also appeared that the government's previously stated resolve to preserve good agricultural land was weakening. However, the government still was promising in 1974 that it would soon complete a provincial plan which would provide an over-all strategy for growth for the province, and which would provide a framework within which the various regional and local municipalities could plan.

In the provincial election in the fall of 1975, the Conservative government lost a considerable number of legislature seats and found itself in a minority position. Because of these election losses, the government began a reappraisal of its planning strategies. In the spring of 1976, the government released a series of studies and policy statements relating to provincial planning in general, and agricultural land preservation in particular.[10] In essence, these statements said that the provincial government did not intend to formulate a provincial plan and that land-use planning was really the prerogative of the regional and local governments. Thus, after several years of intensive pre-planning study costing millions of dollars, the provincial government came up with what was essentially a "non-plan".

Concerning the preservation of agricultural land the provincial government made an even more dismal effort. It disagreed with its own staff report that good farmland was being urbanized at an alarming rate and employed special consultants to prepare a report which said that urbanization of agricultural land was a relatively insignificant problem. The responsibility for preserving agricultural land was shifted back to the regional and local governments.

To provide some relief from real estate taxation, the provincial government has initiated a tax rebate program which returns 50 per cent of the municipal taxes levied on land that is actively being farmed. If the land is sold for development within a specified time, the farmer must repay the rebate plus interest. There are other grant, subsidy and marketing programs, but this piece-meal approach has been deemed inadequate by the farm organizations of the province.

Without a provincial strategy of encouraging and directing growth to poorer and non-agricultural areas, and without an effective policy to guarantee farmers an adequate income, it is unlikely that regional and local governments will be any more successful in preserving agricultural land in the future than they have been in the past.

The British Columbia Farmland Preservation Policy

British Columbia is not richly endowed with good agricultural land. The best farmland is in the same southern valleys where urban growth and related urban recreational activities are greatest. Moreover, because of an inadequate planning controls in the past, low density urban sprawl is more rampant in British Columbia than anywhere else in Canada. In the twenty-year period prior to 1972, it was estimated that 10,000 acres of prime agricultural land a year was being lost due to urbanization. It was also estimated that in the Lower Fraser Valley alone, an additional 3,000 acres of land were being converted to hobby farms and country estates which have very low agricultural productivity.[11]

Shortly after a new N.D.P. (New Democratic Party) government was elected in 1972, it announced that the provincial government would introduce legislation to prevent the rezoning of farmland to urban uses. Immediately after this announcement, there was a rush of rezoning applications in an attempt to have farmland rezoned for urban purposes before legislation could be passed. As a result, in December, 1972, the government passed an Order-in-Council prohibiting any subdivision of farmland from that date until further orders to the contrary.

In the spring of 1973, the government passed its Land Commission Act which had four main objectives: (i) the preservation of agricultural land for farm use, (ii) the preservation of greenbelt lands in and around urban areas, (iii) the acquisition by government of certain lands with desirable qualities for specific urban development with the object of restricting the use of such lands for incompatible purposes, and (iv) the preservation of parkland for recreational purposes. Only in the case of agricultural land is the Commission given any zoning or regulatory powers. Greenbelt, urban development landbank or recreational lands can be designated as reserves only after the Land Commission has acquired the property.

The land reserved for agriculture only was determined on the basis of the Canada Land Inventory. Thus all land with potential for agriculture, regardless of its current use, was set aside for farming. The precise designations of Agricultural Reserve lands were made by the Regional Districts after careful study of land capability ratings and local needs. Hearings were held in every Regional District to insure public participation in the decisions. The designations made by the Regional Districts were reviewed by the Land Commission, and finally ultimate approval was given by the provincial government. Once the lands are designated as Agricultural Reserves, they cannot be used for any purpose other than agriculture or some activity considered to be compatible with the intent of the Act. The primary criterion for compatability is that the physical capability of the land to produce agricultural crops is not permanently damaged by the proposed non-farm use, that is, the land use can be changed should the land be needed for food production in the future.

In determining the boundaries of the Agricultural Reserves, allowance was made for urban areas to expand, permitting up to five years growth into agricultural land where deemed necessary. Thus, in the short term, conversion of agricultural land to urban purposes has continued to the extent that the boundaries of the long-term Agricultural Reserves have not yet been reached. The Land Commission, therefore, can only be effective in stopping urban encroachment onto agricultural land when all of the land exempted for urban purposes has been used up.

Responding to pressure from farm groups, the N.D.P. government passed several acts in 1973 to assure the farmers that, having had their land frozen for agricultural use, they would be able to make a fair income from their farming activity. These were the Agricultural Credit Act which provides for loans and guarantees of loans for purchase of land and improvements on it, and the Income Assurance Act which provides guaranteed returns to farmers for products sold.

The greatest potential weakness of the Land Commission Act would appear to be the great discretionary powers of the Cabinet of the provincial government. The Cabinet may exclude land from an Agricultural Reserve without a public hearing, without approval of the Commission, and without application from a local government. If a Cabinet were to change its view concerning the desirability of preserving agricultural land, the whole intent of the Land Commission Act could be undermined. To date (1976), there have been no signs of the government changing its priorities concerning agricultural land. It is noteworthy that the Social Credit government, which replaced the N.D.P. government in 1975, in its first year made no changes in the Land Commission Act and did not use its discretionary powers to bypass its intent.

It is too early to make any definitive evaluation of the British Columbia effort to preserve agricultural land. However, the original land freeze proved a very effective method to prevent zoning agricultural land for urban purposes until the necessary legislation was passed. In other jurisdictions, so much damage is done between the announcement of intent concerning the management of resources and the actual passing of legislation, that it is tantamount to locking the barn door after the horse is stolen. At this point in time, the combination of the Agricultural Reserves together with guaranteed farm income legislation appears to be the most effective way of preserving agricultural land yet devised in Canada.

NOTES

1. For a definition of urban fringe, urban shadow and urban field, see L.H. Russwarm, "Urban Fringe and Urban Shadow", in R.C. Bryfogle and R.R. Krueger (eds.) *Urban Problems*, Toronto, Holt, Rinehart and Winston, 1975.
2. L.O. Gertler and J. Hind-Smith, "The Impact of Urban Growth on Agricultural Land: A Pilot Study", *Resources for Tomorrow Conference Background Papers*, Ottawa, Queen's Printer, 1961.
   A.D. Crerar, "The Loss of Farmland in the Growth of Metropolitan Regions of Canada", *Resources for Tomorrow Conference Background Papers*, Ottawa, Queen's Printer, 1961. This paper is reprinted in Krueger *et. al.* (eds.) *Regional and Resource Planning in Canada*, Toronto, Holt, Rinehart and Winston, 1970.
3. J.L. Nowland and J.A. McKeague, "Canada's Limited Agricultural Land Resource", p. 109 in this volume.
4. "Urban Growth and Resources Workshop A", in *Resources for Tomorrow Conference Proceedings*.
5. Maurice Yeates, *Main Street, Windsor to Quebec City*, Toronto, Macmillan, 1975.
6. Lower Mainland Regional Planning Board, "The Economic Costs of Urban Sprawl" in R.C. Bryfogle and R.R. Krueger (eds.) *Urban Problems*, Toronto, Holt, Rinehart and Winston, 1975.
   This study defines "urban sprawl" as scattered development, including ribbon development, premature subdivisions, and scattered urban land uses, with an overall density of less than 3.5 people per acre.
7. Lower Mainland Regional Planning Board, "What Price Suburbia?" in R.C. Bryfogle and R.R. Krueger (eds.) *Urban Problems*, Toronto, Holt, Rinehart and Winston, 1975.
8. C.M. Kitchen, "Ecology and Urban Development: The Theory and Practice of Ecoplanning in Canada", in G. McBoyle and E. Sommerville, (eds.) *Canada's Natural Environment: Essays in Applied Geography*, Toronto, Methuen, 1976.
   ——————, "The Role of Ecological Appraisal in Urban Development", in R.C. Bryfogle and R.R. Krueger (eds.), *Urban Problems*, Toronto, Holt, Rinehart and Winston, 1975.
9. *Design for Development* (Phase I, 1966 and Phase II, 1968). Both are available from the Provincial Government Publication Office, Toronto. A summary of these policy statements and other provincial planning activities up to 1970 are found in R.S. Thoman, *Design for Development in Ontario: The Initiation of a Regional Planning Program*, Toronto, Allister Typesetting and Graphics, 1971. See also, R.R. Krueger, "The Regional Planning Experience in Ontario", in R.C. Bryfogle and R.R. Krueger (eds.) *Urban Problems*, Toronto, Holt, Rinehart and Winston, 1975.
10. *Ontario's Future: Trends and Options*, Toronto, Ministry of Treasury, Economics and Intergovernmental Affairs, 1976.
    A Strategy for Ontario Farmland, Toronto, Ministry of Agriculture and Food, 1976.
11. David Baxter, "The British Columbia Land Commission Act — A Review", *Urban Land Economics* Report No. 8, Vancouver, Faculty of Commerce and Business Administration, U.B.C., 1974. The short summary appearing in this paper is based primarily on David Baxter's excellent review and personal communication from him in February, 1976. An illustrated brochure entitled, "The B.C. Land Commission: Keeping the Options Open", is available from the B.C.Land Commission, 4333 Ledger Ave., Burnaby, B.C.

11
The Destruction of a Unique Renewable Resource: The Case of the Niagara Fruit Belt

*Ralph R. Krueger**

The Niagara Fruit Belt, which extends along the south shore of Lake Ontario from Hamilton to the Niagara River, produces most of Canada's peaches and grapes, as well as large amounts of apples, pears, plums, cherries, small fruits and vegetables. The physical suitability of the Niagara Fruit Belt has been well documented and need not be discussed in detail here.[1] Suffice it to say that the combination of climate and soils in the Niagara Fruit Belt is superior for most fruit crops to any other orchard district in Canada and to most United States districts outside of California. Most people are surprised to learn that the risk of frost damage to peaches is less in the Niagara Fruit Belt than it is in the "peach state" of Georgia.

The climate zones for Ontario in Figure 1 are based upon the frequency of: (i) temperatures reaching a low of −29°C or −20°F. (critical temperature for a peach tree) (ii) temperatures reaching a low of −24°C or −12°F. (critical temperature for dormant peach buds), and (iii) spring frost during the peach blossom period. Because peaches are the most susceptible to low temperature injury, Figure 1 classifies the most southerly parts of southern Ontario for their physical suitability for growing all tender fruit crops, including peaches, apricots, sweet cherries and grapes. Some of the more hardy fruit crops such as apples, pears and plums can be grown equally well in other parts of the province, particularly along the shores of the Great Lakes. The winter climate of the most south-westerly corner of Ontario (Kent and Essex Counties) is as good for fruit growing as the Niagara Fruit Belt. However, when the spring frost damage records are added, the Niagara Fruit Belt is clearly superior.

---

*Ralph R. Krueger is a professor in the Department of Geography, Faculty of Environmental Studies, University of Waterloo. Although this paper was written specifically for this book, the maps and some of the textual material were taken from a paper by Krueger, entitled "Recent Land Use Changes in the Niagara Fruit Belt", in R.E. Preston (ed.), *Applied Geography and the Human Environment,* Waterloo, Department of Geography Publication Series # 2, 1973. The author wishes to acknowledge the kind assistance of the Niagara Regional Planning staff and Niagara Regional Councillor Don Alexander in providing him with valuable documents and general information. Financial assistance for continuing research on this topic has been provided by Canada Council.

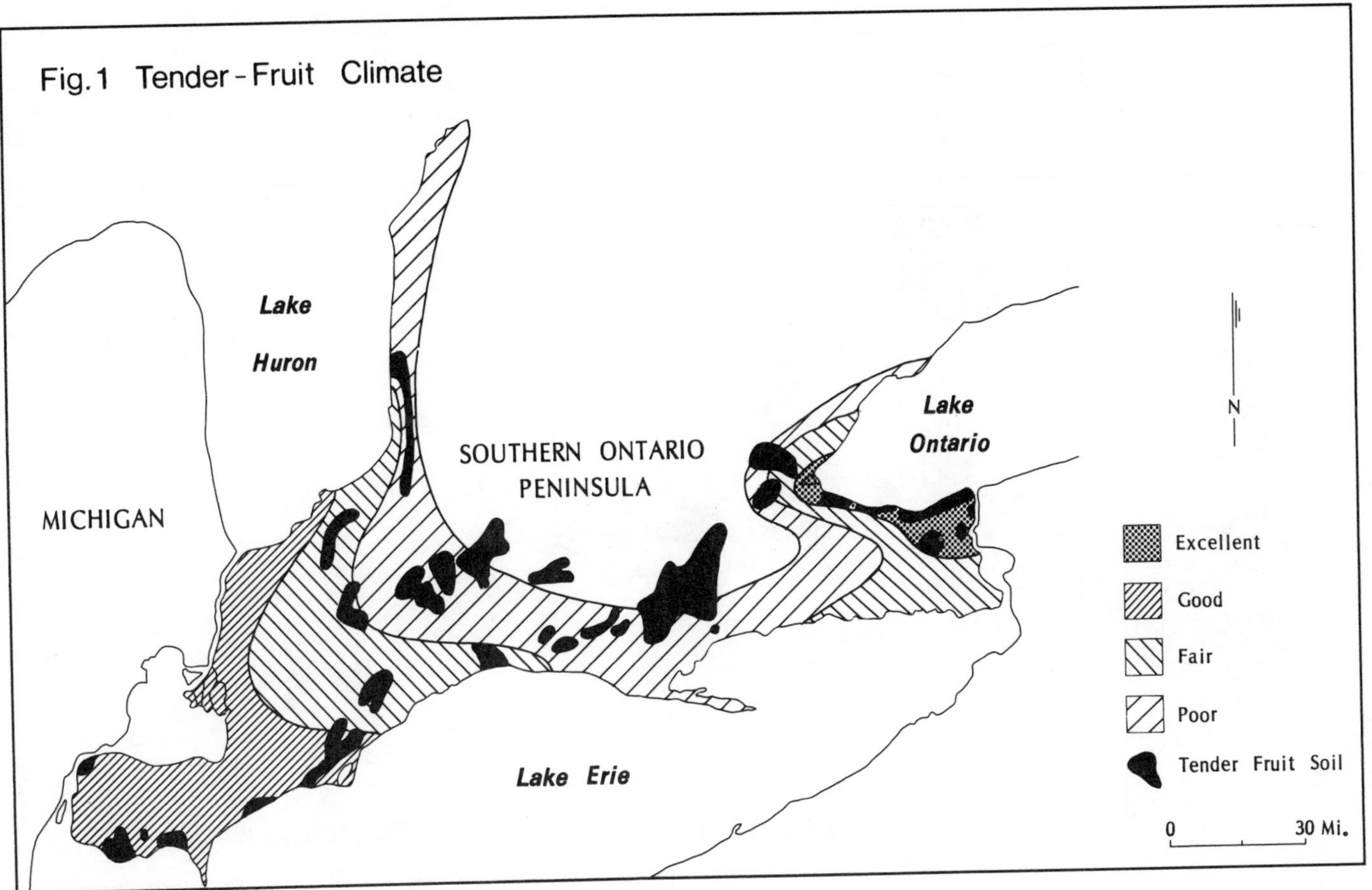

Fig.1 Tender-Fruit Climate

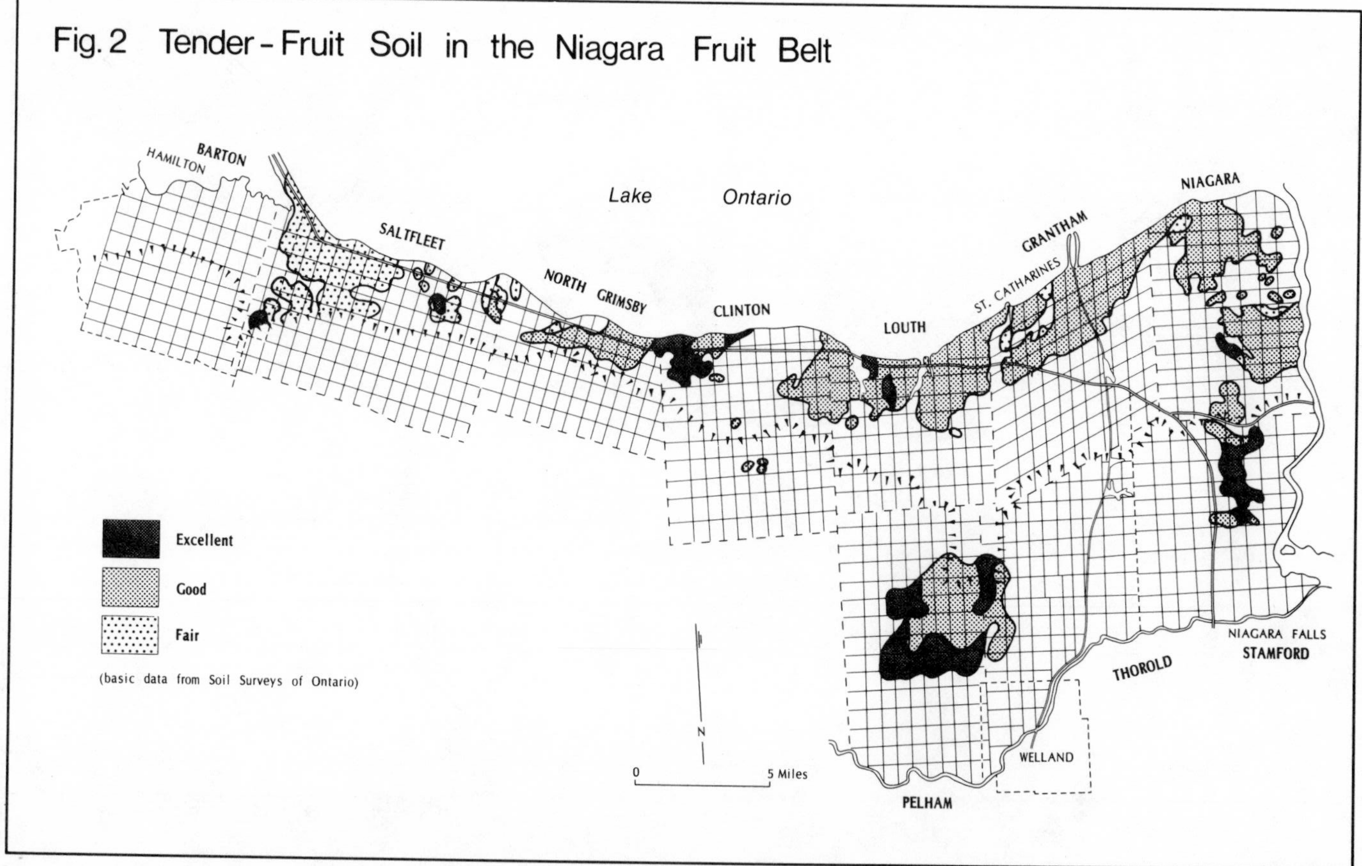

Fig. 2 Tender-Fruit Soil in the Niagara Fruit Belt

Within the Niagara Fruit Belt, however, there are some differences in fruit growing suitability. The eastern end of the Fruit Belt has slightly milder winters than the western end, and those areas immediately adjacent to the lake have less chance of both winter low temperature injury and spring frost damage. The air drainage afforded by the steep slopes in the Fonthill district of Pelham Township gives that area a surprisingly good fruit climate.

As is indicated in Figure 2, only a portion of the Niagara Fruit Belt has the deep well-drained light-textured soils (tender fruit soils) required by peach and sweet cherry orchards as well as small fruits and vegetables. Although peaches and sweet cherries can be grown successfully only on the tender fruit soils, the other tree fruits and grapes can be grown successfully on both the tender fruit soils and on large acreages of other well-drained clay loams in the Niagara Peninsula. It is a fortunate coincidence that the tender fruit soils in the Niagara Fruit Belt are located where the climate for tender fruit crops is most favourable.

Changing Orchard and Vineyard Patterns

Trends in tree fruit and grape acreages are illustrated in Table 1. Between 1951 and 1971 there was a reduction of 9,300 acres of orchard, a decline of 30 per cent in twenty years. Of most significance was the 4,800 acre loss of peaches, because it is for the peach crop that the Niagara Fruit Belt has the greatest comparative environmental advantage. The only fruit crop showing a gain was grapes, which increased by 1500 acres in the twenty year period.

TABLE 1
Niagara Fruit Acreages 1951 and 1971

Fruit Crops	1951 (acres)	1971 (acres)	Change (acres)	Percentage Change
Peaches	14,100	9,300	−4,800	−34
Pears	5,600	5,200	−400	−7
Cherries	4,200	3,200	−1,000	−24
Prunes and Plums	4,700	2,100	−2,600	−55
Apples	3,800	3,300	−500	−13
Total Tree Fruits	32,400	23,100	−9,300	−30
Grapes	20,400	21,900	+1,500	+7
Small Fruits	2,000	300	−1,700	−85
All Fruit Crops	54,800	45,300	−9,500	−17

Note: In this Table, Niagara includes Lincoln, Welland and Wentworth counties and thus includes more than the Niagara Fruit Belt as defined by Krueger. However, only apples spill beyond the Niagara Fruit Belt boundaries to any significant degree.
All data are from the *Census of Canada*. Numbers are rounded off to the nearest hundred.

A series of maps (Figures 3, 4 and 5) shows the 1965 patterns of orchards and vineyards within the Niagara Fruit Belt. Even though some of the townships have been completely annexed by adjacent cities, the township names and original boundaries have been retained for the convenience of reference and comparison. The small blocks are concession blocks and are usually bounded by roads. Within each block, the area of a particular land use was measured from air photos, and was computed as a percentage of the total area of the block.

It is interesting to note that the intensive fruit growing area is not limited to the lake plain north of the Niagara Escarpment. Areas of very intensive orchard and vineyard are found on the well-drained clay loam soils of the Vinemount Moraine that caps the Niagara Escarpment in Saltfleet, North Grimsby, Clinton and Louth Townships, and on the light-textured soils of the Fonthill Kame in Pelham Township. Lesser concentrations of fruit growing are found in Thorold and Stamford Townships. In 1965, almost 40 per cent of the grape acreage was located above the Niagara Escarpment. However, most of the peaches are grown on the tender fruit soils found on the lake plain below the Niagara Escarpment.

A comparison of Figures 3, 4 and 5 with earlier mapping[2] done by the author shows that since 1934, large increases in orchard acreages have occurred on the tender fruit soils. Large decreases have occurred primarily around the cities and towns and along the highways. Most of the vineyard increases have occurred on clay loam soils adjacent to the tender fruit soils and above the Niagara Escarpment. However, between 1954 and 1965, a trend developed to plant grapes on tender fruit soils. This reversal from past trends can be explained by the fact that the newer varieties of European grapes do better on light-textured soils, and the net return per acre from these grapes is greater than from peaches.

The Impact of Urbanization on the Fruit Growing Industry

Besides being uniquely endowed with the physical requirements for fruit growing, the Niagara Fruit Belt is ideally located for industrial and urban development. The area is part of the rapidly growing conurbation stretching from Oshawa around the head of Lake Ontario to Niagara Falls.

The pattern of urban growth in the Niagara Fruit Belt is one of low-density, scattered urban uses, with several nodal concentrations and some corridor tendency along the lakeshore plain (Figure 6). Field observations in 1976, plus interviews with planners in the region, confirm that since 1965 the pace of urban growth has accelerated, and the sprawl pattern has remained unchanged. Each city and town has spread out in all directions and land severances and scattered residential development have continued unabated across the entire Fruit Belt. In his book, *Mainstreet: Windsor to Quebec City*,[3] Yeates shows that all of the census subdivisions of the Niagara Fruit Belt had reached an urban population density in 1971.

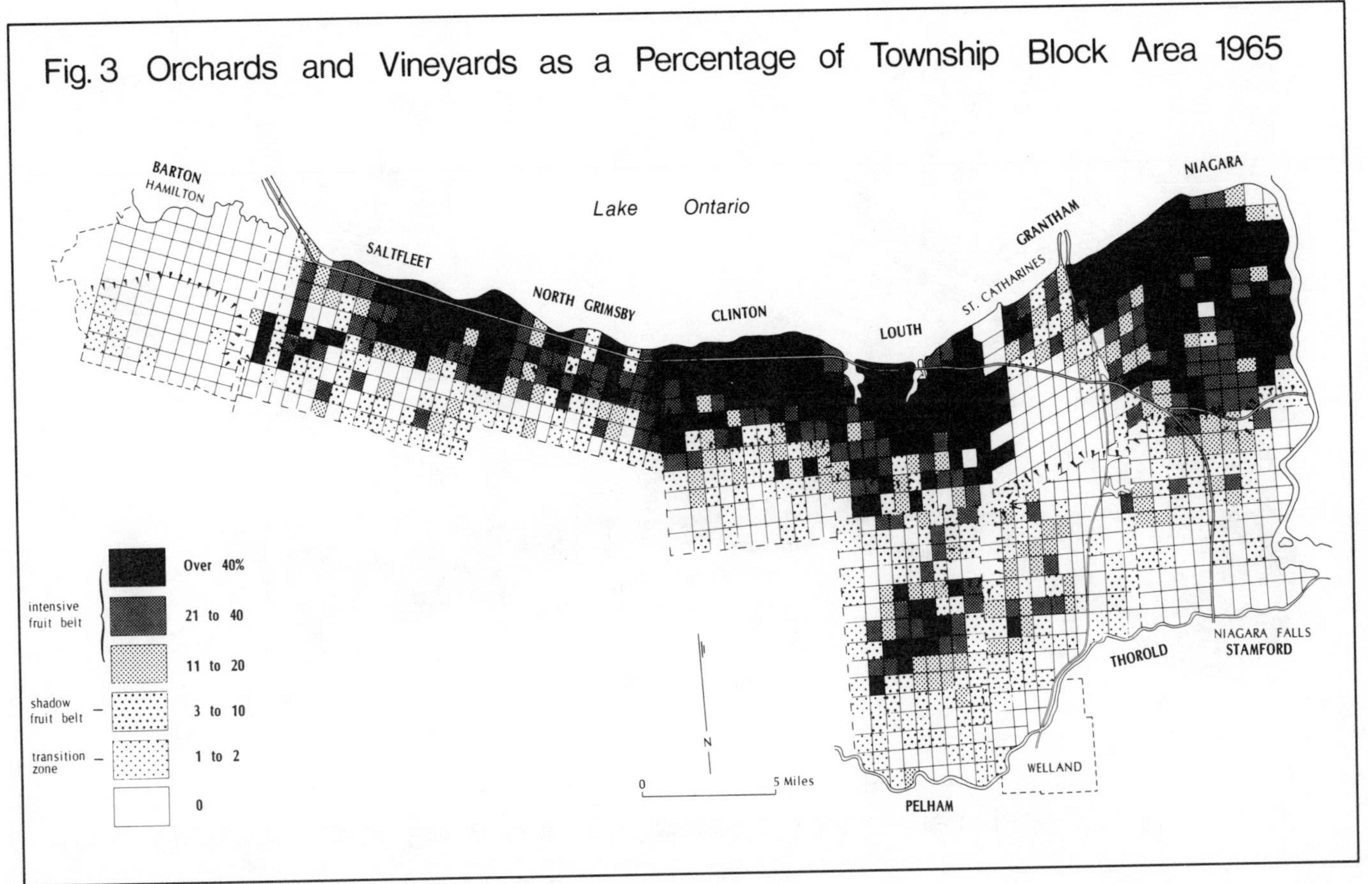

Fig. 3 Orchards and Vineyards as a Percentage of Township Block Area 1965

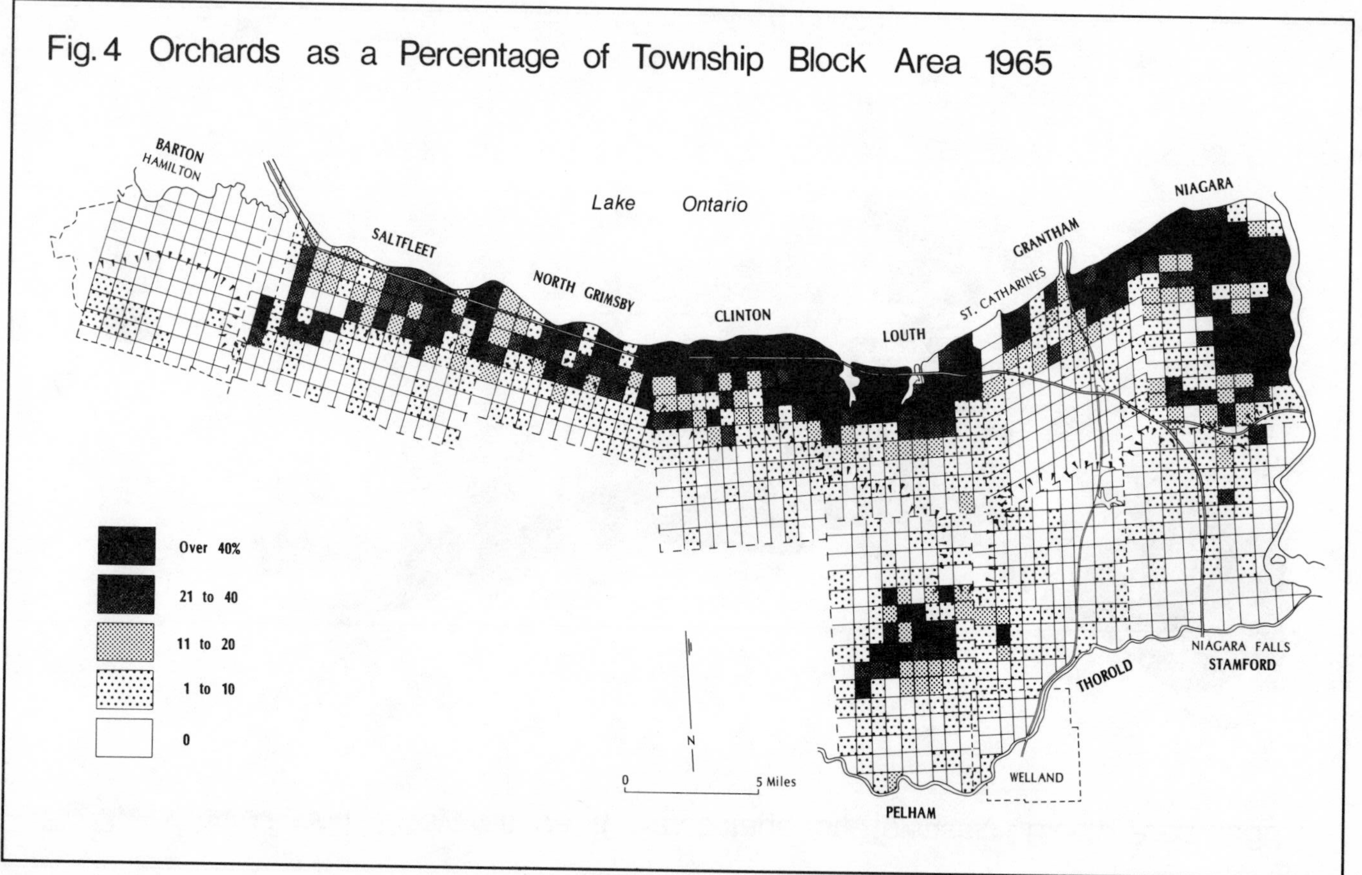

Fig. 4 Orchards as a Percentage of Township Block Area 1965

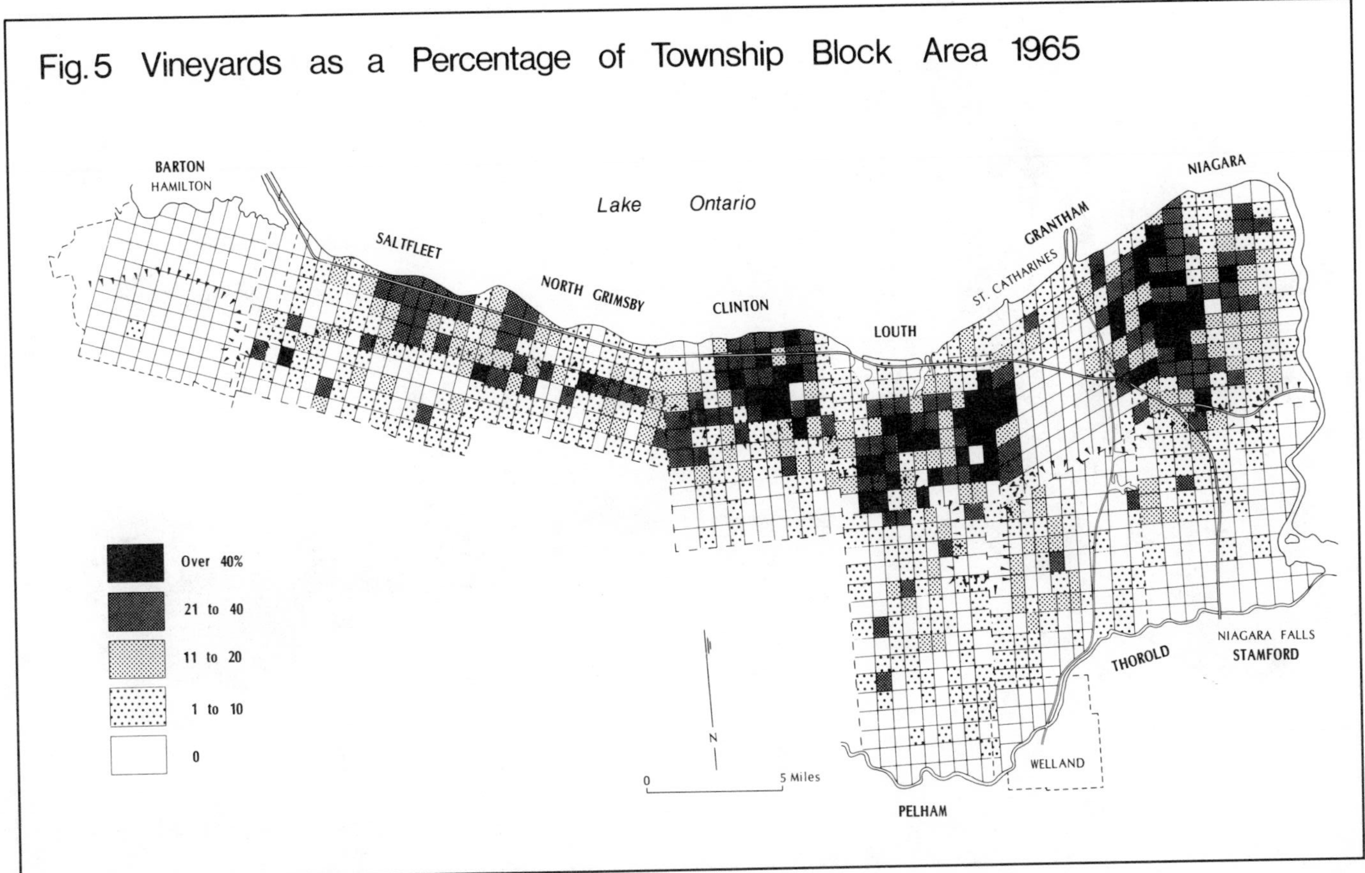

Fig.5 Vineyards as a Percentage of Township Block Area 1965

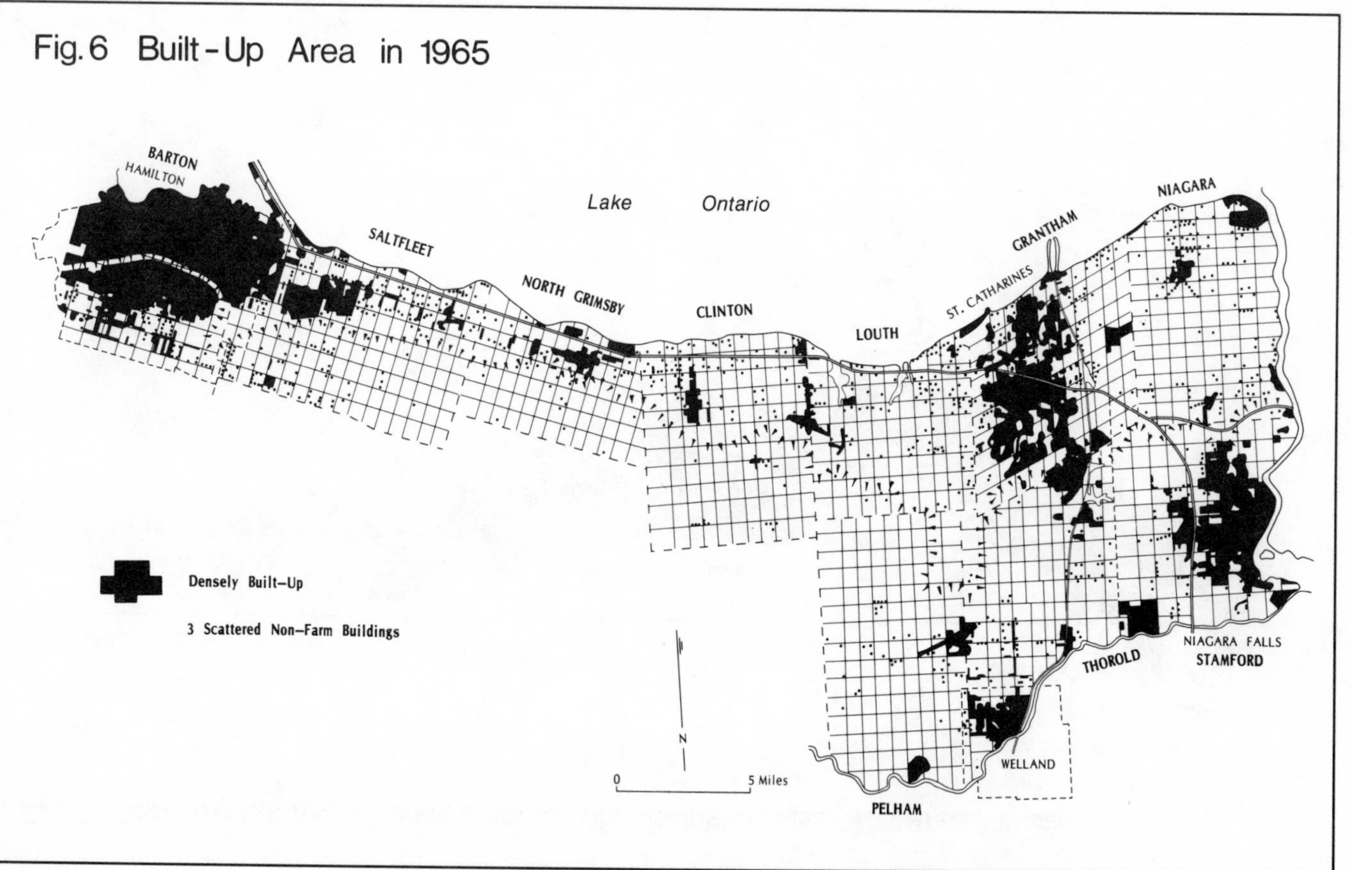
Fig.6 Built-Up Area in 1965
Lake Ontario
BARTON
HAMILTON
SALTFLEET
NORTH GRIMSBY
CLINTON
LOUTH
ST. CATHARINES
GRANTHAM
NIAGARA
NIAGARA FALLS
STAMFORD
THOROLD
WELLAND
PELHAM
Densely Built-Up
3 Scattered Non-Farm Buildings
N
0
5 Miles

Up until 1951, urbanization of agricultural land had relatively little impact on the fruit growing industry. Orchards uprooted for urban purposes were readily replaced in other parts of the region more remote from cities. In fact, census data show that there was an increase in orchard acreage in each decade from 1931 to 1951.

However, a decline in orchard acreage began in 1951 when losses due to urbanization began to be greater than the amount of new plantings. For some time after 1951, peach production kept increasing because of improved yields per tree. However, between 1960 and 1970, peach production declined by about 30 per cent. If the 1961-71 rate of orchard decline continues, the orchard industry will be destroyed by the turn of the century.

While it is very difficult to assess the precise degree of the significance of urbanization as a factor in the orchard decline, there is little doubt that it is the most important one. In an industry which has been caught in a tight "cost-price squeeze", which suffers from instable price conditions, and which faces stiff competition from foreign imports, in many cases the urbanization factor may very well be the "straw that breaks the camel's back." While inertia may be enough to keep a farmer in business despite poor returns from his investment and labour, if he has the opportunity of selling out at a good price, he is likely to do so. Research done by Lloyd Reeds[4] shows that approximately 60 per cent of all full-time orchardists had negative returns to family labour. That is, the net income was less than the interest charges on farm capital. No wonder that farmers are eager to sell their land at about $10,000 an acre.

Reeds also discovered that approximately half of all fruit farms were operated on a part-time basis and that the productivity of these farms was relatively low. Those who are full-time fruit growers have lost confidence in the industry's future, and are unwilling to undertake long-term investments that are necessary to assure continued high production. Thus, it is clear that urbanization has a greater impact on the orchard industry than the decline in orchard acreages indicates.

Because grapes can be grown on a wider variety of soils, more remote from the urban centres, and because of better and more constant market for grapes, they do not face the same threat of extinction as do orchards.

Tender Fruit Soil Occupied by Urban Expansion

The amount of tender fruit soil occupied by urban expansion (Table 2) is even more significant than the decrease of orchard acreage, because this soil, of which there is a limited amount in the Niagara Fruit Belt, is the only type on which the major fruit crop of peaches can be grown profitably. It is these tender fruit soil areas that have the climate and soils combination that make the Niagara Fruit Belt the most valuable horticultural land in Canada. The loss of tender fruit soil is not just a loss of orchards; it is the loss of an irreplaceable renewable resource.

Between 1934 and 1954, urban expansion occupied 2,710 acres of tender fruit soil; between 1954 and 1965, urban expansion occupied 2,360 acres. Thus, while the rate in the earlier period was 135 acres per year, in the later period it was 215 acres per year.

TABLE 2
Niagara Fruit Belt Acreages of Tender Fruit Soil Occupied by Urban Expansion

Township	1934-1954	1954-1965	1934-1965
	(Acres)	(Acres)	(Acres)
Saltfleet	1,050	800	1,850
North Grimsby	100	160	260
Clinton	40	90	130
Louth	140	130	270
Grantham	860	700	1,560
Niagara	140	100	240
Pelham	80	60	140
Thorold	10	20	30
Stamford	290	300	590
Total	2,710	2,360	5,070

Source: Air photos taken in 1934, 1954 and 1965.

It is important to note that the totals in Table 2 include only actual areas occupied by urban uses. They do not include the amount of land taken out of production as a result of real estate speculation that accompanies urban expansion into a rural area, nor the other indirect impact of urban expansion into rural farmland. If we accept the estimate that with present sprawl patterns, for every acre used for urban purposes, two acres are ruined for agricultural use, then the real loss of tender fruit soil between 1954 and 1965 was 7,080 acres, or about 645 acres a year. The rate of urbanization of the tender fruit soils has increased greatly since 1965.

Unfortunately, most of the tender fruit soil is in the path of the low density urban corridor rapidly developing along the lake plain. Any major new service such as another four-lane highway or extensive sewer facilities on the lake plain would greatly accelerate this corridor development and the attendant destruction of the tender fruit soil.

In Saltfleet, Grantham, North Grimsby and Stamford Townships, the urbanization process has gone so far that there is no chance of preserving significant acreages of tender fruit soil. However, in Clinton, Louth, Niagara and Pelham Townships there are areas of tender fruit soil where the urbanization processes are at a sufficiently early stage that there are still prospects of saving some of the prime fruitland for agriculture. Reeds estimated that in the late 1960s there were about 10,000 acres of tender fruit soil that could reasonably be expected to be preserved.

It is clear that the amount of tender fruit soil remaining that is sufficiently free of urban intrusions to make it possible to preserve it indefinitely has been reduced by alarming proportions over the last forty years. Unless drastic changes are made in the direction and pattern of urban growth, the tender fruit soils will completely disappear as an agricultural resource before the end of the century.

Land-Use Planning: Too Little and Too Late?

The first provincial government planning study of competing land uses in the Niagara Fruit Belt was a pilot study of Louth Township in the mid 1950s.[5] In addition to classifying soils according to their fruit growing capability, and studying urbanization trends and impacts on the fruit growing industry, the study team made land-use planning recommendations. Since the study was sponsored by the Department of Agriculture, all the land-use recommendations had to be stricken from the published report so that it would not interfere with the domain of other government departments.

The Louth study was just the first of a multitude of government studies on the Niagara Fruit Belt over a period of twenty years. In every case the results of the studies were either not made public or the recommendations were ignored. Just to give one more example, the Gertler *Fruit Belt Report* was a comprehensive document which included a detailed course of action required to save the best of the Niagara fruitlands. The report was completed in 1968, but was not released by the provincial government until 1972. The government seemed to believe that it was politically safer to hide the report because it was not prepared to take the action required to save the Fruit Belt.

At the same time as the provincial government released the Gertler Report, it released the Chudleigh Report on the economics of the Niagara fruit growing industry.[6] The Chudleigh Report suggested that the future of the Ontario fruit growing industry was bleak indeed unless the federal government negotiated import quotas to prevent the flooding of the consumer market with canned fruits. The Ontario government also stated at that time that the actual land-use planning was the responsibility of the regional and local governments in the area. Thus the provincial government "passed the buck" two ways at once: up to the federal government and down to the regional and local municipalities.

It is true that low-priced imports of fruit are a threat to the viability of the fruit growing industry. Many of these imports come from countries where the fruit growing industry is heavily subsidized. United States' canning companies can undercut Canadian prices because farming costs are lower and the larger market permits a greater volume and thus a lower cost per unit for the canning process. If the federal government is concerned about protecting the Niagara fruitlands then it does have a responsibility to protect the fruit growing and processing industry from unfair competition. It is also true that considerable responsibility for land-use planning falls to regional and local municipalities. However, the management of renewable resources and the ultimate responsibility for the actions of municipalities (which are creatures of the province) lie with the provincial government and it cannot legally or morally abrogate those responsibilities.

The first constructive action taken by the provincial government was the initiation of a local government review which was completed in 1966. Among the many briefs received by the Commissioner of the Niagara Local Government Review was one from the Institute of Land Use at Brock University, which said,

> . . . the rapid urbanization of the Niagara Region poses a serious threat on the continued existence of its agricultural industry . . . studies have all agreed that there is sufficient space within the peninsula to preserve the heart of the Fruit Belt and to meet the foreseeable needs of urban expansion. Despite this, no official action has yet been taken to limit the destruction of the fruitlands. . . .[7]

Nevertheless, in his report the Commissioner indicated that he felt that there was insufficient information concerning the threat of urbanization of the fruitlands, and some of his recommendations actually seemed to encourage urban growth on some of the best fruitland. For example, he recommended that the eastern half of Louth Township be given to St. Catharines for urban expansion, despite the fact that the city had enough land already ruined for agriculture by urban sprawl to fulfill its growth needs for at least another twenty years. (This particular recommendation was later implemented and St. Catharines' major expansion thrust is now going into the prime fruitlands of the former Louth Township.)

The provincial government did not establish regional government in the Niagara Region until 1970. The new two-tier Niagara Regional Municipality (Figure 7) was charged with the responsibility of formulating an Official Plan for the region as soon as possible. Even though a massive amount of study reports existed, the Niagara Regional Council commissioned planning consultants to do a whole series of planning studies. (In defence of the Regional Council, it should be pointed out that in 1970 it did not have access to the comprehensive Gertler Report; as indicated earlier in this paper, the provincial government suppressed its released until 1972.) Finally, in 1973, the Regional Council adopted draft policy statements which included ringing declarations about the need to preserve the prime fruitlands and the desirability of directing urban development to less valuable lands above the Escarpment. However, when the Regional Council got down to the details of its Official Plan, the policy maps indicated that more of the prime fruitland was designated for urbanization than could possibly be used by the turn of the century. A large area of excellent fruitland in former Louth Town-

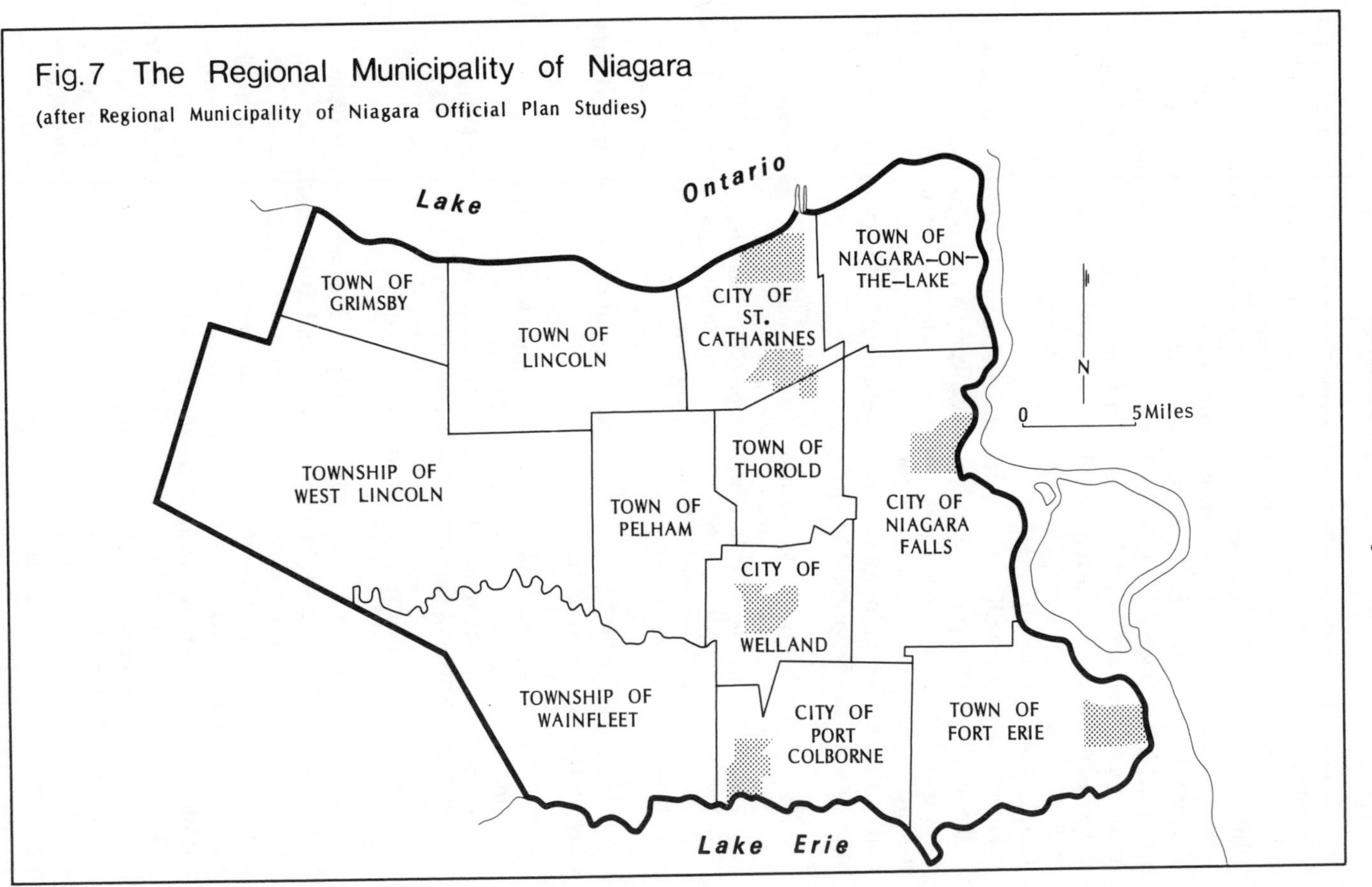

Fig. 7 The Regional Municipality of Niagara
(after Regional Municipality of Niagara Official Plan Studies)

ship was designated for urban uses even though St. Catharines could accommodate its projected urban growth by infilling lands over which urban uses have already sprawled. There were no policies in the Plan which would direct urban growth away from the best farmland. There were no policies in the Plan which would attract urban growth above the Niagara Escarpment. Each municipality was allocated the amount of space which it deemed necessary for its own expansion plans. In fact, more space was allocated for urban expansion than the Region's projected population would require. The proposed Official Plan appeared to be designed to encourage low density urban sprawl and speed up the destruction of the fruitlands.

Fortunately, the NDP party made the preservation of the fruitlands a political issue in the provincial election campaign of the summer of 1975. As a result, Premier Davis was forced to make an announcement that the provincial government would not approve the Region's Official Plan without major amendments. In September 1975, the Minister of Housing wrote to the Regional Council,

> I . . . strongly urge you to consider cutting back urban boundaries, with a view to balancing urban land requirements and the need to preserve as much of the fruitlands as possible. In addition, I would encourage Council to develop a long-term strategy for redirecting growth away from tender fruit and grape lands, as well as other good agricultural lands.[8]

In October, 1975, the Minister of Agriculture and Food reinforced this view by telling the Regional Council,

> In all instances, the underlying principle must be that the best food lands should be retained. While this Ministry is primarily concerned with food land potential, we recognize that some consideration must be given to present use. We would expect, however, in all instances where prime or unique agricultural lands are not retained for agricultural use, their need for other uses be justified.[9]

In short, the provincial government refused to accept the Niagara Region's Official Plan and directed the Regional Municipality to redraw the urban boundaries so as to include less prime agricultural land. After further study the Niagara Regional planning staff reported that the region's projected growth could still be accommodated if the urban boundaries were redrawn to include some 7,000 acres less than shown in the proposed Official Plan. However, Regional Council refused to make major reductions in the amount of land designated for urban development. In the summer of 1976, Council proposed that the urban boundaries be reduced by only several hundred acres. This minor reduction would hardly appear to meet the provincial government's directive "to reduce *substantially* the encroachment of future urban development on this irreplaceable resource." The revisions to proposed urban boundaries are minor compromises only. The thrust of urban development remains the same.

As one of the reasons for its decision, the Regional Council cited financial problems being faced by the fruit growers. The economic plight of farmers is a *short-run* problem. There surely are solutions to farm income problems that do not necessitate destroying prime farmland that would produce food indefinitely. If we look at the costs and benefits in the *long run*, any costs involved in making fruit growing more profitable would fade in significance when compared to the value of produce of this prime farmland for centuries. Neither in moral nor in long-run economic terms can the urbanization of these prime fruitlands be justified, particularly since alternate viable options are open.

At the time of writing, the ball is again in the provincial government's court. The Regional Council has returned its proposed Official Plan without the major changes requested. Time will tell whether the provincial government will stand firm on its original decision or will give in to political pressure from the Niagara Region.

A letter to the Member of the Provincial Parliament for Welland – Thorold (and previously a member of the Niagara Regional Council) asking for his opinion on public support for policies which would preserve the Niagara fruitlands brought the following response:

> As you already know, I am sure, not a single effective step has been taken to preserve the fruitlands. Yet, I am sure that any poll taken in the Peninsula would get at least a 75 per cent response in favour of preservation. . . . There is no doubt that I have the support of the farmers, at least the farm organization, concerning the preservation of good agricultural land. . . . There has been a tremendous change in the attitude of the farm organizations towards the confining of urban development to the poor agricultural land and they now are the single strongest backers of good land preservation. You ask what proportion of the Regional Council really and truly wants to preserve the fruitlands. The answer to that question is, with the exception of Don Alexander, none. There are several who pay lip service to preservation, and in particular instances may vote for some measure of preservation but generally they have little commitment.[10]

There may be some question about the degree of support the general public of the Niagara Region would give to strong policies that would result in the preservation of prime farmland. Certainly they seem to elect a majority of local and regional councillors who have no commitment in that regard. With a lack of leadership from senior governments and a lack of resolve from regional and local governments, it is hard to be optimistic about the chances of saving a significant portion of the Niagara fruitlands.

In the meantime, while governments debate what should be done about preserving the fruitlands, urban development is proceeding as usual. Large new water and sewer projects are being constructed below the Niagara Escarpment right in the middle of some of the best fruitland. The sewer plants are designed (with the concurrence of the Ontario Ministry of Environment) in such a way that they can be expanded substantially in the future. If it is going to take twenty years to effectively slow down urban growth below the Niagara Escarpment, as proposed by the Regional Council, there is not much point in any longer considering preserving the tender fruit soils. By that time they will be almost completely paved over.

Unless action is taken very soon to change drastically the pattern of urban growth, attempts to save some of the unique agricultural resources in the Niagara Peninsula will prove to be a matter of "too little too late".

NOTES

1. R.R. Krueger, *Changing Land-Use Patterns in the Niagara Fruit Belt*, Toronto, Transactions of the Royal Canadian Institute, Vol. 32, Part 2, No. 67, 1959.
   ———, "The Disappearing Niagara Fruit Belt", in R.R. Krueger *et. al.* (eds.), *Regional and Resource Planning in Canada* (rev. ed.), Toronto, Holt, Rinehart and Winston, 1970.
   L.O. Gertler, *The Niagara Escarpment Study: Fruit Belt Report*, Toronto, Ontario Department of Treasury and Economics, 1968.
   For a detailed comparison of the physical characteristics, production statistics, and problems and trends of all orchard regions in Canada, see R.R. Krueger, "The Geography of the Orchard Industry of Canada," *Geographical Bulletin*, Vol. 7, No. 1, 1965. An up-dated summary of this article is found in R.M. Irving (ed.) *Readings in Canadian Geography* (rev. ed.), Toronto, Holt, Rinehart and Winston, 1972.
2. R.R. Krueger, *Changing Land-Use Patterns in the Niagara Fruit Belt*.
3. M. Yeates, *Main Street: Windsor to Quebec City*, Toronto, Macmillan, 1975. See Figure 1.2, p. 11.
4. L. Reeds, *Niagara Region Agricultural Research Report*, Toronto, Ontario Department of Treasury and Economics, 1969.
5. R.M. Irving (ed.), *Factors Affecting Land-Use in a Selected Area in Southern Ontario – A Land-Use and Geographic Survey of Louth Township in Lincoln County, Ontario*, Toronto, Ontario Department of Agriculture, 1957. This study is commonly called *The Louth Report*.
6. E. L. Chudleigh, *Alternatives for the Ontario Tender Fruit Industry*, Toronto, Ontario Ministry of Agriculture and Food, 1972.
7. H.B. Mayo, *Niagara Region Local Government Review, Report of the Commission*, Toronto, Ontario Department of Municipal Affairs, 1966, p. 21.
8. A letter to the Regional Municipality of Niagara from Donald R. Irving, Ministry of Housing, September 8, 1975.
9. A letter to the Regional Municipality of Niagara from William G. Newman, Minister of Agriculture and Food, October 22, 1975.
10. A letter to the author from M. Swart, M.P.P. for Welland – Thorold, December 17, 1975.

12
The Niagara Escarpment: Planning for the Multi-Purpose Development of a Recreational Resource

*John T. Horton**

The Niagara Escarpment is part of a geologic cuesta formation that stretches in a vast arc from upper New York state northward and westward through Ontario and the Great Lakes to Wisconsin. In Southern Ontario the Escarpment forms the most prominent landscape feature and is a unique environmental element in the physical and ecological structure of the province. It extends for more than 250 miles — a relatively narrow ribbon of disconnected cliffs, ridges and woodlands meandering from Niagara Falls and Queenston Heights to the tip of the Bruce Peninsula projecting into Georgian Bay (Figure 1). At various points along its length conspicuous limestone cliffs rise from 300 to 900 feet above the adjacent plains and bays. Its rich mosaic of natural features include sweeping viewpoints, scenic waterfalls, unusual rock formations, cool glens and forests, marshlands, wildlife and distinctive biotic ecosystems.

This more-or-less continuously wooded corridor is unquestionably an irreplaceable resource of inestimable value, particularly so because of its location. The Escarpment lies in the midst of a heavily populated area with a critical shortage of recreational space, where it quite clearly could provide a significant setting for recreational activity of a wide variety. Its southern section traverses the most intensely developed landscape of Ontario — cutting through a continuously expanding urban belt and rich agricultural lands that together comprise the urban-industrial-agricultural heartland of the richest province in Canada.

The Problem

Given its fortuitous situation amid this largest, most rapidly developing urban region of the country, it is not surprising that the Escarpment has increasingly been subjected to competing and frequently incompatible land-use demands. Recreational use of the Escarpment, or rather of its more accessable portions, has been an activity of long standing. Agricultural uses on adjacent lands developed over many decades, including specialized fruit farming on the unique soils of the Niagara Peninsula (see Krueger's paper p. 132); mixed farming, typical of the soils found in

---

*John Horton is an Associate Professor in the School of Urban and Regional Planning, University of Waterloo. This paper was written specifically for this book.

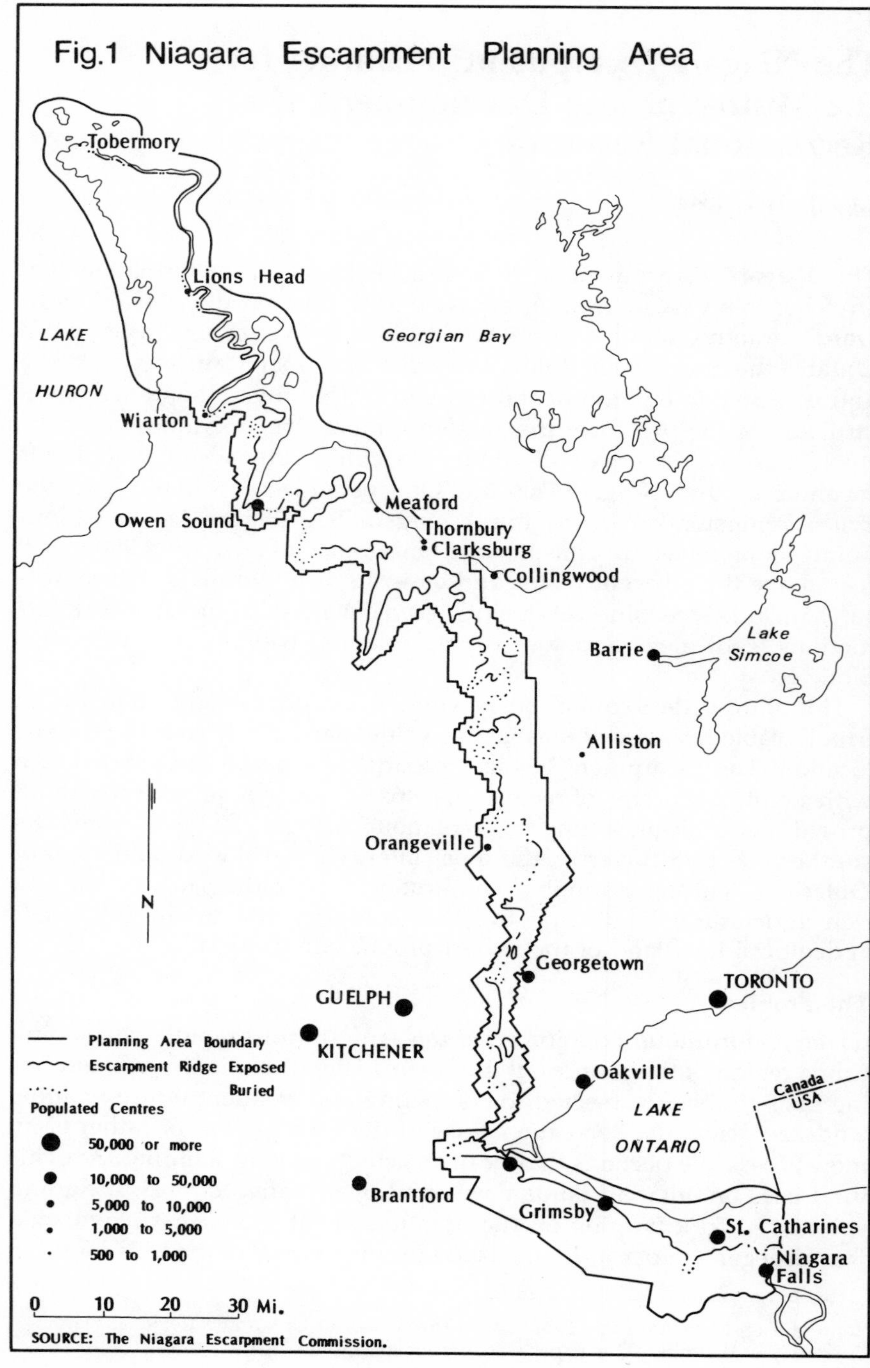
Fig.1 Niagara Escarpment Planning Area
Tobermory
Lions Head
LAKE
HURON
Georgian Bay
Wiarton
Owen Sound
Meaford
Thornbury
Clarksburg
Collingwood
Barrie
Lake
Simcoe
Alliston
Orangeville
N
Georgetown
TORONTO
GUELPH
KITCHENER
Oakville
LAKE
ONTARIO
Canada
USA
Brantford
Grimsby
St. Catharines
Niagara
Falls
Planning Area Boundary
Escarpment Ridge Exposed
Buried
Populated Centres
50,000 or more
10,000 to 50,000
5,000 to 10,000
1,000 to 5,000
500 to 1,000
0 10 20 30 Mi.
SOURCE: The Niagara Escarpment Commission.

the central section; and beef raising on the poorer soils of the Bruce Peninsula. The southern segment of the Escarpment has been for many years the site of an expanding multi-million dollar extractive industry, providing sands, gravels and building stone for the construction industry of much of the central region of Southern Ontario. Urban development, in the Niagara Peninsula in particular, has continued to utilize more and more of the Escarpment lands that stretch between Hamilton and Niagara Falls, with substantial acreages being reserved for future urban growth in that area. Elsewhere scattered urban settlement in the form of non-farm, rural residential development — including both permanent homes and seasonal recreation properties — has been permitted to proliferate unchecked on Escarpment lands.

The Niagara Escarpment cannot be expected to accommodate all of these competing uses without irreparable damage and loss occurring. The demands simply exceed both the spatial and ecological limits of the resource. The fragile and irreplaceable natural elements that together comprise the unique character of this Escarpment region — its soils, forests, geologic features, specialized flora, and its fauna — will not be preserved for the use and enjoyment of present and future generations unless the allocation of lands to various human uses is somehow rationalized.

The problem therefore is one of successfully introducing and applying comprehensive regional planning techniques to ensure the appropriate development of a multi-use natural resource. What should be done to effectively direct and control the future use of Escarpment lands? How should goals and objectives be established and priorities set? Where should the lines be drawn to balance the preservation of the Escarpment and its ecological value with compatible development of at least a portion of its total area? When all of the projected demands represented by past and present trends (recreational, agricultural, industrial and urban uses) cannot be served, and when agreement has been reached as to the acceptable proportions of each, where, when and in what manner should each be permitted to develop?

The basic issue is the preservation of the Niagara Escarpment. The basic challenge is that of devising policies, programs and strategies that, when implemented, will provide an appropriate approach to the long-term development of that resource, employing a multi-use concept of resource planning.

Public Initiatives

During the early 1960s interest was generated in Ontario for establishing a hiking trail, similar to the Appalachian Trail in the United States, that would traverse the entire length of the Niagara Escarpment. Support for the project was largely stimulated by a few far-seeing individuals and the Federation of Ontario Naturalists. In 1960 the Federation established a Bruce Trail Committee, which in 1963 was superceded by The Bruce Trail Association. Its membership included interested members of the public, the Federation, and other naturalist and recreation-oriented organizations. The Association was formed to co-ordinate the voluntary efforts of its members in planning a trail route, obtaining "easements" through the co-operation of landowners, and undertaking the necessary clearing, construction and signing operations. By 1967 the Bruce Trail was completed from Queenston Heights at Niagara to Tobermory at the tip of the Bruce Peninsula. This project was a significant accomplishment, achieved through voluntary public efforts, and undertaken without active government support or funding.

Until the 60s the Escarpment had largely been taken for granted by the general public and by various levels of government — it was viewed as a physical barrier to movement and a landscape feature that retarded development and increased urban servicing costs. With the creation of the Bruce Trail Association this perspective began to change. Their successful efforts, which established an important recreational facility in what had been a beautiful but neglected environmental corridor, were significant in a larger sense as well. The attendant public discussions and publicity served as a catalyst to stimulate a much broader appreciation of the Niagara Escarpment as something unique and invaluable as a recreational resource — one that properly belonged to all of the people of Ontario. There was a perceptible increase in the public's expression of concern for preserving the Escarpment during this period. However, during the same decade there were substantial increases in the degree and rate of encroachment on the Escarpment lands, largely through urban expansion and industrialization. In response to this encroachment there emerged from the public, with its heightened awareness of the implications, and from special interest groups oriented to outdoor recreational activity, a gradually mounting tide of pressure on the provincial government to take immediate steps to protect and preserve the Escarpment.

The Gertler Report

Although Ontario had on-going province-wide programs of land acquisition (through its Department of Lands and Forests and regional conservation authorities), woodland and wildlife management, and the creation of parks and recreation areas that included lands of the Niagara Escarpment, it had indicated no explicit interest in and had made no public commitment to the preservation of those lands. Apart from generalized local and regional official plans that afforded little or no protection and which covered only segments of the corridor, there were no planning programs in Ontario that had as one of their stated objectives the preservation of the Escarpment.

In the face of mounting demands from an ever broader segment of the public and from the media, the province in 1967 appointed a well-known planner, Leonard O. Gertler of the University of Waterloo, to co-ordinate a wide-ranging study of issues and policies relating to the Escarpment area.[1] The primary focus of this interdisciplinary study was the protection of land and the determination of the best means of properly conserving and developing the resources of the Escarpment. It had the distinction of having linked to it a policy commitment from the Premier of Ontario, who announced to the Legislature "a wide-ranging study of the Niagara Escarpment with a view to preserving its entire length — as a recreation area for the people of Ontario."[2] There was thus attached to this undertaking both a position statement by the government and a sense of urgency arising from increased public concern for "a perishable and vulnerable resource."

The Niagara Escarpment Study had three major objectives that emerged from its terms of reference, (1) the delineation of lands to be preserved for their recreational and environmental value, (2) the determination of the means of preservation, and (3) the setting of priorities for preservation action. There was to be careful consideration given to the identification of lands to be reserved for agricultural purposes — with particular emphasis on the rapidly shrinking Niagara Fruit Belt — and to the lands currently devoted to, or projected for, incompatible uses such as quarrying.

An area of approximately 1,800 square miles was subsequently delineated as the study area. Utilizing existing documents, reports and data from related provincial departments and agencies, and information from other sources, the work was completed and the group's recommendations submitted to the government in 1968, within the one-year time period allocated for the Study. The report was one of some import for Ontario, for although it was finished quickly, as requested, it presented a detailed and far-reaching strategy for accomplishing the stated objectives of the government. The Study offered recommendations relating to four areas: (1) a policy for the preservation of land, (2) a program for the development of the Escarpment as a single park network, (3) a sub-strategy for the controlled development of pits and quarries, and (4) an approach to the administration and financing of a comprehensive planning and development program. Recommendations were specific in designating particular lands for acquisition or control, in projecting land purchase costs, in scheduling various steps in the overall strategy, in creating a new planning agency to oversee the program, in outlining necessary changes in legislation to effect the preservation of the Escarpment, and in resolving the existing, sharp resource-use conflicts between recreational, agricultural and extractive activities. It was a remarkable achievement, given the immensity of the task and the urgency attached to its completion. The study group presented the province with a report which not only indicated "what should be done," but "how it should be done, and when."

The Niagara Escarpment Study was something of a substantial departure from what had gone before in the way of land-use and regional planning studies commissioned by the government. Its high visibility and very specificity were major factors in the manner in which it was received by the government. The politicians in power found themselves the recipients of a report, the findings and recommendations of which they had indicated would be made a matter of public record, and which spelled out in unequivocal terms what the government must do — and quickly — to preserve the Escarpment. The report provided a detailed strategy for responding to increasing and obvious losses of irreplaceable escarpment lands on the one hand, and growing pressures for action to halt this encroachment from an ever more concerned and vocal public on the other. At the very least, the completed Study served to give credence to the government's commitment to action.

However, a study which proposed very substantial expenditures at a time of some fiscal retrenchment, the introduction of an extensive land acquisition program, and the imposition of new and restrictive land-use controls over a much larger area than had been anticipated (much of which had been relatively free of development restrictions) concerned and alarmed politicians, developers, and rural landowners alike. The government did not wish to move too rapidly in the face of opposition from these sources and in view of its own uncertainty as to the acceptability, politically and operationally, of many of the report's recommendations. Due to the urgency with which the Study was launched and the time constraints imposed, there had been little or no opportunity to assess the attitudes, views and opinions of the residents and municipal governments in the Escarpment region. It was the province's view that the need for an immediate response to continuing encroachment failed to outweigh political realities and the need for consultation with the electorate in the affected areas. In addition, the Department of Lands and Forests which had its own continuing program of land acquisition, with its constituent priorities for purchases and park development, was not necessarily disposed to agree with and accept recommendations contained in the Niagara Escarpment Study that were at variance with its own planning and commitments. It is not surprising, therefore, that the province did not move to quickly accept and adopt the policies, programs and strategies set forth — inspite of its public commitment to act promptly to save the Escarpment.

The Provincial Response

The government did acknowledge acceptance of the basic principles set out in the Study and ultimately took steps to implement — on a selective basis — certain of its recommendations. Additional funding for land purchases by the Department of Lands and Forests and by conservation authorities was introduced through accelerating the Department's acquisition program and increasing grants to authorities. During the period from early 1968 to late 1972 approximately $7 million was expended for the purchase of 20,000 acres of Escarpment lands — a significant acreage, although substantially short of the amounts and scheduling proposed in the Gertler Study.

In certain sections of the Escarpment municipal official plans were formulated to include some of the preservation measures recommended for use in areas designated for restrictive control of land uses. More specifically, the Study had emphasized the need for three types of control to be implemented, (1) complete control — through outright acquisition, (2) selective control — through the purchase of easements, and (3) regulatory control — through the introduction of use restrictions (land use zoning, etc.). Priorities had been established for specific Escarpment lands based on location, accessibility and relative pressures for conversion, the pressures being greatest in the Niagara Peninsula to the south and in the Bruce Peninsula to the north.

It was found that both prior to and following public release of the Study's findings development and speculative pressures increased noticeably. Land options and purchases were accompanied by the submission of numerous plans of subdivision to the province for approval; these proposals and local official plans both were indicating urban development on lands designated in the Niagara Escarpment Study for acquisition through purchase or easements. The Ministry of Natural Resources (successor to the Department of Lands and Forests in land acquisition) also had recommended purchase of some of the same lands in its program.

By 1972 the situation had reached the point where the Ministry of Treasury, Economics and Inter-Governmental Affairs, responsible for land-use planning in Ontario, felt it had to respond to the actual and potential loss of Escarpment lands by applying, where it could, short-term, restrictive land use regulations.[3] The Ministry introduced two special policy area designations corresponding to the first two of the Gertler Study's control areas. They were made applicable only to those municipalities submitting new official plans and restricted area (zoning) by-laws, or to those requesting amendments to existing official plans. In areas recommended for acquisition no further development was permitted, and in areas designated for purchase of easements it was required that appropriate related agencies review and comment on any proposals for development. Committees of Adjustment and Land Division Committees also were requested to restrict severances on lands recommended for acquisition. Both regulations were to be in force "until the province's management strategy for the Escarpment is defined." As a consequence, a not inconsiderable backlog of subdivision applications — held in abeyance, not approved, or awaiting decisions — began to accumulate in the Ministry's offices. In the face of increasing development proposals, permissive official plans and land severance committees, the Ministry felt it must act.

The conflict between industrial quarrying and preservation of the natural environment of the Escarpment was perhaps the most pointed of all. In keeping with the Gertler Study's recommendations the province moved more rapidly to establish some form of regulatory control. It introduced The Niagara Escarpment Act in 1970 that incorporated many of the provisions suggested for pits and quarries. In 1971 The Pits and Quarries Control Act was passed, strengthening the earlier regulations and governing both the operation and siting of all pits and quarries.

Although these responses by some of the government's agencies were addressed to certain relevant facets of the problem (with varying degrees of effectiveness), they were necessarily partial solutions that failed to provide what was needed — a comprehensive land-use planning program for dealing with the Escarpment founded on appropriate legislation and adequate funding. Since submission of the Niagara Escarpment Study the government had taken little action on the task before it; no over-all goals and objectives had been established for framing a comprehensive policy; the delegation of responsibilities to one or more levels of government for formulating policies and a plan of land use had not been determined; appropriate priorities for land acquisition had not been established; and a system of effective land-use controls, appropriate to the needs of the Escarpment, had not been developed.

The government recognized that it must formulate a policy for the Escarpment that was practical and realistic, and was understandably concerned that a program hastily conceived and implemented would do more harm than good. Yet, it also was aware that early, effective action was needed if key portions of the Escarpment were not to be lost through the effects of competing development pressures.

By early 1972 mounting demands from several sources finally forced the province to act. Developers and municipal councils appealed further for a release of the "logjam" of subdivision applications being held in the offices of the Plans Administration Branch — especially from the Hamilton and Niagara areas. Continuing appeals from a concerned public and the supporting media requested an end to partial, *ad hoc* solutions in order to save the Escarpment; and they were able to point to lands designated for acquisition that had been lost or damaged through failure to act quickly enough. The influence of an aroused public, media, businessmen and local politicians taken together was such that the province found it could no longer fail to respond to the need, and must commit itself to some form of comprehensive action.

In May 1972, four years after receipt of the Gertler report, the province announced the formation of a Niagara Escarpment Task Force to undertake further study of the responses appropriate to the planning needs of the Escarpment area.[4] This study group, consisting of senior representatives from the Ministries most directly associated with escarpment-related programs, was given the following terms of reference: (1) to develop over-all priorities for the acquisition of land by the government, (2) to advise on all such proposed acquisitions, (3) to establish land-use and development standards, examine methods of land-use control, and recommend an appropriate system of controls for the Escarpment, and (4) to advise on all proposals which would produce major changes in existing patterns of land use. This government study was to usher in a period of relatively rapid progress and change.

The Task Force first embarked on a program of citizen involvement (through public meetings, interviews and briefs), to determine the public's response to Escarpment preservation needs and proposals. Although the Niagara Escarpment Study ultimately provided a major point-of-departure for their recommendations to the government, it was largely ignored in the sessions involving the general public in the affected municipalities. The Study was not utilized as a focus for public discussion as either a plan or proposal, and was played down as a potential blueprint for the future of the Escarpment. The exercise was primarily one of going to the people of the Escarpment region to listen to their concerns, opinions and wishes for the area — not to present a specific strategy for government action.

Although the terms of reference given the Task Force were quite extensive, encompassing the full range of vital issues, the study group (depending heavily upon the earlier results of the Gertler Study) was able to submit its findings and recommendations for action by the province at the end of 1972. Following six months of examination and review of the Task Force submission (as well as the Niagara Escarpment Study of 1968) the province announced its comprehensive policy for the preservation of the Niagara Escarpment in mid-1973.

A Provincial Program for Preservation

GOALS, OBJECTIVES AND GUIDELINES

In presenting its proposed program for the Escarpment the province stated as its fundamental goal: "To maintain the Niagara Escarpment as a continuous natural environment while seeking to accommodate demands compatible with that environment."[5] Although the major thrust was to be for preservation, it was not to be the sole purpose of the program, and the policies were to permit agricultural, industrial and urban uses to the extent that they were deemed compatible in any given area of the Escarpment. The government intended its "double purpose. . . policy: not only to preserve this unique area as a wilderness and recreation resource, but also to accommodate other land uses that are compatible with such preservation."[6]

Six objectives were set out which were to serve as practical, working guidelines for assessing and controlling future activity and development in the Escarpment region — whether under provincial programs or municipal and private sector initiatives. These basic objectives — guidelines for the planning program were as follows:

(1) To protect unique ecologic and historic areas
(2) To maintain and enhance the quality of natural streams and water supplies
(3) To provide adequate opportunities for outdoor recreation through the public and private sectors
(4) To maintain and enhance the open landscape character of the Escarpment by such means as compatible farming or forestry and by preserving the natural scenery
(5) To ensure that all new development is compatible with the goal for the Escarpment
(6) To provide adequate access to the Escarpment

Both the primary goal and objectives (and guidelines) were incorporated as integral parts of the legislation enacted by the government.[7]

APPROACH TO PLANNING

The Niagara Escarpment Act of 1973 was passed into law almost exactly six years after the province, with a sense of urgency, commissioned the Gertler report to determine a strategy for planning the future of the Escarpment. In the six months following the submission of the Task Force report in 1972 the government was faced with determining whether existing structures and procedures for land-use planning in Ontario were adequate to meet the requirements of the Escarpment region, or whether modified or entirely new forms and methods were needed — as concluded by Gertler and the Task Force. It seemed clear that existing systems would not be sufficient.

When the province introduced the legislation in 1973 it indicated that its planning strategy would address the unique environmental resources and vexing development issues of the Escarpment with a "new and innovative planning framework", regarding its proposed program as "a significant departure from past practices" in the province.[8] The three key features of the new approach were: (1) the establishment of a new planning region, (2) the creation of a new planning agency, and (3) the introduction of a new planning process. Three important additional elements were: (4) the implementation of a program of selective and limited land acquisition and public ownership, (5) a commitment to meaningful participation in the planning and decision-making processes by the local and regional levels of government, and (6) the assurance of adequate funding to meet the demands of the program.

1. *New Planning Region*

The region to which the new planning approaches were to apply was designated as the Niagara Escarpment Planning Area. The Gertler Study had delimited a corridor extending approximately two miles on either side of the main axis of the cuesta, encompassing all of the major features of the Escarpment and including 1,800 square miles and nearly 1.2 million acres of land. The province adjusted the limits of the region to the nearest legal and municipal boundaries and included all of the Bruce Peninsula, delimiting a planning area of approximately 2,000 square miles and 1.3 million acres (Figure 1).

2. *A New Planning Agency*

In keeping with the conclusions and recommendations of both Gertler and the Task Force, the legislation created a new organization which it entitled the Niagara Escarpment Commission. It was to be "a joint provincial-municipal body" whose primary role and responsibility was the preparation of a comprehensive, master land-use plan for the preservation and development of the Escarpment planning area. In addition it was to co-ordinate and monitor government programs relating to the region, and to serve as a "central source of public contact and reference" on issues affecting the Escarpment and facilitating the making of planning decisions on development proposals.

The province emphasized that one of the essential features of this new agency was the large measure of freedom and flexibility it would exercise in formulating its administrative and operational arrangements, and in securing for itself the best possible planning and support staff. In the latter case, it would be permitted to request the services of key personnel from within any government ministry and to hire additional staff as required.

The Commission was to be comprised of seventeen members. Approximately half that number would be appointed by the government as "provincial representatives", to be broadly representative of the people of the planning area, and the remainder would be appointed as representatives from governments at the local and regional levels.

Because it would be directing "such an important and new planning program" the Niagara Escarpment Commission was made directly responsible to a member of the Cabinet — "since the Cabinet is the final decision-making body of the Government." The new agency was not seen as forming part of a regular formal ministry structure but as a separate agency reporting to the Minister responsible for local and regional land-use planning.

It is important to note that the Commission was not regarded as a permanent feature of the province's organization structure or its ongoing planning activity. When the task of preparing a regional development plan was "substantially completed" (estimated at 1976) the government indicated its intention to transfer responsibilities carried out by the Commission to local governments.[9]

3. *A New Planning Process*

The essential departure from existing planning procedures in Ontario was the introduction of development control. It was concluded that the present system of enforcing planning policies and controlling land uses through restricted area by-laws (zoning by-laws) was unsuited to "a large, varied and environmentally sensitive area such as the Niagara Escarpment." Restricted area by-laws delimit a series of zones or land-use areas and indicate development standards for all the uses permitted in each. The standards are based on the general characteristics or physical conditions of each zone; thus a by-law, as a generalized statement, cannot possibly set out standards that could apply to every individual property if each were to be assessed in accordance with its own particular environmental attributes and context. In this approach, therefore, the important elements of flexibility and detail in evaluating development proposals are sacrificed.

Development control is a system of land-use control in which every proposal for a change in use is studied and appraised on its own merits. If a proposal is considered to be compatible with the planning policies for the area, it is accepted but made subject to special standards designed to properly implement those policies for the area. Although it was recognized that problems might arise during the initial phases of the application of development controls, the government felt that it would provide the necessary flexibility for implementing a comprehensive plan for the Niagara Escarpment Planning Area.

It was indicated that the Niagara Escarpment Commission would be responsible for administering development control, as well as for preparing the master plan for the region. The introduction of development control prior to the completion and adoption of the plan was seen as a means of avoiding the use of a "cumbersome and unwieldy" freeze of all development, and allowing proposals not in conflict with the basic goal of preservation to proceed. The adaptability of this new approach to varying conditions within the region was the primary reason for its adoption in Ontario. As soon as the legislation was passed, parts of the planning area were to be designated as subject to development control regulations; elsewhere, existing land-use controls would continue to be utilized for assessing development proposals.

The master plan was to contain development controls or guidelines for policies concerning any or all of:

— the economic, social and physical development of the area (including land and water management, population distribution and density, pollution control, the designation of major land uses, provision of parks and major servicing, transportation and communication systems)
— the financing and scheduling of public works (provincial or municipal)
— the co-ordination of provincial and local planning and development activities
— the regulation of private developments to ensure that they will be compatible with the plan

If the stated goal of Escarpment protection was to be achieved it was recognized that the provincial policies — as stated by the master plan — must be pre-eminent in the control and development of the entire planning region. Therefore, the plan, once approved, would become legally binding on all governments and take precedence over local plans. It followed that all existing plans were to be modified to bring them into conformity with the Escarpment plan, and where official plans had not been implemented by the local municipalities, their preparation and adoption could be required by the province.

In looking at the growing scarcity of recreational resources (and the rapidly accelerating demand), the government took steps to ensure that the master plan would include policies protecting good harbour areas and shorelines and public access to them. Also the province, in consultation with the Bruce Trail Association, was to determine the best route for the Trail and ensure its protection and proper use.

Provision in the master plan for the control of pits and quarries was regarded as an important element in its implementation. It was stressed that the importance of the Escarpment as a source of sand, gravel and stone for the Central Ontario Region would have to be recognized, even though it was disruptive to the natural environment and clearly "incompatible with the accepted policy of preserving the Niagara Escarpment." The government established a "Pits and Quarries Restrictive Zone" in the planning area, which immediately, and later through the master plan, would prohibit new pits or quarries. Provision was made for the possible relocation and site rehabilitation of existing operations in the zone that were found to be in serious conflict with the Escarpment goal and objectives. The master plan would also designate "Mineral

Resource Areas" in the corridor where new sites would be permitted.

A brief reference was made to agriculture, simply indicating that much of the land in the planning area was currently used for agricultural purposes and would be preserved as such.

No direct reference whatever was made to the thorny issue of urban growth and the increasing encroachment on Escarpment lands in the Niagara-Hamilton section to the south and the Grey-Bruce section of the corridor to the north.

The basic new element in the province's approach to planning the Escarpment was the introduction of development control. The three additional supporting features of the planning framework concerned land acquisition, participation in the decision-making process, and financing of the program.

4. *Land Acquisition Policy*

The province rejected a program of total acquisition of Escarpment lands, based on anticipated costs and the belief that there would be no advantage to changing many existing uses. Rather, its strategy was to be one that featured strong, provincially directed land-use regulations linked with selective public ownership of Escarpment lands. This approach would permit a variety of land ownership and compatible uses, and allow for concentration on the purchase of key areas, where certain features should be preserved most effectively by outright acquisition. Another form of acquisition, the purchase of easements, was seen as particularly applicable for properties along the Bruce Trail.

The government adopted the following priorities for land acquisitions: (1) unique ecologic and historic areas, (2) new recreation facilities (especially park lands near urban centres), and (3) the best route for the Bruce Trail. The province indicated that "a vigorous program" of land acquisition was already underway and committed itself to continuing to place a high priority on Escarpment purchases.

The land acquisition program was tied inseparably by the government to its strategy for preserving the Escarpment — stating that the program "must reinforce the realization of the master plan."

5. *Public Participation*

The province placed great emphasis on the involvement of local jurisdictions in the planning process, stating that the future of the Escarpment was of vital significance to them and that a direct, strong local contribution was essential. Repeated assurances were given that local planning functions and land-use decisions would not be pre-empted. The province indicated that it would work closely with the local governments so that the role of local municipalities in the Niagara Escarpment Commission's master plan preparation would be assured, thereby giving them "a clear advisory role . . . as full participants in the process."

A master plan as a completely "public document" and an "open system" of planning for all to contribute (municipalities, interested citizens and provincial agencies) was promised, with the legislation spelling out procedures for hearings of disputes relating to land-use proposals and for wide distribution and ready access to planning proposals, draft plans, amendments, etc.

The Niagara Escarpment Task Force had pointed out that a joint planning effort of the sort invisioned would require strong local governments as effective participants in the planning of the region. The province responded by indicating that the Niagara peninsula had already been reorganized as a regional government, that new regional governments were to be introduced shortly in the Hamilton-Wentworth, Halton and Peel areas, and that the remaining county governments covering the balance of the planning region (Dufferin, Simcoe, Grey and Bruce) would be strengthened and county planning boards and official plans introduced. At the same time, the province reiterated its intention to ultimately delegate planning powers currently assigned to the Niagara Escarpment Commission to the regions and counties — when they had acquired the requisite planning experience and staff.

6. *Financing*

In addition to the funding required for the operations of the Escarpment Commission, the province anticipated additional expenditures relating to land acquisitions, costs incurred by local governments, and the aggregate industry. Funding for Escarpment land purchases was seen as part of the existing long-term provincial acquisition program. With an estimated 20 per cent of the planning area to be acquired, full compensation was promised to the land owners affected and purchase costs projected at $250 to $500 million.

Payments to local governments were to be made in lieu of taxes on lands owned by the government, and also to offset the cost of modifying existing official plans or, where they were lacking, preparing new ones. No additional major expenses were anticipated for the municipalities of the region, nor were landowners to be subjected to any undue tax burden with the introduction of the Niagara Escarpment Commission.

Although nothing specific was stated, the province indicated that further financing would be necessary if any pits and quarries presently in the restrictive zone were required to relocate their operations to more desirable sites.

The Niagara Escarpment Commission 1973-1976

The Commission established its headquarters in 1973 in the town of Georgetown adjacent to the planning area and west of Metropolitan Toronto. Its initial task was to assemble a planning and support staff from provincial ministries and from outside the government to undertake the primary responsibility of preparing a master plan. It was clearly necessary to curb the continued loss of Escarpment lands and to ensure their preservation during the plan preparation stage; the Commission was in a position to exercise its authority to regulate development in this interim period through the use of development control procedures.

IMPLEMENTATION OF DEVELOPMENT CONTROL

Within the 2,000 square mile and 1.3 million acre Escarpment planning area a smaller section covering approximately 40 per cent of the total area was designated as a restricted, development control area (Figure 2). The environment in this more-or-less continuous belt was deemed to be especially sensitive and in particular need of protection from development. After the area for special restrictive controls and the regulations governing development therein had been defined, recommendations were forwarded to the Minister in mid-1974 with the expectation that they would be accepted and implemented promptly. It was not until mid-1975, however, that the Cabinet finally approved these measures. Among other considerations, concern had been expressed for the size of the development control area, the restrictiveness of the regulations, and the "apparent freeze" on development they represented.

As of June 1975, it became necessary to apply to the Commission for a development permit before new structures or changes in land use could be introduced in the zone. The permit preceeded existing local regulations and procedures but did not replace them, having to be obtained prior to local permits and approvals. The Commission members (appointed from the planning area), on examining each development proposal, could approve, refuse, or add subject conditions (including siting, design, exterior facing, screening, landscaping, grading, completion dates, etc.). Development control guidelines were introduced "to provide a policy framework enabling the Commission to make consistent decisions on development proposals".[10] These guidelines were regarded as being of "an interim nature" and were to be reviewed when the master plan was completed. They were accompanied by policy statements governing development along the Escarpment — in rural areas, in urban areas, on existing vacant lots, in agricultural lands, in recreation areas, on hazard lands, and elsewhere in the planning region.

Provision was made for hearings and appeals to the Minister responsible for the Niagara Escarpment Commission. During 1975 the responsibility for official plans, restrictive area by-laws, subdivision approvals, etc. was shifted from Treasury and Economics to the Ministry of Housing, with the Minister exercising this final right of approval on development within the control area. It should be noted that the Commission had been invested with no regulatory powers regarding official plans,

Fig. 2 Niagara Escarpment Planning and Development Control Areas

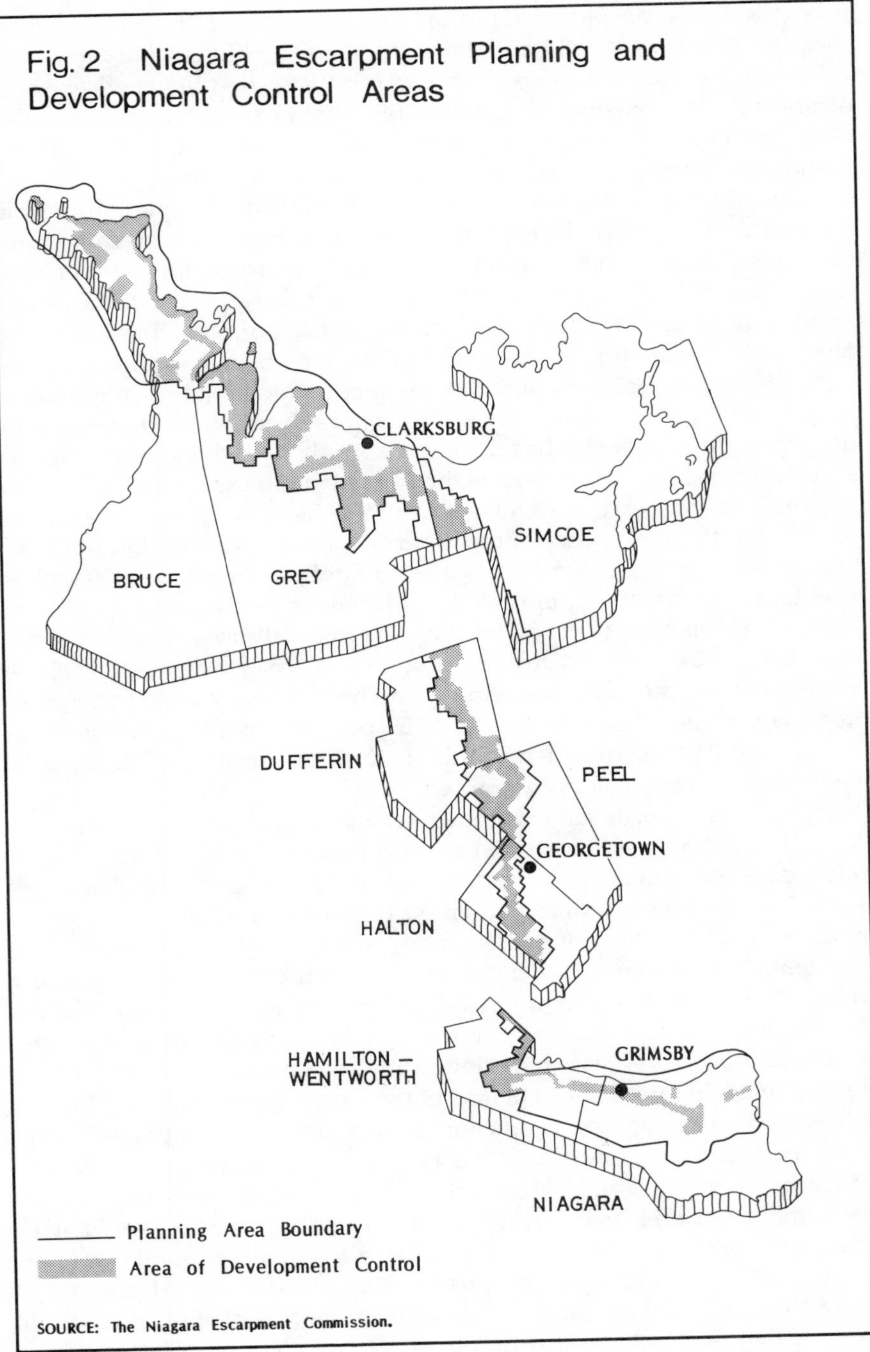

SOURCE: The Niagara Escarpment Commission.

zoning by-laws, or subdivision proposals in the planning area; its role in these matters was strictly an advisory one to the Ministry of Housing.

In addition to the Georgetown central office, two field offices were established at Grimsby and Clarksburg to better serve the public in the administration of development control in the southern and northern sections of the region respectively (Figure 2).

Development control, which really amounts to site planning, was announced by the province as an entirely new and innovative planning tool for Ontario. Although its application to a recreational resource area was a new step, these procedures had, in fact, been in use in the city of London for nearly a decade. Unfortunately their implementation in the Niagara Escarpment planning area has, to date, been less than satisfactory. The Commission declared in its policy statements its intention to refer to local official plans and zoning before deciding on development proposals. In so doing, it has tended to comply with the local provisions and requirements, using them as the context and basis for approvals. An extremely high percentage of applications have been approved and, more often than not, development permits have been granted in sensitive sections of the control area. The Commission's planning staff has generally recommended approvals and denials in a ratio of 25/75. The Commission members have, in turn, consistently reversed that ratio, increasing the approvals from 25 per cent to 75 per cent. Appeals to Minister of Housing have accounted for approximately 15 per cent additional approvals. Thus, in excess of 85 per cent of all applications for development on Escarpment lands in the area designated for special restrictive controls has been granted.

This almost unbelievable situation seems to be explained by two factors, (1) the continued parochialism and limited vision of local officials who see continued development as continued "progress", and are supported in this view by their appointed representatives on the Commission, and (2) the bias of the Ministry of Housing toward increasing residential development wherever possible in the province — including the environmentally sensitive development control area of the Niagara Escarpment. In this present context it is simply not possible for development control — as a planning technique or strategy — to save the Escarpment. In effect, the activities of the Commission and the Ministry of Housing have served to encourage and direct development rather than to inhibit and control it. It has been pointed out that the very existence of the regulations dissuaded some in the area from seeking development permits; that virtually 100 per cent approvals would have been granted by the local municipalities; and, that conditions were attached to certain approved proposals. Regardless, the performance of the Commission in its administration of development control has been regrettable. A much more rigorous and restrictive application of the

Commission's guidelines is greatly needed. Given the basic attitude of Commission members toward development (in their jurisdiction at least) and the existence of permissive local planning regulations, it appears that the government's objectives and guidelines for controlling development were too generalized to be effective.

The attitudes and actions of the Ministry of Housing have served to establish a climate within which residential development is encouraged. The Ministry has approved new subdivision proposals and continued urban expansion in the planning area — against the strong opposition of the Commission's planning staff, some Commission members, conservation authorities and other interested parties. This has done little to justify or support the government's stated commitment to preserving the Escarpment. Urban development proposals on Escarpment lands in the Collingwood, Thornbury, Hamilton and St. Catharines areas have all received the support of the Ministry. Decisions were made following regular planning and approval procedures and on an *ad hoc* basis, without adequate reference to the development guidelines governing the Escarpment area. In the case of the Collingwood area (Castle Glen and Craigleith-Camperdown developments), approvals have been in opposition to government statements of recent years regarding the directing of future growth to existing urban centres along the Georgian Bay shoreline and preserving Escarpment lands from such massive urban-recreational developments. Members of the Commission representing the area and local municipal officials have tended to support the Ministry's position.

The Commission, whose own record in administering development control is not good, finds itself in an operative dilemma regarding official plans and subdivision proposals such as those above. It has advisory powers only and until the completion and adoption of a master plan with suitable restrictive measures to protect the Escarpment it has no means of preventing such developments from occurring — assuming it wished to do so.

MASTER PLAN PREPARATION

The Commission was given until 1976 to complete (or to have almost completed) the comprehensive master plan for the planning area. As the planning staff began its work it became evident that the government had assumed that there was a substantial body of basic data available on the region. In fact, there was almost nothing comprehensive on any aspect of land use; even the data of provincial ministries and agencies were incomplete. It was necessary therefore for the Commission to undertake the time-consuming assembly of this fundamental information.

Certain aspects of the plan were spun off to the Ministry of Natural Resources (segments relating to fisheries, wildlife, parks and recreation, conservation authorities, hazard lands, etc.). The Ministry working in co-ordination with, and more or less under the supervision of the Commission, supplied the staff and organization to produce this portion of the plan.

For its part, the Commission planning staff had been under constant pressure since its inception to adopt local standards and priorities for its master plan. The transfer of the basic elements of existing official plans and zoning by-laws into the master plan would mean that it conceivably could be superceded by local plans, in at least some sections of the Escarpment. The Commission members generally acted in support of such an approach. In the Niagara Region the master plan of the Escarpment Commission was seen as an intrusion on their own official plan. The regional government does not want to be limited by provisions in the master plan (which according to the legislation was to provide guidelines for Niagara). In the other regional municipalities, less advanced in their official plan preparations, a greater measure of coordination and agreement was achieved.

A pro-development perspective has been dominant (as evidenced by the indiscriminate issuance of development permits) during the first three and a half years of the Commission's activity. On the positive side, extensive discussions of proposed master plan policies were an important factor in gradually convincing more members that the Escarpment needed to be protected immediately from scattered non-rural development — and in their municipality, as well as elsewhere. Whether basic attitudes were changed substantially will be reflected, of course, in the provisions and requirements of the master plan to be unveiled late in 1976.

In support of proposed policy statements the planning staff prepared background reports covering various aspects of the plan. These reports ultimately will serve to provide information for the Commission and general public, to generate responses to proposed policies, and to substantiate and elaborate on plan components.

The Act provides for the creation of two advisory committees, appointed by the Minister, to review and comment on the draft plan; one representing municipal interests and one citizens' interest groups. It is presently anticipated that four alternative plans will emerge from this process: (1) the intial draft prepared by the planning staff, (2) two amended draft plans, one each from the advisory committees, and (3) a modified, combined plan merging components of all three. The four alternative plans will then be reviewed by the general public and others and a final plan prepared for approval by the government.

In designating the final route of the Bruce Trail as part of the master plan, the Commission worked closely with the Bruce Trail Association and the Ministry of Natural Resources to determine where the trail should go, how it could be so aligned and what costs would be incurred. By mid-1976 the recommended route had been examined, major conflicts resolved, and a program of land assembly prepared.

The Commission has indicated that agricultural activities will be given a high priority in the master plan, with assurances that good agricultural land will be effectively preserved. However, there seems little doubt that the plan will be ineffectual in preserving the Niagara Fruit Belt, unless the Cabinet intervenes to compel the Regional Municipality of Niagara to control urban expansion in that area.

In looking at the master plan in relation to restrictions on pits and quarries, it seems that the aggregate industry has not been unduly inconvenienced by the Pits and Quarries Control Act of 1973. While the Act essentially placed a freeze on further development, it only applied to new pits and it has been estimated that existing operations had so much land under licence in 1973 that there is really no need (in terms of supply and demand) to begin any new operations. The master plan will no doubt reflect that fact, although it would be possible for the plan to call for the relocation of certain pits.

Regardless of its ultimate value as a statement of practical planning policy for the Escarpment, the master plan in its draft form will undoubtedly serve as a focal point for a great deal of much needed public discussion and debate on the future of the Escarpment. Unless the Escarpment Commission members and the Ministry of Housing are prepared to improve their performance to this point, with the active support of the Cabinet, the adoption of a master plan that will effectively preserve the Niagara Escarpment simply may not occur. The issue is not just one of providing a master plan containing adequate planning policies and regulations; successful preservation also depends very much on the way in which they are perceived and implemented — as demonstrated thus far in the planning area.

LAND ACQUISITION ACTIVITY

The land acquisition program in the Escarpment area suffered from general government cutbacks in spending; there were almost no funds for land purchases as of the end of 1975. In the period 1973-75 approximately 12,500 acres had been assembled by the Ministry of Natural Resources and the area conservation authorities. For the most part they represented the honouring of commitments and the acquisition program in effect prior to the creation of the Niagara Escarpment Commission in 1973. It appeared that lands often were acquired during that period with no clear understanding of the reasons for doing so or for what intended use. By early 1976 total acquisitions (i.e. including pre-1973 purchases) amounted to approximately 72,000 acres — very far from the 20 per cent of 1.3 million acres the province said it intends to acquire.

The Commission has an advisory function only and may not purchase or hold title to any lands in the planning area. In 1974 the staff reviewed the Ministry of Natural Resources' acquisition program and accepted their schedule, with provision made for the Commission to comment on future purchases. Having no plan to indicate acquisition priorities, the Commission could only refer to the general objectives and guidelines established in 1973 by the province. In effect, the Commission was not much involved with land acquisition. Its major input will come through the master plan. When approved, the plan will likely lead to major changes in the Ministry's acquisition priorities and schedule.

The purchase of easements which Gertler saw as a means to substantially lower expenditures has been quite limited and related only to the route of the Bruce Trail. Although this approach may be used more widely in the future, the over-all costs and advantages secured vary little from those of outright purchases.

The entire approach to land acquisition for the preservation of the Escarpment needs re-evaluation and revision. In particular, the on-again/off-again method of attempting to preserve unique and sensitive areas of the Escarpment must be replaced by a guarantee of long-term funding that can be tied to the planning needs and priorities set out in the master plan.

The Niagara Escarpment Commission's primary responsibility and concern was the completion of its master plan for the area. The content and emphasis of the initial draft plan, subsequent changes proposed by the members and their reaction to the public's response would reveal much about their awareness of the issues relating to preservation, their grasp of regional planning principles and practice, and their commitment to doing something effective for the Niagara Region.

Issues and Prospects

The Ontario experience to date in the Niagara Escarpment presents an interesting and timely case study of the issues and forces encountered in planning for the multi-purpose development of a large-scale recreational resource. Although the picture is incomplete and the process in mid-stride, much can doubtless be learned from what has transpired to this point.

The response of the provincial government to a demonstrated and urgent need, ultimately affecting all of the people of Ontario, is disappointing. Its reluctance to act in a quick and forthright manner to the recommendations of the Gertler Study and the early implementation of development control can hardly be excused. When it did choose to act, the legislation (in following most of Gertler's recommendations) was, generally speaking, adequate — particularly its introduction of development control.

The Niagara Escarpment Commission, unfortunately, has failed thus far to act responsibly in its administration of the development control provisions for preserving Escarpment lands. Development control can be made to work and is a decided improvement over previous planning procedures. However, the proper utilization of the technique or tool obviously can be avoided where there is no genuine desire to apply it effectively. Unless there is a substantial adjustment in the Commission's attitudes and approach and the presentation of a master plan that is truly adequate for the needs of the region, the Commission will serve simply as a "window-dressing" agency to oversee the gradual wasting and destruction of a unique and irreplaceable environmental resource.

Time is a major factor. If the Commission members and other municipal officials "become sufficiently educated" to the practical planning needs of the area (e.g. through their involvement in determining plan policies and regulations), it is conceivable that the Commission, with adequate support, could become an effective force for preservation. The question is, will this happen soon enough to save the Escarpment?

The role of the province and its related ministries will be critical. There is a very real need for a reaffirmation of the commitment to preserve the Escarpment given almost a decade ago by Premier John Robarts; in part to offset the continued erosion of confidence and conviction within the region, the Niagara Escarpment Commission, and its own ministries and agencies. In addition to its continuing ambivalent attitudes and responses to the need for sufficiently restrictive controls (especially to save sensitive sections of the planning area), the government seems to have studiously avoided taking a leadership role in the region when nothing less was called for.

The province has overestimated the local municipalities' understanding of the issues and their interest in preserving the Escarpment. Many of the rural municipalities have little or no experience of land-use planning, are not very sympathetic toward regulations that limit individual choices, and regard continued growth and development as a desirable goal. In that context the ready acceptance and support of regulatory measures such as development control is highly unlikely, and the Commission's "quid pro quo" approach to development decisions is quite understandable. To go further and suggest, as the province has, that the functions of the Escarpment Commission be turned over to the local municipalities after adoption of the master plan seems irresponsible.

The dilemma is one of requiring sufficient time to educate, convince and co-opt local municipalities in a program of effective preservation on the one hand, and the increasingly limited time available to successfully stave off the continued loss of Escarpment lands on the other. The solution to the dilemma rests squarely with the province. The necessary initiative, persuasion and positive direction must come, in large part, from outside the region.

NOTES

1. Leonard O. Gertler (Co-ordinator), *The Niagara Escarpment Study: Conservation and Recreation Report*, Toronto, Regional Development Branch, Department of Treasury and Economics, 1968.
2. Leonard O. Gertler, *Regional Planning in Canada: A Planner's Testament*, Montreal, Harvest House, 1972, p. 138.
3. *Special Policy Areas I and II,* (Policy Statement), Toronto, Plans Administration Branch, Ministry of Treasury, Economics and Intergovernmental Affairs, 1972.
4. *To Save the Escarpment: Report of the Niagara Escarpment Task Force*, Toronto, Ministry of Treasury, Economics and Intergovernmental Affairs, 1972.
5. *Development Planning in Ontario: The Niagara Escarpment*, Toronto, Ministry of Treasury, Economics and Intergovernmental Affairs, 1973, p. 6.
6. *Ibid.* p. 33.
7. *Bill 129 – An Act to Provide for Planning and Development of the Niagara Escarpment and Its Vicinity*, Toronto, The Government of Ontario, The Queen's Printer, 1973.
8. *Op. cit. Development Planning in Ontario: The Niagara Escarpment*, p. 10.
9. *Ibid.* p. 13.
10. *Guidelines for Development Control*, Georgetown, The Niagara Escarpment Commission, 1975, p. 2.

13
Canadian National Parks and Related Reserves: Research Needs and Management

*J.G. Nelson**

Introduction

In this review paper the basic aim is to highlight topics and problems where more research would improve management of Canadian national parks and related reserves. The review is largely based on personal experience and study in western Canada, Ontario, the United States, United Kingdom, Central America, New Zealand, and Australia. The relevant literature is vast, often unpublished, and not completely known to me.

A problem in undertaking such a review is how to organize it. What seems to be required is an approach or framework which is interesting and useful to concerned academics, consultants, administrators and citizens of diverse education and background. The framework should provide for as much understanding and interaction among these people as possible.

My own approach to national parks and other land use is basically historical and ecological. It can succinctly be described as studies in land-use history and landscape change. Emphasis is placed on the role and effects of man, especially Caucasian man, and on the relevance of the research results to management.

The terms environment, ecosystem, and landscape frequently arise in such work. Their meanings overlap and they are often used in a confusing manner. In this paper the term *environment* is used only rarely and then in a very broad sociological sense to refer to many things in the world around us: family, nation, noise, parking lots, advertising, sand dunes, eagles, and art.

---

*Dean, Faculty of Environmental Studies, University of Waterloo. This is an edited version of a paper in *Canadian Public Land Use in Perspective,* ed. by J.G. Nelson *et al.*, Proceedings of a Symposium sponsored by the Social Science Research Council of Canada, Ottawa, 1973, pp. 348-379.

Ecosystem is a biological concept which can be defined as the elements and processes interacting with and supporting an organism or organisms in space and time. It refers to the elements and processes that give life to a place over time. It traditionally has involved energy flow and the cycling of phosphorous, nitrogen, and other chemicals through soils, rocks, water, air, plants, and animals. Recently, as biologists have become more sensitive to human effects, they have increasingly applied the concept of ecosystem, and the theory and method of the science of ecology, to mining, lumbering, and other processes associated with man.

Landscape is basically a geographical and architectural concept. The term refers to the assemblage of plants, animals, land-use patterns, and other elements and processes at work at or near the earth's surface at some point in time. Landscape is a manifestation of the ecosystem at a particular time and place. Landscape stresses morphology or structure, mappable forms, and the cultural and biophysical processes accounting for their character and distribution. The concept of landscape is important as it provides evidence of the ecosystem and can serve as a basis for management in national parks and other types of land use.

The Model

A major need in dealing with ecosystems, landscapes, and land use is an organizational framework which will bring order to the maze of possibly relevant theories, methods, and terminology derived from ultimately artificial disciplines such as archaeology, history, geography, economics, botany, and zoology. The model should be broad and integrative, useful to administrators, academics and others. It should be flexible and capable of use at different levels of generalization. One model that seems to meet these requirements consists of four basic parts: ecology; strategies and institutional arrangements; perceptions, attitudes and values; and technology.

ECOLOGY

The concept of ecology is fundamental to the model and focuses attention on the identification of the elements and processes in the system, and the interrelations among them, especially as these pertain to man. The term *ecology* is used in both the physical and cultural sense. It recognizes the potential importance to land use of elements such as plant and animal species, their population and distribution, volcanoes and other landforms, podzols and other soil types, as well as villages, roads, dams, and other human constructs. Ecology comprehends processes such as plant succession, fluctuations or "cycles" in animal populations, wildlife migrations, stream erosion, and eutrophication of lakes. Many of these processes are affected by so-called *physical* and *cultural* agencies. Fire, a physical process, can be caused or influenced by lightning or weather, or by human attempts to hunt, camp, or operate railroad engines. Cultivation of soil was carried out by prairie dogs, bison, and other animals in the pre-Caucasian northern plains, but not to the same extent and degree as later by the "white man" and the plough.

The term *ecology* thus leads in a conscious way to the problem of distinguishing landscape changes independent of man from those dependent on him. The identification of these types of change is no easy task and has become more difficult as man and the various biophysical *agencies* have interacted with *processes* such as fire, flooding, erosion, and earthquakes to affect vegetation, wildlife, landforms, and other interrelated elements of landscape and ecosystem.

This brings us to the verge of the classical question of whether man is a natural or cultural agency. This problem cannot be discussed at length here. It is relevant, however, to national park management, as will be seen later. My own present position is that the term *natural* is confusing and not particularly helpful. Man seems to me to be basically no different from other life in that he is ultimately dependent on air, water and other vital elements, which even the most sophisticated technology must transform from some ultimate biophysical state. Man also has been a part of the ecosystem for tens of thousands of years. He has evolved and changed like other animals and in that sense seems as natural as they are. Having made these comments, it seems that particular concern about man arises when his effects begin to dominate the system, when vegetation, wildlife, and other inter-connected elements and processes begin to become substantially dependent on energy controlled by man and his elaborating technology rather than on sources independent of him.

MAN AS ECOLOGICAL AGENT

The foregoing discussion makes it clear that, in the model used in this paper, man is considered as an ecological agent, an adapter to and a modifier of the ecosystem. However, in order more fully to understand how man adjusts to and changes the world, we must identify and characterize his activities more precisely, in this case in terms of strategies and institutional arrangements; perceptions, attitudes and values; and technology. These categories seem comprehensive, but the distinctions among them are not always clear-cut and can be arbitrary.

STRATEGIES AND INSTITUTIONAL ARRANGEMENTS

Briefly, *strategies* refer to human goals and broad means of achieving them. In the very general sense these goals can be thought of as relating to livelihood (economic), other men (social) and the world, universe or larger environment in which we live (supernatural, religious, scientific). For example, economically we would be interested in knowing whether a group under study was subsistence or commercial in orientation, for the production of a surplus for external markets can lead to much landscape change. Similarly, socially we would be interested in knowing whether a group was basically communal or capitalistic, war-like and aggrandizing, or otherwise, as these traits can have an impact on the system. From the standpoint of the larger environment, we would be interested, among other things, in whether the group was animistic, monotheistic, or teleological in orientation. Christianity, with its emphasis on the idea that the earth was created for the use of man, has been identified, rather inadequately in the light of other contributing factors, as the basic cause of resource and environmental problems in areas such as North America.[1]

The term *institutional arrangements* refers to forms of government, agencies, civil and criminal laws, legislation, and other means of influencing human behaviour and land use. The term includes what have been referred to as "social guides": rules and regulations, penalties and other enforcement, performance standards, subsidies, taxes, and other means of inhibiting or encouraging change.

Also to be recognized as institutional arrangements are social phenomena which often have an indirect and unappreciated effect on land use and landscape. An example is the neutral ground or buffer zone separating native peoples in parts of western North America in pre- and early Caucasian times. Wildlife reportedly was more plentiful in these zones than in a group's home territory where danger of attack was less, and hunting more frequently carried out.[2]

PERCEPTIONS, ATTITUDES AND VALUES

Geographers, anthropologists, and other social scientists have long recognized the influence of man's cast of mind on land use and landscape. Different individuals and groups demonstrably have appraised resources differently in similar ecosystems. Compare the sophisticated civilization of Egypt and the Nile with the corn growers and collectors of the lower Colorado Valley in pre-Caucasian times. In the 1950s this cultural appraisals approach elaborated into studies of individual and group perceptions and attitudes, notably with regard to floods and other hazards to human settlement and economy. Interviews, questionnaires, and other methods were employed to study professional and public perceptions of and attitudes towards levees and other common adjustments to floods.[3] The results were linked with increasing use of floodplains, at even higher cost to the citizen. One consequence of this research has been a broadening of the range of flood adjustments; for example, more emphasis is now placed on zoning, land-use regulations, and other non-engineering techniques.

There are obvious problems in defining and working with the terms *perceptions* and *attitudes*. The word *perception* has often been used to refer to an individual or group's sensory and cognitive impression of a situation. The term comprehends what one "sees", "feels" and is aware of. *Attitudes* are generally seen as being stronger reactions. They are preferences and opinions, based on perceptual or other differences among people. Attitudes may be habitual and overt, quickly and subconsciously acted upon. They also may be rationalizations of an action after it has occurred.

Values are fundamental beliefs and guides to human behaviour, strong influences on the perceptions and attitudes we exhibit toward land use, landscape, or ecosystem. For example, some people basically value growth in income and technology and use such changes as measures of social progress. Others value trees, wildlife, and the rural scene and would oppose growth when it affected these things fundamentally. Obviously any comprehensive approach to land-use problems, national park or otherwise, must involve consideration of such important human influences on decision making.

TECHNOLOGY

This term is often defined as the organized use of knowledge for practical purposes. It is, however, an imprecise term whose usage in the broad sense encompasses much of what we call culture. Various kinds of mechanical and other tools are clearly involved in technology. Some would also extend its meaning to include programs and arrangements necessary for operating machines such as the computer (software). Some of the latter group would also extend the meaning to encompass an entire cultural orientation.

Most technical changes can be classified as mechanical, biological, or chemical, or a combination thereof. In the national parks the outstanding machine in terms of ecosystem effects probably has been the automobile. Exotic plants and animals have been used as tools to "improve" scenery and fishing. Herbicides and other chemicals have also been employed to modify the landscape.

Let us now turn to a brief review of the state of knowledge of Canadian national parks and related public reserves in terms of the four part model: ecology; strategies and institutional arrangements; perceptions, attitudes and values; and technology.

Ecology

The Canadian national park system consists of two basic elements: national and historic parks.[4] The national parks are of greatest interest here. Historic parks are more numerous, but remain little studied. National parks typically are large, often exceeding 1,000 square miles in area, although some such as Pelee, on Lake Erie, and Elk Island, near Edmonton, encompass less than 100 square miles. In contrast, Wood Buffalo National Park, northern Alberta, exceeds 17,000 square miles.

About twenty-nine national parks are located throughout Canada, notably in the west and the Maritimes. Approximately one per cent of the country's land area is in national parks and perhaps five per cent is devoted to both national and provincial parks.

Ontario and Quebec are conspicuous for their small national park area, especially in light of their relatively large populations. Some large provincial parks are found in these provinces but few are managed along "wilderness" lines and they generally are located many miles from cities. Polar Bear Provincial Park, on James Bay, is isolated and wild and has been classed by the Ontario government as a primitive (wilderness) park. Quetico, west of Lake Superior, has recently been classified as primitive, and controls on lumbering, snowmobiling, and other extractive or technical activities introduced. Laurentides Provincial Park, north of Quebec City, appears to have largely escaped industrial effects but is now proposed as the site of a dam and hydro-electric facility. Only four national parks, Wood Buffalo, Kluane, Nahanni, and Baffin Island, are located in the north, where territorial and provincial parks are rare as well. Furthermore, the last three of these exist only on a provisional basis until the native land claims are settled with the Canadian government. A small number of national and provincial parks have been established along the Pacific, Atlantic and Great Lakes coasts.

Large national and provincial parks were created in Canada in two major periods; approximately 1885-1930 and 1955-1973. Less than half the national parks were set up in the first period, chiefly in the west, where the federal government controlled large blocks of public land following confederation in 1867. In contrast, in the east, in 1867, settlement had been underway for decades and most public land disposed of to induce settlement and pay government expenses. However, some large blocks remained in provincial hands late in the nineteenth century, and part was set aside as parkland, notably Algonquin Provincial Park in 1893.

The national and provincial parks created in this first period have since been under heavy pressure for lumbering, mining, power, and other uses. As a result many boundary changes have been made and some parks eliminated.

The second period of park development came after World War II, when rising mobility, incomes, leisure, and other influences all combined to accelerate recreation demand. This pressure resulted in new federal and provincial initiatives. For example, in Ontario in 1955, about twenty parks were in operation. By 1973 the number had increased to about 120. Approximately ten new national parks were identified by the federal government in co-operation with the provinces in the early 1970s. These are chiefly located in the Maritimes and the north where only Wood Buffalo existed prior to 1971. Pukaskwa has been set aside on the north shore of Lake Superior, as well as La Maurcie and Forillon, the first national parks in Quebec. Some of these parks, however, are still subject to negotiation. A major problem often is substantial opposition by residents and interest groups within and around the proposed park area.

Large national and provincial parks of wilderness type are unevenly distributed with respect to population, as well as landscapes and ecosystems (Figure 1). Studies are needed to determine the relative levels of access that citizens in different parts of the country have to forests, highlands, and coasts in public reserves.

A number of landscapes and ecosystems are not included in the large national and provincial parks. Notable gaps exist in the short and mixed grass areas of Saskatchewan and Alberta, the Cypress Hills, the Alberta foothills, the dry southern valleys of British Columbia, the Mackenzie River Valley, the Barren Grounds of the Northwest Territories and the taiga forests of Quebec and Ontario.

Some potential parks are known to have been under consideration for years. One is Val Marie about 100 miles south of Regina. This park would include extensive areas of short grass, rolling glaciated terrain, and rare animals such as the prairie dog. This burrowing rodent appears to have been relatively numerous in the south-western Canadian plains until the introduction of livestock, cultivation, and "pest" control programs. Another potential national park is the forest and lake country of the Bloodvein area, Manitoba and western Ontario. The establishment of such potential parks apparently has been slowed and perhaps blocked by opposition from mineral, agricultural, and other interests.

Surveys have recently been carried out by agencies such as the Canadian Wildlife Service on potential sites for national parks in the north, including the Arctic archipelago: some twenty-nine sites reportedly

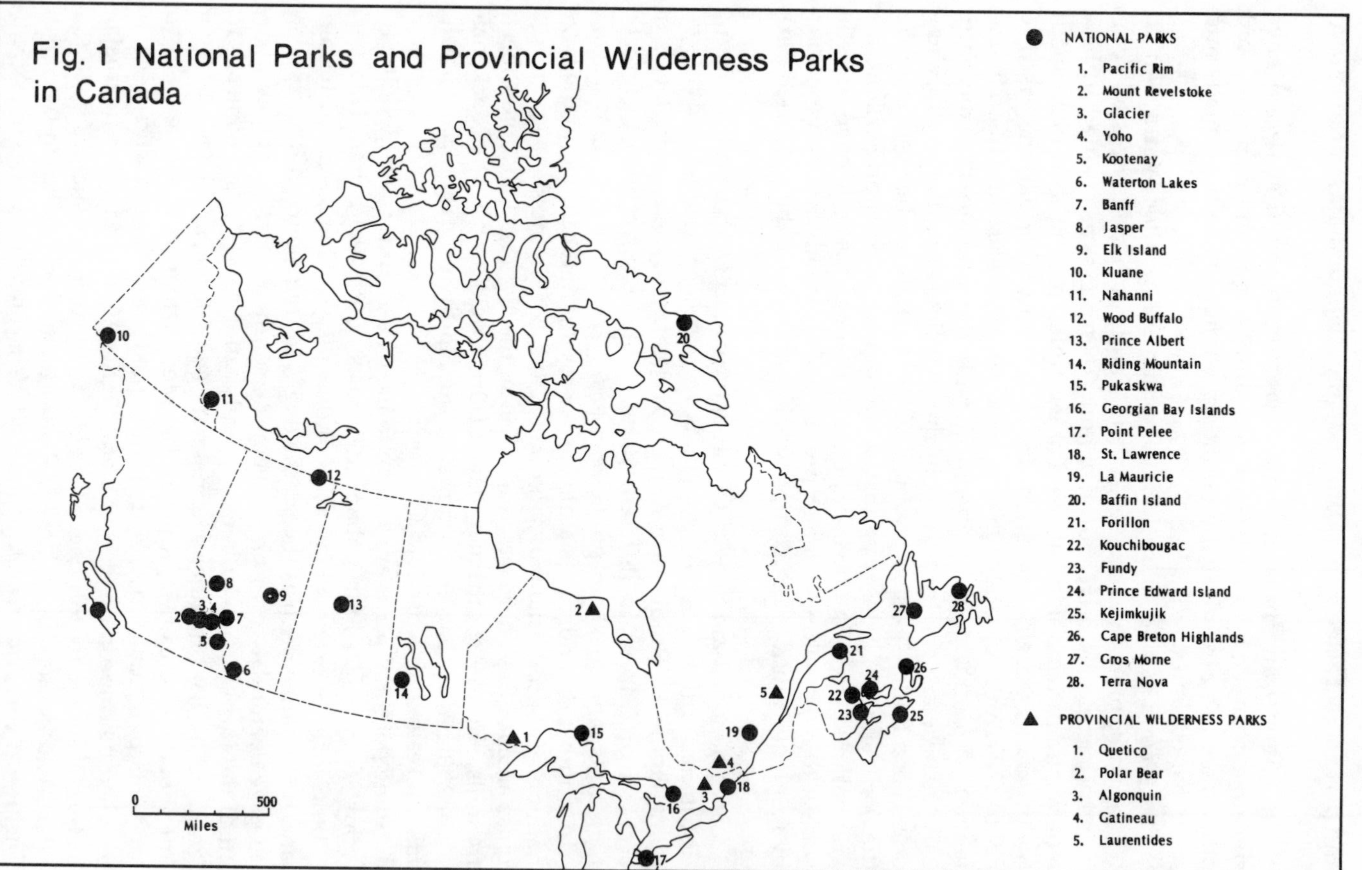

Fig. 1 National Parks and Provincial Wilderness Parks in Canada

were identified in one report. Discussions have been underway for some time about a possible Gulf Island Marine Park in the coastal waters of southern British Columbia. The status of this proposal is vague and possibly has been affected by conflicts with fishing and shipping, including potential effects of oil spills from tankers destined to move Alaska oil to Cherry Point, Washington.

Ecological knowledge of existing and potential national and provincial parks is uneven and inadequate. Older national parks such as Banff, Jasper, and Waterton have long attracted geologists, glaciologists, biologists and, more recently, geographers, sociologists, and other scholars. Much published scientific information is therefore available on these parks, but not always in a form appropriate for management. Important work has been done on the character and behaviour of animals such as mountain sheep and grizzly. This has been used to predict the effects of proposed road construction and other proposals on animals. Yet much remains to be learned about the park fauna, especially the smaller animals upon which the existence of large mammals depends. The vegetation of parks such as Banff and Jasper is still not well understood, although these parks have been in existence for decades. Preliminary forest maps were prepared for Banff in the 1950s. But detailed vegetation mapping in the Bow Valley has been undertaken only recently, by consultants involved in environmental impact studies relating to the proposed twinning of the Trans-Canada Highway. The potential use of such studies to managers is prejudiced by the fact that they appear to have been undertaken after a decision had been made to proceed with a major land-use change; the outstanding questions presumably concern its character and location, not whether the project should in fact go forward. Recently, detailed vegetation studies have been undertaken for Waterton, but nothing appears to be on the immediate horizon for Jasper, Kootenay or Glacier. On the other hand, the National and Historic Parks Branch now has a resources inventory group and is organizing wide-ranging studies of vegetation, landforms, soils, and other landscape elements for use in park planning and interpretation. Relevant studies have also been sponsored on limestone caverns in Banff, Glacier, and other parks. Questions remain, however, about the classifications, the methods, and the scope of this inventory work. Ideally such research should yield a high level of understanding of processes and rates of change so that predictions can be made about the effects of a road or an influx of visitors on plant species, erosion, and other aspects of the ecosystem.

Other relevant elements or processes remain unstudied. A notable example is flooding and associated erosion and deposition. This has caused long-standing problems in parks such as Pelee where many attempts have been made to control wave erosion along the approximately six by one mile peninsula. The history of these attempts and their effects is not well known and remains unevaluated in terms of possibly better flood and erosion control alternatives. Similar remarks could be made about attempts to control stream flooding and erosion in Banff and Waterton, chiefly using engineering methods.

In some parks much inventory data are available to managers, but not enough is known about dynamics. An example is the information on birds of the Pacific Rim National Park area, Vancouver Island. Biologists have conducted bird studies along this coast for years. Much is known about the species that occur and their migration and behaviour patterns. But more knowledge of their ecology is required if the populations of oystercatchers, wandering tattler, tufted puffin, ruddy turnstone, and other birds are to be maintained as recreation pressure increases in this new park. What types of disturbances cause such birds to decline? Can these disturbances be managed effectively? Such questions require detailed studies, including *monitoring*. Inventories should be carried out as soon as possible before or after the establishment of a park, and species with potentially high sensitivity to disturbance quickly identified in terms of numbers and distribution. Observation or monitoring of these populations should also begin quickly so as to measure the effects of recreational and other use and lay the basis for effective management by zoning or other means. Such research can be costly. But early expenditures here might be more useful than investment in rapid and extensive development of roads and other facilities which could attract users in numbers sufficient to cause unwanted and unforeseen deterioration in the features which prompted park establishment originally.

Plants, animals, and other elements and processes of park landscapes are related to past as well as recent conditions. Wildlife species composition and distribution may be changing now as a result of ecosystem changes which began decades or centuries ago, perhaps as a result of the invasion of the Caucasian and his commercial and technical system. Plants and animals now in the park may not have been there some years ago. Animals present earlier also may have become extinct, with uncertain effects on plants or other landscape elements grazed or used by them. In order to identify and understand such changes, and be in a position to make decisions on them, *historical ecological studies* are necessary. Such studies involve tracing changes in human use of an area and its effects on the ecosystem. These studies require some knowledge and expertise in all four parts of the model used in this paper.

In thinking about the value of ecological research it is important to recognize that the results can only *contribute* to a decision, which also will be influenced by other factors, notably the perceptions, attitudes, and values of interested individuals and groups.

Strategies and Institutional Arrangements

As a result of the dearth of historical studies, little is known about the strategies involved in the Canadian national park system. One preliminary study[5] has suggested that the strategies can be thought of as having basically three aims:

1. Architects and planners have aimed to meet the anticipated recreational needs of the people.
2. Business and government have aimed at generating income from Banff and other parks.
3. Some administrators and citizens have been concerned with the preservation and protection of nature or wilderness.

However, existing studies indicate that relatively little research has been done on any of the three aims listed above. Policies aiming at the protection of nature do not seem to have played a prominent part in national park or other land-use management in Canada until the twentieth century. Ontario introduced far-sighted legislation for Algonquin which stipulated the park would be a plant and animal refuge as well as a place for educational, scientific, and health purposes. But, from a very early stage Algonquin seems to have been managed on multiple use grounds, with preservationist thinking giving way increasingly to the pragmatic and the utilitarian. The reverse appears to have occurred with respect to Banff and other national parks. At first Banff National Park was a maze of lumbering, mining, hunting, and other activities. But fire control and other protective practices were shortly introduced. J.B. Harkin began to emphasize the scientific, aesthetic, and spiritual values of the "wild" about 1911, when appointed first Commissioner of Dominion Parks. He developed a strategy for park development which combined an interest in nature and wilderness protection with the development of facilities for tourism and income.

This combined policy of protection and development, which was enshrined in the National Parks Act of 1930, has caused much conflict and disagreement. But it has an interesting ring in relation to the Stockholm Conference of June 1972, with its call for a combination of *Conservation and Development* in resource management throughout the world. Harkin and his colleagues supported strong fire control policies and practices, as well as wildlife protection programs, except for predators and "noxious animals" such as wolves, cougars, and coyotes. His administration also worked for the removal of much of the hunting, trapping, mining, and other extractive activities which had substantially affected wildlife and landscape in Banff and other parks by 1911. Private uses and "rights" in the park were diminished considerably in the years up to World War II. Other moves were made to protect wildlife and "nature". For example, between about 1910 and 1920, three national parks were established in the Alberta grasslands to protect declining antelope population. Later, in part because of an increase in antelope numbers, these parks were eliminated.

Very little has been published on the history of national park institutional arrangements. Originally a separate act was passed for each new "Dominion Park". But comprehensive legislation has been proclaimed and amended on a number of occasions since 1911. The relationship between these legislative changes and changes in policy, practice, and political, social, and other influences on the system remains unknown.

Almost all land in Canadian national parks is publicly owned and has been leased to residents and businessmen in a variety of ways since the 1880s. The leasing system has had a fundamental influence on the character of the national park system. Yet it remains unstudied, except for unpublished consultants' reports on government in the parks, and Scace's work on the development of Banff townsite.[6] Scace's study shows that the leasing system has evolved in such a way as to promote an array of businesses and structures whose growth and distribution are difficult to control, as indeed, are their effects on landscape. A basic change in the system, in order, apparently, to provide for more government land-use planning, and reduce profiteering when leased lots and associated buildings and improvements were transferred, or "sold", was taken to the Supreme Court of Canada by some park residents during the late 1960s, and disallowed. More government success appears to have been achieved in Ontario, where cottagers in provincial parks such as Rondeau, on Lake Erie, have been informed that their leases will be renewed for one more term, whereupon their buildings and improvements will be subject to purchase and/or removal in order to provide for greater public access to beaches and other park resources. Comparative studies of leasing and licensing systems in different parts of Canda, as well as the United States and other parts of the world, would be instructive.

Park zoning systems also deserve study. The Canadian system is a modification of an American model and divides parks into special ecological and cultural, wilderness recreation, natural environment, recreation, and intensive use zones. The descriptions of permissible land use in these zones are very general and vague, and could be improved, especially with regard to controlling the effects of large numbers of visitors and recreation technology. (An improved system has recently been prepared by the Ontario Parks Branch.) A variety of techniques is gradually coming into use to ameliorate such effects, among them the setting of visitor limits, prohibitions against use of non-burnable materials in the back-country, and rotation of trails and campgrounds. Alternative zoning systems, specifically incorporating such techniques, deserve study, as do new park classification systems which more clearly distinguish among park uses and so reduce conflict among them. Various types of recreation are increasingly incompatible with one another and should be spatially or temporally zoned. Scientific work often involves changes in landscape not wanted by other users and so is not desirable in all types or parts of parks.

The public hearings themselves are a prime subject for study. They appear to have developed, like so many other aspects of Canadian land-use policy and practice, from precedents in the United States, specifically the management and planning changes made in that country in the 1950s and early 1960s. The first Canadian hearings were held for Kejimkujik and other Maritime parks, and eventually culminated in hearings for the four Rocky Mountain Parks, Banff, Jasper, Yoho and Kootenay, and for the proposed Village Lake Louise, a project involving hotel and motel construction to accommodate about 10,000 people, largely tourists. The submissions and the records for these hearings are available, as are some park documents relating to decisions made following the hearings. The original purposes, effects, and current status of public hearings, as well as the master planning program, constitute an important research area. This research is relevant to current questions about methods and effects of public participation in decision making.

Methods of assessing the value of national parks and related reserves also deserve the attention of social scientists. Benefit-cost techniques have been applied to many American and overseas reserves. There are problems in applying these techniques to psychological, social, health, and other so-called intangible values. Research aimed at the improvement of techniques is desirable. Few benefit-cost studies seem to have been undertaken on Canadian national parks, although one has been completed for Gros Morne, Newfoundland. This document is restricted to use by park and government officials, a handicap to those interested in more fully understanding the advantages and disadvantages of parks and other types of land use.

Another priority research area is the use of easements and other means of providing public access to private land. The purchase of rights to recreation and other public uses, without having to bear the higher expense of outright purchase, seems attractive at this time of rapidly rising land costs. Easements appear to have been reasonably successful in New Brunswick, but reportedly have encountered problems in Wisconsin. Few detailed studies of easement advantages and disadvantages appear to have been completed in areas where they have been used for some time. Useful case studies could be carried out in areas such as Nez Perce National Park, Idaho, where easements apparently have been combined with public land ownership to create an unusual national park, at least from the North American standpoint. Studies of experience in Britain — where easements and land-use regulations are the basis for the operation of national parks on private land — would be a valuable guide.

An important factor in park management is the relationships between the municipalities, the provinces, and the federal government. One mechanism which reportedly involves the co-operation of the three major levels of government is the CORTS scheme which provides arrangements for research and management of the Trent and Rideau river systems, Ontario. The origin, advantages and disadvantages of this scheme deserve study in terms of their applicability elsewhere.

National park boundary areas, such as the Canmore Corridor, a roughly twenty by five mile stretch leading along the Bow Valley into Banff National Park, definitely require some type of co-operative management and planning. Several years ago when the federal government issued its proposed master plans for Banff and the other mountain parks, very little consultation apparently took place among the provincial government, the Calgary Regional Planning Commission, and other concerned entities. Paradoxical suggestions were made about proposed land-use zoning in Banff in relation to ongoing or planned use on provincial and private land adjoining the park. The Alberta government public hearings held on land use in the Rocky Mountain foothills, east of Banff Park, also seem to have involved little consultation with the federal government, at least in the preparation of background papers.

Perceptions, Attitudes and Values

The first point that comes to mind is that many Canadians undoubtedly are unaware of national parks and other types of public land and have only the vaguest idea of their purposes.

More involved professionals and citizens have greater knowledge but often differ widely in perceptions, attitudes, and values respecting these reserves. Their viewpoints obviously influence their positions on park land-use issues and therefore are very important in decision making. Yet many of their perceptions and attitudes are erroneous in the historical sense, failing to show an understanding of the complexity of park origins and development.

There are those who perceive the national parks as basically having been established for recreation. Many of these people wholeheartedly support the introduction of more roads and other facilities, even though they may cause fundamental changes in the biological character of parks, a central concern of management since at least J.B. Harkin's day. On the other hand, there are those who perceive the parks as "pristine" or "untouched" nature, the protection of which has been the basic goal of park management from the beginning, in the 1880s. Those people generally are opposed to more roads and other development.

Yet park policies, practices, and landscapes clearly have changed through the years. For example, originally in Banff and other western parks, coyotes, wolves, badgers, skunks, cougar, and other predators were regarded as noxious animals. Programs were introduced to control or eliminate them. These programs, coupled with regrowth of poplar, and other vegetation following extensive forest fires in "pioneer days", have contributed to an increase in elk numbers in particular. By 1940, biologists concluded that the numerous elk were overgrazing range. Population control programs were introduced and continue today.

More recently it has been contended that long-continued national park fire control programs have produced extensive ageing forests. This has led, in turn, to suggestions that these policies be terminated and that controlled burning or lumbering be used to encourage the growth of shrub and other vegetation more favourable to many kinds of wildlife.

All these suggestions for change raise questions which require study. Will controlled fires or lumbering have the same effects on vegetation and wildlife as "wild" fires? If introduced, should lumbering be carried out by government or private enterprise? How would citizens perceive and react to lumbering? It seemingly threatens the "wilderness ideal" of national parks which has grown stronger in Canada in recent years.

The foregoing discussion raises the problem of how to define wilderness or, more importantly, landscape goals generally in national parks. Historically, the trend has been to bar or modify lumbering, hunting, and other cultural practices perceived as incompatible with the evolving image of a national park, while otherwise allowing the ecosystem to go on changing, without much thought of end points or landscape goals. In other words, the tendency has been to view national parks as areas where certain human practices do not occur, rather than to think about what type of landscape or ecosystem is evolving as a result of an essentially negative management policy. This approach has led to many unforeseen changes and to much coping and uncertainty among managers and the public.

In studies done in the United States it has been concluded that the desirable national park landscape was that extant when the "white man" came to North America. Recommendations based on such a goal pose certain problems. For one thing, it is not always easy to determine the state of the ecosystem at the time of Caucasian invasion. In western Canada, for example, Indian trade routes made it possible for the Blackfeet, the Shoshoni, and other native peoples to change from a subsistence, stone-age culture to commercial iron-age hunting of beaver and other animals while the European fur trade posts were still hundreds of miles away. A fine temporal division of the Indian and the whiteman's landscape is therefore hard to establish and perhaps not realistic.

Landscapes other than those existing at the time of the Caucasian arrival are also of great intellectual interest, as are longer term evolutionary changes occurring in the environment. Changes in vegetation and wildlife species, in erosion, and in landforms have long occurred in response to changes in climate and other biophysical processes, as well as in response to human activity. In this context, any decision to control or prohibit human activities in national parks can be questioned in relation to indigenous native groups whose hunting, burning, and other actions have had a fundamental place in the ecosystem for centuries. What do we mean by the term "nature" under these circumstances? Is it not quite arbitrary to decide at what point in time human actions and effects are "unnatural" and subject to control?

A final reason for questioning the value of a park policy aiming at the establishment and maintenance of landscapes as they were at the time of arrival of the white man is the lack of enthusiasm such a goal is likely to generate among non-white groups. These peoples are likely to conceive of landscapes that are of much greater historical significance to them.

In the United States and Canada, attempts have been made to deal with the problems of goals through the concepts of era and evolutionary landscapes. Era landscapes are those where disease, fire, and other processes are managed in order to maintain the land as it was at the time of the fur trader, the rancher, or early gold miner. Evolutionary landscapes are those where no human interference is contemplated and the landscape is allowed to change "naturally", independent of man. Such evolutionary landscapes are, of course, still being managed by man, who has simply taken the policy decision not to interfere directly in their development.

Relatively few parks or reserves actually seem to be deliberatley managed as era or evolutionary landscapes, in part because of lack of the necessary historical ecological research. One exception is Yosemite National Park, California, where controlled burning is now being conducted on the valley floor in an attempt to remove the conifers and recreate the oak savannahs of early Caucasian time. In Yellowstone National Park, large evolutionary zones have been set aside where grizzly bear, bison, and other animals roam freely. Recreational use is controlled and human interference is minimized. Some roads traverse these areas, allowing for sightseeing. But visitors are warned not to venture far from cars at risk of injury from wildlife. The policy is to let fire, cyclic variations in animal populations, "over-grazing", and other processes run their course, although if such processes occur on a scale large enough to threaten the viability of a particular species or the character of the landscape remnant as a whole, control measures would be introduced.

Before leaving the topic of perceptions, attitudes, and values, their potential importance in formulating zoning and other land-use regulations should be pointed out. Attempts to employ land-use controls encounter the basic problem of how the kinds and levels of use in an area are to be determined and established. Or, to phrase the problem differently, how do we determine the carrying capacity of a zone or a park? The presence of too many people, or of certain types of activities or machines, for example snowmobiles, can alter vegetation and ecosystems as well as detract from recreational enjoyment psychologically. But how do we measure and determine whether a change in vegetation or wildlife is significant? How extensive must erosion be before it is viewed as dangerous or damaging? Some biologists speak of "irreversible" or "irretrievable" ecosystem changes as a result of human activity. What does this mean in terms of recovery time and character? Will the system never return to something approximating its predisturbance condition, or will this occur in twenty, or forty, or one hundred years? How can one measure and determine when man's enjoyment has decreased significantly as a result of crowding, noise, or some other process? How many people must share this perception before management controls are introduced? Relatively few studies have been carried out on such problems.

Technology

Little detailed research is available on the impact of technology on national parks and related reserves in Canada. Recently the snowmobile and other all-terrain vehicles (A.T.V.) have attracted attention because of their wide-ranging environmental effects. The noise, weight, and mobility of the snowmobile, and its users, have changed vegetation and wildlife. Studies have shown that the vehicle also has affected snow characteristics, soil temperatures, snow melt, soil erosion, noise, and other ecosystem elements and processes.

The snowmobile is of special interest in the light of current concern about technology and environmental impact, for parks managers generally failed to foresee all the direct and indirect effects of the vehicle and the reactions these changes cause among park users. After being introduced rather quickly into Banff and other national parks during the 1960s, snowmobile trails have been drastically reduced in recent years.

The effects of other technology, for example automobiles and trains, is often intuitively grasped but really not well understood quantitatively. Between about 1910, the time of its introduction and 1970 the automobile transformed much of Banff Park. Roads were built along many of the major valleys in the 1920s, and 1940s, allowing access to large numbers of visitors (Figures 2 and 3). These people were then provided with gas stations, motels, restaurants, campsites, and other facilities. The effects of these facilities on wildlife and other aspects of the ecosystem have not been studied in detail. Similar developments occurred in other parks such as Point Pelee, Elk Island, and Jasper.

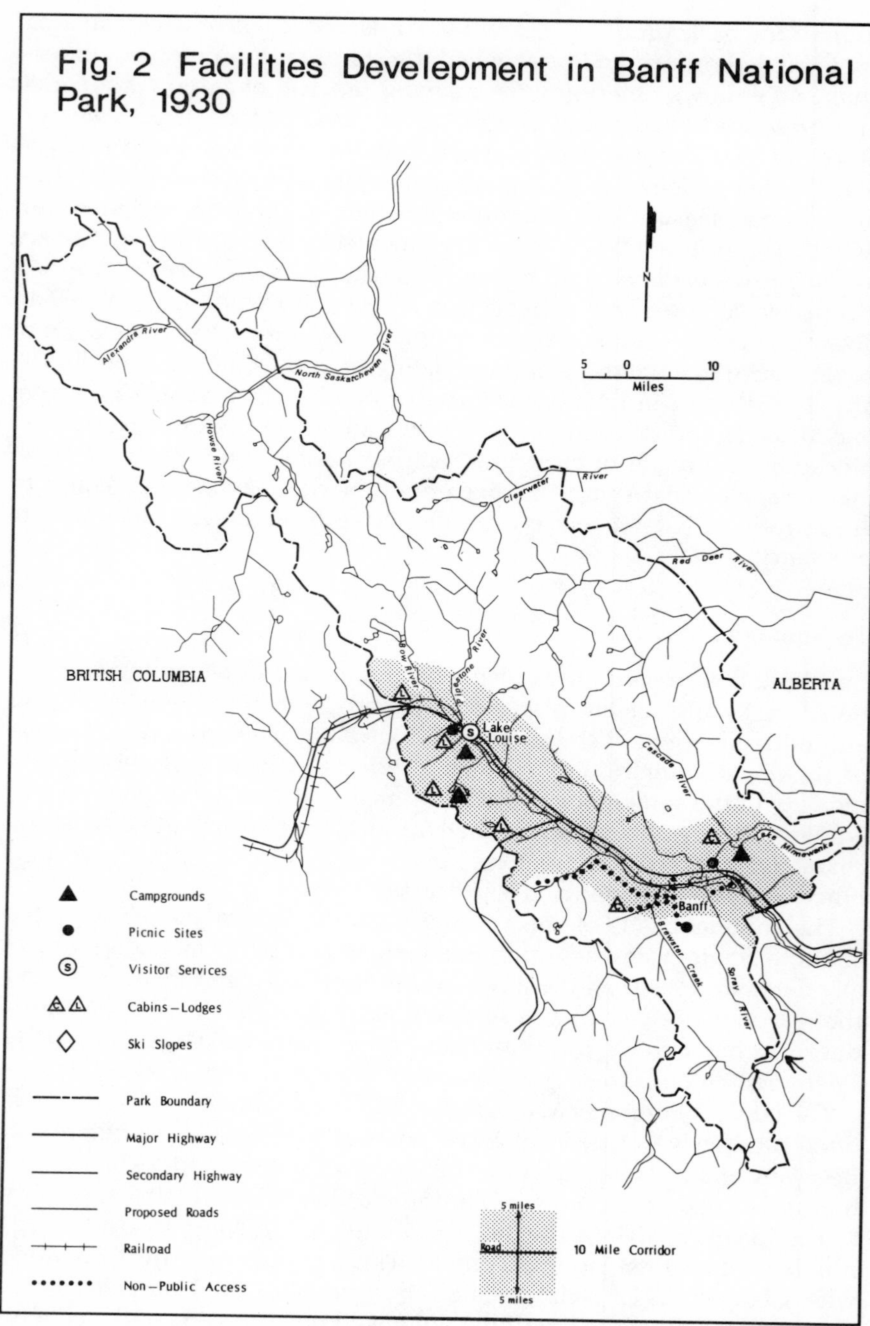
Fig. 2 Facilities Develepment in Banff National Park, 1930
N
5 0 10
Miles
Alexandra River
North Saskatchewan River
Howse River
Clearwater River
Red Deer River
Bow River
Pipestone River
BRITISH COLUMBIA
ALBERTA
Lake Louise
Cascade River
Lake Minnewanka
Banff
Brewster Creek
Spray River
Campgrounds
Picnic Sites
Visitor Services
Cabins – Lodges
Ski Slopes
Park Boundary
Major Highway
Secondary Highway
Proposed Roads
Railroad
Non – Public Access
5 miles
Road
5 miles
10 Mile Corridor

Fig. 3 Facilities Development in Banff National Park, 1971

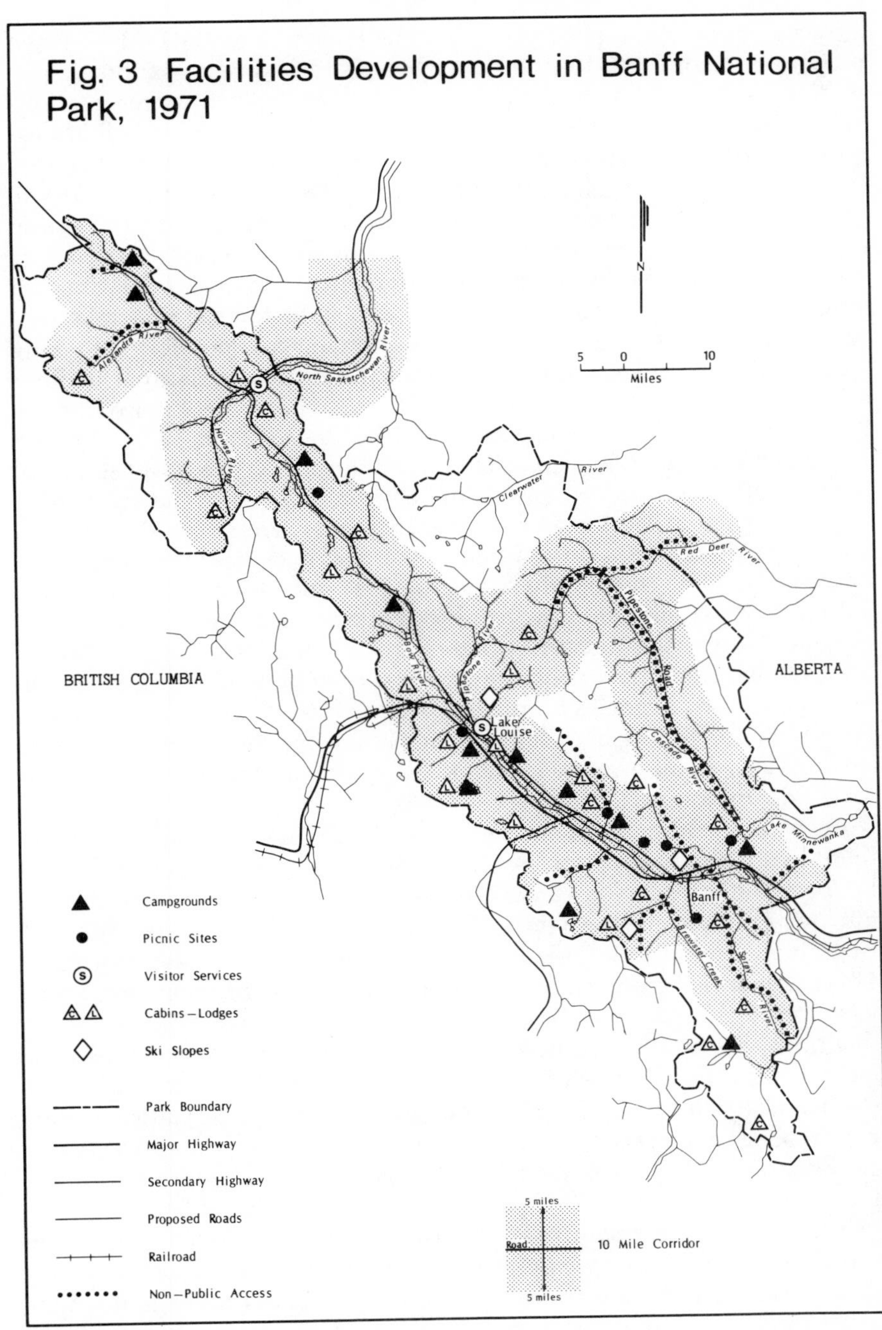

A major change in policy seems to have been made in 1971-72 when proposed major roads for the Rocky Mountain and other national parks were cancelled on the basis of professional and citizen representations about their potential effects on landscape. Major problems still are associated with existing roads as well as townsites, and downhill ski areas, with their high technological load. Greater use of public transport will ease some of these effects, but not others associated with increasing concentration of large numbers of people in small areas.

Such effects have led to the development of environmental impact studies in the U.S. and Canada. The aim is to foresee and take into account as many potential environmental changes as possible in making a decision for or against land-use change. Environmental impact studies are required by law in the United States, where the Environmental Protection Act (E.P.A.) was signed by the President in 1970. This Act requires the preparation of a statement on the effects of a proposed dam, road, or other technology on wildlife or other aspects of the ecosystem. Comments are called for on such things as the "irretrievable" nature of any anticipated effects, long-term loss of resources, and planning alternatives. Initially the biophysical changes were of greatest concern, although the studies are now being extended to include changes in employment opportunities and other social phenomena. In the United States, environmental impact statements are required to be circulated to other concerned agencies for review. The statements are also available to the public for comments. Some changes have been made in proposed projects as a result of agency and citizen criticism, but others have gone forward, unmodified.

Even though Canada does not have Environmental Impact Assessment legislation like that of the United States, a number of environmental impact studies have been carried out in various parts of the Dominion, for example on the James Bay Power Scheme and the proposed twinning of the Trans-Canada highway through Banff National Park. These Canadian studies have certain deficiencies. In most cases they were prepared after a particular land-use decision had been made, so that the opportunity to consider a range of alternatives was limited. The need for the decision often was not demonstrated convincingly. The studies also tend to be hastily prepared and provide insufficient data and analysis for decision making. Some studies have been treated as confidential and not released to other government agencies, nor the public, for comment.

A few very general points should be made in concluding this paper. In my view, much more research on national parks, and other public reserves, is required if we are to understand and better manage this type of resource. Much of the research should be multi-disciplinary, whether carried out by a team of scholars or an individual. Much of the research should also have an applied orientation. Funds should be provided to publish more of the good theses that often remain unused in university libraries. Government departments such as Indian Affairs and Northern Development do not have a publishing program for departmental and consultant reports and should introduce one in order to bring more information to the attention of professionals and the public, in the interest of better decision making.

NOTES

1. L. White, "The Historical Roots of Our Ecologic Crisis", *Science*, Vol. 155, pp. 1203-1207. This paper has been reprinted in several books of readings, e.g. R.M. Irving and G.B. Priddle (eds.), *Crisis, Readings in Environmental Issues and Strategies*, Macmillan, Toronto, 1971.
2. J.G. Nelson, *The Last Refuge*, Harvest House, Montreal, 1973.
3. G. White, "Formation and Role of Public Attitudes", *Environmental Quality in a Growing Economy*, ed. by H. Jarrett, Johns Hopkins University Press, Baltimore, 1966, pp. 105-127.
4. For a number of papers on the history, nature and management of Canadian National Parks see J.G. Nelson (ed.), *Canadian Parks in Perspective*, Harvest House, Montreal, 1970.
5. J.G. Nelson, "Canadian National Parks, Past Present and Future", *Canadian Geographical Journal*, Vol. 86, No. 3, March, 1973, pp. 68-89.
6. R.C. Scace, "Banff: A Cultural Historical Study of Land Use and Management in a National Park Community to 1945", National Parks Series No. 2, University of Calgary, 1972.

14
Land Use in Canada's North

*W.A. Fuller**

Resources

Up to the present, land management in the north has been essentially synonymous with resource management. The traditional categorization of resources into renewable and non-renewable seems to me to be too simplistic and not very helpful. Accordingly, I here propose a six-part classification of resources which will be used in the subsequent discussion of land-use management.

1. SPACE

To a zoologist living space is one of the primary resources required by any species of animal, and many species are known to have elaborate mechanisms for ensuring that space is used efficiently. This is a consumptive form of land use in that during any period of occupancy most other kinds of use are pre-empted.

2. RENEWABLE RESOURCES

These are resources that are capable of providing an annual yield for human use either because they are alive and reproducing, or through recurrent physical processes such as the hydrologic cycle. In all cases the annual harvestable yield is related to the capital stock of the resource. Under proper management only the harvestable surplus is consumed while the capital stock is preserved to provide later yields in perpetuity.

3. RECYCLABLE RESOURCES

According to the law of conservation of matter, chemical elements (except those that are spontaneously radioactive) cannot be destroyed. Thus an atom of iron remains an atom whether it is in combination with

---

*Department of Zoology, University of Alberta, Edmonton. For over a period of thirty years, Dr. Fuller has travelled extensively and has conducted research in Canada's North. This is a slightly edited version of a paper which appeared in *Canadian Public Land Use in Perspective,* edited by J. G. Nelson *et al.* Proceedings of a Symposium sponsored by the Social Science Research Council of Canada, 1973, pp. 153-176.

other atoms in an ore body, or refined, or converted to steel, or thrown in a scrap heap. In principle, at least, it can be recovered and used again and again. The same is true of other metallic ores and of non-metals such as sulphur. Thus, while ore bodies do not renew themselves (except perhaps on a cosmological time scale) the elements they contain can be re-used by man again and again.

4. ENERGY

Energy-yielding materials are usually grouped with minerals as non-renewable resources because, once extracted for use, they are not replaced except, again, on a geological or cosmological time scale. However, energy obeys laws that are fundamentally different from the laws governing matter, the most important of which prohibits the re-use of any given parcel of energy. Thus energy is neither renewable nor recyclable.

5. ESTHETIC RESOURCES

Certain properties of the land or the living community it supports have strong and pleasing appeal to human senses. These esthetic resources differ from all the classes I have considered so far by virtue of the fact that they can be appreciated without being consumed. In other words, the satisfaction of an esthetic need by one individual is a non-consumptive activity that does not necessarily detract in any way from the appeal of the resource to others. The commonest way of "harvesting" esthetic resources is on film, but clearly the resource loses none of its appeal from the mere fact that a photograph has been taken.

6. CULTURAL RESOURCES

Under this heading I include a miscellany of things which a more perceptive intelligence might subdivide into several meaningful categories. I think first of the rich history of the north and the limited effort made to preserve historical artifacts and sites. I remember that in the late 1950s one could drive the Canadian section of the Alaska Highway and see almost no indication that anything important happened prior to construction of the road. The only exception I now recall was a sign at the intersection of the highway and the Dalton Trail which did mention the year 1898. And, if the brief history of European occupation gets short shrift, what of the much longer history and culture of native peoples? Northern natives, in their harsh environment, and dependent as they were on a hunter-gatherer economy, apparently had little time to develop an elaborate culture. Perhaps this makes it all the more desirable to provide opportunities for the present generation to preserve and practise what remains. History provides a link to archaeology and thence to paleontology, both of which depend on relics of the past preserved under special conditions. Accumulations of such relics should be considered resources and given special protection.

Research is a cultural activity in my scheme of things, and the north provides many resources for research activities in many disciplines. I think first of ecological research in areas hardly influenced by technological man, but the range of activities supported by institutes for northern study on several major Canadian campuses testifies to the abundance of research opportunities that the north provides.

Importance of Northern Resources

1. SPACE

At first sight it seems inconceivable that space could be limited or limiting in any way in Canada's north. There is, however, one activity that requires plenty of room and that is wilderness travel. Opportunities to enjoy wilderness are rapidly disappearing from southern Canada so surely one of the highest priorities for land management in the north ought to be the setting aside of wilderness areas. The essence of wilderness travel is to use muscle power only — hiking, pack and saddle horses, canoes, snowshoes, dog teams — thus more than one wilderness area is required. Horses, for example, are the traditional means of summer travel in mountainous Yukon but they are virtually unknown in the Northwest Territories, where the canoe reigns supreme. Wilderness is extremely sensitive to other forms of land use and conflicts will be discussed below.

The only other aspect of space that I wish to comment on concerns urban areas. There are those who foresee tremendous increases in the human population of at least the mid-north with individual communities of 100,000 inhabitants. Surely one must ask, "why"? Traditional services such as streets, sewage, water and electrical distribution are difficult and expensive to provide in the north. Existing communities tend to be, on the whole, rather dreary collections of unimaginative buildings, largely unplanned and frequently wallowing alternatively in a sea of mud or dust. Nowhere is there adequate sewage treatment and this, in spite of the fact that the assimilative capacity of the northern environment is lower than in southern regions even in summer and is virtually nil during the long winter. Much more thought, therefore, needs to go into town planning and policies for encouraging or discouraging urban growth. Alternatives might also be studied. The recent experience of major oil companies with flying crews into and out of the north on a three-week rotation bears close scrutiny. Many developments of short duration could perhaps be done as cheaply and with less impact on the physical and social environments by this means as by establishing semi-permanent towns doomed from the start to become ghost towns.

2. RENEWABLE RESOURCES

Primary renewable resources are soil and water. The products we ordinarily think of as renewable resources are derived secondarily from these two in the presence of solar energy. That statement is no less true of fish and wildlife than it is of wheat or wood. All the renewable resource industries therefore depend ultimately on the fertility of soil, the availability of water and the input of solar energy. When one looks at these three factors in the north it is at once apparent that the base for renewable resource industries is extremely limited. Over all of the high arctic there has been almost no soil developed; in the low arctic there are limited patches of more or less mature soils and in the southern part of the north the soil that develops under coniferous forests tends to be acidic and relatively poor in nutrients. Almost the only fertile soils are lacustrine or alluvial deposits and these are of quite limited extent — along major waterways and in the basins of post-glacial lakes.

Much has been written recently about the phenomenon known as permafrost. I have no intention of reviewing the extensive literature on permafrost here but no consideration of northern land use can fail to take it into account. The term refers to material (whether soil or bedrock) that does not thaw in summer. It is capped by a layer, called the active zone, that does thaw and refreeze annually. Obviously, biological events are limited to the active layer which may range from a few inches to several feet in depth. Where it is very thin plants have only a shallow root zone which never warms above freezing where it is in contact with the underlying frozen material. In addition the annual freeze-thaw cycles cause much movement in the active layer, which, in addition to producing interesting patterns on the surface, may damage underground parts of plants.

Permafrost has geomorphological connotations as well. Its integrity depends upon heat flow into and out of the earth. Any shift in the balance of these two processes will cause permafrost to aggrade or degrade. In the high arctic the balance is almost entirely physical and thus human activity has little effect. In the low arctic and subarctic insulation by living plants or accumulated dead organic matter plays an essential role. Destruction of the insulating layer usually alters the balance in favour of increased thermal input and thus leads to degradation of permafrost and the resulting visual scars on the landscape.

Secondly, precipitation is low throughout both Territories. Much of the high arctic would be classified as semi-desert if precipitation were the only factor, but since evaporation is also very low and permafrost prevents deep penetration of water, the amount of water available to plants is kept deceptively high. Even the best-endowed parts of the north have no more precipitation than the driest parts of southern Alberta or Saskatchewan.

Finally, the input of solar energy has features that are unique to the north. Everyone is familiar with the periods of zero input north of the arctic circle and the corresponding periods of twenty-four-hour illumination. Not everyone, however, recognizes the importance of the low angle of incidence of the sun's rays associated with the long days. In essence, this means that the intensity of incoming radiation is low which tends to offset any advantage of long hours of illumination.

If we were to begin our year at the winter solstice, then half of the energy received at any point on the earth's surface will have fallen by the time of the summer solstice. Over much of the arctic the land is barely free of snow by June 21 and the ocean is ice-covered until very much later. Arctic lakes, too, retain their ice cover well into July and the ice may be snow-covered until the summer solstice. Light penetrates clear ice, and biological production in oceans and lakes may commence long before the water surface is exposed. But snow is not very transparent to light and thus, when arctic seas and lakes are snow-covered until mid or late June, they may be essentially unable to derive any biological benefit from half of their annual energy budget. (This is not to deny that they receive physical benefits in the form of melting of snow and ice and warming of their waters.)

There is a popular misconception that the north is teeming with wildlife. There are probably three main reasons for this misconception. In certain limited localities, such as Creswell Bay on Southampton Island, or the snow goose nesting area on Banks Island, there are concentrations of nesting birds, and the visitor to such an area is impressed by their productivity without realizing that the number of such unique areas in the entire arctic can probably be counted on the fingers of both hands. Early travellers sometimes found themselves in the midst of a caribou migration and again received an erroneous impression of superabundance, not realizing that thousands of square miles off the migration routes were totally devoid of caribou. Finally, there are temporal, as well as spatial, pulses of abundance. About one year in four lemmings reach superabundance and provide a food base for ermines, arctic foxes, snowy owls and jaegers, so that the tundra may be teeming with life. But the picture is very different during the other three years of the cycle when lemmings virtually disappear.

The abundance of fish in northern lakes has also been greatly exaggerated. The growth and maturation of fish in cold, nutrient-poor waters is extremely slow, and once the standing crop that has accumulated over many years is exploited replacement takes a long time.

Thus severe limitations on the factors of biological production ensure that renewable resources will never be abundant. This conclusion could lead to either of two conflicting policy choices. In view of the limitations we could dismiss renewable resources as unimportant; or we could take the opposing view that the limited areas of moderate to high productivity should be given special attention. I favour the second alternative and would advocate a particularly high priority for the limited parcels of arable land and limited areas of wildlife and fish habitats. With careful planning and proper encouragement the land in the north could provide a significant part of the staple foods needed by northern residents.

A final brief word might be devoted to debunking schemes for turning the north into a breadbasket by such devices as irrigation, massive use of fertilizers and pesticides, and use of as-yet-undeveloped, early-maturing crops. Apart from severe economic constraints, such schemes never consider the energy cost associated with intensive agriculture. Until we solve our energy supply problems we should not consider exacerbating them by devoting large amounts of energy to schemes for fertilizing the north.

3. RECYCLABLE RESOURCES

From the time of the Klondike gold rush there has been a tradition in the north that its real wealth lay in its minerals. Mines and miners have therefore expected and received special treatment in the form of direct subsidies, tax concessions, land give-aways and almost complete exemption from regulations aimed at reducing the environmental damage they cause. A critical look at the real costs and benefits of mining in the north is long overdue. The mere existence of the special measures I have already mentioned seems to me to constitute a *prima facie* case that it is not economic. The search for minerals has, in the past, been associated with devastating forest fires (accidental or deliberate?), with poorly engineered roads running at will across the landscape, and with claim boundaries neatly (?) run by crawler tractor. Functioning mines have produced a lunar landscape in the Klondike, serious air pollution in Yellowknife, water pollution from inadequate management of tailings ponds, and finally ghost towns.

On a global level, and again in view of the energy situation, it is clearly time to give greater emphasis to recycling rather than mining *de novo*. For most minerals the energy cost of recycling is very much less than the cost of refining the original ore. Economists are soon going to be forced to face up to the necessity of doing cost-benefit analysis in units other than dollars. This might be a good place at which to start.

I think it obvious from the foregoing that I would favour close examination of the place of extraction of recyclable resources in a land management scheme. Based on the considerations I have raised above, I suggest that such an examination might topple mining from its present lofty place in the spectrum of land uses in the north.

4. ENERGY

Evidence now indicates that the north has three kinds of energy sources — water power, fossil fuels and uranium. Hydro power has been used in the Klondike since the early years of this century, and for varying lengths of time at communities such as Mayo, Yellowknife, Whitehorse and Pine Point. Advocates of hydro developments point to the lack of air, water and noise pollution as major advantages and tend to play down both changes in natural communities and loss of esthetic and historical values that constitute major disadvantages.

Unfortunately, there is a nearly perfect coincidence of potential hydro sites and sites of outstanding esthetic interest. Falling water is a prime attraction for both kinds of user. How then can conflict be avoided? The only suggestion I have to make is that an inventory of all potential hydro sites be undertaken along with an assessment of the probably effects of development. Then a decision should be taken to devote certain sites to power production and to preserve others for their natural beauty. There might be a third category of sites on which a decision was deferred. The present and projected distribution of both recreational and power needs and alternative methods of satisfying each should be thrown into the decision-making equation.

Exploration for, and probable development and transportation of, fossil fuels in the form of oil and gas is currently the hottest topic in the north, and indeed, throughout much of Canada, and the debate is likely to go on for some time yet. I only want to review very briefly some of the effects of this development on the land and then make a few very general suggestions.

To search for hydrocarbons requires geophysical exploration which in turn requires thousands of miles of lines over which seismic crews will operate. If carelessly done such lines can cause degradation of permafrost resulting in visual scars, geomorphological changes and possible ecological effects. Some careless seismic work has been done in the Canadian arctic, but examples may be getting rarer thanks to public outcry and the ensuing attempts of industry to keep its public image shining.

The real threat in geophysical work lies in its extent; probably several hundred thousand miles of lines will be run. Surely only the best techniques, producing the least possible disturbance, can be tolerated. The legal instrument for achieving such a result, the Land Use Regulations under the Territorial Lands Act, was watered down before passage at the request of the oil industry and over the objections of conservationists.

A second phase in petroleum exploration is to drill an exploratory well in a formation that appears to be favourable geophysically. Such a well site will occupy two or three acres which will end up in utter desolation. However, the number of exploratory wells will likely only be a few hundred. The resulting damaged terrain will amount, literally, to widely scattered pinpoints on a map of the Canadian arctic. This necessary damage, then, even though severe, can be tolerated much more easily than the less severe but extensive damage resulting from careless seismic activity.

But there is another chapter to the story of exploratory wells. Several tens of tons of equipment must be put in place before a well can be drilled. In many cases drilling rigs are moved overland on winter roads. Even though snow and ice protect the frozen land surface to some extent, the comparatively large volume of heavy traffic frequently results in deep rutting. There appears to be no means of reducing this disturbance other than to keep haul roads as short as possible.

New problems will arise when oil or gas is found in commercial quantities and industry goes over from exploration to production. Depending on the sulphur content of the fuel, there may be a greater or lesser amount of air pollution with sulphur dioxide, a gas that is particularly toxic to lichens that constitute a major portion of the northern flora. Networks of feeder lines will connect wells to trunk lines. Since they will carry hot oil they cannot be buried in permafrost, and if located above ground they will constitute an additional hazard to animal movement.

Finally, if hydrocarbons are to be exploited they must be transported to market and the transportation corridor constitutes a form of land use. Crude oil and gas pose different kinds of problems, but if we proceed to develop arctic fossil fuels, both sets of problems will have to be solved because, ultimately, both forms of fuel must be harvested together.

Energy policy demands decisions that far transcend the land-use problem. Should we export arctic energy or save it for our own future use? Should hydrocarbons be burned at all or are they more valuable as lubricants and feedstocks for petrochemical industry? Since the world supply of conventional petroleum can now be measured in decades, when do we go to unconventional sources such as tar sands or entirely new energy sources such as the atom or the sun? Such questions should have been considered before we began the singleminded drive to produce conventional hydrocarbons by conventional means. The question now is: is it too late to reconsider?

There are already strong indications that we are likely to go to the atom for energy in the near future. Proponents of nuclear energy play down its hazards, including the difficulty of safely storing waste products for as long as 250,000 years. The morality of bequeathing our descendants such a deadly legacy seems doubtful to me, but I cannot recall reading a single statement on this question by a humanist or a social scientist. In any event, the north is known to contain large amounts of uranium and if we opt for nuclear power there will inevitably be renewed interest in its exploitation. It is at least conceivable that the decision to go ahead with nuclear power will be taken in an energy crisis situation, in which case the pressure to exploit uranium deposits could lead to overriding of land-use policies and safeguards for environmental management.

5. ESTHETIC RESOURCES

The difficulty of preserving esthetic resources is well illustrated by the example of falling water. By what means do we preserve a waterfall for its beauty rather than sacrifice it to power development? I contend that the outcome of any attempt to quantify the respective values will be a tautology of the units adopted. In traditional dollar terms it can always be shown that the economic value of the power produced is far greater than that generated by visiting tourists. If we use a unit of energy for our analysis we will get the same result. However, if we invented a new unit of "esthetic satisfaction," say, then the result would surely be reversed. The conclusion I draw from this is that quantification of values is at best pseudo-science. The case for preservation of esthetic resources must rest on value judgement alone. Most of us have a deep inner need for beautiful surroundings at least occasionally; therefore, we should preserve some of the outstanding beauty spots of the north.

Clearly, esthetic resources are a major base of the tourist industry which is increasing in economic importance in both territories. The increase in tourism is generally seen as a good thing, but a word of caution is in order. Despite my earlier claim that appreciation of esthetic resources is not necessarily a consumptive form of land use, experience in various parts of the globe has shown that too many tourists, by their mere physical presence, can severely damage landscapes and living organisms. In other words, land has a carrying capacity for tourists as it has for renewable resources. The factors that limit biological productivity are also important determinants of tourist-carrying capacity. Trampling by many booted feet, for example, is enough to trigger changes in permafrost terrain as well as in plant communities. Thus, tourism cannot be looked upon as an infinitely expandable industry although that appears to be the way in which it is viewed by promoters in both industry and government and even by well-meaning, but uninformed, conservationists.

Furthermore, part of the appeal of natural beauty for many people comes from viewing in isolation or with a small group of close friends.

Tourism en masse precludes this and thus dilutes the quality of the experience. Policy for recreational use of esthetic resources should distinguish between mass use and individual use. Both types are needed, but the hardest to justify is always the high quality experience for the small number of people willing to make the extra effort required. But the north has many quiet corners of outstanding beauty, some of which should be preserved, in spite of economic arguments to the contrary, to satisfy the legitimate desire of some Canadians for this type of experience.

6. CULTURAL RESOURCES

Much of what I have said about esthetic resources applies also to cultural resources. Their value is inadequately reflected in the economic mirror; they may be an important base for tourism, enriching the lives of those who appreciate them, they are irreplaceable but can be wiped out by heedless development of other resources; and they cannot usually coexist with other, consumptive forms of land use.

Elements of a Land-Use Policy

1. COMPREHENSIVENESS

There is probably no need to belabour this point. All land north of 60° must be included. Since only a vanishingly small amount of land is now in private hands through right of purchase this should not constitute a problem. Much larger amounts of land have been encumbered by other kinds of agreement such as leases and exploration permits. As Professor Andrew Thompson has argued in the case of petroleum exploration in the arctic, there are sound reasons for renegotiating some of these agreements. Others might be allowed to run to term before being brought under the terms of a land-use policy.

2. INVENTORY

A major effort is required to assemble information on resources and land capabilities into a comprehensive inventory. I suspect that a good deal of the information is already available for at least parts of the north. For example, soil surveys have been completed along most of the major rivers where the best soils are known to occur. It seems likely that all the pockets of arable soil could be mapped in short order. Terrain sensitivity maps have been produced by scientists in the Geological Survey of Canada, with the co-operation of others in Environment Canada, under the auspices of the Arctic Land Use Research program (ALUR).

Again, the coverage is only fragmentary and is keyed to actual or potential developments in the petroleum industry. More recently ALUR has experimented with interpretation of terrain sensitivity from aerial photographs. Preliminary results for parts of the high arctic are extremely encouraging, and because the method is relatively quick and inexpensive, a first approximation of a land-use capability for the entire archipelago seems quite within our grasp. Finally, the Earth Resources Technology Satellite (ERTS) promises to yield useful information for a land-use inventory. The chief shortcoming of ERTS imagery is probably its small scale, whereas its strong points are frequency of coverage (every 18 days) and the multiple imagery that allows for rather detailed interpretation.

The most likely areas for occurrence of recyclable and energy resources are pretty well known through the efforts of the Geological Survey of Canada and industry. Similarly, the Water Survey Branch of Environment Canada has accumulated stream flow measurements on most of the rivers that have hydroelectric potential.

Forest inventories have been completed along major rivers where the best tree growth occurs and the Canadian Wildlife Service has sponsored an Ecology Map Series containing a great deal of information on wildlife resources in selected areas directly in the path of imminent development. The ecological information tends to be superficial and episodic and the coverage is far from complete, but it is a base upon which to build.

Even esthetic and cultural resources have received some attention. The recent announcement of new National Parks at Kluane, Nahanni and Baffin Island is an encouraging development. Some information exists in government files concerning half a dozen sites in Yukon and at least one other outstanding area (the East Arm of Great Slave Lake) in the Northwest Territories. But these developments are largely due to the initiative of a few people both within and outside of government, and do not in any way constitute even the beginnings of a systematic search for sites of prime esthetic interest.

I suspect that the situation is similar with respect to historical and archaeological resources. Certainly there has been an effort to locate any sites of interest that lie along the proposed routes of arctic pipelines and highways, but I suspect that a great deal remains to be done in the way of systematic inventory.

One area in which an attempt has been made at systematic study is in a search for areas of outstanding ecological interest to serve as benchmark sites and areas for future ecological research. Under the aegis of the International Biological Programme teams of ecologists have catalogued and briefly described areas that would be desirable as Ecological Reserves. Negotiations have been underway for many months with federal and territorial officials, native brotherhoods and industry representatives with a view to securing legal recognition of these areas.

In summary then, a good deal is known about the land-based resources of the north but much more work needs to be done and the new and existing information needs to be integrated into a comprehensive inventory.

3. PUBLIC SCRUTINY

The days of secrecy in land-use matters are surely at an end. Raw data on which the inventory is based must be made public. The policy itself should be open to public comment and public hearing if necessary. Major decisions about land use and disposal of public lands should also be exposed to public view before final dispositions are made. Nor will it suffice to hold hearings only in Ottawa. The people whose lives will be affected, northerners, must have a voice in such decisions.

4. ENFORCEABILITY

A land-use policy that cannot be administered and enforced is obviously of little use. The present Land Use Regulations have some serious deficiencies that have been pointed out by conservationists and ignored by government. One of the most serious is lack of an absolute requirement to post a performance bond. The discretionary power of the Minister to require a bond seems to open the door to the possibility of influence or pressure which a weak Minister might find impossible to resist, and when no bond is required a major trump card is stripped from the hand of the enforcement agency. Secondly, the regulations as they now stand are much too lenient with the mining industry. The mining lobby was successful in raising the weight limit of vehicles that may be used without requiring a Land Use Permit. They were also successful in increasing the limit for storage of explosives and altering other proscriptions that essentially exempt most mineral exploration parties from the provisions of the Regulations. Since most of the terrain damage associated with mining, as with petroleum, occurs during the exploration phase, these are serious shortcomings. Finally, the onus placed on land-use Inspectors under the present regulations is extremely heavy. It is a serious responsibility to shut down an operation costing tens of thousands of dollars per day for breach of regulations, and the Inspector in the field is a relatively minor official. Some way must be found to involve more senior officials and the decisions of field personnel must receive strong backing right up to the Ministerial level. Unfortunately, that backing has been lacking in two or three cases known to me, perhaps because the Minister is at the same time responsible for promoting development and enforcing of regulations that tend to control or restrict development.

5. IMPACT ASSESSMENTS

Clearly no land-use policy can be implemented successfully in the absence of impact assessments preceding every major development. Such assessments should not be primarily environmental, as is the case in the United States and under the Northern Inland Waters Act, but should be aimed at determining whether the proposed development is compatible with land-use policy and what its impact on other forms of land use is likely to be. In many cases, but perhaps not all, the public should be given the opportunity to comment at some form of hearing as suggested under point three above.

6. FUTURE OPTIONS

Last, but certainly not least, policy should be designed to keep open as many options as possible for future generations. A most important corollary of this statement is that irreplaceable resources, such as those of esthetic or cultural value, should not be lightly destroyed, because their destruction removes for all time the possibility of their enjoyment by future generations. In most cases future generations will not benefit from the alternative development which is likely to have a short life and bring major benefit only to the present generation and perhaps its immediate descendants.

If we were to act in accordance with this principle our concern for future generations would also be reflected in our impact assessments which would have to contain a statement of future options foregone in the event that a particular development were to occur now. We would also ensure that when developments were approved they were carried out using only techniques that would not produce permanent, undesirable changes in landscapes or living ecosystems, so that at the end of the exercise the land would be available, unimpaired, for the next use. A case in point is geophysical surveys in connection with exploration for petroleum. When properly done all signs of disturbance disappear in a decade or so. When badly done the scars will be visible for centuries at least. In the first case the land can revert to wilderness when the oil is all gone, whereas, in the second case it will be impossible to escape the evidence of human activity over very large tracts of land.

Some Problems in Land-Use Management

1. NATIVE CLAIMS

In my view native land claims must be settled before any other action can be contemplated. The "problem" of native claims has always seemed to me to be a non-problem. In my simplistic approach to the question it is clear that the native peoples did occupy the land when the first European explorers and traders arrived. The lands were never taken by right of conquest and it is inconceivable that people living off the land would knowingly have ceded that land by treaty. Legalistic arguments to the contrary, then, fair play demands that we negotiate a fair and equitable settlement.

2. JURISDICTIONAL PROBLEMS

It seems to me that these problems arise at three levels. First, there is constant friction between the federal and territorial governments; second, there are interdepartmental wrangles within the federal government; and third, there are intradepartmental conflicts, at least within Northern Affairs.

I have never been impressed by the claims of "colonialism" made by territorial officials. Although there is clearly political domination by Ottawa, it is also true that federal money predominates in the territorial budgets and, on the whole, the handful of northern residents has been generously treated by the taxpayers of Canada. Having advised both territorial councils, and having followed political developments in the north for more than a quarter of a century, I can only conclude that I am thankful that the powers of territorial legislators are somewhat circumscribed.

Empire building within federal government departments seems to me to be a more serious problem. Whereas major responsibility for northern affairs resides in the Department of Indian and Northern Affairs (DINA), two other departments have major responsibilities north of 60°. These are the Department of Energy, Mines and Resources (DEMR) and the Department of the Environment (DOE). Administration of lands in the Territories is the responsibility of DINA, but some of the technical information on which proper management depends is provided by the Geological Survey of Canada in DEMR, and adverse environmental effects of a land-use operation become the responsibility of DOE. Water management and research and management in forestry and fisheries reside in DOE along with research on wildlife, whereas actual management of game is a territorial function. Conservation, including national parks, comes under DINA but the scientists best able to advise on conservation matters are in DEMR and DOE. In addition to these major inputs Agriculture (through its soils people), Transport (which looks after airports and river and sea navigation) and, more recently Defence, all have a stake in northern development. The major weakness of this arrangement seems to be that DINA must depend on other departments for nearly all of its technical advice. Since DINA (and its forerunners) have always been a junior portfolio whereas Agriculture, Transport and DEMR are senior posts, it cannot always be easy for the Minister of DINA to obtain the advice he requires.

An attempt is being made to co-ordinate interdepartmental functions through a high level interdepartmental committee which has clearly had some success and, in principle at least, could ensure that the Minister of DINA got the advice he needs. But even if co-ordination is less than perfect, the interdepartmental problem is probably less serious than the clear conflict of interest that occurs within DINA where development and conservation are encompassed within one and the same branch which is clearly dominated by the development faction. When the Assistant Deputy Minister sits on the Board of Directors of Panarctic Oils what chance is there that one of his land-use Inspectors will call a halt to a Panarctic operation over a breach of Regulations? This anomaly has been pointed out repeatedly by citizen groups such as the Canadian Arctic Resources Committee and I understand that a reorganization is taking place within DINA that may lead to greater separation of these two functions.

3. PUBLIC ATTITUDES

Our attitude to land has developed over the scant couple of centuries since the industrial revolution and has come to be accepted, as part of conventional wisdom. Basically, the conventional wisdom treats land and its resources in purely economic terms as a commodity to be managed for maximum short-term monetary gain. This philosophy has led to tragic mistakes in land management in southern Canada and elsewhere which, in turn, prompts successive Ministers of Northern Affairs to utter pious assurances that those mistakes must not be repeated in the north. I fail to see, however, how we can avoid mistakes until we banish the philosophy that provides rich economic rewards for those who perpetrate those mistakes. Under the present system mistakes are compounded by a system of positive feed-back that makes each successive mistake profitable.

More than a quarter of a century ago Aldo Leopold argued for a "land ethic" that would set rules for the man-land relationship in the way that religious thinkers have dealt with man-God and man-man interactions. The theme has been taken up more recently by Lynn White in his well-known essay "The Historical Roots of our Ecologic Crisis," and by Garrett Hardin in his equally well-known "Tragedy of the Commons."[1] The central theme of this philosophy is that a sense of stewardship for land must replace our present predatory approach. Such a reversal of attitudes flies in the face of economics but is not incompatible with ecology.

Ecological systems are regulated by negative feed-back which implies that mistakes are penalized rather than rewarded. Regulation leads to a kind of long-range stability that nevertheless permits slow change (evolution). In principle, the biosphere can continue to function as long as it receives a supply of external energy from the sun, which astronomers tell us, may be another five thousand million years. Whether man remains a part of the biosphere for so long depends in an important way on whether he can adopt an ecological strategy in his dealings with the land community.

NOTES

1. G. Hardin, "Tragedy of the Commons", *Science*, Vol. 162, pp. 1243-1248. This paper has been reprinted in several books of readings, e.g. *Man and Resources*, published by the Canadian Council of Resource and Environmental Ministers, Montreal, 1972.

15
Northern Development: Some Social and Political Considerations

*Peter J. Usher**

Canada today is embarking on some of the most enormous resource development projects the world has ever seen. These include the James Bay hydro project, at a cost of $6-10 billion, if not more; the proposed Mackenzie Valley gas pipeline, at a cost of $5-8 billion (depending on whose estimates you care to believe); the Churchill River diversion; and several other proposed developments such as gas and oil pipelines from the High Arctic, development of the Athabasca Tar Sands, metal mining on Baffin Island and so on. The Mackenzie Valley pipeline, enormous as it is, is merely the tip of the iceberg so far as total proposed investment in oil and gas development is concerned. It seems that we are increasingly prepared to commit a significant proportion of the gross national product at a single stroke to any one of these projects.

As a school boy, I was both awed by and enthusiastic about such then-unprecedented development projects as the railway to Labrador and the St. Lawrence Seaway. The latter cost less than $500 million. Truly we have made a quantum jump since then, as we now contemplate several projects each costing ten to twenty times that amount. What are all these projects going to mean to Canadians? How intelligently will they be discussed as the political decisions on these issues are made.

Our decisions in the resource development field in the coming years will have as profound consequences for the future of Canadian society as a whole and in its parts as any other decisions we could possibly make. We will soon see whether we are to be an independent nation or a colony, what kinds of environment we are to have in this vast but no longer so unspoiled country, and how we treat minorities in our society and whether the areas they inhabit will be decent places to live.

I want to talk today about the impact of this kind of development on the North, with particular reference to the Mackenzie Valley pipeline,

---

*Peter J. Usher, a geographer, serves as Consultant to the Committee for Original People's Entitlement in Inuvik. This paper has been reprinted, with minor revisions, from an article entitled "Geographers and Northern Development: Some Social and Political Considerations," *Alternatives*, Vol. 4, No. 1, Autumn, 1974, pp. 21-25. It was originally presented as a paper at the Annual Meeting of the Canadian Association of Geographers, May 27, 1974.

and the role that geographers and other professionally trained people play in it.

Much has been said elsewhere about the environmental impact of the Mackenzie Valley pipeline, but I will add a few words about this as it affects native northerners. One hears much in the south about the supposed environmental impact of the pipeline itself. In fact the impact of the pipeline on permafrost, terrain and vegetation may be the least worrisome problem. Its impact on some fish and wildlife species is of more concern, although if the final outcome is an all-Canadian pipeline with no link to Prudhoe Bay via either the Arctic Coast or the mountains, some of these problems will be reduced. I say this with the proviso that it is easier to write adequate environmental regulations and provisions for pipeline construction than to enforce them. The experience with the Territorial Land Use Regulations (and other similar statutes and regulations) is that enforcement is a serious problem, partly because of expense and logistics, and also because there is at times an evident lack of concern on the part of enforcement agencies. This is particularly true of the Department of Indian Affairs and Northern Development, which has the dual role of encouraging such development and at the same time regulating it in the public interest.

What is of much greater concern to native people, however, is that the pipeline is not an isolated construction project unrelated to other activity. At the very least, the construction of the line is dependent on massive exploration and development activity in the Mackenzie Delta and on the Arctic Coast. The proving of sufficient gas and oil reserves involves extensive seismic exploration, drilling activity and, later, the construction of a network of feeder lines, roads, scrubbing plants and associated facilities. Seismic exploration alone has been a source of major concern to native people due to the destruction of vegetation, the disturbance of terrain, the blocking of creeks and the (at least temporarily) reduced availability of some game species in some locations. Many of these effects have not been scientifically evaluated, nor are there adequate plans to do so.

The prospect of off-shore drilling in the Beaufort Sea is another matter of grave concern to native people. In February, 1974, the Committee of Original Peoples Entitlement (the local native rights organization in that region) issued a statement calling for adequate environmental research and prior consultation before any off-shore drilling was permitted. It is evident that the gas pipeline is but the thin edge of a wedge. Oil development and transport seems an inevitable second step, one fraught with many more environmental hazards than natural gas. This is why the evaluation and debate about the gas pipeline project must not be conducted without consideration of the far broader developments already associated with it, as well as those it will surely entrain.

It may be supposed by many that since native people are now almost all living in settlements, and since many of them have jobs, the land and its resources are of declining importance to them. My own research in recent years indicates that this is definitely not the case. There are still small communities almost totally reliant on land-based resources, and in larger communities hunting provides a significant proportion of people's food. This food is highly valued for both nutritional and cultural reasons, to say nothing of its economic importance. The commitment to land-based resources and the way of life they sustain has not diminished among native people.

There is no immediate prospect that large numbers of southerners will choose to make a permanent home in the North. Most native people, on the other hand, have no desire to live anywhere else. They are therefore very naturally concerned to ensure that the North will be a decent place to live not only for themselves but for future generations. The maintenance of the land and its resources is of fundamental importance in ensuring that this will be the case. They are thus vital components of future development, even though their role in northern life has changed and will continue to do so.

Much publicity has been given in the south to native land claims. While these claims have a political and economic basis, we would be very much in error if we supposed that large cash settlements are what native people seek primarily. They do not view their land simply as a commodity to be exchanged for cash. It is the permanent basis of their welfare and security, and will not be lightly traded off.

One of the reasons the land is important is that, in the experience of the people of the Western Arctic and Mackenzie Valley, the white man's economy is by no means stable or reliable. Boom and bust have characterized economic development in those areas from the fur trade and whaling days to the present. The construction of the DEW Line and of Inuvik are but two recent examples. Jobs can come and go, but the land is always there. This is a significant element in the way local people look at development.

One of the major selling points of the pipeline is jobs for native northerners. Certainly there will be a large number of short-term jobs available, although Canadian Arctic Gas Study Ltd. (CAGSL) projects only about 200 man-years of employment directly generated in the operations phase. Essentially only the lower categories of jobs will be immediately available to native northerners, although doubtless in the longer term some will, because of training and experience, obtain senior level jobs. Since the regional labour force numbers only a few thousand, even the operations phase of the pipeline could employ a not-insignificant part of it. And there will be related developments which could employ more.

But what is the larger significance of such employment to the region? Past experience shows that massive short-term employment in the North has severe dislocating effects on both the communities to which workers are drawn and the ones they leave. It also shows that though the temporary influx of cash in the form of wages may be high, there are neither the traditions nor the mechanisms to develop local capital accumulation which alone can provide the means of transforming local resources into real wealth. Parenthetically, it seems to me a common error in economic impact assessments of short-term projects to confuse the generation of temporary high cash flows with the accumulation of real wealth. We have little evidence that large-scale resource development in any of the hinterland areas of Canada leads to long-term, balanced development in these areas.

There are a number of negative social impacts of short-term wage labour. One is the disruption of small community viability by a "decapitation" effect, whereby the most able members are drawn off. And there is the disruption of family life due either to the husband's absence from home or the move of the whole family to unfamiliar surroundings. Community life, relatives and friends are of profound importance to native people. Training for certain jobs often implies a commitment to mobility which is alien to native life. Many families have found that the economic benefit of wage employment is largely or completely offset if the husband is unable to hunt enough food for his family. It is also true that if the temporary influx of high wages and the resulting spending patterns cannot be maintained, many people feel they are worse off than before. Unrealistic expectations are set up, and these cannot always be fulfilled. The CAGSL application states that the pipeline and associated developments will be qualitatively different from those which have preceded, and will in fact provide the stability and growth which have not previously occurred. I for one do not find these arguments convincing, and it would seem that further research and evaluation are required.

It is inevitable that there will be an enormous influx of transient workers from the south. Although CAGSL proposes to provide health, housing and recreational facilities in self-contained construction camps, the impact on small communities cannot be completely eliminated. Inevitably, there will be increased problems of alcohol, sex, drugs and racism, and the associated disruption of family and community life. And there will be many transients not directly involved in the construction phase who will gravitate to major northern centres. These people will place heavy demands on local goods and services which will push prices upwards; this is already happening in Inuvik, particularly for housing. Such local inflationary effects certainly tend to offset increased wage benefits.

Politically, development has brought and will continue to bring an increased sense of alienation on the part of native people. Many, especially in the larger centres, feel they have become superfluous in their own land. Their previous knowledge and experience are devalued, and as white administrators and entrepreneurs exercise an ever-tightening grip over every aspect of town life, native people feel they have lost control over their own destiny. In the smaller centres people fear that their community may one day become like Inuvik or Fort Simpson, yet feel that at present, there is little or nothing they can do to prevent unwanted development. There have been recent political developments among native people aimed at counteracting these trends. Yet any massive influx of southerners will soon ensure that native people lose even the possibility of political control in the North by virtue of becoming a minority in their own land.

Undeniably, there has emerged in the larger, racially mixed settlements an ethnic-based class system. There is little prospect that future resource development will alleviate this situation, much prospect that such development will exacerbate it. In short, if the present drift of events continues, the North will not be a pleasant place to live in five or ten years' time. This is not to deny that many positive social developments are occurring in the North, but they seem to me to be happening in spite of, or in reaction to, the pipeline and related developments, and not as a positive result of them.

So much for my own views on the social and economic impact of the pipeline, which are after all only in part based on intensive research. The rest are those of a concerned and (I hope) intelligent layman who happens to be in a good position to see what is going on. What does all this mean to geographers and other experts, individually and collectively? Can they or should they have a role to play?

I would suggest at the outset that whatever role geographers, or other professionally trained scientists, play in the North, it cannot be entirely neutral. I do not wish to engage in a detailed critique of geographical writing on the Canadian North, but certainly much of it reflects the Canadian imperial vision of the North as our last frontier. Although there may be a debate about what should occur on this frontier and how, rarely does this debate flow from the basic proposition that native people have never relinquished ownership of the North, and that they might have full political rights to determine the future of their own society and territory rather than being colonial subjects of a supposedly benign federal government. Most general accounts of the North or of specific human activity there tend to accept recent developments and trends as inevitable if not desirable. Many geographers also teach courses in the North. I no longer have any idea what the content of these courses is, but certainly they will have some impact on the future life of the people who live in the North.

While the geographer's role from afar may be rather limited, some may have a more direct involvement. Along with other scientists, we may be increasingly required to act as advisors, consultants or expert witnesses in relation to massive development projects like the pipeline. These projects are characteristically presented as political *faits accomplis*, and only subsequently are we invited to participate in impact studies or evaluations. As we become involved in such endeavours, I think it is essential that we ask: who is sponsoring them? who will get to see them and use them? why were they commissioned? I know of no impact study without an ideology and set of assumptions, explicit or implicit. These are generally crucial to the study and hence to the people whose fate hangs in the balance, although perhaps that is over-dramatic since, when the real political decisions have to be made, impact studies are often used more for window dressing than as real input to those decisions.

Virtually every impact study I have read either assumes explicitly that development will occur, or shows very clearly the sponsoring agency's bias in favour of development even where a hypothetical "no development" case is considered. In the case of the Mackenzie Valley pipeline, we have several thousand pages of impact studies by government and industry which purport to evaluate the impact on terrain, hydrology, vegetation, wildlife, the national economy and the northern economy and society (although, I might add, they contain very few pages on the latter). CAGSL obviously wants to build the pipeline. The government, which is ultimately responsible for assessing the pipeline, has, long before the evidence is in, committed itself to its construction, and actively engages in propaganda to that end. Hence the government sees itself as evaluating not whether, but how best, to build the pipeline. Most consultants and members of assessment boards also see their role not as advising whether or not to build the pipeline, but how this may be done with the most benefit and the least harm. These stances in fact constitute ideological biases and assumptions which are built into the resulting studies.

I am not suggesting that this prejudices the specific conclusions of these studies. Usually that is not the case. Rather, this prejudices the kind of options that are examined. If we accept development and "progress" as unquestionable givens, even if we are a bit sympathetic to the people affected, we will tend to gear our impact studies to the "least harm, most benefit" option, and even explicitly exhort native people to make the best of what is coming, to adapt in whatever ways are necessary to maximize the benefits they could potentially realize from development. But suppose we carefully examined the implications of such options as native peoples having full property and sovereignty rights over their lands? Or native peoples mobilizing politically to prevent unwanted development? Or native peoples having substantial control over any kind of development to ensure that it is in their own best interests? I haven't seen any impact studies like that. Aside from the fact that such studies are extraordinarily difficult to finance, perhaps this is because the idea that human beings are servants of capital, and indeed that is as God ordained it, is very deeply rooted in our society.

Must we accept these projects in their major outlines, and be content to suggest minor changes to eliminate the most obvious hazards? Who will then examine the alternatives? Who will ask the basic questions, let alone answer them? Do we need gas now for export or gas later for Canada? What is meant by "acceptable" limits to environmental damage or social disruption, and to whom are these limits acceptable? To what degree can metropolitan Canada be allowed to ride roughshod over the needs and aspirations of local people (even though the government's recent northern development policy nobly states that meeting these needs and aspirations is its first priority)? Are these questions to be left solely to vitally interested but non-professional groups whom we can then in our scientific wisdom and detachment dismiss?

It seems that the real decisions to be made are usually moral, not technical. And the problem of leaning on the crutch of "objectivity" or "value neutrality", as well as limiting the scope of our inquiries to our "professional competence", is that our approach can too easily become amoral. A recent consultant's study on the pipeline anticipated that "during the transitional phase of development, racism, as a function of economic discrimination, will increase." No recommendation followed. What recommendation could follow, save that if southern interests are incapable of getting oil from the North without inflicting racism on the local inhabitants, they should wait for the oil until they are capable.

When does our scientific integrity become public amorality? When does one become aware of the misuse of scientific endeavour and act against it? How often do those of us doing research for public or private interests engage in — perhaps unwittingly — self-censorship? How far can we really see beyond our own class, professional or cultural biases? How often do we hesitate to bite the hand that feeds us, because we have to worry about where the next job or research grant is coming from? I am not suggesting that impact studies ought to consist of partisan propaganda, but they should not shy away from the really important issues on the grounds that these are somehow beyond the scope of inquiry. It is all too easy for us to say, "that question does not come under my terms of reference; that's not my job." Or as we often hear in our own profession, "oh, but that's not geography." If every one abdicates the responsibility to look beyond the supposedly narrow confines of his professional training, then whose job is it to look at the larger picture? After all, geography does occasionally claim to be an integrating science.

Many social scientists are of the view that their role is simply to present the information, and that it is the job of the government (or whoever else asks for the information) to decide what to do with it. My own experience in government was that this simply did not work. Nobody cared about the information except to blind the public with it if it were favourable, or suppress it if it were embarrassing.

The real problem, I think, is that examining the social and economic impact of some specific action is relatively meaningless unless it is done in the context of some larger vision of what society is or ought to be. We can suggest all manner of consequences flowing from all manner of options, but it is hard to evaluate these without some clear goal or vision in mind. Perhaps what is really needed is that larger vision (which is not amenable to technical analysis and is not achievable by placing ourselves in neat little slots), so that any proposed activity can then be measured in terms of whether it helps or hinders the realization of that vision.

Certainly this is difficult. It is especially so when a development is proposed by one society, the impact is to be felt by another, and there is no agreement between the two about the standards of evaluation. For assuredly, there are groups of people in this country who do not place individual gain above collective good, and mobility above community, and who do not see the transformation of their own society in the direction of the bourgeois liberal industrial model as either desirable or inevitable.

It would appear that the only people thinking seriously about a different plan for the future of the Mackenzie Valley are the native people. Their concern for balanced, long-term development under their own control is expressed by the land claims issue which they have struggled to bring forward and now seek to resolve. Native northerners not only have some vision about their future and their society, they also want people to help them realize it. Even though they have learned to be wary of social scientists and people with similar technical skills, they still have expectations of them. They would like such people to help them articulate their situation and their vision to the outside world with which they must inevitably deal, and to give them technical information, advice and support they need to realize their vision of the future. If they could commission research, instead of government and industry, maybe we would see the types of study I mentioned before.

Must we, as scientists and professionals, always work within the confines of the "reality" laid down by the growth ethic, and keep our private regrets to ourselves? Can we not insist that other groups besides government and industry be heard when the major development decisions are to be made, and make our technical expertise available to them when asked?

The Mackenzie Valley Pipeline Inquiry being conducted by Mr. Justice Berger could set an important precedent in the way resource development decisions are made in Canada. I think it is both our responsibility and in our interest as professionals to ensure that during these hearings all evidence is carefully gathered and evaluated, that those parties without massive financial and propaganda resources have the full opportunity to participate in that process, and that no irrevocable political decisions be made before that process is completed.

As it becomes the trend to involve professionally trained people in research and evaluation related to the impact of major development projects, we have no alternative but to become more aware of the political environment in which we will be operating. As the luxury of isolation disappears, our talents will be more and more open to prostitution, and our integrity will be more and more tested. I hope that in the future we will be able to look back and say we survived with honour.

Section IV
Water

Introduction

Commenting in the introduction to the first Canada Water Yearbook in 1975, Madame Jeanne Sauvé observed that "water . . . has played a historic role in the development of Canada, and it will continue to be a major factor in the nation's future."[1] Nevertheless, she cautioned that increased demands are placing heavy pressure on the quantity and quality of water in densely settled parts of the country. Administrative, jurisdictional and constitutional issues combined with conflicting demands for water need to be overcome. Problems to be faced range from water quality, flood plain management, hydropower development, comprehensive river basin planning and management to basic research. The papers in this section touch upon some of the management problems with which Canada is faced today and will face in future years. They cover the various perspectives discussed in Section I and illustrate a number of assessment and decision viewpoints discussed in Section II.

Each empirical study is interesting in its own right as specific resource management problems are illustrated. However, these studies have general implications for decision making and suggest a host of questions demanding attention. Some of the questions take the following form.

— Why have the federal and provincial governments made so little progress in developing comprehensive water policies? Indeed, are such policies even needed? Do decision models help to account for an apparent lack of policy?

— Are the nature and magnitude of water supply and demand adequately documented?

— What are the major water management issues in Canada? Are they the same in all parts of the country? Have they stayed the same or changed over the years? Will the issues of tomorrow be similar or different from those of today?

— What opportunities and problems are there in realizing international management of boundary waters? Does the existence of international problems make national and provincial policies more or less needed?

— When competing and conflicting uses for water exist, how should choices be made between them? Do we even know enough about the biophysical aspect of water and related land resources to appreciate the implications of creating huge man-made lakes or causing province- or country-wide diversions? How do assessment techniques aid decision makers in this regard?

— What expectations and role should individual citizens and organized interest groups have in the management of Canadian water resources? To what extent should data collected by government and private organizations be made available to the public?

— What is the theoretical range of management strategies available for any given aspect of water management? Why do decision makers consistently seem to concentrate upon a narrow range of options when other alternatives are no more expensive or disruptive?

— Why is there apparent reluctance to review plans, programs or projects in order to learn from experience? Why is the emphasis nearly always upon tomorrow with minimum attention to evaluating the past?

— Are experiences transferable from one part of the country to another? Or, are needs, customs, laws and attitudes too different across Canada to allow successful experiences in one place being implemented in another region?

Quinn, writing from the viewpoint of a federal civil servant, states that Canada does not have a national water policy. He discusses various reasons for the lack of policy — jurisdictional divisions, attitudes toward water — and then analyzes the Canadian approach to water management. His analysis evolves in two stages. First, experiences in the United States and Canada are compared. He argues that Canadians could learn much from the Americans whose management approach has been characterized by numerous comprehensive national studies including inquiries open to the public, inventories conducted at national and regional levels, and systematic evaluation of programs and projects. In contrast, Quinn suggests that the Canadian approach is only starting to incorporate such considerations.

In the second part of his review, Quinn examines Canadian water management policy and practice since 1960. He divides the period into three periods: 1961-1966, when the emphasis was upon water supply, single-purpose development of water potential through large projects, discussion and rejection of water export to the U.S., and investigation of possible inter basin diversions within Canada; 1967-1970, when the orientation changed towards water quality issues, new administrative arrangements and legislation (Canada Water Act), and agreement on three joint federal-provincial comprehensive river basin studies (Okanagan, Qu'Appelle, Saint John); 1971-, when the focus shifted to water being considered as only one aspect of an interrelated environment, emergence of environmental impact assessment, flood plain studies and continued attention to water quality. Recognizing the concept of an environmental web, Quinn suggests that perhaps a national water policy would now be of little use and that a national environmental policy is needed of which water would be one part. He then offers several principles upon which a national policy might be based.

The Skagit Valley, straddling the British Columbia-Washington border, provides the focus for an internationally oriented study. In his study, Perry documents the attempts of several citizens' groups to block Seattle City Light from raising the High Ross Dam on the Skagit River and thereby flooding part of a valley in British Columbia perceived to have high recreational, educational and scientific value. The controversy has boiled since 1969, when a group of Vancouver-based activists, supported by academics, began a campaign to stop the dam. The subsequent battle has ranged from Vancouver and Seattle to Washington, D.C., and has involved two federal governments, the IJC, a state government, two provincial political parties, and a municipality.

The Skagit Valley is indeed a lesson in environmental politics. It illustrates that the time required for approval of major projects can be lengthy and costly. Environmental impact assessments often appear to be overwhelming in detail and length. But assumptions can be made which lead to questionable conclusions during assessments. The role of politics in resource management emerges clearly, especially in the maneuvering of the Social Credit and NDP governments in British Columbia. The Skagit also shows that an aroused citizenry, willing to invest the time, money and effort to become well-informed, can have an impact upon the decision process.

A second paper by Quinn considers both national and international concerns. Focusing upon water transfers, Quinn argues forcefully that there is little chance for water exports from Canada to the United States. The Canadian governments have consistently maintained that export is out of the question until Canadian needs are understood better. Furthermore, the United States has placed a moratorium on all studies of regional water transfers until the late 1970s when it is hoped U.S. needs and supply sources will be identified.

Quinn suggests that the water needs of southern Canadians pose a more serious threat to the ecology, economic development and social patterns of northern Canada than do the needs of the United States. He believes that southern Canada would like to tap the water resources of the North to meet growing demands. And yet, Quinn is bothered by the fact that northern Canadians have not had the opportunity to indicate whether they wish to export their water southwards. Many of the same issues that arise concerning development of a Mackenzie Valley pipeline for oil and gas export occur. What would be the effect of water export projects upon northern wildlife, vegetation and native people? Who has the responsibility to make export decisions? What would be the benefits and costs at national and regional levels? These and other questions need to be answered before Canadians look to northern areas for future water supplies.

Damage by floods has been substantial across Canada, and has led to the federal and provincial governments agreeing on a joint flood hazards program for the late 1970s and 1980s. The study by Nelson *et. al*. illustrates some of the problems which occur in dealing with the management of areas subject to flooding. Although this study relates to flooding during 1972 along the Lake Erie shoreline, the implications have general application.

In assessing the strategies towards flood management in the study area, Nelson *et al.* draw conclusions supported by investigations elsewhere. It was found that strategies generally lacked appreciation of ecological processes, over-relied upon structural solutions (e.g. dams, dykes), were conceived in a crisis atmosphere, utilized financial arrangements which do not make recipients appreciate the costs, and failed to evaluate systematically economic, social or biophysical impacts.

Along the Lake Erie north shore, particularly the Rondeau and Point Pelee peninsulas, the study reveals that drainage initiated in the late 1800s was the first of several human modifications to the environment which has increased the potential for flooding. Drainage allowed wetlands to be farmed when climatic conditions were ideal. However, in times of high water these reclaimed lands still become inundated, with greater losses since they are inhabited. These losses generated a demand for seawalls, dykes and other structures to protect the drained areas. Again, these structures serve a purpose, but are inadequate in exceptional flood years. At the same time, the structures reduce the recreational value of the areas. Who, for example, would like a ten-foot high, twenty-foot wide rock wall on the beach between his cottage and the water? The study then considers non-structural alternatives such as public land acquisition. The costs of various strategies are compared and the structural ones are not obviously superior to some of the alternatives.

Jaakson considers a similar problem when dealing with water fluctuations on natural and man-made lakes, particularly those used for recreation. He maintains that agencies established to manage reservoirs comprehensively are an ideal which could be applied to natural lakes where frequently a variety of government departments end up working at cross-purposes.

As evidence, Jaakson examines the approach used for shoreline management around Lake Diefenbaker. He describes the variety of land-use controls employed to ensure that damage to human lives and buildings is minimized while recreational opportunities are maintained. He then investigates the Trent Canal reservoir-lakes in the Haliburton Highlands of Ontario. These controlled lakes, which supply water to the Trent Canal, have the control functions managed by a federal agency. Conversely, land adjacent to the lakes is managed by the provincial government. The result has been sale of land for cottages along lakes which experience considerable fluctuations due to their supply function. Jaakson considers the feasibility of transferring the Lake Diefenbaker experiences to these smaller lakes with a basic concern to improve the multiple use of the water resource.

Day's article, like Jaakson's, is focused at a local or regional scale. He maintains that we too often concentrate upon planning for the future rather than assessing what was right and wrong with earlier decisions. In this spirit, he re-assesses the Parkhill Dam and Reservoir, completed in September 1969 inland from Lake Huron. He compares the benefit-cost analysis done prior to the project with benefit-cost analysis based on data he collected in 1971 and 1972. His conclusion is that post-project reality suggests the dam and reservoir was a questionable investment with many benefits over-estimated and costs under-estimated.

The dam was justified mainly on the basis of flood control, water supply and recreation benefits. Day's analysis shows that only four of twenty-three farmers have benefited directly from the flood control function of the dam and that the town of Parkhill has received minor advantages. He also shows that financing arrangements led to a large subsidy being given to a few people. Based on this assessment, Day indicates that projects should be examined in a regional context, that those who will gain should be identified before construction, that non-structural alternatives should be considered, and that financing arrangements should be modified.

Mackintosh's paper represents a study in which a multi-disciplinary attempt was made to incorporate biophysical concerns into a local level resource management decision. The Hanlon Creek is a small 7,300 acre watershed adjacent to Guelph. Although currently agricultural and the site of a wild fowl park, its proximity to Guelph makes it a logical place for urban expansion. In fact, urban encroachment has started, and an expressway transects the watershed. The purpose of Mackintosh's study was to determine the impact of the expressway on the creek's ecology, and to estimate the long-term ecological impact of urban expansion upon the creek.

In this paper, Mackintosh describes the procedure which was used in the study. Groundwater, soils, vegetation and wildlife were studied as well as leisure and recreation needs. The inventory and analysis shows the intricate balance in a natural system, and how changing one part of the ecosystem will lead to change in others. What is worse, problems arising from changes do not show up for several years, usually after it is too late to do anything. Mackintosh believes that such studies as his, applicable at any scale, can identify sensitivities and help resource managers design in a way which will minimize disruptive effects. He also feels that such work can only be done with a team of people from a variety of disciplines.

NOTES

[1]Mme. Jeanne Sauvé, *Canada Water Yearbook 1975*, Ottawa, Information Canada, 1975, p. 3.

16
Notes for a National Water Policy

*Frank Quinn**

To the best of my knowledge, a formal statement of national water policy has never been articulated for Canada. Perhaps this is all the more apparent today by contrast with policy statements recently made in other important fields, like energy and foreign affairs. In any event, the federal government is petitioned from time to time by editors and writers to take the lead in formulating something similar with regard to the national water situation.

Two compelling arguments might be advanced for the present state of affairs, i.e., the failure to develop a coherent national framework for water policies as opposed to specific policy applications such as the restriction of phosphate in detergents. The first is that Canada is still a young country in terms of economic development where the water resource is visibly abundant and the demands upon it, at least until recently, have been relatively small. If this were once an acceptable excuse, however, it is becoming less so all the time. The second reason is more durable: our politically reinforced regionalism. Jurisdictional divisions between the two senior levels of government in Canada are in most respects more formidable than in Britain or even in the United States. This must have become apparent to anyone who followed British Columbia's success in changing the terms of the Columbia River Treaty negotiations between 1961 and 1964. Historically, the sheer size (or isolation) of most provinces facilitated the independent development of their water wealth. The extensive federal agency structures dominant in water management in many countries have not evolved in Canada. Before considering the nature of national policies and programs, therefore, it will be essential to develop an appreciation of the sovereign status of the ten Canadian provinces in respect to their water resources.

Other matters will be relevant to this discussion — a reference to U.S. water policies and practices for contrast; a summary of trends in modern

---

*Frank Quinn is Head, Social Studies Section, Water Planning and Management, Environment Canada, Ottawa. Originally published under a similar title in the proceedings of the *Geographical Inter-University Resource Management Seminars*, Waterloo, Wilfrid Laurier University, Department of Geography, Vol. 4, 1973-1974, pp. 11-23, this paper has been revised and updated by the author.

water management; a checklist of desirable elements to be included in framing national policy.

These are presented largely as personal notes. It should be understood that these notes are the product of one public servant's limited experiences and views at the federal level. The perspective would almost certainly be different from a provincial capital or even from Ottawa if some of my colleagues were to address the same topic.

Canada-United States Contrasts

Perhaps the most significant difference in the way the two countries approach water policy is the more deliberate attempt within the United States to come to grips with the issue.

Periodically, national commissions or like bodies are created by President or Congress for the specific and announced purpose of critically reviewing and recommending improvements on the nation's water policies and programs. This has happened at least twenty times since the turn of the century, the latest example being the National Water Commission which reported in 1973.[1] P.L. 90-515 (1968) charged the Commission to tell the nation "what it has done right, what it has done wrong, and what it is not doing that it should be doing." Canada has undertaken nothing of this magnitude for water resources, although we have mounted royal commission investigations, white paper proposals, and nationwide conferences on related topics like energy, transportation and multiple-resource use.[2] Presumably water is not as much a problem for this country as it is south of the border.

National assessments of resources and resource policy in the United States are characteristically conducted in open, public view, often by personnel drawn from outside the public service. Confidentiality of reporting is not as evident as in Canada where intra- and intergovernmental task forces act with more (some might say excessive) discretion to protect Cabinet solidarity. The American public has an advantage of access to information and, more frequently than in Canada, an opportunity to participate and respond to findings and recommendations.[3] To mention again the example of the National Water Commission: terms of reference and funding were embodied in law; the preliminary plan of study was discussed in public conferences where alternative suggestions were invited; all commissioned documents were released as received during the course of investigations; progress reports were published annually; and a draft of the final report was made available to the public for review and comment at regional meetings three months before the Commissioners finalized their recommendations.

The regular agency functions of the U.S. Government and the nature of federal-state programs have sometimes been profoundly affected by such investigations. Itself the product of an earlier national assessment, the U.S. Water Resources Council was created in 1965 as a federal co-ordinating agency. It has inherited and earnestly pursued at least two functions which have no real counterparts in Canada. One of these is to maintain a continuing assessment of the adequacy of water supplies to meet present and future requirements nationally. Much of this work is accomplished through supporting federal-state basin commissions which prepare comprehensive regional development plans. Detailed regional projections of water need across the nation are currently underway. No similar assessment of water supplies, problems and future needs has been attempted in Canada, although federal officials frequently alluded to this task in the latter half of the 1960s as a means of buying time against a perceived water export threat from the United States, and also as an essential information base for building a "national water policy".[4] In fact, no systematic effort resulted before 1970 and an internal federal survey about that time aborted under the weight of departmental reorganization and other budget priorities.

Secondly, the Water Resources Council is responsible for improving the elaborate guidelines which exist for federal water project evaluation in the United States. Benefit/cost analysis, with all its faults as practised, has long been a prerequisite for Congressional approval. More sophisticated principles and standards for planning and evaluating water-related projects have recently been released by the Council after several years of testing and public hearings.[5] If Canadian governments have not yet implemented some of the more questionable projects that can be found south of the border, it is not because we have applied more systematic criteria for evaluating them. We have no standard guides, no consistent criteria, although there have been attempts to develop them in the benefit/cost area. Likewise, there is no assurance that water-related proposals are routinely and consistently analyzed for economic and environmental feasibility before federal or provincial agencies announce them.

Much of the difference between our countries, of course, is a matter of history and geography, following from the longer experience and greater needs of the American people as regards water. Until recently, Canadian demands have been small upon a resource which is abundant (except in the southern Prairies) and the provinces and territories large or isolated enough to develop supplies without conflict with neighbouring jurisdictions. No superior court was needed, as it has been so often in the United States, to separate and limit provincial autonomies for the greater national benefit.

But more significantly, the stronger authority at the federal level allows the U.S. Government to adopt a national leadership role not apparent in Canada. States' rights, under the American Constitution and its repeated interpretation in court, do not approach the status of provincial rights in Canadian waters.

Jurisdictional Division and Political Accommodation

The legal framework for water management in Canada has been conditioned almost entirely by the British North America Act which was the instrument of our Confederation in 1867. A reading of that Act leads one to draw a distinction between the proprietary and legislative rights of governments to water, that is, between who owns the resource and who can legislate regarding its use.[6] This distinction is unimportant only in the northern territories where the federal Parliament retains complete jurisdiction. Elsewhere, the provinces *own* the resources. As owners, they may authorize and license development, regulate flows, and levy fees for most uses. The federal government, on its part, can legislate exclusively with regard to navigation and fisheries, concurrently in matters of agriculture, and indirectly in regulation of interprovincial and international undertakings, including trade.

What this early legislation could not foresee, of course, were the modern needs for multiple-purpose development and the interdependencies in the economy and ecology of water use across broad regions. Nor have the courts ever been important in Canada in defining or extending jurisdictional limits or in establishing principles for water allocation. Many questions of water law have never reached the courts; indeed there has been no litigation on interprovincial waters except incidentally to disputes over other matters. Federal legislation generally tends to be permissive in response to provincial needs.

In Canada, a comprehensive approach to water management is almost by definition a joint federal-provincial approach. To suggest that the two levels of government should proceed separately under their respective powers is to miss the point. There are practical as well as constitutional responsibilities to consider, especially where large-scale, multi-purpose developments may be beyond the technical and financial capacity of some individual governments and where they may have significance beyond the jurisdiction of a province. Engineering, economic and environmental factors loom so large today that it would seem almost mandatory for Canadian governments to co-operate where possible for mutual advantage rather than fight over the grey areas of legal uncertainty. In short, the federal and provincial governments must work out their water relations in a political setting in which jurisdictional separation is bridged, more or less successfully, by co-operative arrangements.

To the extent that intergovernmental co-operation is effective in realizing potential opportunities and in forestalling crises, or at least in responding to them quickly, then courts and legislatures need not define so closely the limits of future action.

A Personal History of Modern Canadian Water Management

For the sake of argument, three periods are selected to represent modern trends in Canadian water management. We begin at 1961, the year in which the Resources for Tomorrow Conference provided a national forum for intergovernmental dialogue and public education.

A word of explanation may be in order about this gathering, assembled at the request of the Prime Minister. RFT did not initiate a new period of resources management so much as underline the values which had already taken root and which would under its aegis become more widely disseminated. The Conference papers reflect a positive atmosphere, one where opportunities were recognized for regional economic gains through the development of natural resources. The theme of the conference was set early:

> . . . our concern is not just with resources alone but with resources in relation to capital and labour, and our complex of institutions as they all, in turn, relate to the objectives of growth. . . . We must be able to turn resources into income and employment opportunities.[7]

If "economic growth" was the theme, "multiple-use" and "co-ordination" were the means most often alluded to. A careful review of the proceedings, however, suggests that multiple-use development was more slogan than guidebook for river basin management; the complementarity of different uses of water for cumulative benefit seems to have been better appreciated than the conflicts and trade-offs that finally must be made. The focus on intergovernmental co-ordination led to agreement among the federal and provincial governments to create the Canadian Council of Resource Ministers (CCRM, now CCREM to include environmental concerns) which is apparently now fading into obscurity after several years of useful service. The early years of the Council saw special attention given to water resource publications.

PERIOD I: SUPPLY ORIENTATION, 1961-66

If RFT reflected a general feeling of optimism about the potential benefits of Canadian resources development, then water projects were already among the more impressive symbols of progress in that direction. Although the three decades of 1950 through 1980 may with justification be termed the great dam building era in Canadian history, in fact most of them were completed, under construction or committed in principle before or during the early sixties. The largest of these included Mactaquac (N.B.); Churchill Falls (Nfld.-Lab.); Manicouagan

(Quebec), St. Lawrence Seaway and Power (Quebec, Ontario); Winnipeg Floodway, Churchill-Nelson (Manitoba); South Saskatchewan (Sask.); Columbia Treaty, Peace (B.C.).

A philosophy prevailed that Canada was wealthy in water and that the main challenge lay in making it available for use by means of structures for storing and/or withdrawing it from nature. It was important to put this resource to work for the self-evident needs of a young and growing economy. Technical considerations relating to the provision of water supply were therefore given priority. These were heady days for the practitioners of water development who were almost entirely engineers and hydrologists.

Initiative for project construction invariably developed at the provincial level. A sense of "nationalism" prevailed in the larger and wealthier provinces, most currently in Quebec and British Columbia where the legislatures established public corporations to take over private companies and to spark new regional development by harnessing the hydro-electric potential of their major rivers.

Federal involvement was important but limited. A role of national leadership was maintained in provision of financial and technical assistance to certain provincial proposals; in collecting and analysing data nationally on water levels and flows; in research on the hydrologic cycle and on impacts of engineering and other activities of man; and in joint investigations with the United States on boundary water problems. One instrument for financial assistance was the Canada Water Conservation Assistance Act of 1953. A product of its time, the CWCAA was biased toward structural development, specifically flood control, and allowed federal authorities only to accept or reject provincial proposals on a rigid cost-sharing basis. ARDA was a more lenient federal benefactor for many provincial projects and others were supported on an *ad hoc* basis.

The United States was both a positive and negative influence on Canadian water policy and planning during this period. Under a national power policy announced in Ottawa in 1963,[8] surplus power could be exported on a long-term basis to U.S. markets as a means of underwriting the capital cost of large hydro programs to be extended into remote areas of the provinces, on rivers like the Peace and Nelson. Previously such exports had been discouraged in the fear that repatriation would be difficult or impossible; now the concern was that Canadian hydro development should be accelerated before nuclear power captured the international market. Secondly, Canada's senior governments responded cautiously but negatively to water export overtures which began with the NAWAPA scheme from Los Angeles in 1964 and continued through a number of variations for several years.[9] Official views were not influenced, at this time anyway, so much by the social or environmental disruptions such schemes would cause Canadians as by the belief that we should explore alternatives to continental thinking in terms of large-scale diversion possibilities within this country. Hence, Alberta formulated its own provincial water redistribution plan in 1965, called PRIME. And the federal government arranged to jointly investigate potential water supplies in the north with Ontario in 1965 and with the three Prairie provinces in 1967.[10] These were purely investigations of water supply and engineering feasibility, reinforcing the orientation already prevalent in Canadian water management, as opposed to systematically evaluating trends and conflicts in water uses or future needs. According to tradition, it was only sensible to avoid social issues until the physical dimensions of feasibility had been established (even if this took several years).

PERIOD II: PROSPECT FOR CHANGE, 1967-70.

Although dam construction continued at an impressive pace and inventories of potential water supply were extending ever northward, not everyone was pleased. In the experience of many Canadians, water was proving neither an inexhaustible nor an indestructible resource. The distress suffered by established communities and their environmental bases by the Columbia and Peace projects in British Columbia, the worsening pollution of the lower Great Lakes by urban-industrial effluent, these and other instances were causing widespread alarm and calls for corrective action among the Canadian public. The water export controversy only accentuated a lack of official preparedness for responding to present problems by raising the specter of future problems and needs.

Initiatives taken by the federal government in this period were mainly organizational and legislative.[11] The prime water responsibilities federally were consolidated in 1966 into a water sector within the Department of Energy, Mines and Resources. An "interim" Interdepartmental Committee on Water was created and chaired by EMR to co-ordinate all federal agency programs before their submission to Cabinet.

A federally organized Canada Centre for Inland Waters at Burlington and a university research support program were both founded at this time to produce practical solutions to water related problems through interdisciplinary (primarily scientific) research. The Centre focused first on Great Lakes eutrophication and waste treatment problems and contributed substantially to an eventual water quality agreement on the Lakes with the United States.

With the limitations of previous federal-provincial arrangements and the poor record of the CWCAA specifically in mind, as well as a recognized need to become more comprehensive, federal ministers spoke of a pending "national water policy" and of enacting a new Canada Water Act. In 1967, EMR Minister Pepin offered to carry out at federal expense a comprehensive basin planning experiment with the province(s) in each of the major regions of Canada. These would embody the spirit of the forthcoming Canada Water Act, and were negotiated as intergovernmental cost-shared agreements covering the Okanagan, Qu'Appelle, and Saint John Basins before the proclamation of the Act in 1970.

In the Prairies, solid agricultural support for traditional PFRA water development programs was sufficient to resist a takeover of this agency by EMR water sector. However, PFRA was instructed to negotiate the transfer to the provinces of major irrigation works it had constructed and continued to operate, after rehabilitation; also to redirect its programs toward community water supply and sewage works, including the infra-structural needs of native settlements.

Meanwhile, the Canadian Council of Resource Ministers sponsored a national conference on the issue of pollution and briefly took up the matter of water pricing. EMR itself sponsored seminars on water demand forecasting and on perceptions and attitudes in resources management.

The uncertainty of the times and rapidity of change carried into the drafting of the Canada Water Act from 1967 when it was intended solely as enabling legislation for more flexible federal-provincial arrangements in consultation, initiative and the adoption of modern planning techniques including public involvement; in short, more socially oriented and comprehensively planned basin development. By 1970 when it became law, the Act's emphasis had shifted markedly toward water quality management.[12] Regional water quality management agencies were to be established sequentially by the federal and provincial governments to set objectives, standards, schedules and effluent fees. By this time the pollution issue had made such an impression on Cabinet that the Act was only one of six new pieces of legislation dealing with that subject, and one of the five dealing with water pollution.

There seems to have been less organizational-legislative reform in water administration among provincial governments during these few years. It must be recognized, however, that some provincial governments (especially Ontario) were already operational in the area of water quality monitoring and waste treatment facilities before federal authorities "discovered" pollution as a national issue about 1969.

PERIOD III: CAUGHT IN THE ENVIRONMENTAL WEB, 1971-?

In the fall of 1970, the government of Canada announced its intention to create a Department of the Environment, consolidating a number of renewable resource agencies just as the 1966 reorganization had consolidated water responsibilities. Similar departments and agencies were created in most provinces. Of course, many agencies with important resources development functions necessarily remained outside the formal environmental structure, leaving the task of co-ordination as important as ever.

Environmental policy was intended to be holistic, i.e., greater than the sum of air, water, land, forest, wildlife, fishery policies. It was expected to favour planners and co-ordinators with broader skills, to give status to integrators over single-resource operators. Behind the rhetoric, however, old professional biases persisted as each functional group struggled to preserve its identity and expertise, reluctant to restrain its own special relations and commitments to supporting interests. The great majority of personnel in the new organization still function as managers, researchers and operators of programs in water, wildlife, etc., while relatively few are principally concerned with regulation of development and protection of the natural environment.

The cosmetic role of current federal-provincial environmental impact assessments in relation to major hydro developments is evidence that governmental decisions continue to be motivated by other goals. All of the recent election campaigns also indicate the lack of clout of environment as an issue in this period of widespread concern over employment and inflation. It remains potent locally, however, and has become accepted at higher levels of decision making as one more factor for consideration. For those who expected greater things in 1970, the realization must come that environmental impact assessments will continue to be made at the discretion of governments and not at the risk of interfering with political commitments; and that governments are reluctant to experiment much further with "public participation" as a means of determining the social acceptance of major resource developments.

It is difficult to characterize this period in water management terms both because of its currency and the confusion of disparate federal and provincial activities underway across Canada. These latter consist of: (a) scattered investigations directed toward establishing comprehensive basin management plans; (b) environmental impact assessments of major hydro projects, largely after the fact of political commitment to development; (c) monitoring and research in water quality, implementation of discharge regulations and financial aid for municipal and industrial treatment facilities; (d) continued construction of storage reservoirs and dykes to advance new regional development or protect existing floodplain investment. A telling example of cross-trends can be drawn from new federal Cabinet interest in broader strategies to flood problems to include hazard mapping and incentives for land-use regulations, motivated by the possibility of transferring increased responsibility for consequences to the local level; meanwhile the same government has extended its funding commitment for dyking miles of shoreline along Lake Erie and the lower Fraser River. Dyking proceeds without serious consideration of alternative measures and, in the Fraser case, after removing requirements for local financial contribution to the works.[13]

Overall, it is apparent that the prestige attached to water management in the 1960s has been eroded within the environmental umbrella organizations. The "water crowd" became for a time a target for attack for its historic engineering bias and insensitivity to environmental relations, a condition now improved by the beginnings of reform in the direction of comprehensive basin planning.

Elements of a National Water Policy

The events of recent years raise the question of whether it is worth the time and trouble to formulate a national policy for water or whether this will be handled better as a component of national policies for the economy and the environment. It is suggested here that the latter are larger policy areas or frameworks which will lack applicability unless they can draw upon, as well as provide context for, the identified needs and plans specific to each major resource. One might consider that these are mutually reinforcing levels in a policy hierarchy.

Another objection to formulating a national water policy should be briefly considered. Given the milieu of overlapping jurisdictions and the periodic need for policy adjustments as new circumstances arise or unexpected results occur, an official statement of national water policy in other than the most general of terms may not be attractive at the political level. We do not need motherhood statements, of course, but we do need flexibility. Canadian experience has been reasonably successful in applying particular policies where and when appropriate to the situation (e.g., flood relief, regional development assistance, waste treatment loans) and in changing these as considered necessary. *It remains, however, to draw from our varied policy applications an assurance of national direction which can be consciously supported by the Canadian population*. The very exercise, of course, forces us to think beyond the confines and immediacies of existing problems.

If the preceding doubts can be overcome, who should logically participate in formulating an acceptable policy framework? The task is not a prerogative of the federal government by reason of its superior authority. "Federal" is not synonymous with "national", especially in the area of natural resources policy; agreement among the eleven senior governments on the substance of a Canadian water policy would be critical to its political life. Nonetheless, the initiative for formalizing such a policy would logically be taken at the federal level, where alone there is a recognized responsibility for the welfare of all Canadians and a corresponding interest in the interregional distribution of policy consequences. The federal leadership role is in the nature of providing the forum and moderator for discussions aimed at consensus, exercising influence rather than imposing jurisdictional superiority, even in matters affecting international relations. Usually it has been an international stimulus (Stockholm; Law of the Sea) which brings the federal and provincial levels together to develop a national position. In the event that some provinces cannot be interested in joining a policy forum, the federal government can still meet with the remaining provinces individually and jointly, summing up the extent of consensus as a first cut toward national policy.

Although the drafting exercise may be an intergovernmental responsibility consisting of proposals and counter-proposals, opportunities should also be available at the outset for public and interest group views, and before completion for public hearings and review. In this way the product may legitimately reflect a larger degree of popular understanding and acceptance.

The above approach will have the double advantage of clarifying the role of different levels of government in water management as the courts and governments individually are unable to do, and of establishing the necessary basis for public participation in water-related decisions.

Without attempting to prescribe limits for or elements of a national water policy, the following suggestions are raised for consideration:

1. Adoption of a more forward outlook which deliberately and systematically anticipates the water problems and needs of Canadians in the future. What are our longer-term objectives and interim targets likely to be? What alternative futures can be identified? These should be translated into water demands, for which a number of solutions can be proposed and consequences elaborated for public review, then policy choice.
2. Commitment to evaluate the effectiveness of ongoing water-related programs and intergovernmental arrangements (federal-provincial, international), including analysis of the distribution as well as the magnitude of benefits and costs, and comparison of program results with original projections and policy expectations.

   It has become painfully apparent that federal and provincial water agencies continue to be diverted by the immediacies of problems specific to time and place. Probably 95 per cent of our planning is reactionary with almost no organizational responsibilities assigned either to (1) long-range planning or (2) routine evaluation.
3. Integration of water with broader regional, and especially land-use planning. We are approaching the end of an era in which water

control developments have had important impacts on land use through navigation, irrigation, power, drainage and flood control. Increasing recognition must now be given to the crucial influence of land use on water resources. Building regulations, land zoning, discharge permits, standards surveillance, hazard insurance, intake metering and pricing, demand forecasting — all of these tools and processes will require a more sophisticated understanding of the regional economy beyond the water's edge. Integration with related considerations at the national level would include national policies of taxation, trade, investment, and immigration.

In retrospect, all of these suggestions lead back to the philosophy of comprehensive water management, a philosophy which has been widely adopted in principle and initiated experimentally on a limited river basin scale. Probably its major political disadvantage is its long-term evolution which is not amenable in the interim to responding, as we are currently used to, one year to pollution, a second year to energy needs, a third to floods. That is not to say that all of these situations cannot be accommodated by a comprehensive approach; they can and should be. But the centrifugal forces of single-minded crises continue to overpower.

As practised on a sequential basin-by-basis scale, comprehensive water management has been necessarily slow to win acceptance. There has been little corresponding progress at the national level. It is one thing to encourage local participation in planning, and to allow for variation in management according to conditions of water availability and demand, but it is too much to expect that operational personnel at a regional level can perfect analytical techniques and develop policies for broader application. Why wait until the need for principles and policies becomes obvious to all in the passage of time, then formulate them incidentally and incrementally out of the findings of ongoing basin investigations? What is argued here is the advantage of supplementing the insights of such investigations with a national overview. That overview, a policy framework for Canadian water management in the last quarter of the twentieth century, can only dimly be perceived at present by anyone.

NOTES

1. U.S. National Water Commission, *Water Policies for the Future*, Washington, Government Printing Office, 1973.
2. Canadian Council of Resource Ministers, *Proceedings of the National Conference on "Pollution and our Environment"*, Ottawa, Queen's Printer, 1967.
3. R. T. Franson, "Governmental Secrecy in Canada", *Nature Canada*, Vol. 2, No. 2, April/June, 1973, pp. 31-34.
4. Canada, *House of Commons Debates*, Ottawa, Queen's Printer, Sept. 2, 1964 (7575-7576); June 28, 1966 (6995-6997); April 3, 1967 (14472-14475); Oct. 10, 1968 (1022); Feb. 24, 1970 (4006-4008).
5. U.S. Water Resources Council, "Principles and Standards for Planning Water and Related Land Resources", *Federal Register*, Vol. 38, No. 174, Sept. 10/73 Part III, 24778-24869.
6. D. Gibson, "The Constitutional Context of Canadian Water Planning", *Alberta Law Review*, Vol. 7, No. 1, 1969, pp. 71-92.
7. Hon. Walter Dinsdale, "Historical Perspectives and Expectations of the Conference", *Proceedings of Resources for Tomorrow Conference*, Vol. 3, p. 7.
8. Canada, *House of Commons Debates*, Ottawa, Queen's Printer, October 8, 1963 (3299-3301).
9. F. Quinn, "Water Transfers: Must the American West be Won Again?" *Geographical Review*, Vol. 58, No. 1, Jan. 1968, pp. 108-132.
10. Inland Waters Directorate, Environment Canada, *Northern Ontario Water Resources Studies*, (Summary Report on Engineering Feasibility and Cost Investigations), Ottawa, 1973; and Canada, Alberta, Saskatchewan, Manitoba, *Water Supply for the Saskatchewan-Nelson Basin*, Summary Report, Ottawa, 1972.
11. J.W. MacNeill, "Assumptions Made by the Canadian Government in Establishing Strategies for Environmental Quality Improvement", *Managing the Environment*, edited by A.V. Kneese, S.E. Rolfe and J.W. Harned; New York, Praeger, 1971.
12. E.R. Tinney and R.J. Van Loon, "Canadian Federal Water Resource Policy", *Water Management*, Paris, O.E.C.D., 1972.
13. Fraser River Board, British Columbia and Canada, *Annual Report, 1973-74*, Ottawa, 1974.

17
The Skagit Valley Controversy: A Case History in Environmental Politics

*Thomas L. Perry Jr.**

In 1969, if one had asked an average British Columbian for the past year's highlight, a likely response might have been the completion of the mammoth W.A.C. Bennett Dam at Portage Mountain on the Peace River. Had one inquired, on the other hand, about the Skagit Valley a blank look would have been the best one could have expected.

In the 1970s, the Skagit Valley became an environmental *cause celebre* in British Columbia, a continuing headache for politicans in Seattle, Ottawa, and Washington, D.C. as well as Victoria. An important wilderness resource in its own right, it is far more significant as a symbol of the changes which have occurred in British Columbians' attitudes toward the resources and environment of their province. Where so recently both press and public hailed hydroelectric power projects as monuments to progress, new dams and other large-scale resource developments are now eyed with a wary suspicion, particularly when they involve the export of energy resources to the United States. Bennett Dam and the Columbia River Treaty projects, once seen as keys to the good life, are now more often regarded as embarrassingly permanent relics of an era of monumental shortsightedness.[1] The Skagit Valley controversy has been both product and invaluable catalyst of the environmental revolution in British Columbia.

Why did a small and little-known valley attract so much attention amidst a wealth of other seemingly more important environmental issues? Why have British Columbians had to fight so hard to regain a piece of land which was originally theirs? The answers to these questions form a complex and curious history, but may also provide some valuable lessons in environmental politics and the need for more rational decision-making processes where the environment is on trial in Canada.

---

*Thomas Perry is a past Co-ordinator of the Run Out Skagit Spoilers (ROSS) Committee. This paper is an edited version of an article with the same title published in *Alternatives*, Vol. 4, No. 3, Spring 1975, pp. 7-17, 33. The author has revised and updated the original article to include events up to the end of March 1976.

An Introduction to the Skagit

The Skagit River Valley is situated ninety miles east of Vancouver, at the limit of the populous Lower Mainland region (Figure 1). Lying in a gap between the mountain ranges which separate coastal B.C. from the interior of the province, it is a heavily glaciated U-shaped trough whose extraordinary flatness, gentle gradient, and low elevation distinguish it as a physiographic rarity in a region dominated by high mountains and precipitous V-shaped valleys.

Coastal and interior ecological zones overlap in the Skagit, resulting in an unusually diverse flora and fauna. A number of plants and animals occur in the valley at the limit of their range, including such rare and valuable species as the California rhododendron, which is limited to this one occurrence on the B.C. mainland. The Skagit supports dense populations of recreationally important animals such as deer, bear, beaver, and birds, all highly visible on the valley floor, and the river is famous for a high quality trout fishery which is unique in the region. As early as the 1930s the Skagit's ecological diversity was recognized by nature clubs from Vancouver which held summer camps in the valley.

Almost all of the Skagit Valley is Crown owned, and despite considerable recreational use and selective logging in recent years, the valley has remained in a basically wild and natural state. The contrast of high surrounding mountains with a flat valley floor and the exceptional beauty of the Skagit River give it superb scenic qualities. This combination of public tenure, favourable topography, ecological diversity, scenery, and proximity to Vancouver makes the Skagit uniquely important as a recreational, educational, and scientific resource for the Vancouver region.

Rising high in the mountains of Manning Provincial Park, the Skagit River flows south across the International Boundary into Washington State, reaching the sea some eighty miles north of Seattle. In Canada, the river is wild, but south of the border, the Skagit is impounded by a series of three hydroelectric dams owned by the Seattle City Department of Lighting. Ross Dam, uppermost of the three, creates a twenty-two mile long reservoir which extends one mile into Canada when full. Each fall, it is drawn down to generate electricity and provide flood storage capacity. At full drawdown, Ross Reservoir retreats nine miles down the valley, exposing thousands of acres of ugly mudflats. Drawdown continues until early May, when spring runoff begins to fill the reservoir, but full pool is not usually reached until late June.

Comprehensive development of the Skagit River's power potential was envisaged by Seattle Light as early as 1906, and Ross Dam was conceived with the intention of achieving this potential by stages. The final stage would heighten the present dam by 123 feet, extending Ross

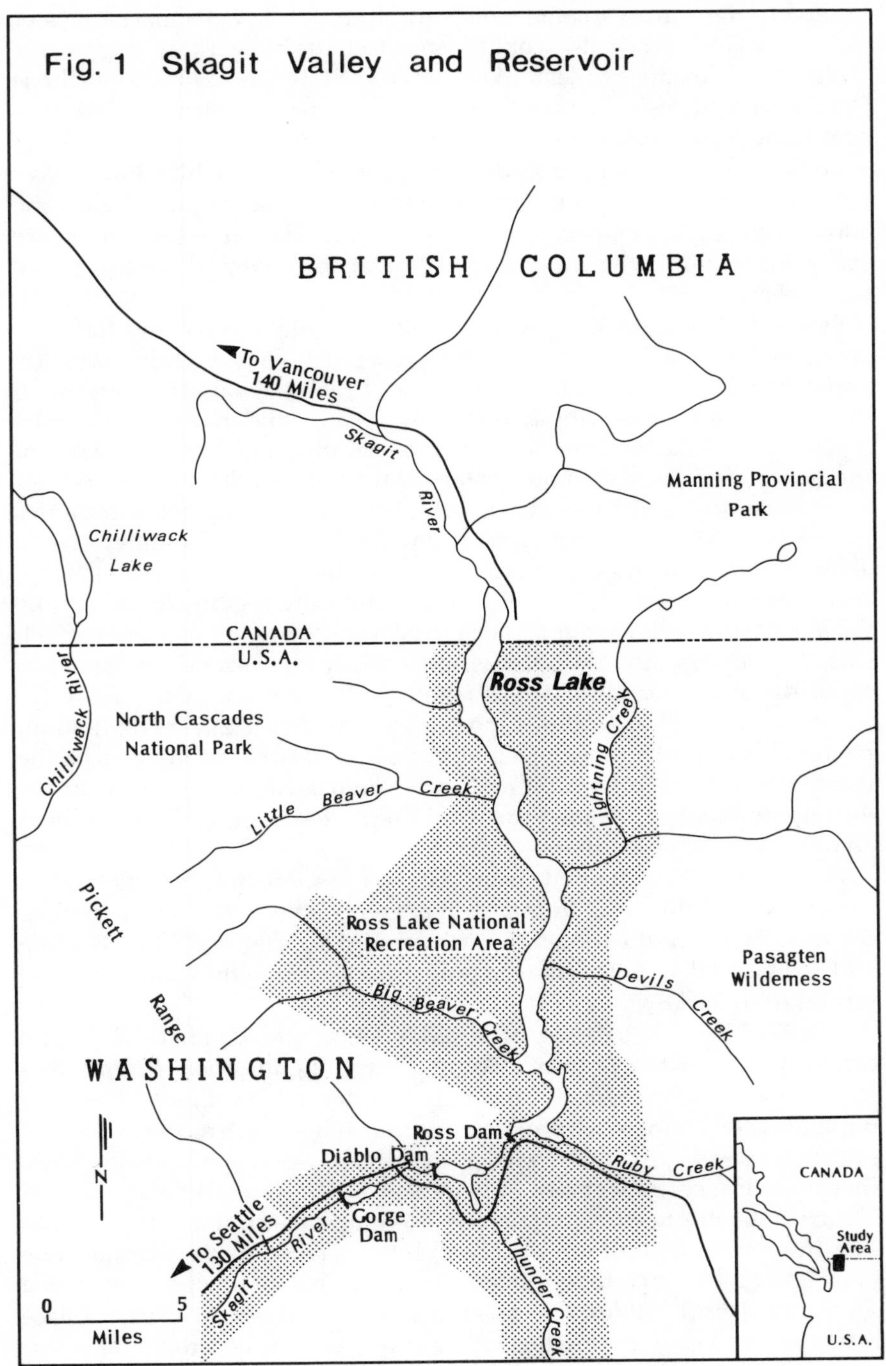

Fig. 1 Skagit Valley and Reservoir

Reservoir eight miles up the valley and inundating 7.3 square miles of Canadian land. Flooding would also affect the wilderness Big Beaver Valley south of the border in Washington State. In return, High Ross Dam would furnish an additional 35 MW of firm power and 294 MW peak generating capacity.

Some effects of the proposed flooding are obvious, while others have been the subject of long and expensive investigations. From the conservationist's perspective, the most important consequences are self-evident, while the conclusions of detailed ecological studies are all but irrelevant.

Essentially, the flooding would replace a unique river and flat land environment with a commonplace reservoir — something already superabundant in the Vancouver region. Much key habitat, along with the best sites for observing and studying plants and animals, would be replaced by a lake for three summer months and mud flats for the rest of the year. The Skagit's unique potential for nature education and other non-consumptive uses of its diverse wildlife and plant communities would be effectively destroyed. Inundation of ten river miles would eliminate the stretch best suited for river fishing, canoeing, picnicking, and camping, a resource irreplaceable within the region. Over half the flat land in the valley would be lost, forcing recreational use into a much smaller and less attractive area and reducing the Skagit's potential to serve the needs of families with young children and the elderly for whom B.C.'s mountainous topography is often a severe limitation. Finally, the key advantage of a long recreational season conferred by the valley's low elevation would be lost, since drawdown of the reservoir during nine months of the year would replace wilderness scenery with an ugly expanse of mudflats.

What would be gained from High Ross? Some modulation of drawdown would result from a larger reservoir volume, but the bulk of the mudflats would be shifted north from Washington to B.C. Boating and swimming opportunities would increase, but these are scarcely rarities in coastal B.C.

Considering the balance of gross effects, the detailed ecological consequences of the project assume a lesser significance. Would deer populations suffer drastic or only moderate declines? Would a population crash follow inundation of trout spawning grounds, or could the fish move to other spawning areas upstream? How many rhododendrons, rubber boas, or American redstarts would be drowned? Naturally such questions retain some importance, but a danger exists that in focussing attention on the minute details of the costume, one may ignore the fact that the emperor has no clothes! If our finest recreational and wilderness areas are sacrificed for a commonplace reservoir or a sea of mudflats, is it really any consolation that only a few deer will die and the redstart can fly to another valley?

This dichotomy of approach has marked the Skagit controversy throughout its development. From the start, public, press and environmentalists have perceived the issue in simple terms. A beautiful valley was to be sacrificed to supply affluent, if not profligate Americans with still more cheap energy. Environmental consultants for Seattle Light, on the other hand, have concentrated their attention on the detailed ecological effects of the project, largely ignoring the fundamental issue of wise resource use. Since governmental agencies investigating the issue have tended to adopt a similar approach, environmentalists have had to pursue a dual strategy, combining critical analysis of the detailed environmental impacts with activities designed to remind both public and government that the key issues are basically simple.

Some of the lessons of this campaign may be useful in other more important environmental battles, but before examining them in detail it is worth reviewing how a Canadian valley came to require such intensive effort for its repatriation.

The Long Road to Sellout

If few British Columbians had even heard of the Skagit Valley when Ross Dam first erupted into the public limelight in 1969, Seattle City Light was hardly so naive. For over fifty years, the municipally owned utility had included the Canadian Skagit within a grand design for the integrated hydro-electric development of the Skagit River system. In 1929, Seattle acquired the only privately owned land in the valley, and in 1930 the B.C. government lent its assistance by placing a Crown reserve on all lands within the proposed flood basin in Canada. Construction of Ross Dam began in 1937, to a design which would permit staged elevations to a final height of 1,735 feet above sea level.

World War II provided a sudden incentive to develop more electric power, and in 1941 Seattle applied to the International Joint Commission (IJC) for authority to raise Ross Dam and flood into Canadian territory. Established by the Canada-U.S. Boundary Waters Treaty of 1909, the IJC is a commission of three Americans and three Canadians which regulates projects involving international water bodies such as the Great Lakes, the St. Lawrence Seaway, or the Skagit River.

Traditional IJC procedure would have demanded advertised public hearings in the affected areas of both countries, and the notification of concerned officials at all appropriate levels of government. Unfortunately for the Skagit, the IJC response to Seattle Light's application was remarkably lax. A single public hearing, lasting less than two hours, was held in Seattle in September 1941. Of the six Commission members, three were absent, including the Chairman of the Canadian Section. Most of the hearing time was consumed by Seattle Light's technical presentation, while discussion of environmental effects of the dam was limited to a one-minute statement by the British Columbia Game Commissioner. Having never before heard of the project, he was unable to comment on the effects of flooding except to note the inevitable loss to "one of the best fly fishing streams in the whole of British Columbia." B.C.'s government did not oppose the project, subject to the condition that "suitable and adequate provision be made for the protection and indemnity of all interests in British Columbia that may be injured by construction or operation of the works."

Seattle Light's plans for the Skagit were news to the representative of the Canadian External Affairs Department, who had no immediate comment but assumed "that we will have an opportunity of presenting a brief later, after we have had a chance to study the details of this project as presented this morning." As it turned out, External Affairs never did offer a subsequent comment, presumably due to its preoccupation with more urgent matters of war.

That the 1941 hearing was really little more than a formality is apparent in a comment of the Chairman of the IJC's American Section. In closing the hearing, he apologized to Seattle Light that "ordinarily the Commission would attempt to make a provisional order authorizing you to proceed." In deference to the absent Chairman of the Canadian Section, however, decision was reserved for a later meeting of the Commission.

In January 1942, the IJC issued an Order of Approval authorizing the proposed flooding in Canada, on condition that Seattle and British Columbia arrive at a binding agreement for compensation of the province and private interests in B.C. It is important to realize that this Order, issued during an urgent wartime crisis after minimal consideration, is still the basis for Seattle Light's contention that it has legal authority to flood the Canadian Skagit.

Negotiation of compensation turned out to be a far more difficult and capricious process than expected, and since the end of the war relieved any urgent need for the power from High Ross, final agreement was not reached for twenty-five years. The intervening period was not, however, without incident. Seattle proceeded with the second and third stages of Ross Dam, and by 1949 its present elevation of 1,615 feet had been attained. In 1947 the B.C. Legislature passed an act authorizing Cabinet negotiation of an agreement without further reference to the Legislature, and by 1952 a tentative agreement had been reached allowing Seattle Light to flood the Skagit Valley for 99 years in exchange for a single cash payment of $255,508 and clearing of the reservoir basin. Just as the accord was to be signed, however, a provincial election toppled the Coalition government and began the twenty-year reign of Social Credit.

The events of the next two years constitute one of the strangest chapters in the Skagit story. W.A.C. Bennett, the new Premier, delayed signing of the agreement while reviewing provincial power policy. In August 1952 General A.G.L. McNaughton, Chairman of the IJC's Canadian Section, wrote to Bennett suggesting he reconsider the proposed accord in light of the different provisions of an IJC Order concerning Waneta Dam on the Pend d'Oreille River. Bennett's response is not clear. While negotiations with Seattle City Light had proceeded by May 1953 to the point that the City Council ratified the $256,000 agreement, British Columbia for some reason continued to stall the signing. In June, Seattle lost patience. Closing the flood gates at Ross Dam, it raised the reservoir to 1,600 feet, illegally flooding 500 acres of Canadian territory. B.C. ignored the violation.

In the fall of 1953, after a new election returned Social Credit with a parliamentary majority, B.C. suddenly informed Seattle that the compensation agreement was no longer acceptable. Premier Bennett had by this time realized the enormous value of downstream benefits provided by water storage in Canada, and was concerned that the proposed agreement with Seattle could set an awkward precedent for impending negotiations on hydro development of the Columbia River.

The issue came to a head in April 1954, when the U.S. Section of the IJC proposed that B.C. be compelled to accept $255,508 as full and final compensation for the flooding. British Columbia countered that no agreement had been signed, and General McNaughton termed Seattle Light's flooding into Canada a violation of Canadian sovereignty and the IJC's own 1942 Order. The up-shot was that the IJC refused to enforce a compensation agreement, while B.C. agreed to accept $5,000 per year as interim settlement for the 500 flooded acres, pending final resolution of the compensation issue. Seattle Light made a final attempt in 1958 to have the IJC impose a settlement, but this was again rebuffed. By now, British Columbia was determined to postpone negotiations until conclusion of the Columbia River Treaty, and to assure itself of a share of the downstream benefits in any compensation accord.

Ratification of the Columbia River Treaty in 1964 established the principle of shared downstream benefits and finally opened the way to a settlement in the Skagit case.[2] Considering how long the B.C. government had stalled Seattle's plans, the terms of the final agreement are truly astonishing. If the Columbia Treaty was a bad deal for Canada, the Skagit settlement signed by B.C. Resources Minister Ray Williston on January 10, 1967 was a dead giveaway. For an annual rental of $34,566 (or its equivalent in power), clearing of the flood basin, and replacement of an existing road, Seattle Light gained the right to flood 5,716 acres of prime Canadian land and to save itself $1 million per year on the cost of building alternative electric generating capacity. A regular meeting of the International Joint Commission in April 1967 "noted" the agreement, without formally considering or approving it, and for Seattle City Light fifty years of planning finally seemed to have been rewarded.

The Storm Breaks

Only a small article on a back page of the *Vancouver Sun* announced the selling of the Skagit in 1967, and the valley was promptly forgotten. Yet two years later, when Liberal M.L.A. David Brousson raised a question about High Ross Dam in the provincial Legislature, a storm of protest erupted. Environmental consciousness in B.C. had increased dramatically, thanks partly to a world-wide environmental awakening, and also due to the resource development policies of the Bennett government in the sixties.

A key initial stimulus to public opinion was the compensation agreement's stark injustice. If few British Columbians had ever heard of the Skagit Valley, it was obvious to most that the province had been skinned once again. The yearly rental of seven dollars per acre was less than the Skagit's value as a Christmas tree farm, and $35,000 compared pitifully with the $1 million Seattle expected to save each year by raising Ross Dam instead of choosing an alternative. (By 1974, the putative saving from High Ross had escalated to $4 million per year.)

Organized protest against High Ross came first from the North Cascades Conservation Council (NCCC), a Seattle coalition of environmental groups. In November 1969, a dozen B.C. outdoor and environmental associations formed the Run Out Skagit Spoilers (ROSS) Committee, and the battle for the Skagit began in earnest. Ever since, the campaign has been distinguished by a unique blend of genuinely spontaneous public concern, continuous surveillance and occasional leadership by the ROSS Committee, and consistent publicity from a sympathetic press.

Despite the opposition, had High Ross Dam been a B.C. Hydro project it almost certainly would have been completed years ago. With the IJC and B.C. approval obtained, only internal American regulatory processes remained in Seattle Light's way. To proceed with High Ross, Seattle City Light requires approval from its parent, the Seattle City Council, and most important, from the U.S. Federal Power Commission. The Washington Department of Ecology also has an advisory role, but has no power to stop the project. Ironically, these American proceedings have offered Canadians their most fruitful means to oppose the flooding of the Skagit.

In 1970 the first hearings ever held on environmental effects of High Ross took place before the Utilities Committee of the Seattle City Council. In contrast to the IJC's two hour 1941 hearing, opposition to the project was fierce, and for the first time Canadian public opinion was represented. From the beginning, opposition concentrated on two main issues: the environmental destruction which Ross Dam would entail, and the illusory nature of the solution to Seattle's already high electric demands which High Ross' 294 MW would provide. A debate in the full City Council followed the hearings, but despite the Mayor's opposition to the project, the Council decided by a narrow margin to proceed.

With this, Seattle Light formally applied to the Federal Power Commission for a licence to raise the dam, and commissioned environmental studies in both Canada and the U.S. to satisfy the requirements of the U.S. National Environmental Policy Act. For its Canadian studies, Seattle City Light retained a small firm of consulting foresters without previous experience in environmental impact assessment. Interestingly, the original contract signed in March 1970 calls for "management, engineering, forestry, and public relations services", nowhere mentioning truly objective environmental impact assessment. By fall, the consulting firm had published the first of many glossy reports and began a public relations campaign designed to show that British Columbians would benefit with increased recreational opportunities from High Ross Dam!

Meanwhile, the Skagit had attracted enough attention in Canada that Environment Minister Jack Davis threatened to invoke the Inland Waters Act to prevent the flooding. He soon discovered, however, that its powers could not apply to projects already approved by the IJC. For his part, B.C. Resources Minister Williston insisted that a valid contract had been signed with Seattle, and refused to oppose the project. Indeed, he invited bids for clearing the flood basin, postponing the logging only under heavy pressure in the Legislature and the press.

To counteract Seattle Light's PR campaign and the B.C. Government's refusal to lift a finger against the dam, a demonstration was organized in the Skagit Valley in mid-October 1970. Three thousand people turned up on a cold rainy day, and the Skagit suddenly gained status as a national issue.

Hearings of the Washington State Ecological Commission in March 1971 added more fuel to the controversy, as dozens of witnesses from both Canada and the U.S. testified for two days in nearly unanimous opposition to High Ross. Along with the organized presentations of the ROSS Committee and NCCC, a remarkable number of individuals spontaneously turned up to state their views.

The federal government, meanwhile, found itself in a difficult position. It faced the complication of an apparently legal contract between Seattle and B.C. and the provincial government's approval of High Ross. Characteristically, "quiet diplomacy" prevailed, as External Affairs convinced the U.S. State Department to permit referral of the Skagit case back to the International Joint Commission. When the terms of reference were announced in April 1971, environmentalists found to their dismay that the IJC was asked to "make recommendations for the protection and enhancement of the environment and the ecology of the Skagit River Valley not inconsistent with the Commission's Order of Approval dated January 27, 1942". Put bluntly, the IJC was not to be allowed to alter the decision it had reached after a single two hour hearing thirty years before!

To many, the IJC reference seemed like cynical opportunism on Ottawa's part; but perhaps it represented a clever and calculated gamble, for despite its unpromising beginning, the IJC's inquiry ultimately led to a key turning point in the controversy over the Skagit Valley's future. Three full days of hearings in Vancouver and Bellingham, Washington in June 1971 began the IJC's reconsideration of the case. This was the first public hearing ever held on the Skagit in Canada, a fact of which the Commissioners were soon abundantly, if not painfully, aware. Presentations by the ROSS Committee, NCCC, and their member organizations covered every aspect of the High Ross issue from environmental effects to energy ethics. Even the legal basis of the 1967 compensation agreement and the earlier IJC Order of Approval were questioned. Seattle Light was also well represented by a team of lawyers, and presented a slick new report from its Vancouver consultants. While the federal Environment Department sent a representative to oppose High Ross, the B.C. Government ignored the hearings and prevented its civil servants from presenting the results of their studies on the effects of flooding. But once again, the spontaneous response of the public was perhaps the most impressive. When a group of businessmen from the small town of Hope, B.C. endorsed the dam, for example, they were followed to the podium by a housewife who had signed up over 1,200 of the town's residents on a petition against the project!

Once past the public hearings, an IJC professional study team was given three months to assess the environmental effects of High Ross. Concurrently, an Opportunities for Youth grant enabled a team of students at the University of B.C. to prepare the first reasonably comprehensive statement of the case for preserving the Skagit. This report, if only by providing a bulky document to stack up against the masses of glossy literature produced by Seattle Light, seemed to significantly enhance the credibility of the conservationist position.

In December 1971, the IJC's 191-page report was finally released.[3] Considering the terms of reference with which the Commission had been saddled, the report is a remarkable document. The IJC found that "seen in a broad social context, the Skagit Valley is an uncommon and non-restorable area and has important social values." While most individual elements of the Skagit's environment could be found elsewhere, "few valleys, if any, are equivalent to the complete Skagit Valley." Much of the report dealt with detailed ecological effects, but significantly, the Commission attached considerable importance to "social and option values" including the value of a wilderness valley to the city dweller who never intends to visit, but simply enjoys knowing that the valley remains in its natural state.

In effect, the IJC seemed to be bending over backwards to condemn High Ross without violating the terms of reference of its inquiry. When the Washington Department of Ecology nearly simultaneously announced its official opposition to the dam, the outlook for the Skagit suddenly looked much brighter. Unperturbed, Seattle City Light continued to lay the ground for its formal application to the Federal Power Commission by expanding its environmental studies into a full-fledged impact assessment, including the study of fish, wildlife, climate, forestry, and recreational effects of High Ross on both sides of the border.

A last ditch attempt by the NCCC to have Seattle City Council stop the project in the spring of 1972 was foiled when the Council Chairman prevented a vote after yet another hearing. B.C.'s Social Credit government, by now thoroughly embarrassed by the deal it had concluded, still stubbornly refused to make any move to save the Skagit.

Suddenly in August 1972, the entire balance shifted as a new NDP provincial government swept into power on a program largely dedicated to modernizing the environmental and resource policies of the Bennett era. In November the new Resources Minister, Robert Williams, officially announced the government's intention to prevent the flooding of the Skagit Valley, beginning a curious shadow boxing campaign between British Columbia and Seattle Light.

The B.C. government apparently hoped that a firm statement of its opposition to High Ross, combined with renewed pressure on the U.S. from Ottawa, would induce Seattle Light to simply abandon the project as a lost cause. The utility saw things otherwise, insisting that it had a valid contract with British Columbia which could not be cancelled without damages of six, ten, or even fifty million dollars. Calling B.C.'s bluff, it filed preliminary testimony on engineering, economic, and environmental aspects of High Ross Dam with the Federal Power Commission in January 1973.

The ROSS Committee, taking the B.C. government at its word, had meanwhile effectively disbanded. By fall 1973, with FPC hearings relentlessly approaching, there was still nothing concrete to block High Ross, and conservationists in both Washington and B.C. again began to stir. Once more the provincial government countered with a bluff, announcing in mid-October the creation of a 144 square mile Skagit Valley Recreation Area, including all of the land proposed for flooding. But Seattle Light remained undaunted, and by now preparations for the FPC hearings were too far advanced to be stopped.

Federal Power Commission Hearings

With 1974 began the most intense and interesting phase of the Skagit Controversy, as the Federal Power Commission (FPC) announced that its long-awaited hearings on High Ross Dam would finally begin. The ROSS Committee and NCCC, both registered as official intervenors before the FPC, were caught unawares, having assumed that a negotiated settlement was in the offing. Ottawa had contemplated participating, but ultimately decided that intervention in an internal U.S. regulatory proceeding would be diplomatically inappropriate. Instead, a statement was relayed to the FPC conveying Canada's "hope" that the Commission would refuse Seattle's application to raise the dam. British Columbia announced that it considered the 1967 agreement with Seattle invalid and did not recognize FPC jurisdiction over the Canadian Skagit. While officially boycotting the hearings, it allowed two civil servants to testify as independent expert witnesses called by the staff of the FPC.

In March, with hearings imminent and no prospect of any Canadian involvement, the ROSS Committee requested a stay in proceedings and launched a desperate appeal to both federal and provincial governments for funds to intervene actively. The FPC granted a delay until April 23rd, and three weeks before the start of the hearings, Ottawa suddenly released a total of $35,000 to the ROSS Committee. A Seattle environmental lawyer was immediately retained, and preparations for the hearings begun on an emergency basis. South of the border, the North Cascades Conservation Council and Washington Department of Ecology also geared up for the hearings.

Federal Power Commission proceedings have four main phases, each serving distinct purposes. Initially, the Commission staff assesses the feasibility of a project and prepares its own Environmental Impact Statement. Next, an FPC administrative judge holds open hearings to sample public opinion in the area affected by the project. Evidentiary hearings follow, in which expert witnesses for both the applicant and any intervenors give sworn testimony on engineering, economic, environmental, or any other matters of concern. This testimony is subject to cross-examination and rebuttal and must be substantiated by any available technical studies. At the close of testimony, lawyers for the applicant and intervenors prepare summary arguments, the judge rules on the application, and the decision is submitted to the Federal Power Commission itself for ratification or reversal.

Theoretically, this adversary system has several important advantages. Critics of a project, along with the FPC, gain full access to information compiled by the developer which might otherwise remain secret. Assumptions, methods, data, and conclusions of any studies used to justify a project are subject to intense scrutiny. Opponents have ample opportunity to explain and defend their views, and the validity of their objections can likewise be tested. The fact that evidence is given under oath presumably encourages professional consultants to present their conception of the truth honestly and resist pressures from either side. In the event that a project is approved, the process affords excellent opportunities to identify any important problems requiring further study or mitigation.

In practice, the adversary process is considerably less than perfect. Most important, it requires some equivalence between the resources of a project's proponent and those of its critics. Seattle City Light spent over $4 million on preparations for the FPC hearings on High Ross, while the combined expenses of its opponents were less than $75,000. Withholding of crucial technical reports until the last possible moment and prepping of expert witnesses to avoid admissions damaging to the client have also shown the difficulty of ensuring that the evidentiary hearings fulfill their role of elucidating the truth. The system is cumbersome, time consuming, and expensive, and much time and effort are wasted on trivial details irrelevant to the primary issues. Nevertheless, the High Ross case has constituted the first reasonably meticulous scrutiny of a major environmental impact assessment in British Columbia, and has demonstrated that an adversary system has much real merit.

FPC Administrative Judge Allan Lande opened public hearings in Bellingham, Washington on April 23, 1974. Forty-four Canadians representing environmental, sports, labour, and business groups testified, all but one against High Ross Dam. Statements of opposition were also received from fifteen Lower Mainland municipalities. When the hearings shifted to Seattle, 110 Americans filled three days with testimony, again nearly unanimously opposed to High Ross.

Confronted with evidentiary hearings less than a month after receiving funds to intervene, the ROSS Committee suddenly found itself faced with a task for which Seattle Light had been preparing meticulously since 1970. The hundreds of pages of written testimony filed a year earlier by the utility had to be reviewed for cross-examination and expert witnesses found to present the case against High Ross. Fortunately, the response from B.C.'s academic community was highly enthusiastic. On less than a week's notice, four professors from Simon Fraser University and the University of B.C. agreed to review Seattle Light's testimony, prepare their own written evidence, and appear before the FPC in Seattle. Despite severe cross-examination by Seattle Light's team of attorneys, they presented a strong case in favour of the unique physiographic, ecological, recreational, and educational values of the Skagit which would be destroyed by High Ross.

The hearings next shifted to Washington, D.C. for testimony from

Seattle Light witnesses. A review of the engineering feasibility studies from High Ross commissioned by the ROSS Committee revealed some interesting deficiencies in both structural and geological investigations. High Ross would be the 24th highest dam in the world, and the most highly stressed arch dam ever built, yet its novel design is unprecedented, and investigations of the weak rock abutments have been minimal in comparison with other recent dams of its type.

By June, Judge Lande knew that he had stumbled into a hornet's nest. Noting that after eighteen days of hearings, "I am right where I started, in dead center. I don't know who is right and who is wrong," he remarked, "As I was observing you people, various questions entered my mind. We have a very difficult problem here. Usually in a license project case some people want a project performed and others are against it. We have a third dimension here and it is called 'Canada', and every time you look at it you wonder, 'What am I going to do about it?' "

With the resumption of hearings in late June, attention turned to environmental and economic aspects of High Ross. A Seattle economic consultant testified that alternatives to the dam, such as gas turbines, nuclear, or coal-fired plants, would cost at least $4 million more per year, and claimed that energy conservation or new pricing policies would be ineffective in reducing Seattle's load growth below its current 2% per annum. Environmental consultants stated that High Ross would not seriously affect the Skagit fishery and wildlife, and that recreational potential would increase with a larger reservoir!

As questions were raised on cross-examination, new data and reports suddenly emerged which, if not actively withheld by Seattle Light, certainly had not been volunteered for inspection by intervenors. Some of these, though submitted to the FPC as much as a year earlier, were not furnished to the ROSS Committee until a matter of days before the responsible witnesses appeared on the stand for cross-examination. University experts who reviewed these reports on the ROSS Committee's request again found abundant technical flaws which provided fruitful avenues for embarrassing questioning. Some examples are worth considering, since they may well be typical of environmental impact studies performed by supposedly objective consultants. If anything, the studies of the Skagit Valley conducted by Seattle Light's Canadian consultants probably have been more intensive and meticulous than most. The expenditure of $1 million on this small valley certainly would exceed, on a per area basis, that on almost any other project in Canada.

From the start, reports by Seattle's Canadian consultants have been seriously biased. Consultant reports have consistently ignored resource values which would suffer from High Ross, while emphasizing those which would benefit. For example, little or no recognition is given to the special significance of wilderness flat land or the unique appeal of a wild river for fishing, canoeing, or general recreation, but the joys of summer fun on a reservoir are highly touted. (Somehow, the drawbacks of a nine-month drawdown are conveniently forgotten.) By focussing on technical details, the reports divert attention from the major issues. Superficially impressive studies of the distribution and abundance of fish, wildlife, and unusual plants obscure the central point that the regionally significant resource is the unique land and stream environment of the Skagit, not the population density of any particular species.

In cases where the consequences of High Ross are not amenable to scientific prediction, the consultants consistently adopt self-servingly optimistic assumptions. We are confidently assured, for example, that displaced trout will migrate to new spawning areas available upstream, but not alerted to the distinct possibility that they may not. Techniques used to estimate fish and wildlife numbers are frequently biased and estimates are based on arbitrary assumptions and insufficient or demonstrably unreliable data. The consultants present as fact conclusions which could never be published in a scientific journal on the basis of the data presented.

Finally, the consultants' reports have not been above outright distortion and misrepresentation. For example, a report by a recreational consultant implies that 33 valleys within 100 miles of Vancouver could be considered alternatives to the Skagit, neglecting to mention that almost all are either physiographically dissimilar, totally inaccessible, privately owned, or already ravaged by logging. Other reports, judging from conversations with former employees of the company, appear to have been "sanitized" in editing, to conform to the needs of the client. For example, preliminary data indicating adverse climatic effects of High Ross Reservoir were omitted from a study purporting to show no changes in microclimate.

While FPC hearings dragged on through the summer of 1974, important developments continued in the political arena. On June 25th, the government of British Columbia unilaterally requested the International Joint Commission to rescind its 1942 Order of Approval of High Ross Dam. A detailed legal brief argued that the Order is invalid on technical grounds, and asked the IJC to restore the Skagit River to its natural level at the boundary, a move which would cost Seattle as much as $500,000 per year in power benefits gained from present water storage in Canada. Uncertain how to react to this unprecendented challenge to one of its own rulings, the IJC requested legal opinions from Canada, the U.S., and Seattle. Also in June, the U.S. Department of the Interior suddenly announced its official opposition to High Ross Dam.

To maintain public and media interest in the Skagit case, the ROSS

Committee arranged a premature victory celebration for July 28th. In conjunction with the "First Annual International Skagit River Canoe-In and Picnic", the B.C. Government staged an official dedication ceremony for the Skagit Valley Recreation Area, which includes the 4,720 acres which would be flooded by High Ross. After the ceremony, three provincial Cabinet Ministers joined more than a hundred other canoeists and kayakers on a six-mile stretch of the Skagit River which would be flooded. Seattle City Light Superintendent Gorden Vickery, invited to the Canoe-In as an official guest of the ROSS Committee, declined to attend the event, thereby providing front-page publicity in a Seattle newspaper. But if the Canoe-In was useful in reinforcing the provincial government's determination to preserve the Skagit, its point seemed to be lost on Seattle's Light consultants. Despite national press coverage of the event in Canada and an ongoing survey by field employees, Seattle's chief recreational consultant testified on oath ten days later that the Skagit River cannot be canoed safely in July!

Simultaneous with its challenge to Seattle's legal right to flood the Skagit, British Columbia tendered the olive branch. A letter from Resources Minister Williams to the Mayor of Seattle offered to buy back the 1967 compensation agreement at present value, purchase Seattle Light's land holdings in the Canadian Skagit at their market price, and consider provision of alternative energy to the city. Some sort of negotiations were apparently commenced, although no hint of their progress has yet emerged. Hedging its bets, the provincial government furnished the ROSS Committee with $25,000 to continue full scale intervention in the FPC proceedings.

Hearings continued in Washington through the fall of 1974, returning to Seattle in January for rebuttal testimony by intervenors. ROSS Committee witnesses, this time backed by several months of preparation, attacked Seattle City Light's studies on fisheries, climatic, and recreational effects of High Ross, and the lack of serious consideration of alternatives to the dam. U.B.C. geographer Dr. Olav Slaymaker used a satellite photograph to show logging damage to many of the thirty-three "alternative" valleys proposed by the consultants, while colleague Dr. John Hay revealed that Seattle City Light was planning a weather modification program in the upper Skagit basin whose principal effects might be felt in B.C. Significantly, Seattle City Light's lawyers went to considerable lengths to undermine the rebuttal testimony. In February the hearings returned to Washington for Seattle Light's rebuttal testimony, finally terminating on March 5, 1975 after accumulating some 9,827 pages of testimony.

Meanwhile, in a surprise move, the U.S. State Department joined Canada and B.C. in supporting the International Joint Commission's jurisdiction to reconsider its Order of Approval and the 1967 Agreement. The IJC deferred further consideration of B.C.'s appeal pending the outcome of negotiations between the province and Seattle.

On June 30, 1975, negotiating teams finally met in Seattle to explore the possibility of a settlement. The City called for provision of energy and peaking power equal to High Ross at equivalent costs, while British Columbia reiterated its unequivocal opposition to the dam, brandished the threat of its legal action before the IJC, and withdrew to consider its position. A November 10th letter from the Deputy Minister of Lands set forth B.C.'s objections to the 1967 Agreement and a daring proposal for settlement. Basing its case on the Columbia River Treaty precedent, the letter argued that in principle the $6,670,000 annual value of High Ross should be shared equally between Seattle and B.C., indicating an appropriate rental would be $3,335,000 per year, in contrast to the $34,566 provided by the 1967 Agreement. Declaring the latter "financially unconscionable" but rejecting a settlement based merely on improved compensation, B.C. proposed a three point substitute:

1. Permitting Seattle to maintain its present 20 feet of storage within Canada for a rental of $315,000 per annum (50% of the current value) retroactive to 1954. For its part, B.C. would return all rental payments made under previous agreements and reimburse Seattle for studies made pursuant to the 1967 Agreement. No further flooding would be allowed.
2. Creating an international park to which B.C. would contribute 80% of the annual payments received from Seattle. These funds would be shared equally between British Columbia and Washington State agencies responsible for the park. B.C. would purchase at fair market value Seattle's land holdings in the Canadian Skagit.
3. Offering to Seattle at market price B.C.'s share of benefits from extension of a new hydro-electric project on the Pend d'Oreille River which could generate additional energy by flooding a small area in Washington State.[4]

Needless to say, Seattle did not jump at this proposal, and only one month later, the N.D.P. was replaced by a new Social Credit government in British Columbia. As the year ended, the Skagit once again seemed in danger when the *Seattle Times* quoted a Social Credit functionary as predicting its eventual flooding. To the surprise of many, however, new Premier William Bennett announced his opposition to High Ross and insisted that negotiations with Seattle would continue.

On February 4, 1976, nearly two years after commencing his investigation, FPC Judge Allen Lande ruled in favour of Seattle's application to raise Ross Dam. His decision, requiring ratification by the Federal Power Commission itself, was quickly appealed by intervenors, and the new B.C. government granted the ROSS Committee $5,000 to pursue its case. Should the FPC confirm Judge Lande's ruling, opponents would retain the option of appealing to the U.S. courts.

Meanwhile, British Columbia's challenge to the 1942 IJC Order of Approval remains in limbo. Fearful that reconsideration of the Skagit case might open a Pandora's box of other disputed decisions, the IJC is clearly reluctant to proceed with the case. Presumably, it will continue to exert indirect pressure on B.C. and Seattle to come to a negotiated solution.

How the conflict will be resolved remains to be seen. Seattle Light estimates costs to date of $9 million, basing its claim partly on expenditures made in anticipation of High Ross even before the 1942 Order of Approval. A 1975 energy planning study suggested that the city's need for new peaking power is not as critical as formerly supposed, but Seattle still is not likely to relinquish its bargain agreement on High Ross without a fight. Many Canadians must surely have been warmed to see a provincial government for once determined to avoid the quick and easy sellout and insist on an honourable settlement, but the new government of B.C. may not be so determined. Ultimately, the federal government may contribute to a compensation accord, or the IJC may yet be forced to reopen an undistinguished chapter of its past. Doubtless the Skagit's future will largely depend, as it has throughout the last seven years, on the intensity of public reaction to the threat of its destruction.

What useful lessons emerge from the fight to save the Skagit? Is the case relevant to other environmental issues in Canada, and has it really merited such intensive effort by conservationists through six years of controversy?[5] To the last question, the answer is emphatically yes. The Skagit case has furnished valuable lessons for specific environmental battles and has raised important questions for general environmental policy in Canada.

Lessons for Citizen Action

First, the case has shown the power of a concerned public to win an environmental battle against seemingly overwhelming odds.[6] Few if any of those originally involved would have predicted success when the fight against High Ross began in 1969. Faced with a provincial government which approved of the dam, a federal government known for its timorous approach to U.S. incursions on Canadian sovereignty, and a power-hungry utility used to getting its way, it might have seemed sensible to abandon the Skagit as a lost cause. Yet year by year stalling by citizens on both sides of the international border delayed the project long enough for government attitudes to catch up with those of the public.

Time and again, the utility of public hearings for raising important environmental and social issues has been demonstrated.[7] Repetitive hearings before powerless commissions may be frustrating in the extreme, but they furnish invaluable opportunities for a sympathetic press to return the controversy to the public eye. Combination of occasional theatre with a basically honest approach is crucial to maintaining media interest in an issue.[8] Attack, rather than defence against the developer's initiatives, and newsworthy events such as a demonstration generate publicity, yet reporters are wary of environmentalists' exaggerated claims. A national television reporter's expression of delighted surprise when the Skagit lived up to its billing speaks for the importance of not overselling an issue.

The unique lessons of the Skagit case, however, have arisen from the recent Federal Power Commission proceedings. Under the relentless skepticism of a lawyer's eye, impressive and bulky consultants' reports which once seemed impervious to criticism have been revealed as specious, unscientific, inadequately substantiated, and at times outright dishonest. The confident predictions of bought environmental impact assessments have not stood up to the adversary system's test of truth. University experts have proven eager to volunteer their time and expertise to the critique of technical reports, and to research and testify for the conservationist case.

The implications for environmentalists are clear. We must not be intimidated by environmental impact assessments which at first glace seem to have left no stone unturned. Any such study is likely to have flaws and, as likely as not, the key issues have not been uncovered, but *covered over*. Citizens should not hesitate to ask for help from the universities. Academics are often waiting for a chance to involve themselves in the public interest, and they are, after all, supported by public funds. While finances sufficient to retain full time legal counsel were invaluable to the ROSS Committee in the Skagit case, it is significant that the most valuable technical assistance came from the voluntary efforts of academics.

Environmental Policy Implications

The Skagit case also raises important questions about general environmental policy in Canada. These include the need for professional standards, a conservative ethic, and independent review in environmental impact assessment, and the question of the proper balance between common sense and technical detail in environmental decision making.

Environmental consulting as a recognized profession is relatively new in Canada. In recent years, dozens of consulting firms have sprung into existence to capitalize on a lucrative and expanding market. In contrast to established professions such as engineering, architecture, law or medicine, environmental consulting is governed by no professional standards or code of ethics. No requirements exist for contracts between consultants and their clients to specify full and honest disclosure of the facts, regardless of their convenience to the client. No standards govern the design, performance, and reporting of investigations, such as those which determine whether a research paper is acceptable for publication in a scientific journal. No sanctions against incompetence and dishonesty protect either the public or the profession's reputation. Since developers who purchase environmental studies are often more concerned with fostering good public relations or meeting government requirements than in learning the real environmental impact of their projects, the need for such professional standards in environmental consulting is particularly urgent. Consultants whose concern for excellence exceeds their pecuniary motives have a responsibility to themselves as well as the public to clean up the profession promptly and effectively.

Another contrast between environmental impact assessors and the traditional professions is the role of healthy conservatism. Engineers, doctors, scientists, and the judicial system routinely employ *conservative* assumptions when predicting the behaviour of a system. Thus dams, buildings, and other structures are over-designed in the interest of safety, while drugs are withheld from market if there is even the slightest question about their net benefit. Scientists avoid drawing firm conclusions until the evidence in their favour is overwhelming, and juries are supposed to give defendants the benefit of the doubt. Environmental impact assessment, in contrast, is rife with *optimistic* assumptions. Where the effects of environmental change are still in question, consultants all too often assume the best, assuring their clients and the public that there is really nothing to worry about. Seattle City Light's studies in the Skagit, discussed earlier in this article, provide many examples of this practice.

It can well be asked whether continued use of this double standard is acceptable. Conservative assumptions in engineering, law, and medicine are designed, of course, to protect *human* life. Since the usual rationale for environmental impact assessment is surely the preservation of environmental quality *for man*, conservatism should be the ethic here as well. Where legitimate doubt remains, perhaps the worst case, rather than the best, should be assumed.

This brings us to the importance of some general mechanism for independent review of environmental impact assessments in Canada. Federal Power Commission hearings on High Ross Dam have served this purpose in part but, as we have seen, the adversary process has major shortcomings. It is inefficient, wasting much time, money, and effort on trivial problems, and it depends on persistent and adequately financed intervention by environmental groups. In the U.S., the Environmental Protection Agency has begun to provide independent reviews of environmental impact statements, a recent example being its sharp criticism of the Atomic Energy Commission's EIS on the breeder reactor program.

But who is filling this role in Canada? What guarantees that environmental impact studies serve to reveal, rather than obfuscate the facts, and facilitate truly wise resource management decisions? Who, for example, will test the adequacy of environmental studies on the Mackenzie Pipeline, Syncrude project, Arctic oil wells, the nuclear energy industry, development of northwestern B.C.? Traditional government agencies cannot be relied on, since they too often are subject to pressure from politicians eager for development, witness the suppression of the Alberta civil servants' critique of Syncrude or the forced absence of Environment Canada scientists from the Berger Inquiry hearings. Environmental groups have neither time nor resources to attend to more than a fraction of the issues which must be considered, and adversary forums like that of the FPC are seldom available. The freedom of information tradition available to American environmentalists does not apply in Canada.

A recent publication of the Science Council of Canada calls for an independent agency specifically mandated with the critical review of environmental impact assessments.[8] With a review board of this type, government authorization of a project could be withheld at least until the adequacy of environmental studies has been certified. This requirement might also encourage governments to suspend the real decisions on resource developments until environmental effects have been weighed against economic benefits, rather than using environmental studies merely as after-the-fact sops to placate an aroused citizenry. Establishment of a formal legal requirement for environmental impact assessments and of avenues for legal challenge to EIA's by citizens would also contribute to more meaningful environmental protection. Tax changes which encourage charitable donations to environmental organizations, or direct government subsidies, are vital if citizen groups are to realize their potential for independent constructive criticism.

Sophisticated new arrangements to ensure the scientific credibility of environmental impact studies would, however, be of little value without some concomitant change in perspective in controversies involving the environment. Here again, the Skagit case has an important lesson. From the beginning, environmentalists have maintained that the issues are fundamentally simple. In its own way, City Light has shared this approach, and two million dollars worth of environmental studies has in no way altered the views of either side. Eschewing value judgements in the name of "professionalism", however, the environmental consultants have so narrowed and distorted their perspective that they have essentially missed the point of the controversy. From a fundamental choice between a rare natural environment and a commonplace artificial one, they have reduced the Skagit controversy to a numbers game involving fish, wildlife, and man-days of recreation. Perhaps it is time to restore a common sense perspective to environmental decision making and to stop shrinking from the value judgements which underlie our decisions whether we recognize them or not. If the Emperor has no clothes, let us admit he is naked without further ado!

NOTES

1. For another view concerning the impact of changing attitudes towards resource development programs, with specific reference to the Skagit Valley, see W. M. Ross and M. E. Marts, "The High Ross Dam project: environmental decisions and changing environmental attitudes", *Canadian Geographer*, Vol. 29, No. 3, Fall 1975, pp. 221-234.
2. Provisions of the Columbia River Treaty and its implications are discussed in W. R. D. Sewell, "The Columbia River Treaty: some lessons and implications", *Canadian Geographer*, Vol. 10, No. 3, 1966, pp. 145-156. Other views about the treaty may be found in H. L. Keenleyside, "Columbia River power project", *Canadian Geographical Journal*, Vol. 71, No. 5, November 1965, pp. 148-162, and R. W. Johnson, "The Canadian — United States controversy over the Columbia River", *University of Washington Law Review*, Vol. 41, No. 4, 1966, pp. 676-763.
3. International Joint Commission, *Environmental and ecological consequences in Canada of raising Ross Lake in the Skagit Valley to Elevation 1725*, Ottawa and Vancouver, International Joint Commission, 1970-1973.
4. Press Release, Minister of Lands, Forests and Water Resources, Victoria, December 18, 1975, containing letter dated November 10, 1975 from Norman Pearson, Deputy Minister of Lands, to Edmund J. Wood, Administrative Assistant to the Mayor of Seattle.
5. Another resource development project initiated in the United States with environmental implications for Canada is the Garrison Diversion irrigation project in North Dakota. Irrigation water draining into the Souris and Red Rivers may degrade these streams which in turn could cause damage to health and property in Manitoba. For an account of the Garrison Diversion project see A. M. Josephy, "Dr. Strangelove builds a canal", *Audubon*, Vol. 77, No. 2, March 1975, pp. 76-112.
6. To maintain perspective, it should be noted that environmentalists have not been successful on every occasion in British Columbia. For example, they were unable to stop a mining firm from dumping tailings into an inlet on Vancouver Island. Details of this unsuccessful effort by environmentalists may be found in A. R. Lucas and P. A. Moore, "The Utah controversy: a case study of public participation in pollution control", *Natural Resources Journal*, Vol. 13, No. 1, January 1973, pp. 36-75. A more general assessment of the impact of the public is contained in D. Draper, "Environmental interest groups and institutional arrangements in British Columbia water management issues", *Institutional arrangements for water management: Canadian experiences*, edited by B. Mitchell, Publication Series No. 5, Waterloo, University of Waterloo, Department of Geography, 1975, pp. 119-170.
7. Two studies which assess the effectiveness of public hearings relative to the International Joint Commission are: D. Swanson, "Public perceptions and resource

planning", *Perceptions and attitudes in resource management*, edited by W. R. D. Sewell and I. Burton, Ottawa, Information Canada, 1971, pp. 91-97, and M. Sinclair "The International Joint Commission and its relationship with the public", *Institutional arrangements for water management: Canadian experiences*, edited by B. Mitchell, Publication Series No. 5, Waterloo, University of Waterloo, Department of Geography, 1975, pp. 83-116.

8. For example, former M.L.A. Dave Brousson relieved the tedium of the FPC's public hearings by taking the offensive against Seattle Light. Raising for the first time Seattle's illegal flooding of Canadian land in 1953, he threatened to file a motion requesting Seattle Light be ordered to lower Ross Reservoir back down to the international border. In the same vein, a Canadian logger who supervised Seattle's original clearing operations in the Skagit raised an exciting, if last ditch, possibility for stopping the flooding. Citing the 1967 compensation agreement's specification that all labour within Canada must be performed by B.C. residents, he warned that a union boycott of the required clearing operation would prevent Ross Reservoir from being raised even if the dam were built! One of the keys to success in popularizing the Skagit issue was the "news sense" of people like Brousson and the colour provided by individuals like the logger.
9. T. J. F. Lash, G. Filteau and P. A. Larkin, "On doing things differently: an essay on environmental impact assessments of major projects", *Issues in Canadian Science Policy*, Vol. 1, Ottawa, Science Council of Canada, 1974, pp. 9-15.

18
The North Also Thirsts: Countering the Threat of Water Export

*Frank Quinn**

The International Picture

The thirst of this continent's southern deserts and central plains has been working its way northward since the turn of the century. Along the way, many well-watered basins have fallen under its shadow; some have resisted more successfully than others. The outcome is uncertain.

Los Angeles sent out agents in 1906 to purchase water rights in Owens Valley, 200 miles to the northeast. It was only a matter of time before southern Californians, by the sheer weight of their numbers, would overwhelm their neighbours north of San Francisco Bay and bring the Sacramento's tributaries down to the desert. Irrigation districts on the Great Plains began to reach across the Rocky Mountains and other divides. Denver, Dallas and Salt Lake City soon followed suit. [1]

Farther north, the South Saskatchewan project and Qu'Appelle diversion served to reduce the area of Palliser's Triangle of aridity. Still, no inter-basin diversion anywhere in the west crossed a state, provincial or national border. And the Canadian north, "where God had not sufficiently divided the land from the waters," was far from the action as the decade of the 1960s dawned.

There followed a sequence of events in rapid succession which projected the vision of long-distance water movement to its zenith within five years. The longest argument ever heard before the U.S. Supreme Court terminated with a decision on Arizona v. California *et al.* in 1963 which returned the whole problem of southwest water allocation to the political arena. Adverse reaction to a federal plan led to a rash of alternative proposals that looked farther north for sources of still unappropriated water. Simultaneously, a drought diagonally across the country made life temporarily difficult along the shores of the falling Great Lakes and the Atlantic seaboard.

---

*Frank Quinn is Head, Social Studies Section, Water Planning and Management, Environment Canada, Ottawa. This article is a slightly revised version of a paper with a similar title which originally appeared in the *Transactions 1970: thirty-fourth federal-provincial wildlife conference,* held in Yellowknife, N.W.T., July 14-16, 1970, and published by the Canadian Wildlife Service, Department of Indian Affairs and Northern Development, pp. 57-62.

By this time it appeared that every consulting engineer and even some academics with the time to spare were making paper projections. Most of these concentrated on making the Columbia, Missouri or Mississippi tributary to the southwest, or James Bay tributary to the northeast; but some saw an opportunity to go all the way, solving in one massive campaign all the water problems of the west, the east — indeed the whole continent.

In almost no time, it became fashionable to speak of co-ordinating governments nationally and internationally for the purpose of conveying millions of acre-feet of water over distances of thousands of miles and pumping lifts of hundreds of feet for costs which climbed into billions of dollars. The water rush to the north had begun (Table 1).

Although they continued to capture headlines, the tide began to flow out on continental water promoters about 1968. The Columbia Basin states, aided by conservationists, were successful in turning back all bills in Congress which attempted to include studies of the feasibility of major inter-regional diversion; a moratorium of ten years was declared on such studies.[2] The Texas Water Plan, which proposed to import 17 million acre-feet from east Texas and the lower Mississippi, was set back by the failure of a bond amendment. And Canadians officially and unofficially rejected the suggestion that their waters were "continental resources".

Federal and provincial governments in Canada appear to have been in consistent agreement on the following points:

1. There is no identifiable market as yet for Canadian water in the United States. All diversion proposals are privately sponsored; none has the endorsement of the U.S. government which has made no offer to the government of Canada even to discuss the question.
2. Canada would be unwilling to negotiate any sale of water at present even if there were a market, because Canadian water supplies have not been adequately inventoried and Canadian water requirements into the future have not been assessed.
3. Federal and provincial governments must agree before any international negotiations could begin.
4. Canadian waters will never be sold under conditions which would jeopardize their permanent ownership and their repatriation if and when needed in Canada. Therefore they will not be sold as part of a total energy package.

Federal ministers' remarks in the House of Commons[3] agree closely with those made by provincial officials over the same period of time. It is essential to understand the attitudes of both levels of government because, under the terms of the B.N.A. Act, jurisdiction over resources is divided and both levels of government have a veto power on water export from the country.

TABLE 1

Private Proposals for International Water Transfer

Proposal (author)	Year proposed	Water source	Water destination	Vol. of div. in millions of ac. ft.	Estimated cost in billions of $
Grand Canal Plan (Kierans)	1960	James Bay dyked, rivers "recycled" southward	Great Lakes region of both countries; possible further transfer southward	17+	?
Great Lakes-Pacific Waterways Plan (Decker)	1963	Skeena, Nechako & Fraser of B.C., Peace, Athabaska, Saskatchewan of Prairie provs	Great Plains and Great Lakes region of United States	115	?
North America Water & Power Alliance or NAWAPA (Parsons)	1964	Primarily the Pacific & Arctic drainage of Alaska, Yukon and B.C., also tributaries of James Bay	Southern Prairie Provinces, Great Lakes, almost all of United States, northwest Mexico	110	100
Magnum Plan (Magnusson)	1965	Peace, Athabaska & N. Saskatchewan in Alberta	United States, via Souris River in North Dakota	25	?
Kuiper Plan (Kuiper)	1967	Peace, Athabaska & N. Saskatchewan in Alberta, Nelson & Churchill in Manitoba	Great Plains and other states south of Canadian Prairies	150	50

TABLE 1 *(continued)*

Central North American Water Project or CeNAWP (Tinney)	1967	Mackenzie, Peace, Athabaska, N. Saskatchewan, Nelson & Churchill	Great Plains and southwest states via North Dakota	150	30-50
Western States Water Augmentation Concept (Smith)	1968	Primarily Liard & Mackenzie drainages	All seventeen Western states via Rocky Mountain Trench	40	90
NAWAPA-MUSHEC or Mexican-United States Hydro-electric Commission (Parsons)	1968	NAWAPA sources + lower Mississippi & Sierra Madre Oriental Rivers of S. Mexico	Virtually all of occupied North America	287 (NAWAPA + MUSHEC)	?
North American Waters, A Master Plan or NAWAMP (Tweed)	1968	Yukon & Mackenzie Rivers, drainage to Hudson Bay	Prairies, Great Lakes and all of United States	1,500	?

TABLE 2

Interbasin Water Diversions: Canada*

River diversions	Location	Average annual amount mill. ac. ft. (sq. mi. dr. area)	Purpose (formerly) now	Year Estab.
A. Affecting Canada				
1. Allagash to Penobscot	Maine	?(270)	(log driving) power	1841
2. L. Michigan to Illinois R.	Illinois	2.31	(navigation) sewage	(1848) 1910
3. St. Mary R. to Milk R.	Montana	.18	dilution irrigation	1917
B. Existing in Canada				
1. Nechako R. to Kemano R.	B.C.	2.17	power	1952
2. L. St. Joseph to Winnipeg R.	Ontario	2.02	power	1957
3. Long Lake to L. Superior	Ontario	1.01	power	1939
4. Ogoki R. to L. Superior	Ontario	2.82	power	1943
5. Megiscane R. to St. Maurice R.	Quebec	? (263)	power	1953
6. Indian R. to Humber R.	Newfoundland	.15	power	
7. Grey R. to Salmon R.	Newfoundland	.69	power	1967
C. Under Construction in Canada				
1. Naskaupi & Canairiktok to Hamilton R.	Labrador	? (4384)	power	1968-
2. Victoria & White Bear to Grey R.	Newfoundland	1.87	power	1968-
D. Under consideration in Canada				
1. Porcupine to Peel to Rat R.	Y.T., N.W.T.		power	
2. Yukon to Taiya or Taku	B.C., Alaska		power	
3. McGregor R. to Peace R.	B.C.		power & flood control	

TABLE 2 *(continued)*

4. Churchill R. to Nelson R.	Manitoba	24.55	power	1969-
5. Shuswap R. to Okanagan R.	B.C.		supply, dilution, etc.	
6. Alberta's PRIME study	Alberta		supply, etc.	
7. Fed.-Prov. Sask.-Nelson study	Prairie Prov.		supply, etc.	
8. Northern Ontario study	Ontario		supply, navigation, etc.	

*First-order diversions only are indicated, i.e., those which result in flow reaching the ocean by other than its natural channel. Second-order diversions, such as that from the South Saskatchewan to the Qu'Appelle, and lower orders, such as those effected by canal feeding right down to the individual user's different points of intake and outflow, are not shown. Note that most existing diversions serve power uses and required only minor construction activity to bring about, whereas future diversions will serve supply and other purposes to a greater extent and will probably require longer conveyance facilities and more sophisticated management.

A conclusion which can be offered at this point is that no Canadian waters will figure in any plan developed in this decade to satisfy American thirst. The thrust of schemes like NAWAPA toward the Yukon and Mackenzie will remain no more than lines on a map. The first reason is that the challenge from the dry southwest has been beaten back at the first line of defence, i.e., by those well-watered basins within the United States, like the Columbia and the lower Mississippi, which are reluctant to share their wealth.

The U.S. Congress is currently engaged in environmental quality matters and will not even consider studying inter-regional diversion feasibility in the west before official moratorium on that subject ends in 1978, at which time a reconnaissance survey of water supplies and requirements will have been completed state by state. In other words, the U.S.A. will be engaged in some basic homework determining its needs and alternative ways of satisfying them.

Another reason international discussions cannot proceed in the near future, mentioned above, is that Canada must carry out its own water inventory and consider its own alternatives. In this respect, northerners may have more to fear from the demands or indifference of their southern neighbours inside this country than from those who live outside. It will be imperative for the north to participate in Canadian water planning in the 1970s.

The National Picture

The budgets of federal and provincial water agencies have increased significantly in the past five years, in part to accelerate the national hydrometric network and expand it northward, and to assess the possibilities of increasing water supplies in the southern regions of the country by storage and diversion.

A basic fact of our geography is that approximately 60 per cent of Canadian run-off is carried by rivers flowing northward, while 90 per cent of our population is concentrated within 150 miles of our southern borders. As local resources are developed to capacity in the southern interior of British Columbia, the prairies and the lower Great Lakes-St. Lawrence, interest has increased in dipping more deeply into the northern reservoir for water and power needs. A beginning has already been made in interbasin diversions (Table 2), and more studies are underway.

Of most significance to joint federal-provincial investigation are the Saskatchewan-Nelson studies and the Northern Ontario studies. Both have been underway for some time; both are dominated by considerations of hydrology and engineering; neither is exemplary of the kind of comprehensive planning which the federal government is struggling to implement today. The determination of potential additional supply for the Saskatchewan-Nelson by storage and/or diversion from the north, supplemented by data on engineering projects costs, "will not . . .result in a comprehensive development plan on the basis of which projects could be selected for implementation."[4]

Economic, social and environmental studies assessing the effects of any diversion on the area of origin as well as on the potential receiving area must obviously precede any such implementation. Perhaps most important, northern representation and participation must be active in any studies which investigate northern waters.

The means are at hand. Two legislative measures which Parliament has recently passed into law speak to the question of improving consultation among federal-provincial-territorial governments and affected interests. These are the Canada Water Act and the Northern Inland Waters Act.[5] Contrary to popular belief, the Canada Water Act is not devoted entirely to cleaning up the Great Lakes and other pollution problems; it aims for co-operative arrangements with provincial and territorial agencies toward developing comprehensive water planning, planning which will evaluate all users and potential users of the resource and alternative means of achieving a satisfactory balance among them. Goals and priorities will be established as a first step by high-level consultative committees among the governments, not left to later determination when the results of physical investigations are in.

The Northern Inland Waters Act will complement the Canada Water Act by providing regional water authorities, the Yukon and Northwest Territories Water Boards. These boards will consist of the senior federal water officials in each territory and officials from the territorial governments. From now on, the territories are assured a stronger voice in any studies or proposals relating to the use of northern waters, whether such use is intended in the region or out of it.

There are lessons to be learned from Bennett Dam and Southern Indian Lake, lessons which might yet be applied in making studies such as that of the Saskatchewan-Nelson more comprehensive. Otherwise, the traditional judgements of the past will prevail: that the highest use of water is in reclaiming the drylands, that a river whose flow has been controlled by dams is always preferable to one which fluctuates freely. The 1970s are imposing extra demands on environmental planning for which past experience is inadequate. It will no longer be good enough to "win a few, lose a few". Governments cannot continue to guard their independence of action before the fact, then co-operate out of panic and pressure afterward.

Pressure on northward-flowing rivers will intensify. Fortunately, past experience provides some lessons (often of how not to go about it) and legislation exists for better consultative arrangements between jurisdictions. What balance do northerners want among conflicting demands?

Those who would divert water southward to the prairies of the American drylands frequently speak of thirst in physiological terms of life and death, of economies that will decline without new water.

For what does the north thirst? What kind of development, what protection for its unique character of peoples and resources? The rest of the country knows too little, not only about what problems large-scale diversions would bring the north but also about what opportunities northerners might develop without diversions.

NOTES

1. F. Quinn, "Must the American West Be Won Again?" *Geographical Review,* Vol.58, No. 1, Jan. 1968, pp. 108-132.
2. U.S. Congress, *Colorado River Basin Project Act,* P.L. 90-537, 82 Stat. 885, Washington, 1968.
3. Canada, *House of Commons Debates,* Ottawa, Queen's Printer, Sept. 2, 1964 (7575-7576); June 28, 1966 (6995-6997); April 3, 1967 (14472-14475); Oct. 10, 1968 (1022); Feb. 24, 1970 (4006-4008).
4. Canada, Alberta, Saskatchewan, Manitoba, *1969 Annual Report of the Saskatchewan-Nelson Basin Board,* Regina, 1970.
5. Canada Water Act, R.S.C. 1970, 1st Supp. C. 5. *Northern Inland Waters Act,* R.S.C. 1970, 1st Supp. C. 28.

19
The Fall 1972 Lake Erie Floods and Their Significance to Resources Management

J. G. Nelson, J. G. Battin,
*R. A. Beatty and R. D. Kreutzwiser**

Research on human adjustments to 1972 and earlier floods in the Rondeau-Erieau and Pelee-East Marsh areas (Figure 1) on the north coast of Lake Erie reveals:

1. That significant ecological elements and processes associated with flooding are not well understood by resource managers and the public.
2. That a relatively narrow range of expensive engineering (structural) adjustments has been used in attempts to control flooding and related ecological elements and processes.
3. That such adjustments have generally been introduced in a crisis atmosphere, during periods of high-water level on Lake Erie.
4. That financial and institutional arrangements have been developed to support perpetuation of engineering adjustments, notably by spreading their cost among increasing numbers of Canadian taxpayers.
5. That no detailed evaluation of the economic, social, or biophysical (environmental) benefits and costs of these adjustments has been undertaken by any government agency associated with their use.
6. That engineering adjustments generally appear to be justified on the grounds that they promote food and agricultural production, but without adequate evaluation of: (1) returns which could be derived from comparable public investment elsewhere (opportunity costs); (2) the discriminatory character of the investments; (3) the recreation and environmental costs of using engineering adjustments, or the "technological fix"; (4) alternative adjustments, including land use controls.

---

*J. G. Nelson is Dean of the Faculty of Environmental Studies at the University of Waterloo. This paper reports on part of a research project conducted while Nelson was a professor of geography at the University of Western Ontario. Battin, Beatty and Kreutzwiser were all graduate students at the University of Western Ontario at the time of the study. The authors wish to acknowledge financial support from the National and Provincial Parks Association, Parks Canada, and Canada Council. This paper is an edited version of one with the same title published in the *Canadian Geographer,* Vol. 19, No. 1, Spring 1975, pp. 35-59.

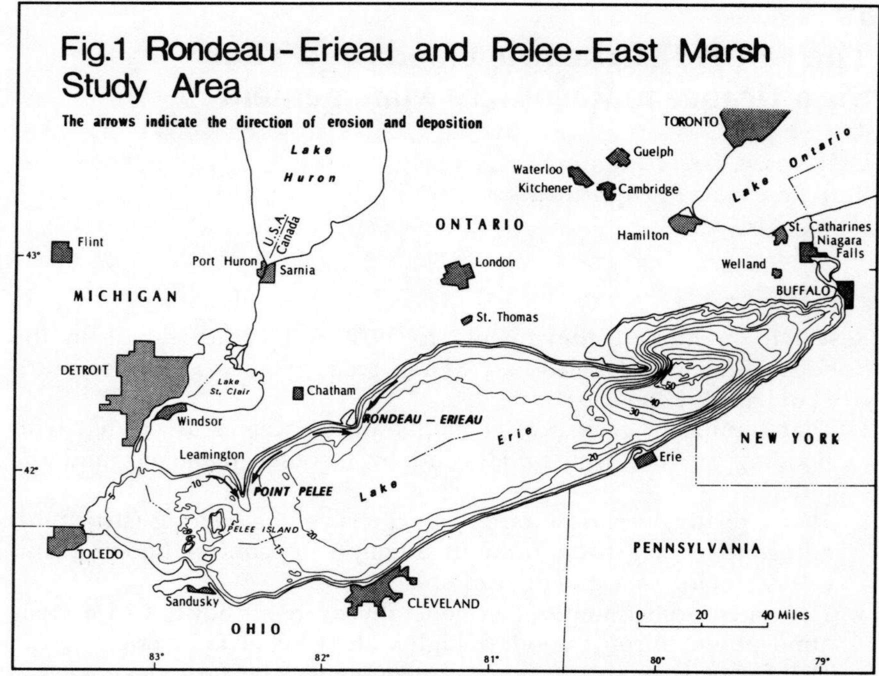

Fig.1 Rondeau-Erieau and Pelee-East Marsh Study Area

The arrows indicate the direction of erosion and deposition

A number of recommendations are made as a result of our research:

1. Impending large-scale diking and other engineering projects especially on marsh lands along the north Erie shore, Lake St. Clair, and the Lower Thames should not go forward until detailed benefit-cost and environmental impact studies are carried out and further careful consideration has been given to hazard insurance, land-use controls, and other alternative adjustments.
2. The results of the aforementioned studies should be circulated to interested individuals, groups, and agencies, and fully discussed at public hearings before decisions are made.
3. No large-scale drainage, flood, or erosion control schemes should be undertaken in Ontario in future without evaluating a wide range of alternative adjustments and their economic, social, and environmental benefits and costs in the manner just described.
4. A detailed review of policy, legislation, and institutional arrangements relating to drainage, flood, erosion, and other adjustments should be initiated in the near future, notably with respect to coastal lands. In this review, especially careful consideration should be given to: (1) reducing the proportion of senior government financial subsidy for structural and other hazard adjustments; (2) introducing guidelines for the use of senior government hazard funds at the municipal level.

5. Consideration should also be given to other policy and institutional changes, including: (1) public purchase or land-use control of coastal lands identified as very susceptible to flooding, erosion, and marsh conditions; (2) introduction to new co-ordinating legislation, for example, a Coastal Land Use Act; (3) establishment of an Ontario Hazards Commission to develop consistent policies, guidelines, and procedures for senior government involvement in selecting, financing, and introducing hazard adjustments.

Reviewers of an earlier version of this paper have suggested that recommendations 4 and 5 do not recognize the promise inherent in existing agencies and institutional arrangements, for example, the conservation authorities. The reviewers also suggest that the establishment of new agencies may be unduly complicating and expensive, and that we should be more precise in discussing any new institutional arrangements. To some extent these criticisms are well taken. However, research thus far leads us to conclude that existing organizations either are not fulfilling their potential or are inadequate in some ways. Hence our recommendation for a detailed review of hazards policy, especially in coastal areas. The report of the Ontario Select Committee on Land Drainage is helpful in this regard.[1] But the committee's terms of reference precluded focusing on coastal lands and the flood and erosion hazards of prime concern in this study.

Floods and the Ecological Setting

Problems of human adjustments to Great Lakes shorelines are often perceived in terms of flooding rather than shore erosion or associated processes. Yet full understanding of the hazard problems facing man in such areas requires an appreciation of all major interrelated ecological elements and processes at work along the coast.

The two study areas, Rondeau-Erieau and Pelee-East Marsh, are located near Rondeau and Point Pelee peninsulas, two of the largest land masses jutting into the lake (Figure 1). These peninsulas consist of low-lying marshes and higher beach-dune complexes, or sand bars. The marshes are generally quite extensive, occupying more than 60 per cent of the peninsulas at times of high water. Both marshes and bars owe their character and distribution to the three basic interrelated processes of erosion, deposition, and lake level fluctuation, all of which have been operating for thousands of years.

Flooding and erosion are both closely related to the underlying process of lake level fluctuation. Two basic types of fluctuation occur. The first, or short-term fluctuation, may last a few hours to a few days and involves tilting of the lake's surface due to winds or pressure. Lake Erie is especially susceptible to this type because it is shallow and oriented nearly parallel to the prevailing winds. Variations of 9.5 feet have been recorded at Fort Erie during a five-day period. Short-term fluctuations are especially noticeable when synchronous with long-term fluctuations.

The second basic type of fluctuation is long term. Lake Erie rises and falls over the years for a variety of reasons, including changes in evaporation, precipitation, groundwater flow, run-off, and crustal tilting. Man has exercised some influence through diversions, dredging, consumptive use, and regulation of the level of Lakes Superior (1921) and Ontario (1958).

The rise and fall of the lake causes variation of hundreds of feet in the extent of the marsh areas. Vegetation, wildlife, and other ecosystem elements and processes adjust to this change. During extended periods of low water, large formerly marsh areas are exposed to the atmosphere. Willow, silver maple, ash, and other species of the wetland borders extend into the drying marsh, along with deer and other essentially land animals. During long high-water periods, trees fringing the marsh are damaged or killed, and fish, turtles, and other animals move onto what once was dry land to spawn and feed. Erosion also becomes very noticeable in places along sand bars and shores during high water. The rise and fall of lake levels is therefore a process of fundamental importance because of its regular effects on a network of ecological elements and processes in Pelee Peninsula and similar areas on the north Erie coast.[2] Human interference with lake levels means interference with an array of interrelated elements and processes.

Human Adjustments to North Erie Shore Ecology

Archaeological research indicates that for centuries native peoples have been using Pelee and other parts of the north shore for hunting, fishing, collecting and gathering, and more recently for corn production and agriculture.[3] There is little to indicate that lake level fluctuations, flooding, and erosion caused the Indians any serious difficulties. They simply appear to have moved their camps and activities in accordance with the rise and fall of the lake.

The first European invaders merely crossed Pelee, Rondeau, and other peninsulas while travelling between Montreal, Detroit, and points west. Their hunting, and the introduction of the fur trade and the European commercial system, undoubtedly took a quick toll of deer, muskrat, and other life formerly so numerous on the peninsulas. But the early travellers and traders do not seem to have made adjustments to north shore ecology that were fundamentally different than those of the Indians.

European agriculturalists began moving into the wetlands, marshes, and sand bars of the peninsulas in the early 1800s. Among the earliest at Pelee were French-Canadians who had an economy and life style rather different from the English who followed them. The French-Canadians built houses near the dunes and beaches and stressed fishing, trapping, and the raising of free-ranging cattle, pigs, and other livestock, rather than cultivation. But cultivators and horticulturalists began to press into wetland areas in the late 1800s and soon introduced the first fundamental adjustment to north shore ecology: drainage.

DRAINAGE

Early drainage projects in the 1850s and 1860s were of small scale. They were undertaken by individuals using ditches, or simple subsurface drains of rock, brick, or wood. These efforts appear to have been concentrated on the higher, imperfectly drained wetlands and were of no use in "reclaiming for agriculture" the large ponds and marshes which covered many square miles near the peninsulas and river mouths.

In the 1860s, 1870s, and 1880s, a number of interrelated changes made it possible to drain and use these coastal marshes for agriculture. Of much significance were changes in technology. The development of tile and the introduction of large steam-powered dredging machines and pumps made it physically possible to attack the large marshes which had previously been beyond the settlers' capabilities.

However, the new technology was expensive and beyond the means of individual settlers. New institutional arrangements were needed if it was to be applied. In the 1860s, 1870s, and 1880s, a number of financial, legislative (Drainage Acts), and organizational changes made it possible to combine the efforts and funds of many individuals and implement large-scale drainage schemes.

Provincial legislation empowered municipal governments: (1) to grant permission for projects within their jurisdiction, upon petition from interested farmers and given the submission of a favourable engineering report; (2) to secure loan funds from the provincial government at low interest rates; (3) to levy taxes on all ratepayers within the area of the drainage scheme in order to maintain the large municipal drains.

In 1894-5, some 4,729 acres of land, including 2,804 acres of marsh near Point Pelee in Mersea Township, were drained and protected from lake flooding by dikes. The scheme was petitioned by 39 local landowners and cost approximately $23,000. Of the total acreage drained, about 1,200 acres was in what is now known as the East Marsh Drainage Scheme (Figure 2).[4]

In 1913-14, some 1,600 acres of marsh were drained in the Rondeau area of Harwich Township, to form a major part of the Burk Drainage Scheme (Figure 3). This scheme also was petitioned by local landowners and cost about $43,000. Lake Erie was held back by a lakeshore dike and Rondeau Bay was excluded by a railway embankment. The lakeshore dike served as the first road link to the nearby village of Erieau.

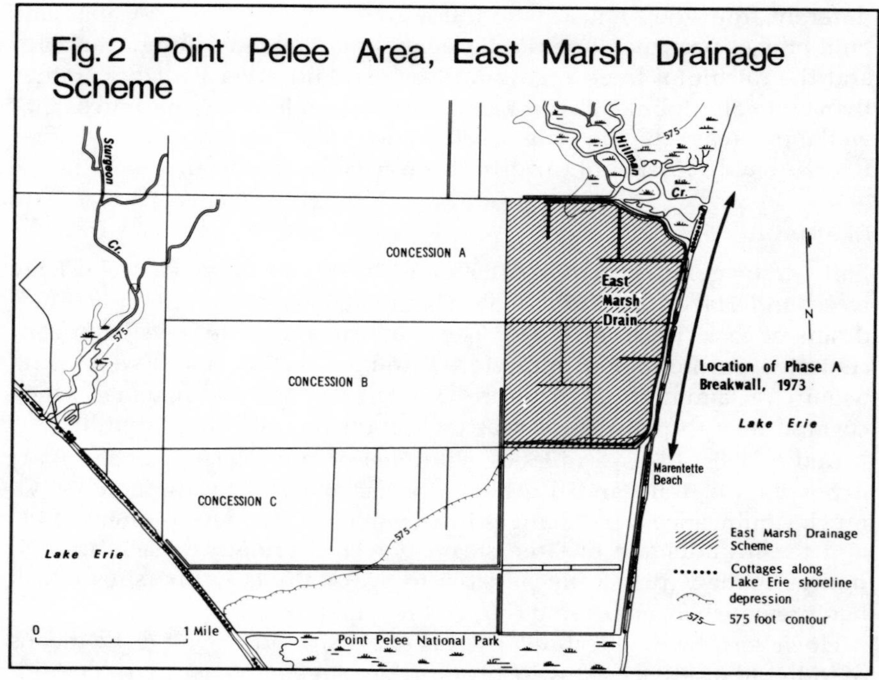

Fig. 2 Point Pelee Area, East Marsh Drainage Scheme

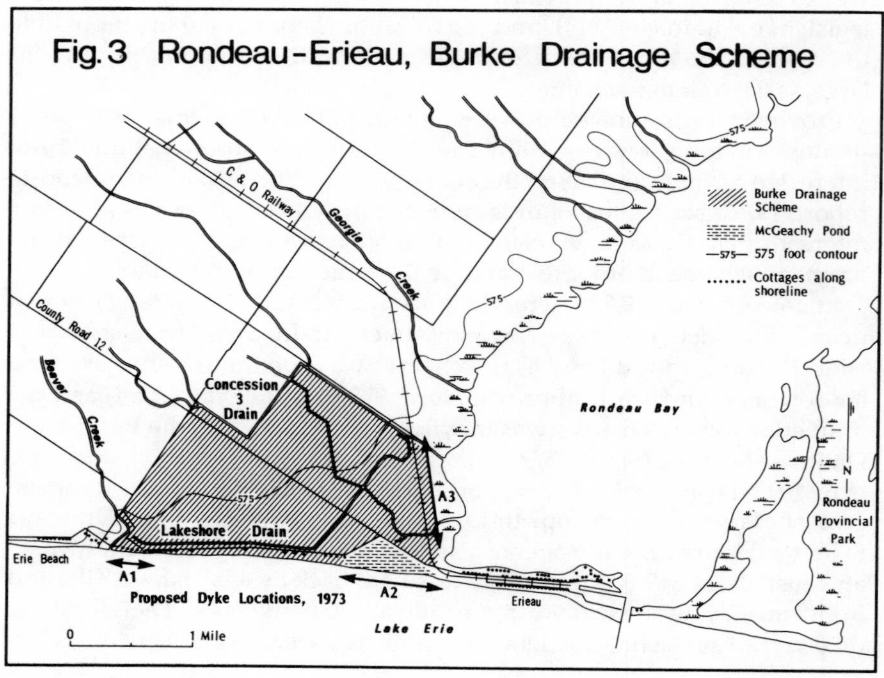

Fig. 3 Rondeau-Erieau, Burke Drainage Scheme

Since initial drainage, about 120 cottages, some of which date from the 1920s, have been constructed along the lakeshore road between Erie Beach and Erieau. Approximately 45 cottages also have been built along the sand bar separating the East Marsh Drainage Scheme from Lake Erie.

ATTEMPTS TO CONTROL SHORELINE POSITION AND COASTAL PROCESSES

The development of these large drainage schemes on former marsh lands, located inland from naturally moving beaches and dunes, has led to the second major type of adjustment to north Erie shore ecology: attempts to control the position of the shoreline and to prevent flooding, erosion, and other processes associated with lake level fluctuations.

Details of this second type of adjustment can be demonstrated by organizing data on flood responses in the Rondeau-Erieau and Pelee-East Marsh areas in terms of the model developed by White, Burton, Kates.[5] Responses are divided into four basic classes: modify the cause; modify the hazard; modify the loss potential; adjust to losses (Table 1). Certain responses classified under modify the cause, modify the loss potential, and adjust to losses have been employed on the north Erie shore — for example, diversions, control of inflow and outflow, warning systems, public relief, and individual loss bearing — but the emphasis has been on modifying the hazard. Responses within this general class are predominantly engineering or structural in character. Their construction has mainly been possible because local projects have been supported by substantial low-interest loans, subsidies, or other payments from the provincial and federal governments. Floodproofing (for example the stilting of cottages), zoning, and other alternatives generally have not been used, although some municipalities have recently considered land-use regulations.

STRUCTURAL ADJUSTMENTS, HIGH WATER LEVELS, AND CRISIS ATMOSPHERE

Figure 4 illustrates that dikes, breakwalls, and other structures are built chiefly during high lake level periods when shoreline erosion and flooding are perceived widely as a serious threat. A crisis atmosphere prevails and local residents and politicians are called upon to provide funds to build the traditional protective structures. Most of the repairs take the form of rebuilding embankments, seawalls and groynes. Federal and provincial financial assistance is provided through the Municipal Drainage Act, and the Provincial Aid to Drainage Act. Figure 4 also indicates that, in spite of the introduction of such structures, the natural processes of erosion and flooding have continued and will continue to be a problem which cannot be eliminated even with substantial increases in public funding of engineering adjustments.

In order to provide a more complete understanding of decision making during a high-water stage, attention will now be directed to the 1972 autumn floods which occurred when Lake Erie was at a very high level (Figure 4).

TABLE 1

Theoretical and Actual Range of Adjustments in the Two Study Areas*

Modify the cause	Modify the hazard	Modify the loss potential	Adjust to losses		
			Spread the loss	Plan for the loss	Bear the loss
Weather modification	*Seawalls*	Flood proofing	*Public relief*	Flood insurance and relief funds	*Individual loss bearing*
Channelize the lake	*Groynes*	Zoning and land use regulation	Subsidized insurance	Tax write-offs	
Diversions	*Dikes*	*Forecasting*	*Tax write-offs*		
Control inflow and outflow	*Breakers* and bars	Warning systems	Government purchase of land and property		
	Rip-rap	*Temporary* and permanent *evacuation*			
	Gabions	Subsidized relocation			
	Land fill and landscaping	*Building codes and design*			
	Flood fighting				
	Beach nourishment				
	Various loans and payments from senior governments for the above				

*Adjustments that have been used in the Pelee-East Marsh or Rondeau-Erieau areas (actual range of adjustments) are printed in italics.
Source: Adapted with modifications from: T. F. Saarinen, "Environmental Perception," in I. R. Manners and M. W. Mikesell (eds.), *Perspectives on Environment*. (Washington, D.C.: Association of American Geographers, 1974), p. 272. Various issues of the *London Free Press* and *Windsor Star*, Harwich and Mersea Township Files, and field observations were used in compiling the actual range of adjustments.

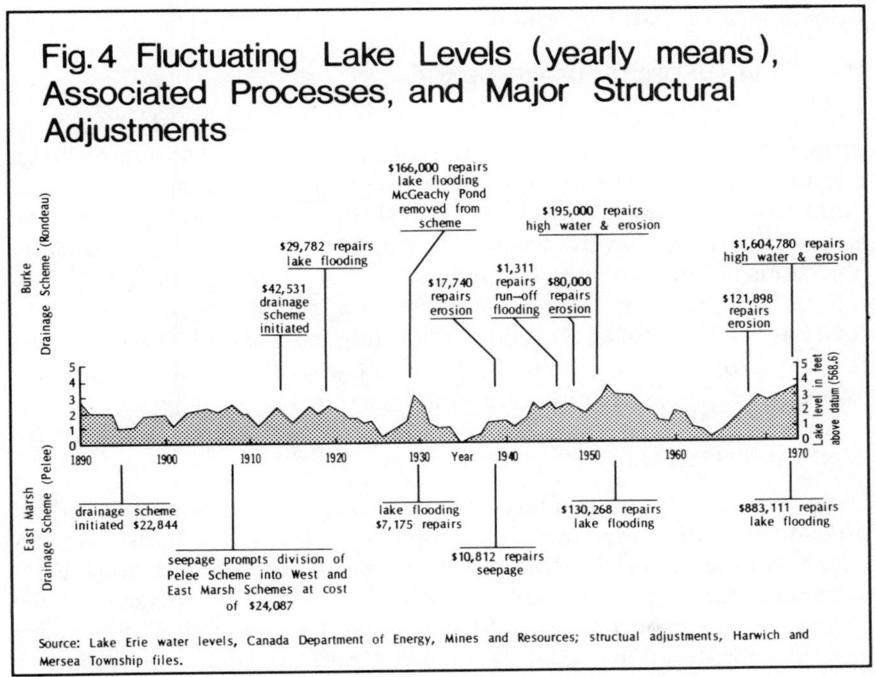

Fig. 4 Fluctuating Lake Levels (yearly means), Associated Processes, and Major Structural Adjustments

Source: Lake Erie water levels, Canada Department of Energy, Mines and Resources; structual adjustments, Harwich and Mersea Township files.

The Fall 1972 Floods

On 14 November 1972 an intense low-pressure system passed south of Lake Erie, generating steady winds from the northeast at approximately 40 knots, peaking to 55 knots. Owing to the high wind velocity and 200-mile fetch over the lake, the water at the western end of the lake rose an estimated 4 feet above the already high level.

At Point Pelee waves reportedly were 10 feet high and brought about erosion, evacuation of residents, flooding of about 2,000 acres of nearby farmland, and damage to cottages and homes. Damage to cottages in the Pelee area was estimated at $250,000.

In the Rondeau-Erieau (Burk) area, waves washed over dikes, but much water was carried away by ditches and little farmland was actually flooded. Some cottages along the dike road were damaged or destroyed.

Total damage from the 1972 floods in southwestern Ontario has been estimated at approximately $5,000,000, although the basis for this estimate is unknown.[6]

Within three days of the onset of flooding, Ontario's Premier and Natural Resources Minister had both inspected the damage along much of the north Erie shore and had promised financial aid. The media gave the floods and the plight of farmers and cottagers wide publicity.

Response to the Fall 1972 Floods

PROCEDURES UNDER THE DRAINAGE ACT

Under the Drainage Act, a standard procedure is used to process proposals for repair and construction of dikes and other structures in an existing drainage scheme: (1) landowners in the scheme petition the municipality to have work done; (2) the municipality orders an engineering report on the work; (3) a public meeting is held to consider objections to the engineering report; (4) the municipality accepts or rejects the report or asks the engineer for alterations; (5) a court of revision is held to hear objections regarding assessment to landowners for the proposed work; (6) higher-level appeals can be made, for example, to the county judge and drainage referee.

RONDEAU-ERIEAU AREA AND HARWICH TOWNSHIP

In its response to the problem, Harwich Township followed standard procedures and waited for the completion of an engineering report, which was submitted in July 1973. Separate recommendations were submitted for areas A1, A2, and A3 of the Burk Drainage Scheme (Figure 3). The report for area A1 recommended removal of 29 cottages and dike construction on the cleared property. Cottagers were offered a total of $41,530 in compensation, ranging from $250 to $5,876 per cottage. Many cottagers considered this compensation totally inadequate in relation to current market values.[7]

Under the standard procedures of the Drainage Act, the cottagers were able to launch an appeal against this recommended solution. The cottagers were well-organized and secured wide publicity, including a full-page article in the Toronto *Globe and Mail*.[8] A lawyer, experienced in drainage matters, was retained to make the necessary appeals. Cottage owners voiced opposition to the proposed solution at Harwich Township council meetings and the court of revision.

Subsequently the ARDA (Agricultural Rural Development Act) branch of the Ontario Ministry of Agriculture and Food, the source of provincial and federal funding for the proposed adjustment, indicated its lack of support and pushed for an alternative. A revised engineering report was submitted for Area A1 recommending location of the dike on farms inland from the beach. This recommendation was accepted by Harwich council in February 1974.

PELEE-EAST MARSH AND MERSEA TOWNSHIP

In its response to the flood and erosion problem in the Pelee-East Marsh area, Mersea Township used the emergency provisions in the Drainage Act. The township council ordered an engineering study, but also authorized immediate construction of a breakwall prior to the completion of the report, and without holding a public hearing. The breakwall is a large stone block structure, approximately ten feet high and twenty feet wide, built shoreward of the cottages, separating the cottagers and any other recreationists from the lake. The structure is inflexible and certainly will appear paradoxical when the lake level falls.

The breakwall cost about $720,000 and would have been out of reach of Mersea Township without promise of substantial (90 per cent) federal-provincial financial assistance. The breakwall was constructed along approximately 1.5 miles of sand beach located within a few thousand yards of heavily used Point Pelee National Park, whose bathing and swimming resources would have been significantly increased if the alternative of purchasing the cottage and beach property had been adopted. With the breakwall a quick reality, however, the East Marsh cottagers, even if they had been organized like those at Rondeau-Erieau, had little opportunity to affect the decision. Unlike the Rondeau-Erieau cottagers, they could not influence the size, character, location, or cost of the breakwall. Nor have they so far been able to reduce the $750 to $3,000 per cottage property assessments levied by the municipality to help pay its 10 per cent share of the cost of the structure. In this context, it should be recognized that the cottagers were declared ineligible for the 90 per cent subsidy allowed farmers through ARDA channels. Moreover, the breakwall undoubtedly lowered at least some cottage property values, although these already were decreasing with rising public awareness of flood and erosion problems associated with high lake levels.

COST AND BENEFITS

The Pelee-East Marsh breakwall is obviously of greatest benefit to farmers living on drained marshland just inland from the beach and cottages along the shore. Data on engineering adjustment expenses are presented in Table 2. These data underline the fact that a small area of agricultural land was protected at very high cost, largely borne by Ontario and Canadian taxpayers. In fact the 1972-3 federal-provincial subsidy was $960 and $550 per acre in the Rondeau-Erieau and Pelee-East schemes respectively. These payments, and others made in past years, very probably exceed the value of the land for agricultural purposes.

Certainly the 1972-3 and earlier municipal, provincial, and federal costs of draining and protecting the Burk and East Marsh schemes have substantially exceeded the current market value of the farmland designated for protection after the 1972 floods. Consultation with local real estate firms and knowledgeable government agencies suggests that the 1972 price of organic (muck) and mineral soils in the Burk scheme

TABLE 2

Adjustments to the Fall 1972 Floods, Rondeau-Erieau and Pelee-East Marsh

	Rondeau-Erieau	Pelee-East Marsh
Drainage scheme and area of agricultural land involved	Burk, 1,378 acres	East Marsh, 1,124 acres
Nature of adjustment	Stone-covered berm on cottage property (A1); stone-covered berm along McGeachy Pond (A2); stone berm along C & O railbed (A3)	Stone breakwall on beach (Phase A); open drain (Phase B); berm along Hillman Marsh (Phase C)
Total cost of adjustment and cost per acre of agricultural land	$1,604,780 $1,165 per acre	$883,111 $786 per acre
Amount of ARDA subsidy and subsidy per acre of agricultural land	$1,325,952 $962 per acre	$624,075 $555 per acre
Number of cottagers affected	29 cottagers (Area A1) to be removed and compensated $41,530	45 cottagers and 20 lot owners assessed $112,635 for breakwall
Procedure under Drainage Act	Standard procedure — engineer's reports considered — report for A1 rejected under pressure from ARDA	Emergency procedure – engineer's report considered after adjustment completed
Current status of project	Revised engineer's report for A1 accepted — will not involve cottage removal	Project completed — cottagers are appealing court of revision decision on assessments
Total cost of adjustments to date (in constant 1973 dollars)		
Exclusive of 1972-73 adjustments	$2,064,268	$1,044,031
Inclusive of 1972-73 adjustments	$3,669,048	$1,927,142

Sources: Engineer's reports by Todgham and Case and William Setterington; *London Free Press* and *Windsor Star;* Harwich and Mersea Township Files. Constant 1973 dollar conversions based on general wholesale price index (including gold). See M.C. Urquhart and K.A.H. Buckley (eds.), *Historical Statistics of Canada* (Toronto, Macmillan, 1969); and Statistics Canada, *Prices and Price Indexes,* 1960-74 (Ottawa: Information Canada).

was about $2,000 and $500 per acres respectively. With about 878 acres of mineral and 500 acres of organic soil designated for protection, the total value of this farmland is estimated at approximately $1,400,000. This is slightly less than the estimated costs (Table 2) of the 1972-3 flood and erosion adjustments for the Burk scheme and substantially less than has been spent on construction and maintenance since the beginning of the Burk scheme in 1914. Township files contain data on expenditures since that year. In Table 2 these have been summarized and converted to 1973 dollar equivalents using the general wholesale price index.

As another indication of the costliness of the 1972-3 structural adjustments, consider that the 29 cottage properties alongside dike A1 could have been purchased for about $180,000 in 1972. This estimate is based on realtor opinion and our estimate that in the fall of 1972 ten cottages were each worth about $8,500 and nineteen cottages each about $5,000. Costs of protective measures for the A1 section of the Burk scheme are in the $300,000 range.

Thus, the 1972-3 and earlier federal-provincial grants and subsidies strongly favour a small group of farmers whose numbers are hard to calculate exactly because of the small size of some farm units, family operation, and other difficulties. Today approximately forty owners are involved in each scheme, although most of the 1972-3 benefits accrue to less than ten major landowners. Government grants or subsidies for the costs of engineering adjustments for acreage in just one farm operation in the Burk scheme amount to about $240,000.

PUBLIC OWNERSHIP

Such large individual subsidies are very difficult to justify and raise the possibility of public ownership. If the land were purchased by government, it could be farmed through lease-back or other arrangements, or maintained for recreation or conservation purposes. Government ownership would certainly make it possible to allow these lands to flood and erode in a natural manner during high water levels and to be farmed at lower lake levels. Government ownership would reduce the need for constructing and maintaining dikes and other structures. Of course engineering adjustments provide income and employment which would have to be foregone to some extent under new managerial arrangements.

SOURCE OF FUNDING

The federal-provincial assistance for the 1972-3 engineering adjustments was provided in a rather extraordinary manner. The federal contribution of 45 per cent was funded by the Department of Regional Economic Expansion (DREE) through Ontario ARDA. DREE was created in 1969 basically to fight regional economic disparity in Canada.[9] ARDA was founded in 1961 to meet the needs of poorer Canadians, chiefly farmers, living in rural areas.[10] Neither agency seems particularly appropriate for the funding of large-scale engineering adjustments to floods, erosion, and high lake levels in a relatively well-to-do part of Canada. Further to this point, on 31 December 1968, the Ontario Ministry of Agriculture and Food discontinued its ARDA program for drainage in southwestern Ontario and began to concentrate on lower-income eastern and northern Ontario.

To use ARDA as a mechanism for providing assistance to the Pelee-East Marsh and Rondeau-Erieau areas required two amendments to the Federal-Provincial Rural Development Agreement, 1970-5. Both of these were made by Order-in-Council and were not subject to debate in the legislature or among the public. Under the first amendment, projects eligible for ARDA assistance were extended to include flood protection by diking and river channel improvements. Under the second amendment, the total costs to be shared by the federal and provincial governments were increased from 66-⅔ per cent to 90 per cent.[11]

THE DRAINAGE ACT AND ITS ADMINISTRATION

Although adjustments were funded through ARDA, they were administered through the Ontario Drainage Act. Several problems with this Act make it questionable as an administrative mechanism for flood protection measures. For example, no provision exists in the Drainage Act for the purchase of land. As a result, in Harwich Township, had the proposed diking taken place, cottagers would have retained title to their property and paid taxes, but would have lost their cottages as a result of the construction of a dike on their land.

Appeal procedures under the Act are inadequate. In both Harwich and Mersea townships, the court of revision is composed of the township's council members. The people who provisionally adopt an engineering report therefore consider objections to the assessment levied under the report. Moreover, the emergency provisions of the Drainage Act work to block objections from landowners not favouring adjustments.

Examination of the recent Select Committee report on drainage in Ontario indicates that some of these procedural problems could continue in future. The committee has recommended no basic change in the functions or membership of the court of revision. Appeals beyond this court are now directed to the county judge or drainage referee. The Select Committee has recommended that a new body, the Ontario Drainage Appeal Tribunal, be established to exercise many of the present powers of the county judge and drainage referee. In particular this tribunal would hear appeals from any decision of the court of revision, certain assessment appeals, appeals on refusal of certain loans, or on the grounds that a proposed scheme does not meet some of the requirements of the Drainage Act, as well as other matters. Such a tribunal could be quite effective, provided that its membership is chosen with due regard to the need for independence and also possible conflicts of interest. The Select Committee makes no recommendations on membership other than to say that no maximum should be set and that members should be appointed by the Lieutenant-Governor-in-Council.

Administratively, relatively little provincial planning and control is possible through the present Drainage Act. No benefit-cost analysis or environmental impact statement is required, and engineers do not need to justify drainage projects on agricultural or other grounds.

However, the Select Committee on drainage has recommended that benefit-cost and environmental impact studies be required for drainage projects. Such requirements, if implemented by government, would be a definite improvement. More significant benefits undoubtedly would accrue if the environmental impact statements were prepared by means other than those favoured by members of the Select Committee. They envision that a statement would be produced by a committee of three people appointed by the municipal council and consisting of two government representatives and an "impartial ratepayer resident in the municipality" who would be chairman. Preferably the government members would be from the Ministry of Agriculture and Food, and the conservation authorities. A possible representative of the Ministry of the Environment is given lowest rank, whereas many outside observers would probably feel that such a person should be a required member of an environmental impact assessment committee. Whether such a locally oriented committee could consistently produce broadly based, high-quality environmental impact statements is problematical. If funds were available for staff and consultants, prospects would seem better. A further requirement for the holding of public hearings on proposed major projects would also allow a wide range of interested individuals and citizen groups to bring their own perceptions, values, and learning to bear on proposed land-use changes.

Another major difficulty is that the Select Committee does not appear to take its own environmental impact statement recommendation seriously. Studies upon which the statement would be based seem to be envisioned as proceeding along with the project, with little or no anticipation that difficulties could arise. The idea that a pre-project study might stall or prevent a project, or that problems encountered in construction or operation might result in project cancellation, is conspicuous by its absence from the Select Committee report.

The following illustrates the Select Committee's basic views on the environmental impact statement:

> While the Committee is not completely persuaded that agricultural drains have great environmental impact in every case, it is prepared to recognize the possibility. Accordingly, the Committee recommends that an environmental impact statement on every new drain proposed in Ontario be filed with the council of the municipality in which the drainage works is proposed. The Committee feels that in many cases the environmental impact committee's report to council will be merely a brief statement to the effect that the work has been completed and that the conclusion is the environmental impact is nil. The environmental impact committee would, it is expected, make a more detailed and more formal report where there are complications.[12]

An Ontario ARDA official has suggested that flood and erosion control projects may be administered by conservation authorities in future. In this context, Harwich Township applied to the Ministry of Natural Resources in February 1973 to have shoreline areas included in the Lower Thames Valley Conservation Authority. In Essex County, petitions led to the creation of the Essex Region Conservation Authority in July 1973. The possibility of additional flood aid was a motivating force in both cases.

The influence of the conservation authorities could result in a widening of the range of flood adjustments employed along the north Erie shore. The authorities have used land-use adjustments in the Toronto area, for example. The authorities also have supported purchase of large floodplain areas in the Thames and other valleys and maintenance of much of this land in open space and other uses less likely to suffer heavy damage with flooding. On the other hand, a federal-provincial agreement has been concluded for the impending construction of more than $16,000,000 worth of dikes, breakwalls, dams, and other structural adjustments to river and lake flooding and erosion in the Lower Thames Valley and St. Clair Region Conservation Authority regions.

Detailed research reports on the need for these structural adjustments, any available alternatives, and estimates of the economic, social, and environmental benefits and costs associated with the alternatives should be circulated to interested government departments and made available to citizens for critical discussion at public hearings before any final decisions are made.

Summary and Interpretations

In summary, the evidence in this study indicates that financial and institutional arrangements for flood, erosion, and other hazards, especially on reclaimed marsh lands along Ontario's Great Lakes coasts, are in need of careful study and some changes.

A review is urgently needed of the provincial and federal grants (or subsidies) system which has supported adoption of increasingly costly dikes and other engineering adjustments, notably at times of high lake level in a crisis atmosphere. The concentration on a narrow range of dikes and structural adjustments, to the neglect of land use and other possible responses, arises from the long-time, and ultimately hopeless, conviction that lake levels, flooding, erosion, and other natural processes can be fixed and controlled.

In Pelee-East Marsh and Rondeau-Erieau, and presumably in other areas as yet unstudied, past large-scale structural adjustments are difficult to justify on economic, social, or environmental grounds. They involve large public subsidies to a relatively small number of individuals, largely farmers. In the Burk and East Marsh drainage schemes, the relatively high hazard zones total approximately 1,200 acres of drained organic (formerly marsh) soils. These lands produce mainly onions and other crops, which can be grown elsewhere without subsidy. The continued use of dikes and other structures has contributed to the reduction of north Erie shore marsh lands to a small area, and so to the loss of fish spawning and nursery areas, as well as waterfowl and other wildlife habitat. The significance of marsh losses to the decline of sturgeon and other fish populations in Lake Erie unfortunately has not received the attention accorded the effects of over-fishing and pollution. Structural adjustments also have led to destruction of large beaches valuable for private and public recreation.

Very large hazard grants or subsidies may sometimes be justified, although it is difficult to think of specific instances. In areas such as Pelee-East Marsh and Rondeau-Erieau the often heard claim that such agricultural lands are needed to feed Canada and a starving world founders on the fact that the areas involved are very small, and that they might well produce more fish, waterfowl, and other food if left as marshes.

Under present arrangements, the federal and provincial governments have introduced no formal safeguards or guidelines for use of hazard or drainage grants at the local or municipal level, although Ontario ARDA and other senior government personnel are in a position to attend local meetings and influence decisions, as for example in Harwich Township in 1972-3. Yet the ultimate decision on how the grants are to be used remains with the municipality, especially in a crisis situation when political pressures are high and use can be made of convenient legislation such as the emergency provisions of the Drainage Act.

Any system of guidelines will be perceived by some as an "infringement on the democratic right of residents to choose their own solutions to local problems" and as yet another example of the steady incursion of provincial and federal bureaucracies into local affairs. Such a position surely is truly tenable only if accompanied by a willingness and ability to pay for a large proportion of the costs of local decisions. When the great proportion of these costs is borne by the citizens of Ontario and Canada generally, then decisions should be subject to guidelines and careful review by higher governments, as well as by interested citizen groups, preferably through advisory committees and/or public hearings.

A need also exists for greater co-ordination among government departments at all levels. In the Pelee-East Marsh area, for example, the 1972-3 decision to build a $720,000 breakwall ruined a potentially purchasable beach of significance to managers of heavily used Point Pelee National Park. The National Park personnel were given no opportunity to participate in this decision. The introduction of structures at Rondeau-Erieau bears a similar relationship to heavily used nearby Rondeau Provincial Park.

More specifically, this study supports increased use of detailed benefit-cost and environmental impact statements. The background research should be conducted in a scientific manner by a process which involves highly qualified professionals as well as consideration of a wide range of alternatives, including the option to do nothing.

Use of advisory committees and public hearings in reviewing these studies provides a means for all affected groups to present their perceptions, values, and information prior to a decision. Public hearings are especially important for major projects largely financed through low-interest loans, grants, or other public subsidies.

Other policy and institutional changes worthy of careful study include:

1. Means of public purchase or land-use control of coastal land identified as highly susceptible to flooding, erosion, and marsh conditions.
2. Possible establishment of co-ordinating legislation and/or agencies, for example, a Coastal Land-Use Act which requires lower-level governments to produce a land-use plan before receiving further provincial or federal grants, or the creation of a North Erie Shore Land-Use Commission. The advantages and disadvantages of such potential institutional arrangements should be compared to what is presently possible under existing arrangements, for example, conservation authorities.

An Ontario Hazards Commission could establish policies, guidelines, and procedures for senior government involvement in selecting, financing, and introducing hazard adjustments. This, in turn, could reduce the direct and immediate pressure often placed on provincial and federal administrators and politicians after a major flood or other hazard. Politicians are frequently urged to arrange for grants or compensation on an *ad hoc* basis after buildings, crops, or other land uses have been damaged or destroyed. The 1974 Grand River floods in the Cambridge area, Southern Ontario, resulted in such damages, and in the establishment of an *ad hoc* committee of inquiry to advise government on this problem.

NOTES

1. *Agricultural Land Drainage in Ontario*, Final Report of the Select Committee on Land Drainage, Legislative Assembly, Toronto, June 1974.
2. *See*, for example, C. Drysdale, *Point Pelee Environmental Management*, Leamington, Parks Canada, 1973; H. A. Regier and W. L. Hartman, "Lake Erie's Fish Community: 150 Years of Cultural Stresses", *Science*, Vol. 180, 1973, 1248-55.
3. D. L. Keenlyside, *Late Prehistory of the Lake Erie Drainage Basin, the Point Pelee Region*, Ottawa National Museum of Man, Archaeological Survey of Canada, 1972.
4. Township of Mersea, By-law 523, 19 March 1894, and *Windsor Star*, 23 June 1951.
5. I. Burton, R. W. Kates and G. F. White, "The Human Ecology of Extreme Geophysical Events", *Natural Hazard Research Working Paper*, No. 1, Toronto, University of Toronto, Geography Department, 1968.
6. *Windsor Star*, 1 Nov. 1973.
7. Todgham and Case Limited, Report to Harwich Township re Burk Drainage Works Embankment Protection, Area A1, 23 July 1973.
8. *Globe and Mail*, 13 Sept. 1973.
9. D. Jamieson, *Regional Economic Circumstances and Opportunities in Canada*, Ottawa Department of Regional Economic Expansion, 1973, p. 1.
10. James N. McCrorie, *ARDA: an Experiment in Development Planning*, Ottawa, Canadian Council on Rural Development, 1969, p. 8.
11. *Federal-Provincial Rural Development Agreement*, April 1970 to 31 March 1975, and ARDA Branch, Ontario Ministry of Agriculture and Food, ARDA Project Proposal, *Flood Control for Agricultural Lands, Townships of Harwich, Pelee and Mersea*, 15 January 1973.
12. See Note 1.

20
Riparian Land Management in Saskatchewan and Ontario

*Reiner Jaakson**

Lake and reservoir shorelines and other riparian interfaces are important water resources, and their planning and management are key issues today. Also, most summer outdoor recreation is strongly dependent on water. It is generally estimated that the large majority, perhaps some 75 per cent, of these activities are water-based, water-oriented or, at least, enhanced by a proximity to water.[1] Not surprisingly, therefore, land areas adjacent to water have become the foci of intensive activity and development, requiring innovative riparian land-use planning concepts and adaptable new administrative mechanisms if conflict between uses and environmental overload is to be avoided.

The well-established mechanisms of land management on large government initiated multiple-purpose reservoirs provide good examples for the administration of natural lake shorelines where planning has long been inadequate. On large multiple-purpose reservoirs a project agency, frequently established for the purpose of managing reservoir land and water, expropriates land to be flooded, delineates shoreline safety elevations and land-use zones, and implements subsequent development control. In contrast, around lakes and other natural waterbodies, provincial line departments attempt to tackle complex riparian problems, using development control and land management legislation that is intended for general planning and is unsuited for the specific purpose of lake planning and shoreline administration.

This paper consists of three sections. Both the first and second section deal with a case study of widely divergent shoreline land-use planning and land administration practices. The first case study is of "Lake Diefenbaker", the multiple-purpose South Saskatchewan River Reservoir, where an established framework for shoreline planning has proven to be successful. The second case study is of the Trent Canal water

---

*Reiner Jaakson is an Associate Professor in the Department of Urban and Regional Planning at the University of Toronto. This paper is an edited version of an article which appeared with the same title in *Institutional arrangements for water management: Canadian experiences*, edited by B. Mitchell, Publication Series No. 5, Waterloo, University of Waterloo, Department of Geography, 1975, pp. 173-207.

storage reservoir-lakes in the Haliburton Highlands region of Ontario, where, in spite of strong involvement by both the federal and provincial government, riparian planning has been inefficient. Using the case studies as examples, the third section sets forth a series of general proposals for the improvement of shoreline land-use planning and land administration.

The South Saskatchewan River Project

The reservoir for the South Saskatchewan River Project, commonly referred to as "Lake Diefenbaker" (and so named in the balance of this paper), is used as an illustration of the Saskatchewan case study of reservoir land-use planning. It is the prototype from which all other similar regulations in the province stem.

In 1952 a Royal Commission reported on the feasibility of creating a reservoir on the South Saskatchewan River.[2] Having examined the benefits and the costs of such a project, the Royal Commission concluded that the economic returns would not be commensurate with the costs of the project, even though the project would yield social returns which were not subject to measurement. On July 25, 1958, however, an agreement to create the reservoir was signed between Canada and Saskatchewan.

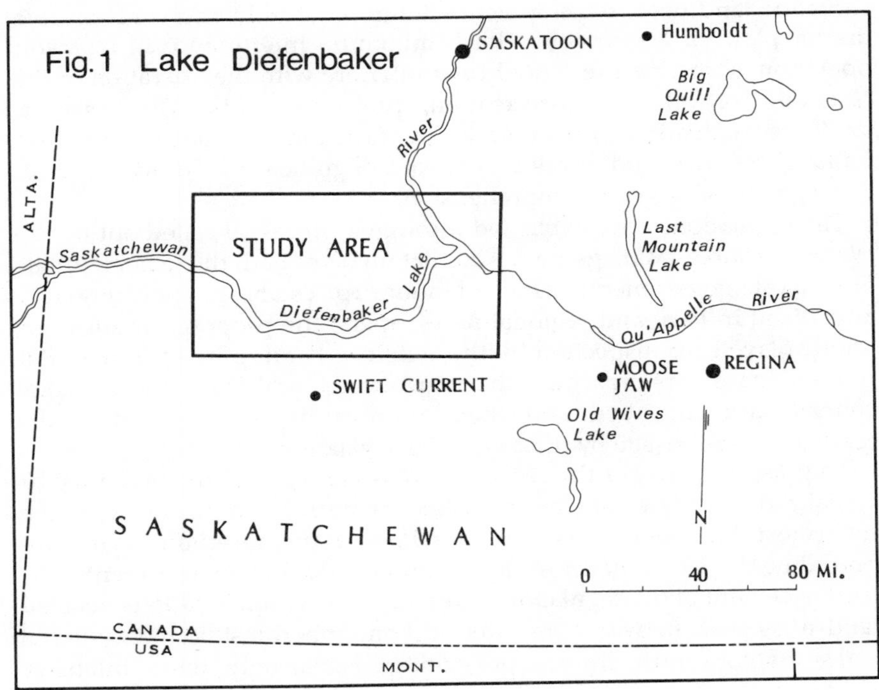

Fig. 1 Lake Diefenbaker

Lake Diefenbaker has a storage capacity of 8 million acre-feet of water, is approximately 150 miles long, and has close to 500 miles of shoreline (Figure 1). The water level in the reservoir can fluctuate up to 28 feet. The project cost, set at $125 million, has been shared between the two levels of government (Canada 75 per cent, Saskatchewan 25 per cent, the Saskatchewan share not to exceed $25 million).[3] The federal government was responsible for the design and construction of the physical facilities of the project, while Saskatchewan was to undertake the planning and the development of the project benefits: irrigation, hydro-electric power, flood control, domestic and industrial water supply and recreation.

Reservoir Land-Use Control

Authority for riparian planning in Saskatchewan derives from the section entitled "Reservoir Land Use" in the Water Resource Management Act, 1972. To date, riparian land-use regulations have been established around Lake Diefenbaker, as well as at a number of smaller reservoirs in various parts of the province. The regulations fulfill three objectives. First, safety: shoreline development should not suffer damage from flooding, water action, slumping or sedimentation. Second, efficiency: to establish efficient relationships between various shoreline land uses, development should be orderly and conform to a master plan for a reservoir. Third, minimum interference in reservoir operation: shoreline uses should not interfere with the operation of the reservoir for other, non-recreation, project benefits. The reservoir land-use regulations incorporate the functions of zoning by-laws, building by-laws, and development control guidelines. To say the least, the regulations are very comprehensive.

The regulations are established through a process, spelled out by the Water Resources Management Act, that involves both the general public and local government. The intention to establish regulations is advertised in local and regional newspapers; the proposed regulations are displayed for inspection by the public; a hearing is set to consider written comments regarding the regulations; local Rural Municipality councils are consulted and their approval is required before the regulations are passed by the provincial legislature.

To grasp the crux of the reservoir land-use regulations, they may be visualized as a series of concentric lines (Figure 2). In this analogy, the innermost line represents the shoreline of the reservoir water impoundment. The outermost line from the shoreline represents the furthest extent of the regulations, and includes within it various detailed land-use zones. Between the outermost and innermost boundary nest a series of concentric lines representing increasingly more intensive

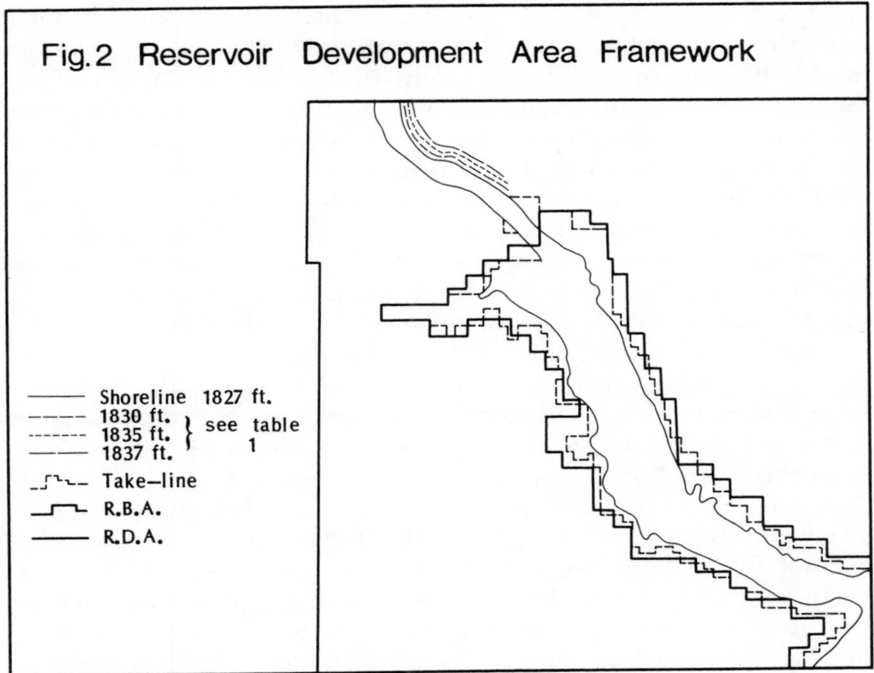

land-use controls as one approaches the shoreline. The regulations that affect land at any given location consist of the regulations which apply at that level in the hierarchy, together with the regulations from each outward concentric line. That is, the regulations are cumulative from the outermost boundary inward. The following description of the reservoir land-use regulations traces the concentric line analogy from its outermost to its innermost boundary.

The Reservoir Development Area

The shoreline land-use regulations, once approved by the provincial legislature, are formally known as Reservoir Development Area regulations. The Reservoir Development Area boundary is the outermost ring in the concentric line analogy, and encompasses all the other more detailed control designations. In 1961 Reservoir Development Area regulations were implemented on a small area surrounding the main dam of Lake Diefenbaker. In 1962, the coverage of the regulations was extended to include the entire 150 mile length of the reservoir. The Reservoir Development Area boundary of Lake Diefenbaker varies between three miles and fifteen miles from the shoreline, and on the average is some eight miles from the water's edge.

The predominant land use around Lake Diefenbaker is grain farming and ranching. Small urban communities in the region serve as agricultural service centers and often also function as nuclei of farm family residences. The foremost goal in the delineation of the Reservoir Development Area boundary around Lake Diefenbaker was to control the future land-use pattern in the region. New land uses, even if only localized in one small area, could influence development in distant locations and thus ultimately affect the entire reservoir region. For example, uncontrolled commercial development, perhaps to cater to tourists along a highway in the vicinity of the reservoir, could seriously interfere with and erode the existing established trading centers.

It is relatively easy to predict with fair accuracy many of the changes in shoreline land use which may occur as a result of the creation of a new, large reservoir, such as the location of provincial, regional and local parks, cottage subdivisions, organized institutional camps and boat launching ramps. However, in the larger region around a reservoir, some distance inland from the shoreline, it is more difficult to accurately predict future land-use changes (Figure 2). Admittedly, an agricultural area located well outside the influence-orbit of the reservoir will most likely not undergo major land-use alterations. Yet, as one moves from this area outside the influence-orbit, closer toward the reservoir, a transition zone where future changes are more likely to occur is encountered. This transition zone extends from agricultural areas outside the influence-orbit of the reservoir, where few if any land-use changes due to the reservoir may be anticipated, to the reservoir shoreline itself where major land-use changes, often for recreation, can be anticipated reasonably accurately. Planning in the transition zone is a problem since it is difficult to predict what land-use changes are likely to occur, and where. The boundary of the Reservoir Development Area at Lake Diefenbaker, as well as at most other reservoirs where the regulations exist, was therefore located to include all of this transition zone, as well as some land beyond it as a buffer to surrounding areas.

The Restricted Building Area

Inside the Reservoir Development Area, perhaps the most important boundary is the Restricted Building Area (Figure 2). In the concentric circle analogy, the Restricted Building Area forms the first ring inside the outermost circle of the Reservoir Development Area. The Restricted Building Area includes land of a varying distance from the shoreline of the reservoir, where slumping and bank instability, sedimentation, and periodic water action make the safe location of buildings and other structures difficult. New construction and alteration of existing structures within the Restricted Building Area must be approved with a building permit issued by the reservoir authority. Background reports on shoreline geology, bank stability, erosion, and sedimentation are used to evaluate, on a site-to-site basis, whether the location of buildings is safe.

The "Take-Line"

The construction of a large dam will impound a body of water which permanently floods extensive areas of land. It is therefore necessary for the project authority either to expropriate land that will be flooded, or alternatively to acquire flood easements from land owners. First, the contour elevation of the water level in the reservoir at full capacity, and the ownership of land below this elevation along the entire length of the reservoir, are identified. Then, based on studies of the geology of the land along the future reservoir shoreline and the future hydrologic characteristics of the water-body, land that may be subject to slumping, sedimentation or other hazards above the full-supply-level contour elevation is identified. The "take-line" is the boundary that encircles all of this land to be acquired ("taken") for the project (Figure 2).

The take-line is the first concentric ring inside the Restricted Building Area. However, the intent of these two boundaries is quite different. The take-line includes land to be flooded as well as land that may be threatened by reservoir water action, slumping, sedimentation, or erosion. The Restricted Building Area, on the other hand, also includes privately owned land beyond the take-line where such hazards are unlikely, but where control over the careful location of buildings is nevertheless desirable.

The Safe Building Elevations

Similar to the previous two boundaries, Safe Building Elevations constitute a series of boundaries nested one within the other. They represent the most intense riparian controls, parallel to the reservoir shoreline. While the Restricted Building Area and the take-line boundary follow the survey grid of sections and quarter sections of land, the Safe Building Elevations, because they are more directly dependent on natural features, follow contour lines. Table 1 outlines the four categories of Safe Building Elevations at Lake Diefenbaker.

In summary, the Safe Building Elevations may be viewed as more detailed development control guidelines inside the Restricted Building Area. As with the other controls discussed earlier, Safe Building Elevations are based on studies of shoreline geology and reservoir hydrology.

The previous sections on the Saskatchewan reservoir land-use management methods will again be discussed in the last section, where riparian planning guidelines for Ontario are outlined.

TABLE 1

Lake Diefenbaker Safe-Building Elevations

Category # 1	Habitable buildings and structures. Minimum elevation *1,835′*.
Category # 2	Permanent non-habitable buildings and structures. Minimum elevation *1,832′*.
Category # 3	Portable non-habitable buildings and structures or permanent non-habitable buildings and structures specially designed to permit short periods of flooding, and developments not susceptible to damage from flooding. Minimum elevation *1,827′*.
Category # 4	All engineered work, public and private, requiring special considerations. Elevation subject to the discretion of the design engineer, who should be guided by consideration of reservoir flood levels, period of maximum levels, minimum reservoir levels and wind effects on reservoir levels.

The Trent Canal Reservoir-Lakes

The Saskatchewan model of riparian land management around Lake Diefenbaker offers direct and very useful suggestions of how riparian land in Ontario, and elsewhere, may be planned and managed more effectively. Although in Ontario there are no water resources schemes of the scale of Lake Diefenbaker, a large number of smaller reservoirs do exist throughout the province. The Saskatchewan type of riparian controls could be adapted to apply to such reservoirs. More importantly, however, the same principles, with only slight modification, apply also to lake, coastal, and river riparian land management. The purpose of this section is to briefly outline an Ontario case study as background to the next section where the two case studies are combined and general shoreline management principles are proposed.

In 1830, an Act of the Parliament of Upper Canada authorized £16,000 to be designated for the construction of "the inland or back waters" of Ontario. Construction of the first locks of the Trent Canal started in 1833 and, with various stages of completion, was terminated in 1918 (Figure 3). Under the British North America Act, 1867, the federal government owned the improvements along the Trent Canal, while the province of Ontario had jurisdiction over the rivers, lakes and shorelands that make up the Trent Canal and its waterway.

In 1903 the Superintending Engineer of the Trent Canal advised the Minister of the Canada Department of Railways and Canals that, in order to ensure a sufficient water supply for the Trent Canal, the federal government should consider the acquisition of a number of dams, owned by the province, on eight rivers and their tributaries north of the canal in the Haliburton Highlands region. An Order-in-Council

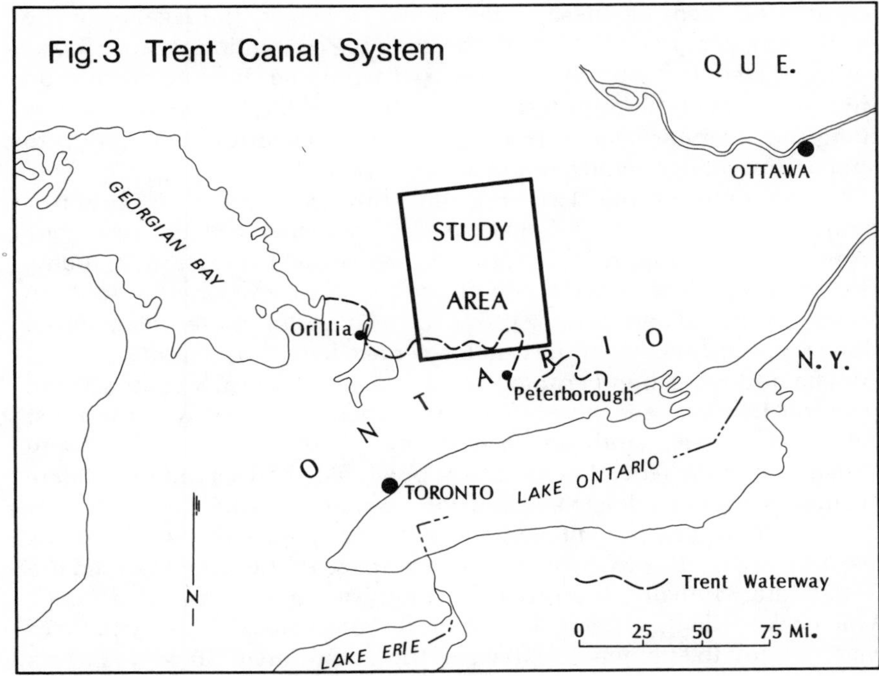

approved by the Lieutenant-Governor of Ontario in 1905 stated that "the Committee of Council advise that certain dams, canals and other works on waters tributary to the Trent Valley Canal heretofore constructed and maintained by the Department of Public Works, Ontario, be transferred to the Department of Railways and Canals, Canada."[4]

There were nine terms to the transfer, of which Clause 7 is particularly noteworthy. Clause 7 gives the federal government the right to build new dams anywhere within the mentioned watersheds, in addition to the dams which existed at the time of the transfer. The transfer agreement makes no mention of any necessary negotiations to approve such new dams; it can only be assumed that at the time of the transfer, no such approval procedures were deemed to be necessary. The federal government today thus has potential control over any new dam-sites within the watersheds north of the Kawartha Lakes. Furthermore, Clause 7 states that "the (Canada) Minister of Railways and Canals shall have the right at any time . . . to increase or decrease the height of all or any such dams."[5] Awareness of this clause must have been lacking ever since 1905, because Ontario has disposed of shore line Crown land for cottage development on most of the affected reservoir-lakes, and has allowed private construction well within the 66-foot road allowances common on many of these waterbodies. However, the legality of the entire transfer agreement, and particularly the contentious Clause 7, has yet to be tested. Politically, of course, it would be difficult to envision any government attempting to do so, because local property owners along the reservoir lakes could organize as a powerful lobby group to oppose any changes which might affect their land.

At the time of the 1905 transfer, the water uses on the two components of the Trent Canal system, the canal and the reservoir-lakes, were very different from the water-uses which exist there today. The canal was originally intended to be a water-transportation route to bring agricultural and forestry products to Lake Ontario shoreline ports. However, this function of the canal never reached great importance, and tourism and recreation became the major uses at an early time. On the reservoir-lakes, at the time of the agreement, forestry was the most important activity and, in fact, many of the dams which were transferred to the federal government previously had served to facilitate the transportation of logs to Haliburton Highland sawmills.

The federal government has authority to operate the water in the reservoir-lakes; the province owns and manages Crown land around the waterbodies. Initially, the province administered a Crown land policy which acknowledged the main role of the reservoir-lakes as a source of water supply to augment the flows of the Trent Canal. Since water was withdrawn from the reservoir-lakes throughout the summer, wide fluctuations of water level (13 feet on some lakes) were seen as constraints against shoreline development for recreation and tourism. However, with the rapid growth of cottaging in Ontario after World War II, and even earlier, the policy of restricting development on the reservoir-lakes was changed. With public pressure to open the area for cottaging, the Haliburton Highlands region, together with the Muskoka District and the Kawartha Lakes, thus became part of the recreation hinterland of urban southern Ontario.

Unfortunately, riparian planning in Ontario in the past has not been significantly different from other general land-use planning practices, and few if any special land-management tools have been used to interrelate the land and the water environments. However, more recently four attempts to improve riparian planning have been introduced. First, public health requirements control cottage sewage and waste-water discharges, and strict regulations monitor the location of septic tanks. Indirectly, the location of cottages themselves can thus be controlled. Second, the Ontario Land Inventory has a comprehensive system to rank and map shoreline recreation capability, and has developed data that now serve to guide lake planning.[6] Third, various methods to calculate lake-carrying capacity for recreation have been formulated, first by Jaakson, then by Hough and Stansbury, and more recently by Dillon.[7] Fourth, a methodology for standardized lake master plans was introduced by the Ontario Ministry of Natural Resources on an experimental basis in 1974, and was applied to a series of lakes in northwestern Ontario. Nevertheless, in spite of these various developments, riparian planning in the province is still inadequate, and needs to be improved. The aim of the next section is to propose a few such improvements.

Riparian Planning Proposals

The riparian management techniques described earlier, using Lake Diefenbaker as a case study, are applicable to most shoreline planning situations. However, an important consideration in the transfer of the techniques is the scale of the land-water interface to which these planning measures are applied. For the purpose of discussing differences in the transferability of the various riparian planning techniques, waterbodies have here rather arbitrarily been divided into four scale categories. The first scale category consists of small lakes, best represented by Canadian shield lakes. The second scale category consists of inland lakes of intermediate size, best represented by the Kawartha Lakes, Lake Simcoe, Rice Lake, and Lake Nipissing. The third category consists of the Great Lakes, the fourth category of marine coasts. The most direct application of the riparian techniques described here is to the small and the intermediate scale lakes, and important transformations of the basic principles have to be made in their application to the Great Lakes or to marine coasts.

In the discussion which follows, some reference is made to the mosaic concept of lake planning.[8] Briefly, the mosaic concept proposes, first, that small-scale Canadian shield lakes cannot be planned in isolation of each other but must instead be treated on a regional basis. Second, the mosaic concept proposes that lake shorelines should remain, as much as possible, in public open space and that development should take place in clusters in the intervening land areas between the lakes. The mosaic concept is more applicable to new, undeveloped lakes than it is to lakes with considerable existing development. If the mosaic concept is accepted as one model to plan small Canadian-shield scale lakes, then the principle of a Reservoir Development Area provides the useful function of co-ordinating development in one area with development elsewhere in a region of lakes. "Reservoir Development Area" has here been changed to "Lake Development Area", since in the current discussion the term refers to lakes and not to reservoirs.

Figure 4 illustrates how Lake Development Areas may be delineated around a group of small lakes. The rationale for the specific location of the boundary around each lake depends on a number of principles, of which only the more general are mentioned here. Many of these

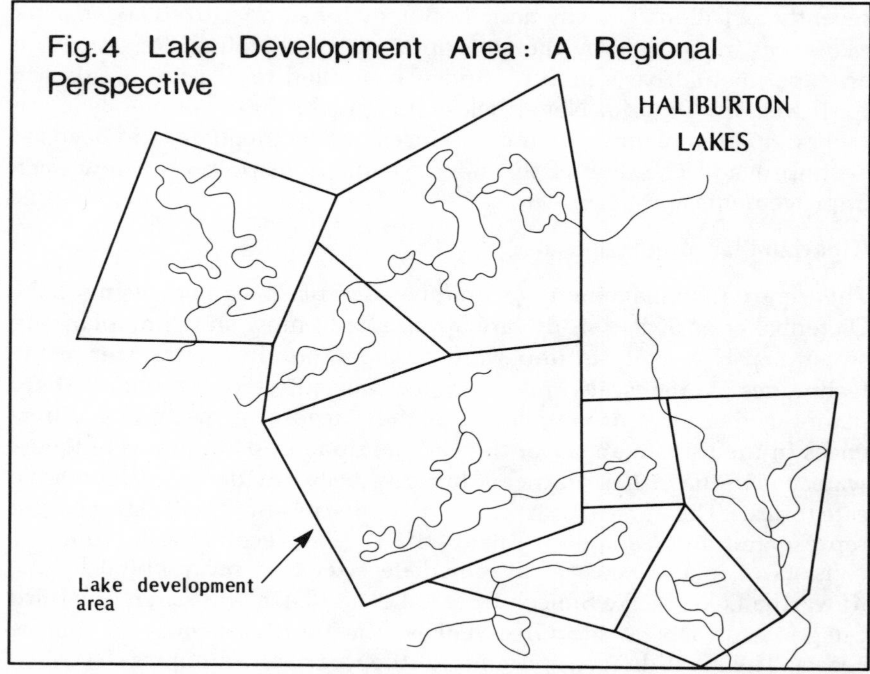

Fig. 4 Lake Development Area: A Regional Perspective

principles are similar to those which guided the location of the Reservoir Development Area around Lake Diefenbaker. In a Canadian shield situation where relatively small lakes are regionally adjacent to each other, the Lake Development Area boundary would be located in the intervening land areas between the lakes, and often also would include smaller lakes within the same boundary. The location of the actual boundary depends on, for example, topography and direction of drainage. Where development is to follow the mosaic pattern, the planned location of cluster cottage colonies must be taken into consideration when Lake Development Area Boundaries are established.

In a region of lakes there would thus be a quiltwork of Lake Development Areas with contiguous boundaries (Figure 5). Planning in such a region may take place at an extensive, an intensive, or an intermediate level of detail. At the extensive level, a large group of lakes, involving a number of Lake Development Areas, would be considered in, for example, planning the network of access roads to various lakes and the phasing of development in the region. While the extensive level thus considers factors common to the region, the intensive level deals more with one specific lake or small lakes hydrologically adjacent to each other and within the same Lake Development Area. That is, the intensive level considers factors unique to each lake.

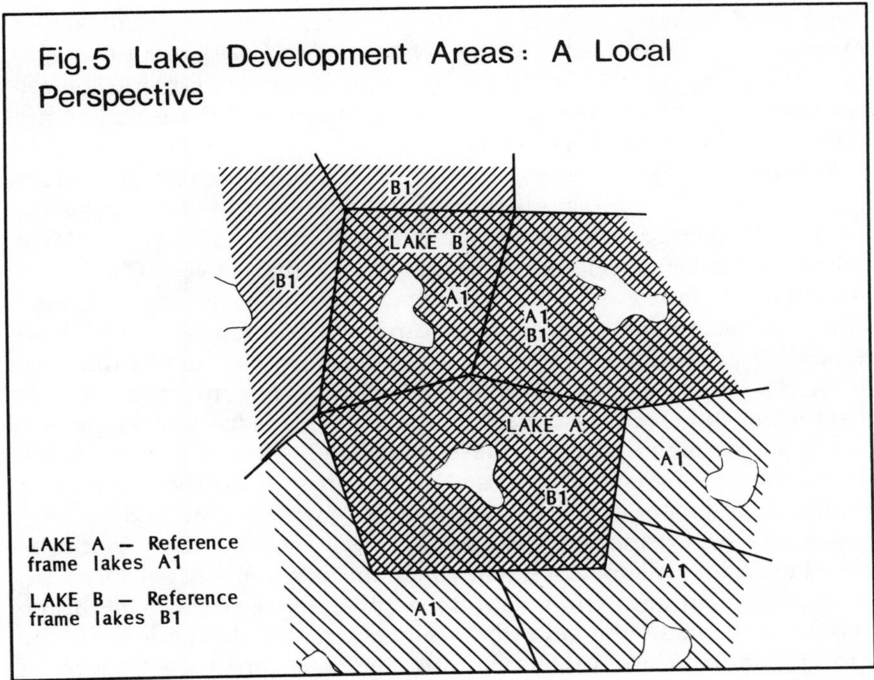

Fig. 5 Lake Development Areas: A Local Perspective

The intermediate scale is somewhat more difficult to envision, but reference to the mosaic pattern of lake development may again be useful. If we accept that the planning of each lake must be interrelated with all the lakes that are regionally adjacent to it, then it is fundamental that the plan for any one Lake Development Area should be related to the land-use plan in each of the adjacent Lake Development Areas. Each Lake Development Area thus has an extraneous "reference frame" formed by the conterminous surrounding Lake Development Areas (Figure 5). Since the system is interlocking, any one Lake Development Area would be included in a number of different reference frames, one each for the Lake Development Area with which it is contiguous. Planning at the intermediate level is also cellular in nature, in that it relates both downward in scale to the intensive level, and upward in scale to the extensive level.

Within each Lake Development Area planning falls into the related but separate categories of land and water surface zoning, and riparian land management and administration. The first category has been comprehensively discussed elsewhere, both for the conventional shoreline development model,[9] as well as for the more innovative mosaic pattern.[10] Although the main theme here deals with riparian planning, its relationship to zoning should also be kept in mind. One important relationship between the two is that riparian management techniques underlay different land-use zones, since they cut across land-use boundaries. Yet, the aims of zoning and of riparian management are quite distinct. Unfortunately, in many areas of Ontario, as well as in other provinces, both zoning and riparian land management are absent or at best inadequately used.

Within a Lake Development Area a key land management mechanism is the Restricted Building Area. Environmental sensitivity to development is frequently mistakenly summarized either as sensitivity that totally precludes development or sensitivity that uncritically allows development. However, there is a broad continuum of sensitivity that allows development, but only on carefully selected sites and with rigorously applied performance standards. One may argue that any development anywhere will have *some* effect on the environment, and that the question really is to measure the relative effects of development, to assess the significance of these anticipated effects, and to define logical bases whereby a proposed development may be rejected or modified. The more clear-cut categories of sensitivity can be dealt with reasonably well using land-use zoning: very sensitive sites would be zoned to exclude all development; where the environment is well suited to development, growth would take place in accordance with the performance standards and the use restrictions demanded by the appropriate land-use category. However, the broad continuum of variable sensitivity demands a more flexible analysis, whereby localized sites on which controlled development could take place may be identified. It is primarily with reference to this broad sensitivity range that the Restricted Building Area is particularly useful.

In the case of the Trent Canal reservoir-lakes, delineation of Restricted Building Areas would help to achieve the following three goals. First, limit further development to prevent over-use on shorelines where the danger signs of environmental degradation are already evident. Second, on lakes where new development may be accommodated, the Restricted Building Area would ensure that careful site selection, and adherence to development standards, take place. Third, since the Restricted Building Area applies both to private and to public activity, it is a particularly useful tool to help assure that private development and private facilities do not usurp the use of a lake by the general non-resident population.

The above discussion deals mainly with the planning of relatively small-scale Canadian shield lakes. With a few modifications, however, the concepts are also applicable to the intermediate scale lakes and to the Great Lakes and marine shorelines. The Lake Development Area and the Restricted Building Area both apply to intermediate scale lakes, but possibly only the Restricted Building Area applies to the two larger-scale water environments.

The application of the take-line concept to waterbodies other than reservoirs is somewhat less clear than is the more straight-forward transferability of the Lake Development Area and the Restricted Building Area concepts. In theory, the take-line defines land to be flooded by the impoundment of a reservoir and additional land that is necessary for acquisition. However, if we expand the definition of take-line to mean any riparian land to be acquired by a public agency, then the transferability of the concept to lake planning in general becomes clearer. The restricted rights that the non-property owning public has on many lakes dictates that comprehensive studies be undertaken immediately to define the demand for public access sites, to inventory existing available sites, to rank the priorities of these sites, and to formulate an acquisition program. In such background studies and implementation schedules, the take-line concept is indispensable as a means to classify desirable existing or future public riparian lands.

A slight alternative to this use of the take-line is its delineation, not for the purpose of shoreland acquisition for public use, but rather acquisition for the purpose of ecological preservation. For example, privately owned marshes and other wetland areas could be inventoried in a way similar to desirable potential public access sites, and acquired under the same or a related program.

The take-line concept is highly adaptable. The general priority ordering of shorelands to be acquired for public use should also include, on lakes that are chronically overdeveloped, a long-range program to transfer some selected properties from private ownership to public ownership. The actual transfers can be implemented gradually under a policy of acquiring private property as it becomes available on the market, if the costs involved and the benefits gained for the public good warrant such expenditures. In other words, the take-line can be used almost as a holding by-law to limit further private development in designated property transfer areas. This approach would not, of course, be without considerable problems, but it may be a valid goal in certain planning situations. Public use of such chronically overdeveloped lakes, where some properties have been weeded out, would have to be closely regulated to make sure that the general public does not impose more of a burden on the lake than did the expropriated private cottage owners. Counts of boats using a lake, and regular water-quality sampling are necessary for such regulations to be successful. Finally, the take-line can also be used to build flexibility into long-range planning, in anticipation of unforseen new trends in recreation and its associated development.

To this point, the take-line has been considered as land to be purchased by a public agency, for public use. However, the take-line is sufficiently flexible that a number of legal alternatives to the purchase of fee simple may be used, without radically altering the basic concept. The Tennessee Valley Authority has created a number of reservoirs on land that remained privately owned, but where the Authority acquired flood easements in lieu of purchasing the land. The take-line could be used to delineate shoreland sites or — in the mosaic model — inland areas where certain well-defined public rights should be acquired through the purchase of easements, such as, for example, easements to disallow the cutting of trees or the alteration of natural features. The take-line in these examples does not delineate land that is purchased but rather land where certain rights have been purchased from private property owners.

It is unfortunate that at the time of the transfer agreement of the Trent Canal reservoir lakes, neither the federal nor the Ontario government saw a need to institute take-line type of riparian controls. Since most of the land around the reservoir lakes was in Crown ownership, the prevalent impression may have been that take-line type of controls were not needed. This impression was administratively convenient during the early years after the construction of dams on these lakes, since little or no development existed at that time. This impression proved wrong, however, once the province subdivided and sold shoreline Crown Land for private cottage development. Had any of the various take-line measures been instituted at the time when dams were first built and the water level in the various lakes raised and regulated, many of the current problems of recreation on these waterbodies could have been avoided.[11] For example, on many lakes, certain stretches of shoreline have shallow beach profiles which exaggerate the effects of water draw-down, and should therefore have been delineated with a specifically designed take-line to exclude them from development. Although the term take-line commonly refers to private land that is taken (purchased) by a public agency, its basic *intent* remains the same even when the take-line is used to delineate land that should be *kept* in public ownership (a "keep" line). Today, the Ontario Ministry of Natural Resources retains ownership of Crown Land around lakes where cottage development is to take place. Fortunately, lots subdivided from Crown Land are leased, not sold, and a Crown Land reserve, usually 25 per cent of the shoreline length of a lake, is retained for general public use. Unfortunately, since the shoreline public reserve tends to consist of areas that are left over after the best shoreline stretches have been chosen for lots, the reserve often is not particularly suitable for public use. It serves more to enhance the lake environment for the private cottage owners, by leaving part of the shoreline in a natural state, rather than providing genuine public use areas.

The last riparian planning lesson from the Lake Diefenbaker case study described here deals with safe-building elevations: specific contour elevations above the water-level to ensure that buildings of various categories are set back a sufficient distance from the water's edge, in order to minimize damage from flooding, erosion, and other reservoir water action. There is a direct adaptation of safe-building elevations to riparian land management in Ontario. Safe-building elevations are desirable on the Trent Canal reservoir-lakes as a means to ameliorate the negative influences of water-level fluctuation on recreation, especially drawn-down during the summer. In shoreline recreation planning on reservoirs, a dilemma exists in that shorelines with a physiography that is more suitable for development and recreation also seem to be most directly influenced by water-level drawn-down, whereas shorelines that are less affected by draw-down are also less suitable for development. Since on almost all reservoirs shoreline development may be adversely influenced by reservoir operation, it is mandatory that safe-building elevations be established to ensure that development is safe and does not interfere with reservoir operation. Riparian property owners who are critical of the way reservoir operation affects them have the potential to become a powerful lobby group to force changes in reservoir operation to conform to a schedule which would suit them better.

Safe-building elevations are also needed on waterbodies of intermediate size and on the Great Lakes shorelines. High water levels which have occured on the Great Lakes strongly suggest the need for building setbacks based on contour elevations above known water-level records. One approach would be to co-ordinate the actions, in this regard, through the International Joint Commission, of the federal, Ontario and the various state governments, to define desirable safe-building elevations and to institute comprehensive enforcement methods at the federal, province-state, and local level. A necessary extension of this action would be to declare various types of buildings, located below appropriately defined safe-building elevations, as non-conforming uses in zoning by-laws, and to curtail further construction or renovation in these areas. A somewhat more extreme, although still desirable, measure would be to institute an acquisition program of unsafely located riparian properties similar to that described earlier with reference to the take-line.

Conclusion

As riparian interfaces of land and water, shorelines play an important role in the economy and lifestyle of most societies. The shoreline is the focal point for regional trade and commerce, transportation, industry, services, residential development, and private and public recreation. With an ever-increasing variety of conflicting lakefront land-use demands, it is now quite apparent that many regions, such as in Ontario along the lower Great Lakes, have almost run out of undeveloped shorelines.

Riparian land management forms a unique variation of the broad field of land-use planning. To effectively interrelate the land and the water environments, riparian land administration necessitates specialized techniques in addition to the general principles commonly associated with land-use planning. Shorelines must be planned and managed as one continuous biophysical system; treating the land and the water as independent units is both erroneous and futile. New land-management tools must be established if riparian areas are to be planned and used effectively. The tools must reflect the role of riparian land as part of an ecotone of overlapping shoreline ecosystems that are vulnerable to environmental deterioration, particularly to intensive development beyond natural carrying-capacity levels. Furthermore, riparian use must be safe and it must safeguard the right of the general public to use water and its associated land areas.

While some of the current weaknesses in lake planning in Ontario may be overcome by means of establishing riparian land-management tools similar to those used in Saskatchewan, new difficulties would also emerge. The Saskatchewan model of Reservoir Development Area management works well when one agency is clearly in charge over a water-resources project. Where no such clear authority exists, administrative chaos could result from the unco-ordinated efforts by numerous, often competing, government departments or ministries. Authority for lake planning would best be centered in one agency, with the role, first, of planning the general framework of regional lake growth and establishing development policy, and second, co-ordinating the activities, in lake development, of other, special purpose, government agencies. The question of policy, above all, is of key importance.[12]

Another direction from which difficulties may arise is public opposition to the Saskatchewan type of riparian controls. Private lakeshore property owners may resent the broader, more regionally oriented, planning of a series of adjacent Lake Development Areas. The solution of problems at any lake would no longer be confined to one area, but there would instead have to be considerably more compromises and trade-offs between different lakes and their diverse problems.

In summary, public rights, controlled private privileges, and ecological harmony are the keystones of riparian planning.

NOTES

1. Geological Survey, U.S. Department of the Interior, *Water for Recreation-Values and Opportunities*, Outdoor Recreation Resources Review Commission, Study Report 10, Washington, D.C., 1962.
2. Canada, *Royal Commission on the South Saskatchewan River Project*, Ottawa, Queen's Printer, 1952.
3. Canada, Department of Agriculture, Prairie Farm Rehabilitation Administration, *South Saskatchewan River Development Project*, Ottawa, Queen's Printer, 1967.
4. Ontario, Department of Attorney General, Order-in-Council 597/52, approved by His Honour the Lieutenant Governor, June 7, 1905, Toronto, 1905.
5. *Loc. cit.*
6. Ontario, Ministry of Natural Resources, *Lake Planning*, Draft No. 3, Toronto, May 1975.
7. R. Jaakson, *Lakeshore recreation planning for cottage development*, M.Sc. thesis, Toronto, University of Toronto, Department of Urban and Regional Planning, 1968; Hough, Stansbury and Associates, *Lake Alert. Phase 2, methodology*, Toronto, 1972; Peter J. Dillon, *A manual for calculating the capacity of a lake for development*, Toronto, Ontario Ministry of the Environment, March 1975.
8. R. Jaakson, "A mosaic pattern of balanced land-water planning for cottage development and lake planning", *Plan Canada*, Vol. 14, October 1974, pp. 40-45.
9. R. Jaakson, "Recreation zoning and lake planning", *Town Planning Review*, Vol. 43, No. 1, January 1972, pp. 41-55.
10. Jaakson, "A mosaic pattern . . .".
11. R. Jaakson, "The influence of draw down on recreation on the Trent Canal Reservoir Lakes", *Water Resource Bulletin*, Vol. 9, No. 6, December 1973, pp. 1225-1233.
12. R. Jaakson, "Planning toward an Ontario Cottage policy", *Forestry Chronicle*, Vol. 50, No. 6, December 1974, pp. 220-223.

21
The Parkhill Dam and Reservoir

*J. C. Day**

For every hundred studies of what might or should be done with a river, there is seldom one that deals with the effects of development. Nevertheless, investigations of past management efforts should be used to give an understanding of the benefits and disadvantages that might result from future integrated water and land-management planning schemes.[1] By 1969 there were 467 large dams in Canada[2] and thousands of smaller ones, but there are few cases in which the social, economic, or ecological ramifications of any of these undertakings has been traced.

This paper reports on the consequences of building the Parkhill Dam and Reservoir, by the Ausable River Conservation Authority (ARCA), on the Parkhill Creek, Ontario.

The Watershed

The Ausable River drains 665 square miles of good agricultural land on the eastern shore of Lake Huron. In its 19th century course, the river extended 110 miles from headwater to mouth. In its lower reach, it ran north to the Town of Grand Bend before turning sharply to the southwest, paralleling the lakeshore for roughly ten miles before entering the lake at Port Franks (Figure 1). An 1875 diversion — the Cut — carried the main Ausable flow directly to Port Franks and in the process drained a small lake southeast of the present Highway 21 route for agricultural purposes. Another entrance to the lake was excavated at Grand Bend in 1892 to create a harbour. As a consequence, the Ausable now discharges to Lake Huron at Port Franks and the Parkhill Creek and other smaller tributaries empty at Grand Bend. Except during floods, there is no surface flow between the Ausable and Parkhill Creek.

Impetus to construct the Parkhill Dam stems from farmers in the lower part of the Ausable River Watershed. Downstream from the

---

*J. C. Day is an Associate Professor in the Geography Department at the University of Waterloo. This paper is an edited version of one with the same title which appeared in *The Proceedings of the Symposium on the Lakes of Western Canada*, Publication #2 of the University of Alberta Water Resources Centre, edited by E. R. Reinlt, A. H. Laycock and W. M. Schultz, June, 1973.

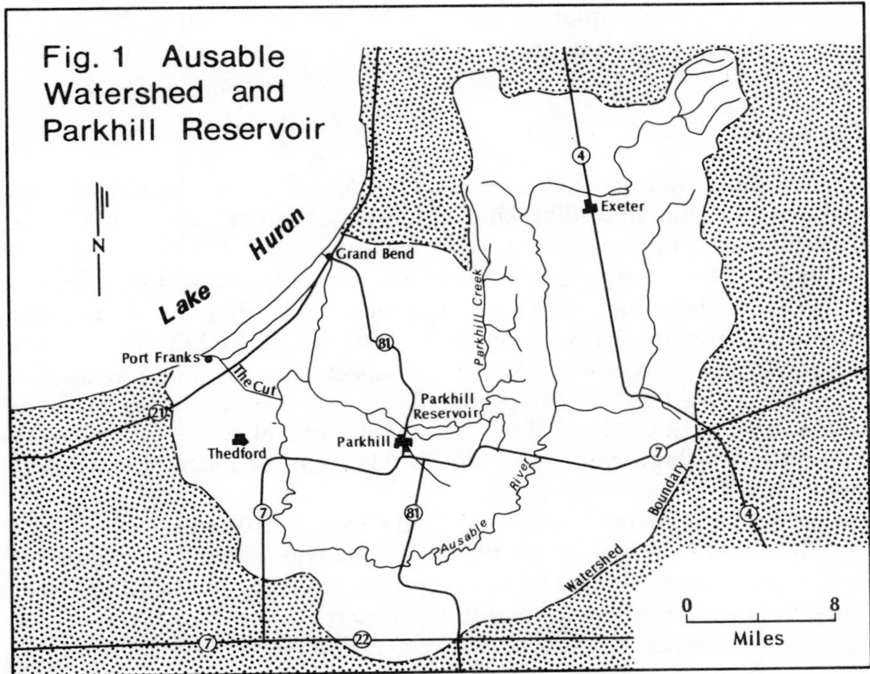

reservoir, the creek flows five miles westward before joining the former main branch of the Ausable. The confluence is in a former lake bottom composed principally of organic deposits and clays (locally called the Klondike area). Agricultural capability of lands downstream from the Parkhill Reservoir is generally high when drained, particularly in the organic soils of the Klondike. As agricultural land uses intensified during the 1940s and 1950s, accompanied by accelerated construction of municipal and farm drainage, it was alleged by farmers that run-off and the flooding frequency of the low-lying Klondike land had increased. Threatened lawsuits to gain compensation for these asserted changes by affected landowners acted as a catalyst to focus attention on the desirability of large-scale water-control measures in the lower Ausable River Watershed.

Since the Authority's first report in 1949, actions to correct watershed problems have been couched within the framework of a comprehensive program of potential land, vegetation, and water management, but solutions to the problem in the lower Parkhill Creek Valley and in the Klondike area have invariably focussed on a series of structural measures to deepen, dike, or dam the rivers. Channel improvements to the Cut in the vicinity of Port Franks (Figure 1) and a small dam near

Exeter have been completed; several other works including three more dams and a river deepening project were recommended. The Parkhill scheme was one of these.

The Project

The Parkhill Dam and Reservoir is a joint federal, provincial and regional government undertaking. It was approved in January, 1967, the construction contract awarded in the same year, and the dam and reservoir were completed in September, 1969. Project repayment obligations, excluding recreation facilities, were divided among the federal and provincial governments and the Ausable Authority approximately in the ratio of 45.75:45.75:8.5 respectively. Since Highway No. 81 was rerouted to pass over the dam, the Ontario Department of Highways contributed to the project an amount equivalent to the cost of realigning the highway across the Parkhill Creek and constructing a larger bridge.

Nearly 52 square miles of the Parkhill Creek drainage basin discharge into the Parkhill Reservoir. At the controlled water level, 1900 acre-feet of storage create a 190-acre lake approximately 2 miles long and 1000 feet wide; the lake surface area expands to 410 acres when the 7,600 acre-feet of flood storage capacity fills.

Anticipated Benefits and Costs

Tangible social benefits were anticipated from construction of the Parkhill project. Flood control was the most important accounting for 60.2 per cent of total benefits; protection of Klondike farm lands was allocated 55.8 per cent and the Town of Parkhill an additional 4.4 per cent for water damage alleviation. New recreation opportunities and a water supply for the Town of Parkhill accounted for 36.3 per cent and 3.5 per cent respectively of total benefits (Table 1).

Between the two project evaluation dates (1959 and 1964), major changes were made in the feasibility analysis. The magnitude of agricultural and flood control benefits expanded while the comparative importance of other purposes declined. The net result was that total benefits increased by 69 per cent to $1.989 million (Table 1). Concurrently, costs rose by 65 per cent to $1.267 million (Table 2). As a consequence, the benefit cost ratio increased between the evaluation dates from 1.53:1 in 1959 to 1.57:1 in 1964 based on a 100-year amortization period at 4 per cent interest.

Expenses attributable to the conservation aspects of the project escalated an additional 48 per cent to $2.494 million during the construction period. This was primarily due to increasing construction and land costs (Table 2).

TABLE 1

**Conservation Benefits and Benefit:
Cost Ratios — Parkhill Dam and Reservoir
(thousands of dollars)**

Element	Estimates			
	1959 (5)		1964 (3)	
Flood Protection:	$	%	$	%
Agricultural	540	45.9	1,110	55.8
Parkhill	87	7.4	87	4.4
Recreation	478	40.7	723	36.3
Water Supply: Parkhill	69	5.9	69	3.5
Total conservation benefits	1,174	99.9	1,989	100
Total conservation costs	767		1,267	
Benefit Cost Ratio	1.53:1		1.57:1	

TABLE 2

Parkhill Dam, Reservoir, and Road Costs (thousands of dollars)

Element	Estimated Cost			Final Cost
	1953 (6)	1959 (5)	1964 (3)	1971 (7)
Construction		824	1,277	2,000
Land		167	250	875
Total	275	991	1,527	2,875
Less Ministry of Highways contribution		248	300	421
Plus operating costs		24.5	40	40
Total conservation costs (*15*)	275	767.5	1,267	2,494

Flood Protection: Agricultural

Flood protection of low-lying land in the Klondike agricultural area is the major purpose of the Parkhill project. It was anticipated that the dam would prevent floods up to, and including, those with a 33-year recurrence interval during June, July, and August, as well as floods with a 10-year recurrence interval during September, October, and November. Based on the assumption that the maximum flood which the Parkhill

TABLE 3

Benefits Attributed to Agricultural Flood Damage Prevention

Land Use	1949 (4)	1959 (5)		1964 (3)		1972 (4)		1972 Proposed (9)	
	Acres	Acres	Benefit ($)	Acres	Benefit ($)	Acres	Benefit ($)	Acres	Benefit ($)
Field crops	?	2,250	405,000	2,250	405,000	3,600	650,000	4,070	850,000
Vegetables	?	200	135,000	1,200	705,000	1,000	590,000	1,830	1,080,000
Not cultivated	?	2,720	—	1,720	—	570	—	570	—
TOTALS	4,470	5,170	540,000	5,170	1,110,000	5,170	1,240,000	6,470	1,930,000

Dam can control would inundate 5,170 acres, flood benefits were calculated to reflect the intensity of cultivation and the kind of crops in this area. Benefits reported in 1959 and 1964 (Table 3) are based on the distribution of vegetable and field crops by elevation within this protected area and the magnitude of average losses suffered by such crops at five periods during the year.

Fundamental to determining the magnitude of agricultural flood control benefits attributed to the Parkhill project is the size of area to be protected from summer floods with a 33-year recurrence interval. The protected acreage was increased 16 per cent to 5,170 acres between the time of the initial 1949 estimate of acreage inundated in the 1947 flood and the first feasibility study in 1959. The same protected area was maintained in the 1964 feasibility assessment and, indeed, until after project completion. However, when repayment obligations were allocated in 1972, the protected area was enlarged again by an additional 24 per cent to approximately 6,400 acres, all of the new area to benefit is in Bosanquet Township (Figure 2).

Agricultural activity expanded rapidly on protected Klondike land after the initial calculation of flood benefits in 1959. Although the 1964 feasibility study suggested that 1,000 acres of vegetables were cultivated on these areas during the following five years, a 1972 survey suggested 800 acres of vegetables to be a more realistic figure. Nevertheless, by that date, all but 570 of the 5,170 acres to be protected from flooding were under cultivation. The result is that flood control benefits expanded 12 per cent over the level anticipated during project approval to $1.24 million (Table 3).

The suggested expansion of benefiting lands to 6,470 acres would greatly enlarge agricultural flood control benefits attributable to the Parkhill project. An estimated additional 830 acres of vegetables and 470 acres of field crops are involved if the proposed benefit boundaries in Bosanquet Township are adopted. Flood control benefits would be increased by 74 per cent over the level anticipated at the time of project approval to $1.93 million.

Field survey data were used in the 1959 feasibility study to check the accuracy of the synthetic flood loss estimates used in deriving flood control benefits associated with the Parkhill Dam. Flood damage records from the 6-year, 1947-1952, period were from the Haig Farm, the major landholder in the Klondike area and a principal supporter of the Parkhill project. When the project feasibility was reviewed in 1964, the same six years of flood loss records were again used to confirm flood damage estimate calculations. This was done even though 11 years of more recent experience were available. (Fifty-six per cent of project benefits were claimed for alleviation of agricultural flooding.)

In an effort to check the accuracy of flood benefits claimed, 58 Klon-

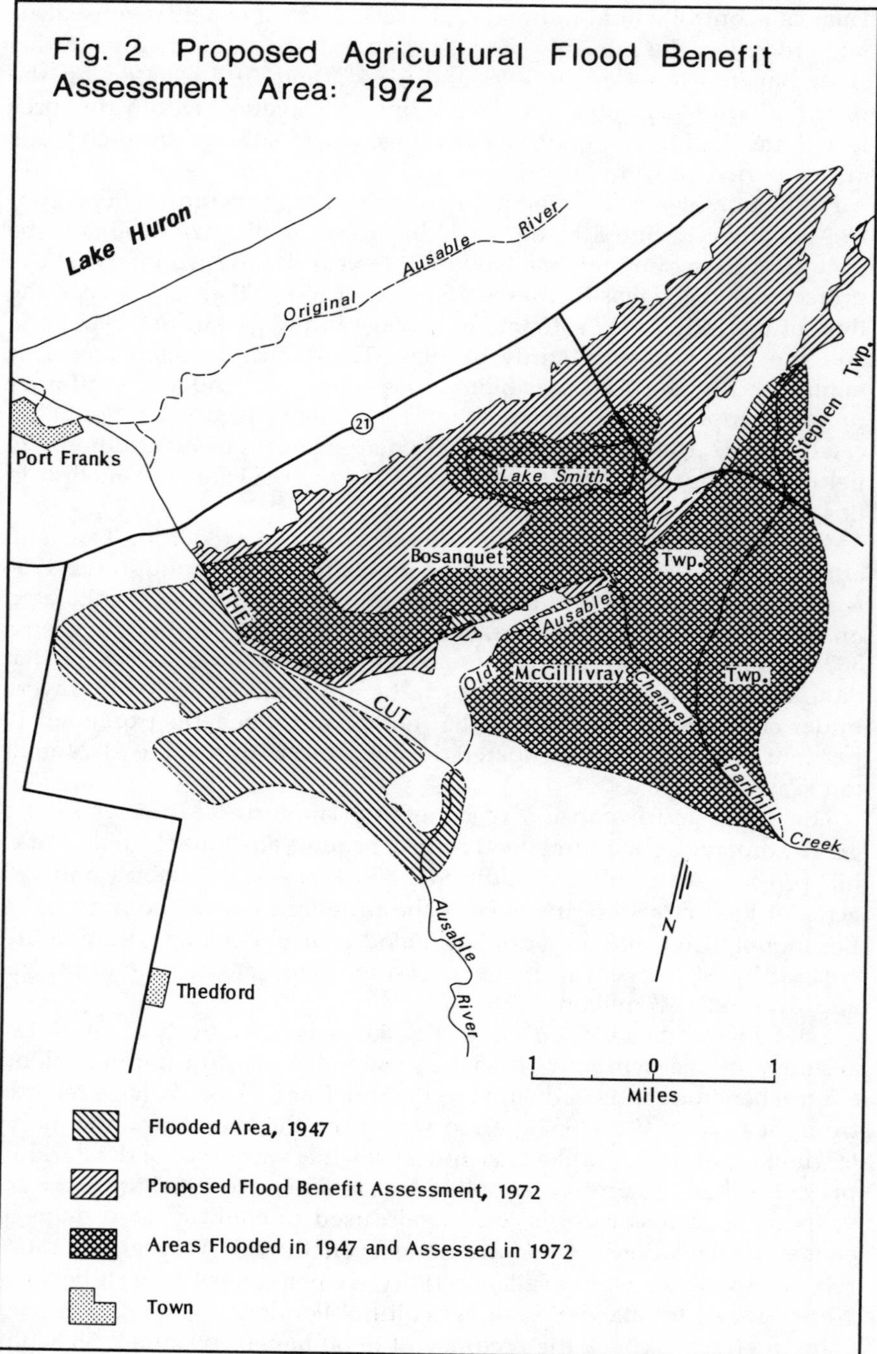
Fig. 2 Proposed Agricultural Flood Benefit Assessment Area: 1972
Lake Huron
Original Ausable River
21
Port Franks
Lake Smith
Bosanquet
Twp.
Stephen Twp.
THE
CUT
Old
Ausable
McGillivray
Channel
Twp.
Parkhill
Creek
N
Ausable River
Thedford
1 0 1
Miles
Flooded Area, 1947
Proposed Flood Benefit Assessment, 1972
Areas Flooded in 1947 and Assessed in 1972
Town

dike area farmers were interviewed. It appears that there is a major discrepancy between the Haig Farm flood loss estimates from 1947-1952 and losses in the subsequent 17 years prior to completion of the Parkhill Dam. During this latter period, subdivision of the low-lying Klondike lands into farms proceeded rapidly. Farm interviews revealed an average annual flood loss of only $7,100 in contrast to $35,000 average annual loss report by the Haig Farm between 1947 and 1952. An additional $2,750 of damages occurred in 1970, the first full year the dam was operational (Table 4).

TABLE 4

Agricultural Flood Losses in the Klondike Area

Year	No. of Farmers Reporting Losses	Source of Estimate	Flood Losses ($)
1947 (5)	1	Haig Farm	62,000
1949 (5)	1	Haig Farm	39,500
1950 (5)	1	Haig Farm	33,325
1951 (5)	1	Haig Farm	5,773
1952 (5)	1	Haig Farm	68,740
1954 (10)	1	Haig Farm	100,000
1967 (11)	1	New Venice Corp.	2,750
1969 (11)	1	Peter's Farm	500
1970 (11)	1	New Venice Corp.	2,750

To check on this apparent difference in reported flood losses, Klondike farmers were interviewed to determine the level of agricultural flood protection benefits they perceive from the Parkhill project (Figure 3). Only 4 of 23 farmers in the area inundated by the 1947 flood believe the dam helps their land (Table 5). Benefits reported result from more rapid drainage of spring floods from the land and hence an earlier seeding date. (It is unknown to what extent improved farm drainage accounts for this difference.) Two of the four own 55 per cent of the land within the proposed 1972 assessment area. Much of their property is the land most subject to flooding in the Klondike. It is planted with low-value field crops. Conversely, most vegetable farmers feel that the project has not been useful, usually because they have never been flooded.

Disenchantment with the project is universal among landholders within the proposed Bosanquet Township assessment boundary but outside of the 1947 flood area, except for one major landholder who was a driving force behind the project. Indeed, it is notable that most farmers who consider the project to be useful own riparian Ausable River land in Stephen Township. Although small areas of their land flood almost annually, they are not assessed for repayment of flood benefits.

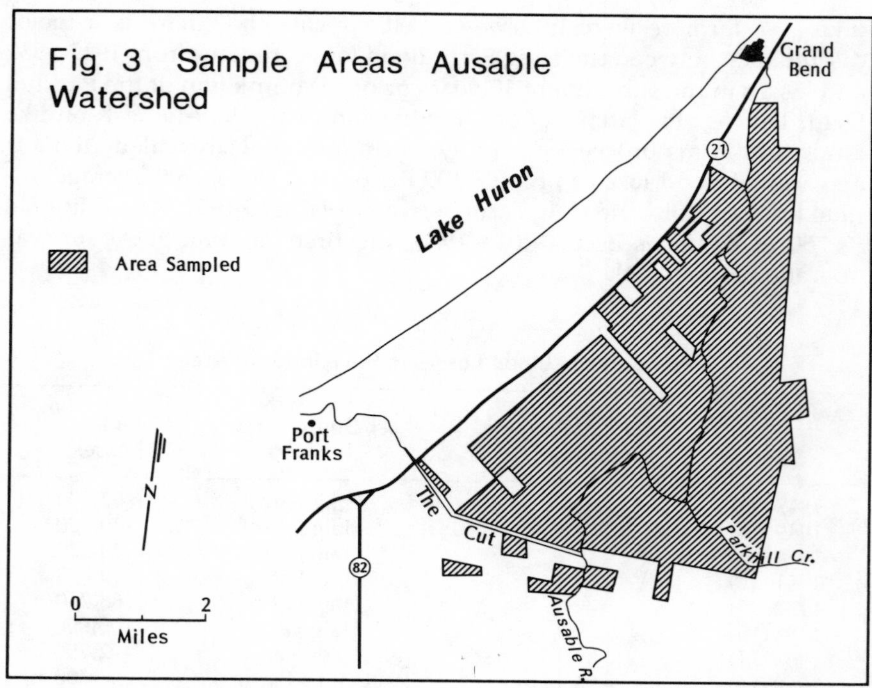

TABLE 5

Attitudes Concerning Agricultural Flood Control Benefits

Responses	Farmers in the 1947 Flooded Area	Farmers Within the 1972 Proposed Assessment Boundary but Outside the 1947 Flooded Area	Farmers Outside the Proposed 1972 Assessed Boundary
Benefit	4	0	5
Not Benefit	19	14	16
—never flooded	15	7	
—flooded but no damage	3	4	
—flooded once	1	3	
TOTALS	23	14	21

Flooding: Parkhill

Flooding has been experienced for some decades in the Town of Parkhill from the Cameron-Gillies Drain which carries run-off from approximately 2,000 acres of agricultural land to the southeast. The confluence of the drain with the Parkhill Creek is two miles west of town. It is important to realize that the Town of Parkhill has never been flooded from the Parkhill Creek (the project site) which passes north of the municipality.

Water damage was experienced in town for several reasons. Initially, houses and business establishments invaded the drain flood plain and bridges under the Canadian National Railway and Provincial Highway No. 81 provided only small openings and poor alignments to permit flows to pass.

In 1952, the Ontario government approved and subsidized improvement of the Cameron-Gillies Drain to improve agricultural productivity and stream flow through Parkhill. This included deepening of the stream channel through the town and for 800 feet westward to increase its carrying capacity. Nevertheless, periodic town flooding was experienced occasionally because of earlier mistakes in establishing the settlement pattern and transportation routes. Merchants averted spring flood damages simply by moving stocks from basements before the annual snow melt.

In the project, flood damage alleviation in Parkhill was valued at $87,000, or 4.4 per cent of total benefits. Losses were all reportedly suffered by nine town merchants closest to the creek and by the highway, railroad, and other small bridges in the town. Of the annual $3,500 of flood damages identified, $1,000 was attributed to spring losses and the remainder to flash summer floods affecting personal property and bridges.

The solution to the town's flood problem was entirely structural. The Cameron-Gillies Drain was dammed about a half mile upstream from Parkhill and a diversion channel was dug to the new reservoir on the Parkhill Creek about a quarter mile to the north. The new dam permits a maximum of 500 cubic feet per second to pass downstream in the drain towards Parkhill, excess flow in the creek is diverted to the reservoir.

To check on the accuracy of alleged flood damages, back issues of the Parkhill Gazette, as well as Ausable River Conservation Authority documents, were reviewed. Interviews were also conducted with more than 50 Parkhill merchants and citizens and with officials of the Canadian National Railway, the Ontario Ministry of Transportation, and the Town of Parkhill to appraise the extent of previous flood losses.

This study suggests that flood control benefits for the Town of Parkhill were grossly overestimated in the Parkhill feasibility reports. The Ontario Department of Planning and Development reported in 1949 that floods were no more than a nuisance to the town.[12] This is confirmed by interviews with merchants and citizens during 1971 and 1972. Only once during more than two decades of local newspaper issues was mention made of flood losses to merchants; a damage estimate was not reported. Field inspection revealed that Parkhill has made no effort to keep vegetation and debris out of the drain and, in fact, it has permitted the installation of pipes which seriously impair flows to cross the stream channel. Nor has the town adopted zoning legislation to prevent more flood plain development. Local merchants, the major group identified as suffering flood losses, have not bothered to flood-proof buildings. Moreover, officers of the Ontario Ministry of Highways, the Canadian National Railway, and the Town of Parkhill report infrequent and minor flood damages to roads or bridges within the town.

Clearly, municipal flood damage estimates were seriously overestimated. Numerous structural and nonstructural adjustments could have been made locally at modest cost to prevent losses from the occasional high stages in the Cameron-Gilles Drain. Thus, a municipal flood-control benefit may not justifiably be attributed to the Parkhill project.

Recreation

It was proposed in the 1959 plan that a 50-acre recreation area fronting on the Parkhill Reservoir be provided with swimming, boating, fishing, and picnic facilities. Recreation benefits were calculated by assuming 40,000 visitor days annually with a gross market value of $.75 per visitor-day, less $10,500 for annual operating costs. In the 1964 feasibility study, the value of recreation benefits attributed to the Parkhill Reservoir was increased by more than 50 per cent by raising the value of a visitor-day to $1.00. By assuming 40,000 visitors annually over 100 years of project life at 4 per cent interest, the present value of recreation benefits amounts to $723,000, or 36 per cent of total project benefits.

The method of calculating recreation benefits in both the 1959 and 1964 feasibility studies introduces serious errors. Associated expenses to realize recreation benefits were excluded. These include the cost of the landscape architect's report to produce a comprehensive recreation plan, the cost of constructing recreation facilities, and the cost of stocking fish in the reservoir.

Following completion of the dam, a recreation consultant recommended an ambitious program which would provide, after a 20-year development period, enough facilities for 2,200 campers and 4,000 day-users simultaneously in the summer, 1,000 winter visitors, and an ambitious conservation education program. The initial estimate of providing these facilities exceeded $2 million or 83 per cent of the total cost of conservational aspects of the Parkhill project.[13]

Shortage of funds will constrain the development of recreation facilities to approximately $180,000 during the first five years of project operation instead of $845,000 as suggested in the consultant's report.

A further error in calculating recreation benefits was that they were not staged in recognition of the fact that 40,000 visitors cannot attend the new reservoir annually until facilities are provided and until large numbers of the public learn about the new facility. If current trends in visitor-days continue, it is estimated that at least five years will pass before the anticipated annual level of 40,000 visitors will be experienced (Table 6). As a consequence, the shortfall in recreation benefits is estimated to be $83,500 in the first five years of operation.

TABLE 6

Parkhill Reservoir Attendance

Year	Expected Attendance	Actual Attendance	Benefit Deficiency ($)
1970	40,000	3,500	36,500
1971	40,000	16,000	24,000
1972	40,000	25,000	15,000
1973	40,000	32,000 estimated	8,000
1974	40,000	40,000 estimated	—
TOTAL			83,500

An additional problem concerns a 124-acre property on the northern side of the reservoir. This private farm effectively divides the northern side of the reservoir land into two parts and makes its management and control difficult. Continued use by its present owner as a hog farm exposes public areas around the reservoir to undesirable odours; it could also adversely affect water quality.

Water Supply: Parkhill

Wells which have traditionally been used for the municipal water source by the Town of Parkhill are heavily contaminated by hydrogen sulphide and iron. In considering alternative sources of supply, the cost advantage of using reservoir water over new facilities to treat well water was estimated to be $69,000. However, the decision was subsequently made to use Lake Huron water supplied by pipeline. In effect, this entire benefit was lost.

Summer Flow Augmentation

It was assumed that construction of the Parkhill Dam would permit a minimum dry weather flow of 10 cfs downstream. However, between 1970 and 1972, the practice was adopted of closing the reservoir following the spring run-off and releasing water only when complaints are received. In effect, this intangible benefit did not materialize because of insufficient capacity of the reservoir to maintain a summer flow without adversely affecting reservoir recreation interests.

A Summary Assessment

Although not many years have elapsed since completion of the Parkhill Dam, important indicators concerning the feasibility of this investment already are apparent. Project architects were overly optimistic concerning costs and benefits to be derived. Total costs are substantially higher than anticipated, the recreation benefit appears smaller, both the municipal flood control and water supply benefits related to Parkhill are unwarranted, while the magnitude of the agricultural flood control benefit is conjectural. Recalculation of the benefit cost ratio, including associated expenditures for recreation facilities, suggests that the 1964 relationship of 1.57:1 has decreased to 0.76:1 at 4 per cent interest (0.52:1 at 6 per cent) (Table 7).

TABLE 7

**Revised Benefit: Cost Ratios —
Parkhill Dam and Reservoir (thousands of dollars)**

Element	Estimates	
	1964	1972 (*14*)
Flood Protection		
Agricultural	1,110	1,240
Parkhill	87	—
Recreation	723	640
Water Supply Parkhill	69	—
Total conservation benefits	1,989	1,880
Total conservation costs	1,267	2,454
Benefit Cost Ratio		
at 4% interest	1.57:1	0.76:1
at 6% interest	1.06:1	0.52:1

Major questions remain in the 1972 feasibility analysis. Flood benefit calculations are based on the 14 years of extrapolated streamflow data available in 1957 when the flood frequency analysis was made. Because of the extremely short data record, future streamflow observations could affect the benefit calculations either positively or negatively.

Also, the agricultural flood protection benefit has been raised slightly from the 1964 calculated level to reflect increased land reclamation since that date. It should be remembered, however, that only four (17 per cent) of the farmers interviewed in this area perceive the dam as useful to them, the agricultural flood protection benefit may prove to be too high. Moreover, if the Ontario Municipal Board rules against the current appeal by affected farmers in favour of the Township of Bosanquet and permits the assessment of a flood control tax on the recently proposed assessment area which is 25 per cent larger than the area initially to be protected, the flood control benefit would be even higher. It is clear, however, that such an unanticipated tax on an area which has not experienced flood damages in the memory of any of the residents, a tax which was announced following completion of the Parkhill Dam, will ultimately work against the support for future conservation actions proposed by the Ausable River Conservation Authority. Such a development should be considered a cost, even though intangible, of the Parkhill undertaking.

Implications

Several kinds of measures may be useful as aids to reaching more realistic decisions concerning the desirability of future dams and reservoirs in Ontario. Better evaluations are necessary than the ones used to justify the Parkhill project. For example, statements explaining the feasibility of, and necessity for, new recreation facilities within a broad regional context would be useful to decision makers, rather than a simple discussion of the activities to be made possible and the number of visitors expected. Formal comments by other provincial agencies such as the Department of Agriculture and Food where agricultural benefits are involved and the Ministry of Natural Resources where fish and wildlife are affected should be mandatory. And other environmental implications of such projects deserve formal discussion.

Another helpful innovation would be to identify as closely as possible the area and the people who will benefit from projects. For example, it may have been useful for decision makers to know that two landowners with 55 per cent of the acreage to be protected from flooding, and the land most prone to inundation, will repay 43 per cent of the local flood protection assessment and only 1 per cent of the total project cost. Failure to identify project beneficiaries and inform them concerning repayment obligations prior to project approval angered Klondike area farmers who are now being asked to pay a special assessment for flood control benefits.

After a quarter century of active dam and reservoir construction in

Ontario, there is a tendency among local conservation authority members, and the public at large, to regard the dam and reservoir as a preferred way of achieving conservation work within river basins. There is also a marked propensity for consultants to overestimate benefits and underestimate costs. As a consequence, the lone field representative of the Ontario Conservation Authorities Branch, the Resources Manager, needs the encouragement and support of head office specialists to ensure that structural measures do not receive special advantage in the evaluation process. For example, less expensive structural and non-structural measures were not discussed as means of alleviating the minor flood problem in Parkhill. Nor was zoning of flood-prone lands by township governments required as a precondition before society spent millions of dollars for the structure to control the Parkhill Creek. Unless the head office professional staff can ensure that a fair evaluation of alternative means of achieving river basin authorities' conservation goals takes place, local project beneficiaries will continue to be overly represented in the decision-making process at the expense of those who pay. This is particularly true in cases such as the Parkhill Dam where the cost share of the Ausable River Conservation Authority was less than 9 per cent of the project.

An important problem relates to the Federal Agricultural and Rehabilitation Development Act (ARDA) which funded more than 45 per cent of the Parkhill project. While ARDA officers insisted that the Parkhill undertaking should be part of a comprehensive and integrated land and water planning effort throughout the Ausable Watershed, they failed to support this notion at the reservoir site. Under the ARDA agreement, structures and land to be flooded were eligible for subsidies. Contiguous land which must also be publicly owned, if society is to realize the maximum benefit from such a project, was not eligible for financial assistance. As a consequence, properties adjacent to the reservoir, including a large pig farm near the recreation area, remain in private ownership.

The concept of the multiple purpose dam and reservoir has come to be regarded as a cornerstone of conservation activities based on river basin planning units in Ontario. This view has emerged over the past quarter century during which time dams were commonly chosen as a means to achieve social change. Like any other device, however, such structural measures are not inherently useful. Their value must be judged in terms of the desired changes they can produce, their precision, and their adaptability to changing social priorities.

This study suggests that the Parkhill project has been a questionable social investment. Its performance, and the experience of a representative sample of other multiple-purpose reservoirs, deserve careful study. This task can be aided by instituting new bookkeeping systems to monitor expenditures and benefits over time. Such information should be used as a guide in evaluating the feasibility of future man-made lakes.

NOTES

1. R. W. Judy, "Economic problems in water resources management in Canada", *Water management research: social science priorities*, by W. R. D. Sewell, R. W. Judy and L. Ouellet, Ottawa, Queen's Printer, 1969, pp. 35-37.
2. International Commission on Large Dams, Canadian National Committee, *Register of dams in Canada: 1970*, edited by H. K. Pratt, 1970, 142 pp.
3. Ontario, Ausable River Conservation Authority, *Brief on water management and watershed development*, Exeter, Ont., 1966.
4. Ontario, Department of Planning and Development, *Ausable Valley Report*, Toronto, 1949, water section.
5. Ontario, Ausable River Conservation Authority, *Brief on flood control measures for the Parkhill Creek watershed*, Exeter, 1959.
6. Ontario, Ausable River Conservation Authority, *Brief re flood control measures on the Ausable watershed*, Exeter, Ont., 1953.
7. Interview with Secretary-Treasurer, Ausable River Conservation Authority, November 7, 1972.
8. Based on 1971 and 1972 interviews.
9. Derived from assessment in Stephen and McGillivary Townships and proposed assessments in Bosanquet Township, 1972.
10. *Parkhill Gazette*, October 28, 1954. A farm official reporting $7,000 damage for the same flood event.
11. Based on farm interviews during 1971 and 1972, throughout the Klondike area.
12. Ontario, Department of Planning and Development, *op. cit.*, water section.
13. Richard Strong Associates, *The Ausable River Conservation Authority Parkhill Reservoir Development Plan, 1968*, Toronto, Richard Strong Associates, 1968.

22
The Hanlon Creek Study: An Ecological Approach to Planning

*E. E. Mackintosh**

Historically, North American cities have been planned as physical systems with little apparent concern for the people who exist within them. Planners have been preoccupied with the infrastructure of the urban environment, often to the detriment of the environment's inhabitants. But increasing awareness about environmental issues and the apparent concern for "quality of life" standards are slowly forcing planners, engineers, and architects to modify their traditional approach to planning to accommodate these concerns.

One obvious outcome of this changing concept is recognition of the role of physical resource analysis in planning decisions.[1] In the past, use of physical resource data for planning has received only limited attention, and little attempt has been made to integrate their findings so as to understand their real significance. Indeed, McHarg is one of the few individuals who has attempted to carry the physical resource concept to the point of integrating it into the urban planning process.[2]

The Hanlon Creek experience demonstrates how an "ecological" or "physical resource" approach can be used to advantage in developing and planning an area.

The Hanlon Creek Study

BACKGROUND AND OBJECTIVES

Hanlon Creek, a small watershed on the southern fringe of Guelph, Ontario (Figure 1), drains an area of 7,300 acres. At the moment the watershed is predominantly agricultural. Kortright Waterfowl Park is located at the mouth of the creek (Figure 2) and depends on the high water quality and base flow in the creek to support its activities. As urbanization of the watershed proceeds, recreational demands on the park will increase significantly.

---

*E. E. Mackintosh is an associate professor in the Department of Land Resource Science at the University of Guelph, Guelph, Ontario. This paper is an edited version of one which appeared in the *Journal of Soil and Water Conservation*, Vol. 29, No. 6, November-December, 1974, pp. 277-280.

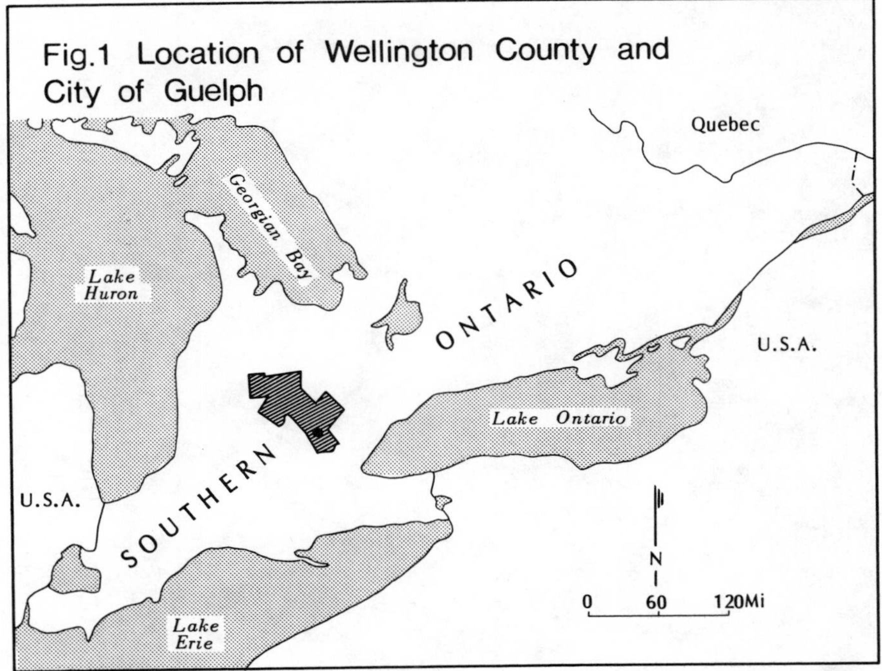

The city annexed part of the watershed in response to forecasted expansion of industry and housing. The watershed was chosen primarily because utility services could be linked to the existing gravity-flow service network.

Location of an expressway within the watershed boundaries precipitated the events leading up to the investigation being undertaken.

The study was undertaken in two phases. Phase A was to determine the effect of the Hanlon Expressway on the ecology of Hanlon Creek. Phase B was to determine the effect of long-range urbanization on the ecology of Hanlon Creek. The study team also was responsible for identifying actions that would mitigate adverse impacts.

Experts in stream biology, terrestrial wildlife, vegetation, hydrology, surficial geology and soils, sociology, and landscape architecture comprised the study team. Each phase of the investigation consisted of an inventory stage, an analysis stage, and a recommendation stage. The physical and biological inputs for both phase A and B were somewhat similar, although phase B was much more extensive. For this reason, only phase B is considered here. It should be emphasized that examples discussed were chosen to demonstrate the usefulness of the approach and do not represent the complete analysis.

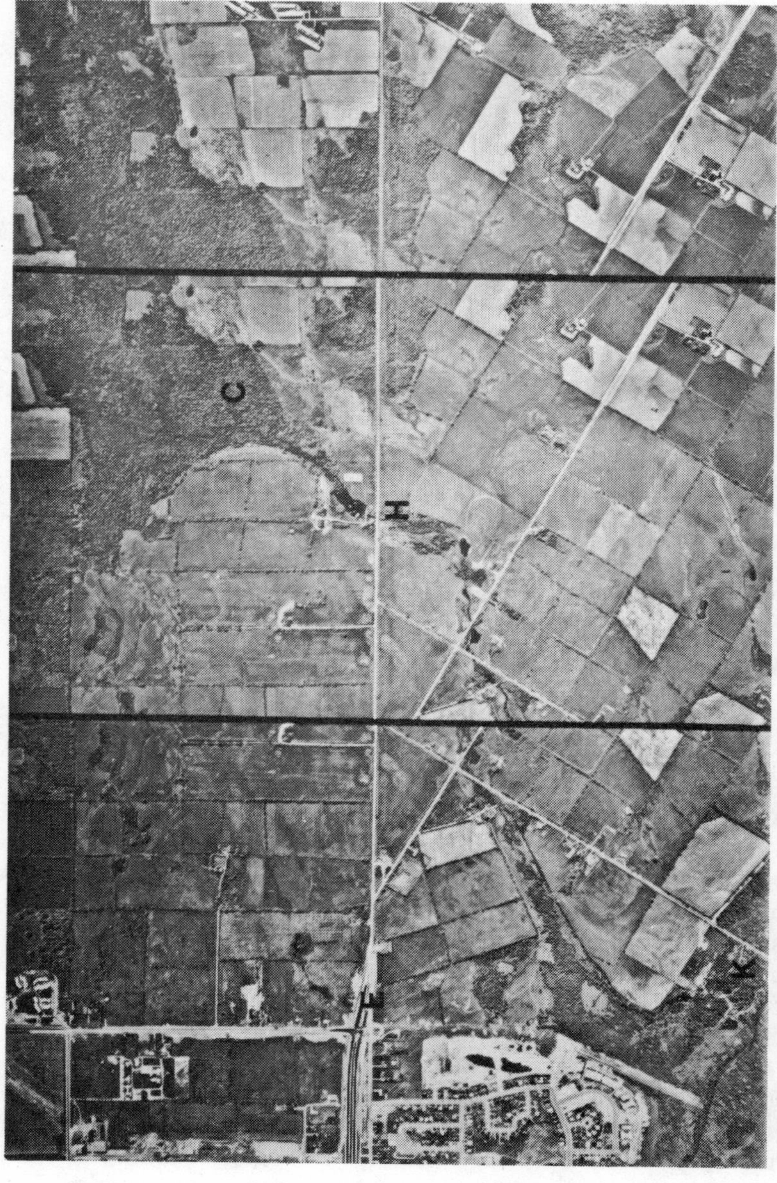

Fig. 2 Aerial Stereo Pair of a Portion of the Hanlon Creek Watershed

C – Cedar woodlot on organic soils
H – Hanlon Creek
E – Completed portion of Hanlon Expressway
K – Kortright Waterfowl Park

PHILOSOPHICAL APPROACH

An investigation of this nature requires a theme or focal point on which to formulate alternative policies or avenues of development. In this instance Hanlon Creek itself served this purpose for a number of reasons: (a) It provided an excellent focal point around which to develop recreation and open space opportunities. (b) It serves as an important water source for Kortright Waterfowl Park. (c) Under policies developed by the Ontario conservation authorities precautions must be taken to preserve and protect major groundwater recharge areas, especially those occurring in the headwaters of creeks and rivers.

The physical and biological investigations were directed toward preservation of Hanlon Creek. The sociological input was directly related to this theme by forecasting the recreational, open space, and park demands on the area.

The obvious extremes for management of Hanlon Creek lie at opposite ends of the spectrum: complete preservation of the watershed as a conservation area or alternatively encasing the creek in a concrete drainage channel. The latter implies total urbanization with no consideration given to water management, while the former implies no development or an absence of urban land use. Neither of these appeared to be realistic. Between them lies a series of more or less feasible alternatives that provide for varying degrees of development and recreational opportunities. It is these alternatives toward which the study team directed its attention.

INVENTORY STAGE

Since the prime study objectives were concerned with maintaining base flow in Hanlon Creek throughout the year, a major concern of the physical resource inventory was identifying (a) sources of waterflow for Hanlon Creek; (b) extent, kind, and distribution of soils and surficial sediments; and (c) major groundwater recharge areas for the creek. Identification of these latter areas allows one to assess the effects of various land use practices on groundwater recharge in the area, hence the creek's base flow.

Flow measurements taken at various points on Hanlon Creek throughout the year established that 50 to 60 per cent originates from lateral seepage. Once this information was combined with soils data (Figure 3), water table levels (Figure 4), and static water levels in wells, it was possible to develop a qualitative model for the watershed. Some of the information gathered showed: (a) The area designated as hummocky sandy loam till serves as a major groundwater recharge area. This is indicated by the coarse texture of the soil and lack of external drainage features in the area. Precipitation is channeled into the enclosed "potholes" and percolates downward to recharge groundwater levels.

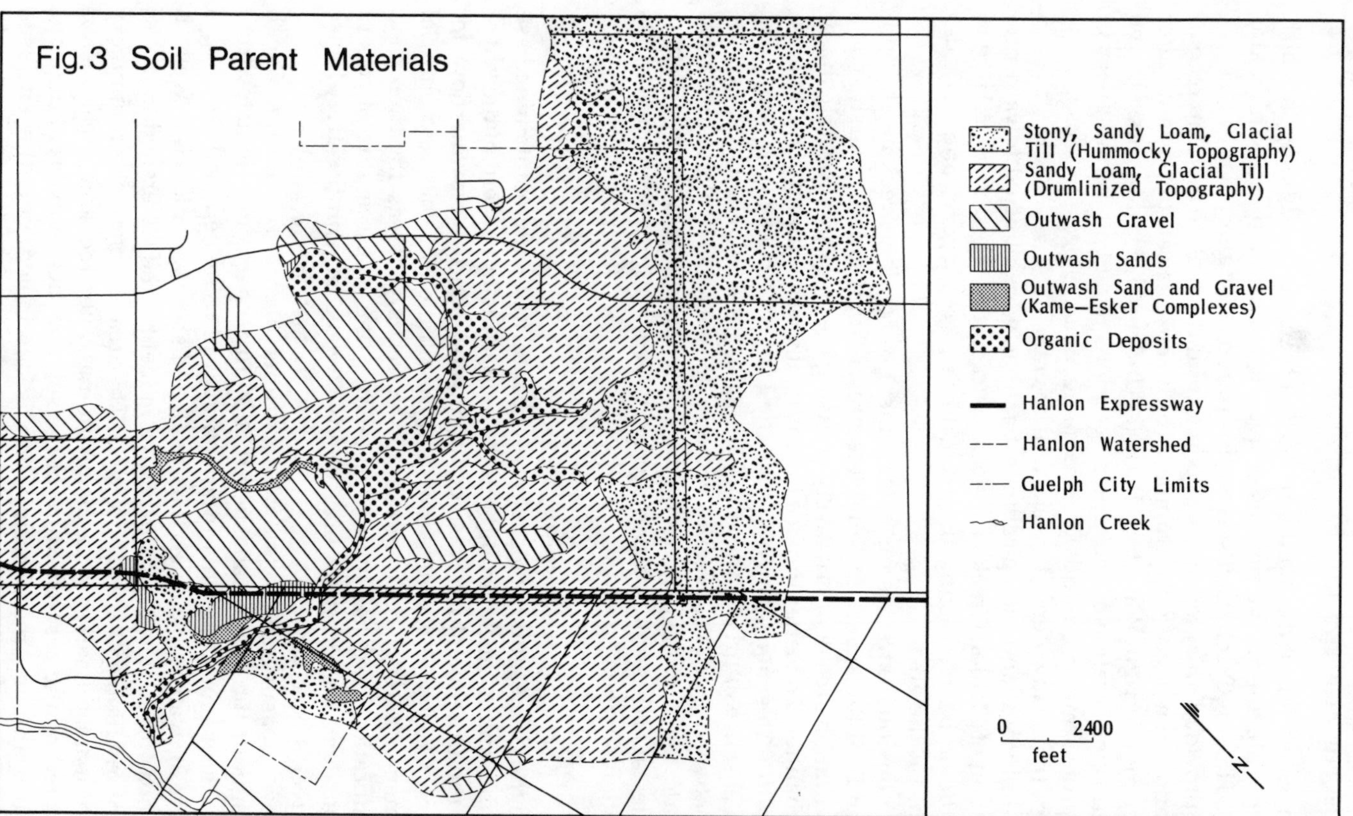

Fig. 3 Soil Parent Materials

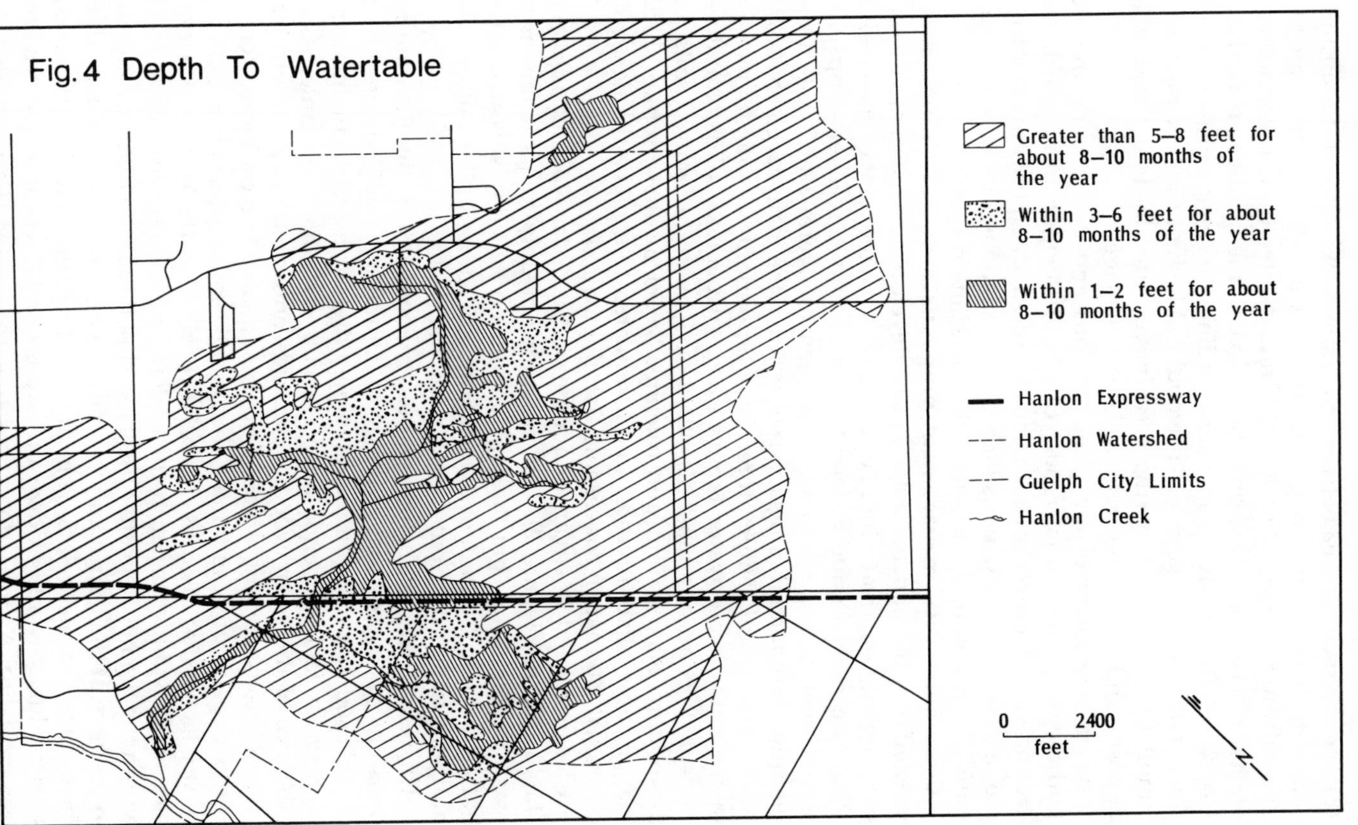

Fig. 4 Depth To Watertable

(b) The intervening area between the hummocky till and the springs are coarse textured outwash gravels that act as aquifers through which groundwater moves laterally. (c) Groundwater from these sediments emerges in the form of springs that serve as the headwaters for Hanlon Creek. (d) The low-lying area surrounding the creek consists of organic soils and contains a large cedar woodlot. Much of the precipitation and runoff from the surrounding area moves laterally into these organic deposits and enters the creek as lateral seepage.

As an outgrowth of mapping the soils and determining the area's hydrology, a conceptual model can be developed from which major groundwater recharge areas can be identified. But more importantly, the model can serve as the basis for recommendations with respect to maintaining a year-round, sustained flow in Hanlon Creek.

Once alternative management proposals have been formulated for streamflow, the aquatic biologist can develop management criteria for maintenance of aquatic life. For example, management of the creek as a trout stream has quite different requirements for water temperature, water quality, and sustained flow than for warm water fish. Consequently, the aquatic biologist is interested in the many facets that control water quality and temperature. Some important parameters measured in the study were water temperature, suspended solids, nitrate and phosphate concentrations, dissolved oxygen, and dissolved salts, such as sodium, magnesium, and calcium. Based on these inputs, further management alternatives can be formulated to achieve the desired recreational alternative concerning fish populations.

Closely related to stream conditions is the cedar woodlot adjacent to Hanlon Creek (Figure 2). The woodlot not only helps maintain cool water temperatures, but the organic soils on which it is located act as a buffer to control sediment entering the stream and filter out or adsorb nutrients in run-off from the surrounding area.

This area, perhaps better than any, demonstrates the intricate relationship or balance that exists in a natural system. Existence of the organic soils depends on maintaining a high water table; maintaining a high water table depends on preserving base flow in Hanlon Creek; existence of the cedar woodlot depends on maintaining present water table relations; and preservation of water quality and cool water temperatures depend on maintaining the organic soils and cedar woodlot.

Any factor that disturbs this balance will alter the system. For example, what would happen if an underground utility line were located within the organic deposits? In all likelihood the water table would drop to the base of the trench and the cedar trees would die gradually due to the change in water relations in their rooting zone. Further, the organic soils gradually would oxidize and expose roots, which would accelerate tree mortality. As the woodlot disappeared, water temperatures would rise and erosion and sedimentation would occur because of increased run-off.

Such changes usually are not evident over short periods of time. Instead, the on-going destructive processes become visually apparent only after several years, at which time it is too late to initiate remedial measures.

ANALYSIS AND RECOMMENDATION STAGES

Once available, the basic inventory data can be collated, analyzed, and development alternatives determined. Arguments can be presented for preserving lands for open spaces and recreational opportunities based on the needs for sustaining the natural system rather than on an indiscriminate basis. For example, it is evident that the organic soils and areas adjacent to these soils with a high water table should not be developed. In addition, much of the area comes within the conservation authorities' flood line.[3]

To this point constraints on development are based primarily on physical data or inputs. It is here that a most important contribution from the social scientist is required. For example, what recreational facilities are required? What is the demand for these?

Most provinces require developers to dedicate at least 5 per cent of the area to recreational activities. Many people consider such allotments to be inadequate, but provincial legislation in most instances is too weak or too vague to cope with the problem. However, documentation of these demands, together with an enumeration of an area's physical limitations, builds a strong case for allotment of land to urban open space and recreational activities, and it could serve as a basis on which to develop new legislation.

Figure 5 shows the allotment of land required for various development alternatives. The recreation alternative delineates what was considered an absolute minimum land area for maintaining a sustained, year-round flow in the creek. Such an alternative would be suitable for warmwater fish populations. The conservation alternative shows the minimum land requirement for maintaining base flow at or near its present level. Under this proposal, one should be able to preserve existing stream quality and water temperature standards. Additional areas corresponding to low-lying, imperfect, and poorly drained soils were recommended for purchase as part of the conservation alternative (shown as "desirable" in Figure 5). "To be replanted" areas correspond to steeply sloping land where erosion control is required.

Other measures in addition to land control obviously are necessary to ensure success of the development alternatives. For example, extensive pumping of groundwater from wells in the watershed should be prohibited. Instead of conventional storm sewer systems, consideration

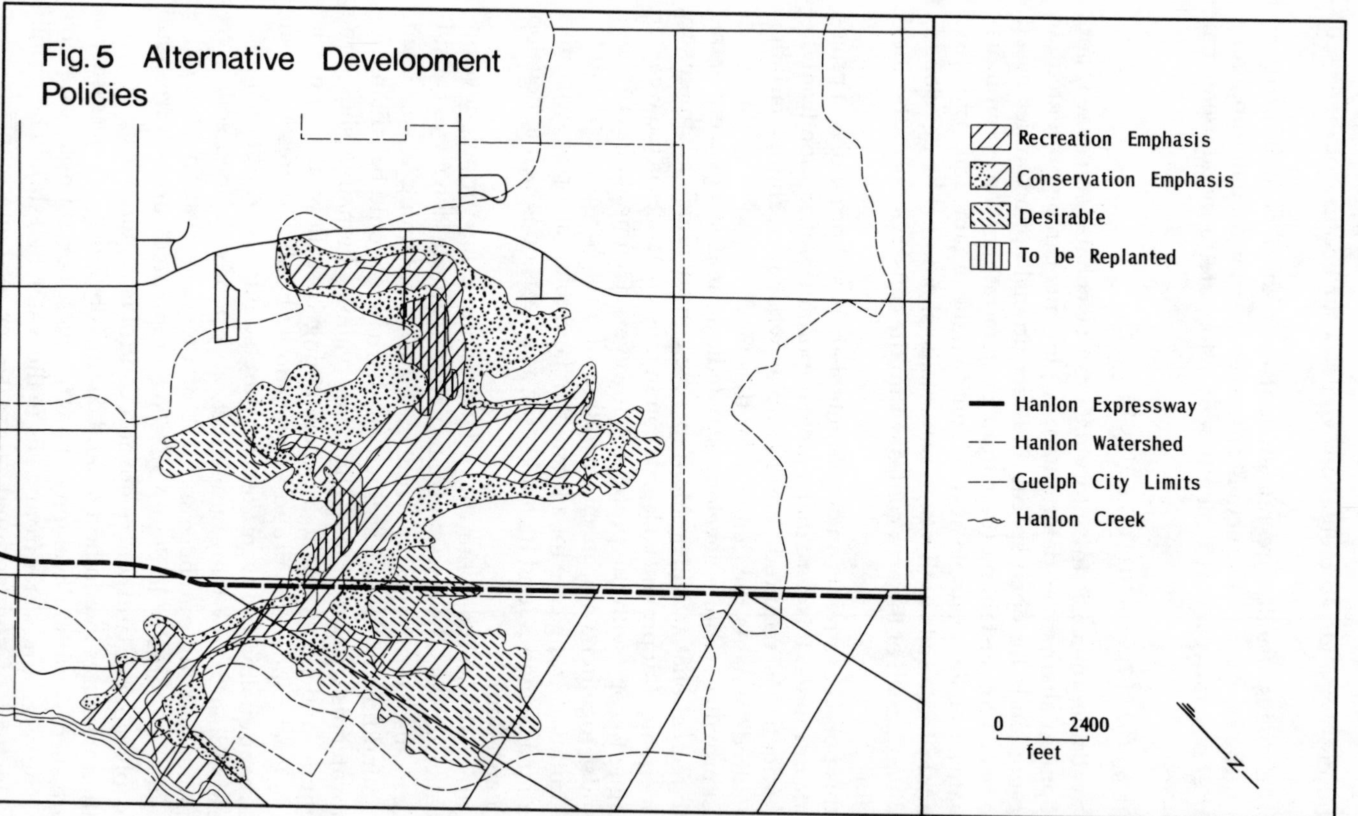

Fig. 5 Alternative Development Policies